PREFACE

The papers in this volume were presented at a National Short Course on Elements of Outdoor Recreation Planning held in Ann Arbor, Michigan, May 6-16, 1968. The short course was co-sponsored by the School of Natural Resources and the Extension Service of The University of Michigan; the Lake Central Region of the Bureau of Outdoor Recreation; the Conservation Department (now the Department of Natural Resources) of the State of Michigan; and the National Association of State Outdoor Recreation Liaison Officers.

Representatives from the co-sponsoring agencies decided that the greatest benefit could be obtained from a national short course if it dealt primarily with general theories and concepts to provide structures within which planning at the regional and state levels could be performed. Correspondence with recreation planners at these sub-national levels supported the position that training sessions in specific methodologies and techniques could be held more appropriately at the regional or state level where there is less variation among applicable techniques. The word "elements" in the title rather accurately indicates that few discussions of "methods" of recreation planning will be found in this volume.

The subjects selected for discussion were organized around two key words in the title of the short course, recreation and planning. About one half of the papers deal primarily with considerations of the nature, significance, scope, and trends of outdoor recreation phenomena. The remaining papers present general concepts about planning, policy formation and administration as these subjects relate to provision of outdoor recreational services. The two parts of these proceedings reflect this division. An editor's introduction to each part presents the general organization and content of that section.

Several people, in addition to the lecturers and discussion group leaders, should be cited for their special contributions to the short course. They are R. Keith Arnold, Justin W. Leonard, J. Downs Herold, Douglas W. Scott, and Alicia Pratt of The University of Michigan; Roman H. Koenings and Robert L. Pierce of the Lake Central Region of the Bureau of Outdoor Recreation; and Ralph A. MacMullen and Norman L. Smith of the Michigan Department of Natural Resources. Also, it is appropriate to express appreciation to the participants, and to other outdoor recreation planners and administrators, who have responsibilities for providing this important social service, outdoor recreation.

Ann Arbor   B.L. Driver

CONTENTS

PART I

OUTDOOR RECREATION: ITS NATURE, SIGNIFICANCE, SCOPE AND TRENDS

PART II

A GENERAL VIEW OF OUTDOOR RECREATION PLANNING, POLICY FORMATION AND ADMINISTRATION

PART I

OUTDOOR RECREATION: ITS NATURE, SIGNIFICANCE, SCOPE AND TRENDS

EDITOR'S INTRODUCTION TO PART I

The papers in the first part of these proceedings attempt to define broadly the nature, scope and significance of outdoor recreation, especially as these dimensions relate to the responsibilities of planners. The objective is to provide, in one group of papers, the general information about outdoor recreation which is necessary for an integrative and comprehensive approach to planning for the provision of this important social service. Because of the breadth of inquiry many related subjects are considered.

Scope of Outdoor Recreation Planning

Driver and Tocher   (Toward a Behavioral Interpretation of Recreational Engagements, with Implications for Planning):

This paper offers a behavioral interpretation of recreation as a supplement to the conventional activity approach. The authors present five descriptors of recreation and postulate that if all five of these descriptors can be applied to any phenomenon it is recreational in nature. The authors maintain that humans have motivations to recreate. They also postulate that these motivations cause recreationists to pursue a recreational goal-object, whether it be a trophy head or temporary escape into a less noisy and more tranquil environment. The conceptualization also includes the suggestion that recreational engagements (activities) are related to the nature of the reward expected and that the responses made by the recreationist in the pursuit of his goal-object are instrumental to his attainment of that goal. Recreation is defined as an experience which exists to the extent that the goal-object is attained. The concepts of goal-states and recreational states are discussed. It is pointed out that different levels of recreational experiences can exist at different locations on the goal-state continuum, which will range from inception of the motivation to gratification of the need to recreate. Implications for recreation planning are considered.

Pierce   (Statewide Outdoor Recreation Planning):

Mr. Pierce, one of the principal organizers of the short course, discusses some of the necessary reasons for taking a comprehensive approach to recreation planning. In explaining the reasons why planners must be aware of the broad implications of their efforts, he discusses some of the general problems facing recreation planners. Regional differences in problems and different approaches to planning are considered. Provisions of the Land and Water Conservation Fund Act of 1965 are related to the responsibilities of state outdoor recreation planners.

Underhill   (Hierarchy of Responsibilities in Outdoor Recreation
             Planning):

Mr. Underhill discusses the roles, responsibilities and functions of different levels of government and of the private sector in providing outdoor recreation services. He makes recommendations and offers positive suggestions on how these responsibilities can be fulfilled. Outdoor recreation planning activities at different levels of government are reviewed. The need for cooperative and coordinative arrangements is emphasized.

Styles   (Variables Which Must be Considered in Outdoor
             Recreation Planning):

This paper addresses itself to the basic variables which should be considered in outdoor recreation planning. It depicts some of the shortcomings of the traditional approaches to planning and calls for more experimentation and innovation. In discussing the social importance of outdoor recreation, Mr. Styles stresses the need for the provision of a range of recreational opportunities within a "balanced recreation system." He argues that in recreation planning greater consideration must be given to changing trends in society, especially those defined by variables related to population, education, urbanization and land uses. He concludes his paper by pointing out that the states will continue to play an increasingly important role in providing outdoor recreational services.

Cultural and Technological Influences on Outdoor Recreation Participation

Burch   (Recreation Preferences as Culturally Determined Phenomena):

Mr Burch urges the recreation planner to take cognizance of culture as a sensitizing agent. He raises the question: why is leisure apparently problematic in our society? Useful insights into possible answers to this question are provided through his comparisons of variations in the perceptions and uses of free time in different cultures, extending from subsistence to post-industrial societies. He identifies some of the accumulative human values and behavioral patterns which train our peculiar incapacity with leisure. In his discussion of cultural variations and social trends in American life which have consequences for recreational planning, he suggests that emphasis on specific activities and things keep leaving planners unprepared. He calls for a greater concentration on occupational, sub-cultural and cultural value associations by pointing out that planners must work with cultural diversity — not homogeneity. In considering the "culture of recreational planning" Burch explains his belief that there "will be an encouraging tendency for recreation planners to shift from reliance on the

4

forestry model to a reliance upon an educational model for directing their actions." He sees a tendency away from interest in things to interest to people. In concluding, he suggests that the recreation planner must expand his cultural vocabulary so that he may begin to expand the vocabulary of the recreationists.

de Grazia   (Some Reflections on the History of Outdoor Recreation):

Mr. de Grazia reflects upon the history of outdoor recreation by raising several queries, among which are: what have people in high cultures of the past done that we do not do, and what do we do that they did not do. After making these comparisons, he proposes that in our urban environments we have achieved much greater success in the "indoors" than in managing and maintaining the quality of our outdoor environments. Mr. de Grazia argues that "only the city can save the wilderness." He suggests that man needs to get outdoors and will do so; unless appropriate opportunities exist for more satisfying outdoor urban experiences, the impact on the wilderness and the countryside will be devastating. We need to provide more opportunities for healthful outdoor recreation within our cities. He concludes with a speculative challenge to outdoor recreation planners by asking what will be the nature and functions of "recreation as a foil for work" for those future people of our society who will enjoy more free time and have fewer needs for such a foil as recreation.

Christy (Elements of Mass Demand for Outdoor Recreation Resources):

Mr. Christy proposes and analyzes five elements of mass demand for outdoor recreation resources. These are (1) ease of participation, (2) a desirable image associated with the activity, (3) characteristics that permit a strong identification with the image, (4) opportunities for demonstrating skills, and (5) a comfortable and efficient use of leisure time. He argues that if a particular form of outdoor recreation activity scores high on all of these elements, the activity is likely to become very popular, measured in terms of mass demand. Throughout the paper, Mr. Christy stresses the need for better understanding of the motivational factors relevant to recreation participation.

Satterwaithe   (Some Functions Recreation Will Play for
    the Individual in the Future):

Miss Satterwaithe discusses three functions that recreation will play for the individual in the future. They are (1) fulfilling or experience testing, (2) skill challenging and (3) forgetting and escape. In addition to calling for greater attention to these functions in recreation planning, she urges that greater consideration be given to the role of technology and to special social groups, such as to the poor and to women.

Davis   (Technological Change and Recreation Planning):

Mr. Davis examines five factors relevant to technological change which are affecting participation in outdoor recreational activities. He offers these as supplements to the four conventional elements (increases in populations, greater amounts of leisure time, more disposable or discretionary income, and greater accessibility, including better transportation). The five elements considered are (1) our shifting cultural viewpoint (philosophy) toward work, (2) changes in productivity per man-hour in all major sectors of our economy, (3) changes in the nature of an individual's work, (4) our difficulty of changing with change, and (5) urbanization. Mr. Davis, in discussing and considering these elements, argues that recreation planners must somehow give greater attention to these determinants of recreational participation as they attempt to "imagine the future."

Economic Considerations Related to Outdoor Recreation Planning

Brazer   (Outdoor Recreation as a Public Good and
              Some Problems of Financing):

Mr. Brazer explores the questions of whether outdoor recreation should be viewed as a public good and how expenditures in outdoor recreation should be financed. The economic definition of a public good is explained, and consideration is given to whether outdoor recreation fits into this definition. Problems of determining which level of government has the primary responsibility for providing certain types of recreational services are considered. The role of the private sector is discussed briefly. Different economic criteria for financing existing facilities and for the acquisition of new facilities to put new resources into use are considered. He examines the application of marginal-cost pricing principles and considers other variables, such as the adverse effects of excessive exclusion costs and the problems of congestion costs. Problems of measurement and of accounting which accompany the application of economic criteria are considered.

Knetsch   (Assessing the Demands for Outdoor Recreation):

Mr. Knetsch reasons that outdoor recreation planning must go beyond the assumption that demand for outdoor recreational services is increasing. He argues that we also need to consider ways of increasing the efficiency and effectiveness of investments necessary to meet these demands. The problems created by planners' equating use, consumption and/or participation rates with economic demand are considered. Mr. Knetsch explains that economic demand is a quantity demanded-price relationship, not a measure of quantity used at frequently minimal or zero cost. He further points out that demand is related to supply and that participation rates, which are frequently called

6

demand by planners, are often no more than reflections of existing opportunities peculiar to a specific region. He argues that most recreation demand studies do not provide means of determining how recreational use will respond to changes in supply. In discussing the relationship between supply and demand, Mr. Knetsch gives some reasons why conventional approaches are used and points out the problems which arise from such approaches. He calls for more true economic demand studies of recreational services similar to those made for other goods and consumer items.

Twiss   (Supply of Outdoor Recreation):

In this paper some of the major supply issues in outdoor recreation are reviewed. Problem areas of supply studies are discussed within the context of their relationship to the overall planning task of identifying and quantifying supply variables. Seven elements of supply analyses are discussed, they are (1) inventory, (2) classification, (3) capacity, (4) location, (5) information handling, (6) program goals, and (7) analysis of data.

Role of the Private Sector in Outdoor Recreation Planning

Horvath (The Role of the Private Sector in Providing
         Recreational Opportunities):

Mr. Horvath, in considering the general role of the private sector in outdoor recreation, discusses several basic characteristics of recreation which have made it considerably different now than it has been in the past. He examines several characteristics of the leisure time market which have implications to private investment in recreation. Types of recreational opportunities appropriate for provision by the private sector are compared to the types considered most appropriate for the public sector. Data from the author's studies in Kansas, Minnesota, and Colorado are presented. Mr. Horvath examines some of the factors underlying participation in recreational activities and discusses his data which show participation by different time categories for both adults and children. Percentage rates of participation and expressed preferences are related to possible investment opportunities for the private sector. Information important to recreation and tourism businessmen is discussed with respect to how planners can better evaluate the possible contributions of the private sector.

Diamond   (The Private Role in the Provision of Large-Scale
          Outdoor Recreation):

Mr. Diamond suggests that the basic problem with private recreation development is "that there are considerably better ways to make a buck." Factors reducing levels of recreational investments by the private sector have been (1) seasonality of recreational enterprise, causing a short amortization period, (2) initial capital investment is generally high, (3) recreational consumption is one of the first items to be trimmed from a family budget, (4) recreation often requires a high labor input, (5) recreation is subject to capricious and unpredictable changes in public tastes, and (6) competition from the public sector, which pre-empted the field. In discussing these factors, Mr. Diamond mentions that consideration of the private sector should include personal expenditures on recreation not just capital investment by private industry. He argues that these private expenditures have received inappropriate recognition because attention has been focused on business development. He suggests that large scale private development has been successful under special situations such as (1) special high quality and high cost recreation, (2) the provision of outdoor recreation with hopes of making money on associated land values, (3) the provision of supplemental services, and (4) concessions on publicly owned land.

Fine   (Tourist Accomodations):

In discussing the resort industry, Mr. Fine mentions that the provision of accomodations for tourists is primarily the responsibility of the private sector and that the provider of these services should operate his business as a retailer does. He should study his product and his customers and make every effort to match the product with the customers' needs and desires. Mr. Fine discusses the characteristics of the resort industry by describing the nature of the product provided and of the consumer using the product. The pertinent considerations regarding the product (the accomodations) are (1) seasonality, (2) small size, (3) few provide dining and roadside services, (4) it is a resort based enterprise with emphasis on waterfront, and (5) the resorts are generally old. Pertinent characteristics of the customer are (1) he spends the bulk of his recreation dollar on accommodations and driving, (2) he increasingly tends to spend less time at any one recreation vacational site and engages in more touring types of vacations, (3) he, if average, is in a recreation party of approximately three people with a third of the parties containing no children, (4) he has a relatively high income, and (5) he generally comes from a professional or managerial class. Mr. Fine also compares the cottage-resort to small farm operations with respect to seasonality, weather, resort depletion, high investment in proportion to amount of annual income, and the family business as a "way of life."

He also discusses the trend in resort business in Wisconsin, mentioning such things as decline in total number of small establishments, increases in larger resorts, the trend towards complete resorts, which offer a wider array of services, and the development of all-season facilities.

TOWARD A BEHAVIORAL INTERPRETATION OF RECREATIONAL ENGAGEMENTS, WITH IMPLICATIONS FOR PLANNING

by

B.L. Driver and S. Ross Tocher

Assistant and Associate Professors, Outdoor Recreation
Studies, Department of Forestry, School of Natural Resources
The University of Michigan

The purpose of this paper is to present a conceptual framework within which the conventional activity approach to recreation planning is supplemented by a behavioral interpretation of recreation. Framework is used within the context of a logical and cohesive structure within which tests can be made to evaluate the phenomena of recreation. As with all concepts, the following are neither true nor false; they are only more or less useful. Hopefully, the reader will find them useful when reading the other papers in these proceedings, especially the ones in Part I.

Recreation Defined

"What is recreation, outdoor or indoor?" This is a question not infrequently asked of recreation planners or by them.

Webster defines recreation as "a refreshment of strength and spirits after toil; diversion or a mode of diversion; play." Webster's definition is rather complete, intuitively acceptable and semantically useful for purposes of communication. It includes the notions of non-work activity, replenishment, change from the routine, pleasure and all the other ingredients commonly attributed to recreation. But how useful is the definition to recreation planners? Obviously, it has general usefulness, but it offers few, if any, specific guidelines for planning and investment scheduling. What criteria does it provide for recommending action? Can we plan for pleasure or for the refreshment of spirits? If so, how do we project the demand? What "spirit-refreshing" facilities do we provide? It is difficult to imagine that agency budgets will include line items for such things as 500 units of play!

Perhaps the definitional problem is not as great as suggested. Private and public recreation agencies have established guidelines for action. Further, they have realistically and pragmatically interpreted their important individual responsibilities. Nevertheless, problems associated with defining recreation have helped cause recreation planners to view recreation as *participation in activities* which, seemingly, are recreational to the participant. Through this approach, fishing becomes recreation, swimming becomes recreation, exercising becomes recreation, and so on.

The activity approach has many advantages, such as the ease of identifying who participates in what activity, when, where, and for how long. However, it suffers disadvantages because it does not make explicit the need to consider other relevant questions: Why is the recreationist participating in the activity?[1] What other activities might have been selected if the opportunities existed? What satisfactions or rewards are received from the activity? How can the quality of the experience be enhanced? In other words, the activity approach frequently assumes that supply defines preferences (and sometimes that supply will generate demand), but it does not question what latent preferences are not being met. It causes recreation planners to focus on supply and give too little attention to demand, which is frequently appraised in terms of past consumption. In summary and somewhat contradictorily, the activity approach is rather passive. This is especially true when projections of demand (participation) are made based on past types and rates of participation.

Even though the activity approach has many practical advantages, is it the only way to conceive of recreation? Perhaps it would be useful to view recreation not as an activity but instead as a psycho-physiological experience measured in terms of recreational responses and/or a mode or process of responses. Under this behavioral approach, recreation will consist of more than participation in an activity.[2]

To develop the proposed behavioral approach, we will make and explain five postulates about recreatation.[3] These non-mutually exclusive postulates are:

1. Recreation is an experience that results from recreational engagements.

2. Recreational engagements require a commitment by the recreationist.

3. Recreational engagements are self-rewarding: the engagement finds pleasure in and of itself, and recreation is the experience.

4. Recreational engagements require personal and free choice on the part of the recreationist.

5. Recreational engagements occur during non-obligated time.[4]

The first postulate states what recreation is. The remaining four serve as descriptors or criteria to differentiate recreational behavior from other forms of human behavior. For this differentiation, *all* of the last four descriptors must be applicable if the action or event (response) is to be considered recreational.

The postulates are arranged in a numerical order of increasing specificity. Number one is a rather generic descriptor with applications to a wider array of human behavior than is number five. The key words are non-obligated time, personal choice and rewarding (not punishing) engagements. Notice the word engagement, rather than activity, is used to incorporate better the psychological dimensions. We might be mentally engaged only.

At the risk of causing confusion we will point out that recreation stands in opposition to work if work is defined as occurring during obligated time and/or is not, in and of itself, (positively) rewarding. For many people, "work" (as commonly defined), is recreational. It is recreational if these people are not obligated to "work" and if the "work" is, in and of itself, rewarding.

Each of these descriptors will now be briefly expanded, explained and related to recreation planning.

Recreation Is An Experience

Introduction:

There are analytical and conceptual advantages in viewing recreation behaviorally. Psychologists define behavior as any observable action (response) of a person or thing (Morgan and King, 1965). Also, it is commonly accepted that most human behavior is goal-directed or goal-guided and that *a person's responses are instrumental in obtaining some goal-object or need satisfaction.*[5] Thus, although we are not always aware of the goal-objects being pursued, it is relatively safe to say that most of what we do is done in the pursuit of a goal-object. These behavioral pursuits, which are observable as instrumental responses, are underlaid by motivations to obtain the goal-object; that is, to consummate or to receive gratification for the need leading to the goal. We can now state that participation in recreational engagements (activities, if the reader prefers) are instrumental in experiencing recreation. Further, it is being postulated that humans are motivated to recreate, that there are psychological and physiological forces, motives, drives, etc., which cause the recreationists to pursue the recreational goal-object(s) and to experience recreation. Implicitly, it is being suggested that motives to recreate can be identified. Let us expand the first descriptor and postulate that recreation is an experience that exists to *the extent to which* the needs or desires to recreate are gratified. It is the experience of attaining special recreational goal-objects. The level of the experience is a function of the goal-state of the recreationist − his condition or situation with respect to attaining the goal-object.

Laing (1967) explains the basic concept being developed in simple language:

We see other people's behavior, but not their experience. . . .

Experience is man's invisibility to man. . . .Experience as invisibility of man to man is at the same time more evident than anything. *Only* experience is evident. . . .

If, however, experience is evidence, how can one ever study the experience *of the other?* For the experience *of the other* is not evident to me, or it is not and never can be an experience of mine. . . .

11

...I wish to define a person in a twofold way; in terms of experience, as a center or orientation of the objective universe; and in terms of behavior as the origins of action. Personal experience transforms a given field into a field of intention and action; only through action can our experience be transformed. . . .

People may be observed to sleep, eat, walk, talk, etc., in relatively predictable ways. We must not be content with observation *of this kind alone.* Observation of behavior must be extended by inference to attributions about experience. . . .

In a science of persons, I shall state as axiomatic that: behavior is a function of experience, and both experience and behavior are always in relation to *someone* or *something other than self.*

Records of participation in recreational activities are simply recorded observations of behavior. But, "We must not be content with observations of this kind alone. Observations of behavior must be extended by inference to attributions about experience. . . ." Actually, we need inferences about recreational experiences supported by data.

Before we attempt to identify some specific motivations to recreate, we will raise a few basic questions: From where do these motivations to recreate come? How do they arise, and why do they take the directions they do? These are difficult questions to which an over-simplified answer will be given. They come primarily from learning based on past experience. To elaborate, the two basic sources of human behavior are instinct and learning. Instinctive behavior stems from inherited characteristics that cause us to perform, respond or act in a certain manner. Learning, the second source of behavior, is defined as a *relatively permanent change* in behavior that is the *result of past experience or practice of the individual* (Morgan and King, 1965). It is now commonly accepted that most human behavior is learned behavior. Even those behavioral patterns which are generally considered to be underlaid by instinct, such as sexual drives or motivations to eat (prompted by hunger pains), are overshadowed by man's sophistication in learning. Taboos on sexual behavior, eating for self-love or for the demonstration of affluence, and the scheduling of meals at a convenient time are examples. That learning and skill development are important aspects of recreational behavior is conventional recreation wisdom. Changes in tastes and preferences for different recreational engagements must be explained by learning. It is also important in the following discussion of specific motivations to recreate.

Motivations to Recreate

To begin this discussion of specific motivations to recreate, imagine that recreation occupies a bi-polar behavioral continuum with needs to escape temporarily or to disengage passively situated at one pole and motivations to engage actively listed at the other pole. Further, imagine that the extent to

12

which either of the polar goal-states is realized is measured in terms of the types and amount of information received externally or generated internally during the recreational experience. Information is used here as a measure of the ability of an individual to make decisions and to discriminate meaning-fully among different values, with these additional degrees of freedom being gained either from the external (sensory) stimuli received or the internal in-ferential and reflective cognitive processes enacted during the engagement.

The motivation to escape — to disengage, re-engage or engage randomly — would then underlie the *re*-creational aspects of recreation. Rather loosely, it can be said that such motivations constitute drives or priming forces which "push" the recreationist from a rather structured (non-random) life space he wishes to avoid *temporarily* into a recreational life space in which he anticipates he can *re*plenish his adaptive energies. For example, he might be escaping an information overload situation and desire a change in stimuli (information) orientation solely for restorative purposes. At the other pole, the motivations to engage actively would underlie the creative aspects of re*creation*. More positive or "pulling" forces attract the recreationist to learn and gain *new* information rather than to escape to change his external informational environments.

The notion of informational environments being both external and internal to the person was presented to point out that the information received must somehow be processed. This processing, at least in part, requires that the new information be related to information that has been received during prior perceptual (learning) activity. This associative process is an on-going cognitive activity of information categorization and storage (Bruner, 1957). These associations help us to develop our mental images (representations or maps of ourselves and our external world). The representations are not dependent on just the environmentally monitored data our perceptors feed to our brain. They are formed and changed in a complex, not well understood and interactive process of reception, association, classification, categorization, reflection and prediction. Thus, the internal environment is important, and each recreationist will process and appraise the information from his engagement according to his individual cognitive style and for his own purposes.

The above bi-polar conceptualization is perhaps useful. However, it is too simplistic and provides limited knowledge for functional planning. Let us develop a slightly different conceptualization of human behavior, so we can leave the bi-polar scheme and view recreation as a response to a multitude of motivating forces which may exist independently or in some combination simultaneously. To do this we will use Gutman's (1967) and Maslow's (1954) hierarchies of human behavioral responses.

Gutman differentiated human responses into six classes defined by the complexity of the behavior. The classes, which are not mutually exclusive, are:

1. vegetative
2. reflexive

13

3. conditioned
4. learned
5. problem solving
6. creative

Vegetative behavior refers to basic physiological behavior, such as the intake of food and excretion of wastes. Reflexive behavior is a relatively rapid and consistent unlearned response to a stimulus, ordinarily not conscious or subject to voluntary control, lasting only so long as the stimulus is present. An example would be the doctor's tap of a hammer on the knee and the well-known response. A conditioned response is produced by a conditioned stimulus after learning. The best example is Pavlov's dog that salivates with no food present when hearing a bell (the conditioned stimulus) if the bell has previously been paired with the presentation of food for some period of time. Learned behavior is as defined before. In addition to conditioned learning, it would include instrumental and perceptual learning. Problem-solving is an even more complex type of learned behavior. It occurs when a situation exists which constitutes an obstacle to need gratification and requires cognitive processes of the individual to arrive at a solution. According to Gutman, creative behavior is the most complex form of human behavior. He defines it as any activity by which man imposes a *new order* upon his environment, frequently his mental environment. It is an organizing activity. More specifically, it is the original act by which that new order or organization is first *conceived* and given expression.

Gutman's schema complements Maslow's hierarchy of man's "lower to higher" needs. Maslow's listing includes physiological needs, safety needs, belongingness and love needs, esteem needs, and the need for self-actualization. Maslow argues that as the lower needs are satisfied, we seek gratification of the next higher need in the hierarchy.

Gutman's and Maslow's ideas are useful in developing a behavioral interpretation of recreation. Both make explicit the multi-dimensional aspects of behavior. Maslow's conceptualization helps explain increasing demands for luxury items and recreational experiences in an economy that is quite rapidly removing constraints on gratification of lower level needs. Both hierarchies, along with judgment, permit us to postulate that in recreational pursuits, we find interesting opportunities to engage in the most complex and "highest" forms of human behavior — learning, problem solving, creativity and self-actualization.[6] Especially relevant to recreation planning is the possibility that these types of behavior might be useful in defining functions of such planning. To follow this thought, let us leave our bi-polar continuum, add to our list of motivations to recreate, relate these motivations to different types of behavior and make inferences about how recreation planning can either help constrain or facilitate the realization of the goal-objects toward which the motivations lead.

What are some other possible (and at this stage of theory development, speculative) motivations to recreate? Desires that one's children may experience certain recreational and/or learning situations can be considered a motivation. Parents and others, such as close friends, may feel motivated to recreate to share those experiences with loved ones. Or people may recreate to *affiliate* themselves with a group. The motivation in this case could be to maintain a social identity or a source of esteem.

Skill development would appear to be another important motivation to recreate. For such engagements, the amount of satisfaction (however scaled) of the recreationist should be positively correlated with the extent to which he felt he was able to apply or develop the relevant skill(s). Such satisfaction can possibly be interpreted in terms of *needs to achieve,* which appear to be important human needs (McClelland, 1961).

The *pursuit of status,* especially the collection of status symbols (such as trophies, rocks, or even photographs), seems to motivate many people into engagements which they find recreational.

Research in psychology suggests that individuals are motivated to recreate in order to satisfy *exploratory needs,* which would contain elements of problem-solving (Berlyne, 1960). Or the exploratory behavior may primarily serve a *creative function,* the rewards of which are the realization that we have established a new order in our environment.

Is the conceptualization thus far relevant to recreation planning? It should be for several reasons. Much is read in our literature about the need to provide a wide array of real opportunities for personal choice. Hopefully, the conceptualization contributes to a better understanding of why different opportunities are pursued and why the array is important. Possibly more relevant is the insight provided about the relationships between motivations, opportunities for engagement and drive consummation, or need gratification. To illustrate, opportunities to escape, to explore, or to collect status symbols, all imply environmental arrangements which differ one from the other. Or the opportunities to gain status might differ from those to create. For example, does not Old Faithful Inn in Yellowstone Park primarily, but not totally, serve the function of providing opportunities to gain status? To be sure, it is an architectural curiosity and has many historical values. But the question still remains, should scarce funds be allocated through public recreation agencies for the attainment of status in a unique area if other opportunities, possibly of higher value, are foregone in the process? The problem is one of determining and ranking the mix of opportunities to be provided.

Several other comments relevant to recreation planning can now be made. First, much behavior is related to the simultaneous pursuit of several goal-objects. These may be complementary and mutually supportive, or competitive and introduce conflict. Thus, we can find learning (a possible goal-object) and recreation happening together and frequently impossible to differentiate. Or we can find the recreationist, especially the tourist, rushing as he recreates.

The planner should recommend the enhancement of opportunities for supplemental or complementary engagements, such as the provision of interpretative and other informational facilities. He should aim to help reduce points of conflict, such as recommending the provision of certain services (lodging, food, etc.). The mix will vary for different types of engagements (i.e., for different motivations to recreate and for different recreational goal-objects being pursued). Second, it might be useful for the recreation planner to view different classes of uses as having different "goal-packages." The goal-packages of an elderly person could differ significantly from those of a teenager.

The Recreation Experience Continuum:

It was stated that the recreational planner has impact on recreational experiences through his influence on the provision of opportunities to pursue recreational goal-objects. But he can also affect the experiences in other ways. To elaborate this statement, let us view the recreationist as receiving value (utility) from the experience — from goal-object attainment. The magnitude of this utility is determined by several interacting factors. The most important ones are the antecedent conditions, which give rise to and determine the strength(s) of the need(s) to recreate; the attractiveness of the goal-object(s); and the nature and consequences of the intervening variables which the recreationist encounters during his pursuit of the goal-object.

To make more explicit how the recreation planner can effect these values, let us elaborate these sources in tabular form. See Figure 1.

The antecedent conditions are those which give rise to motivations to recreate. They are not mutually exclusive and can be considered as priming forces which lead to pursuits of the goal-objects. Environmental stimuli are the conditions or things to which an individual is exposed (e.g. to which he is sensitive) in his ordinary life-space(s). These stimuli are varied and would include among others those measured by variables like density, environmental pollutants, pressures of the job, ethnic "place," and status incongruity. Physiological drives are self-explanatory and refer to such conditions as the need for exercise. They can find their source either in heredity or learning. Hereditary factors also are self-explanatory and refer to conditions, such as differences in neurophysiological make-up or in body structure, which could change the ability of the individual to engage in certain activities, such as strenuous activities. Prior learning has been discussed before. Particularly relevant is the fact that prior learning determines the relative attractiveness of the goal-object — the level of utility expected to be realized from goal-object obtainment. Maturity is here used to mean stability of behavioral characteristics reflected in the differences in latitudes of variation between children and the elderly (Bloom, 1965). The elderly have rather stable and fixed behavioral patterns and less flexibility for *basic* changes in these characteristics. Cognitive style refers to the different approaches various individuals will take in a problem situation.

16

<u>Motivational Conditions and Behavioral Directions</u>

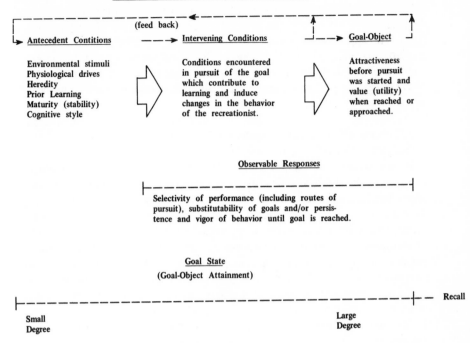

(feed back)

Antecedent Contitions ----> **Intervening Conditions** ---> **Goal-Object**

Environmental stimuli
Physiological drives
Heredity
Prior Learning
Maturity (stability)
Cognitive style

Conditions encountered
in pursuit of the goal
which contribute to
learning and induce
changes in the behavior
of the recreationist.

Attractiveness
before pursuit
was started and
value (utility)
when reached or
approached.

<u>Observable Responses</u>

Selectivity of performance (including routes of
pursuit), substitutability of goals and/or persistence and vigor of behavior until goal is reached.

<u>Goal State</u>
(Goal-Object Attainment)

Recall

Small
Degree

Large
Degree

<u>Recreational-State</u>
(The Recreational Experience Continuum)

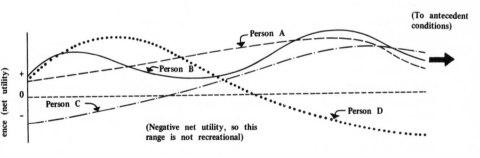

(To antecedent
conditions)

Person A

Person B

Person C

Person D

(Negative net utility, so this
range is not recreational)

Level of the Experi-
ence (net utility)

Figure 1

SCHEMATIC PRESENTATION OF RECREATION BEHAVIOR

The intervening variables are those which the recreationist encounters enroute to his goal-object. They can cause changes in expectations of accomplishing the goal, and through feed-back and learning, changes in the antecedent conditions for subsequent and concurrent motivational states.

The observable consequences serve as measures of behavioral responses. They are appraised in terms of selectivity of performance (such as the activities engaged in and how engaged), the vigor of the response, the persistence in the pursuit of the goal (how long engaged and with what persistence and intensity, etc.), and the substitutability of goal-objects (changes in activity, etc.).

Attainment of the goal-object will consummate the drive for a given motivational state. An example would be reaching the top of a mountain being climbed. The attractiveness of the goal-object relates to the expected value to be received from attaining it. Expected values and actual utility received might differ significantly in either a positive or negative direction. For example, if there is a low level of anticipation, but a very rewarding on-site experience, the difference is positive. Similarly, if the on-site experience is lower than anticipated, the difference will be negative. In either case, the utility from the experience becomes a component of the antecedent conditions for subsequent behavior. Net utility (utility minus disutility) is received from either approaching or attaining the goal-object. It is conceptually possible that net utility might be at its peak before the drive is consummated. For example, we might find the anticipation of and preparation for a fishing trip more rewarding than facing the elements at the stream.

One aspect of the recreational behavioral continuum is not clear in the tabular schema. This is the element of recall, memory or reminiscence. As we see it, this form of recreational engagement may take one or more of three forms. First, it can best be considered as a distinct recreational pursuit with its goal-object(s), at least in part, being reminiscence. This would be the case when we show our trophies or slides to friends. In these situations, the recreational goal-object would be associated with other, and socially determined, goal-objects. Second, the memories may put us on a new recreational continuum in a slightly different way. They may enter as antecedent conditions (not goal-objects) which prompt us in the pursuit of another goal-object similar to the one which gave us the satisfactory memories. Alternatively, the memories might be unsatisfactory and reduce our motivations to engage similarly again. Or the memories might crop up as intervening variables to strengthen or weaken the strength of a drive-state. In both of these two forms or modes of recall, we are on a new continuum if the four differentiating descriptors can be applied. The third form of recall requires that the recreational-behavioral continuum be extended past goal-object attainment as indicated by the dashed line at the bottom of the table. In this case, the recall need not be associated with a new goal-object and is usually a spontaneous engagement to which the separate application of the four differentiating descriptors have little meaning. It would seem that elements of all three of these forms usually exist — they strongly emphasize the educational or learning aspects of recreational behavior.

Based on the above statements, it can be seen that there is a difference between a goal-object, a goal-state and a recreational-state. The goal-object (the trophy, skill development or application, a different environment, etc.) is that with which the recreationist relates to determine the direction and to gauge the progress of his pursuit. His changing perceptions of its relative value affect the strength, persistence, and consistency of responses emitted. These perceptions are determined by the nature of the reinforcement (positive or negative) he receives enroute. Attainment of the goal-object dissipates the drive for that particular motivational-state and some other drive takes over.

The goal-state refers to where the recreationist finds himself at any point in time with respect to goal-object attainment. There are a variety of possible goal-states extending from anticipation (defined in terms of the antecedent conditions) to recall.

The recreational-state is the state or level of the experience. As defined early in the paper, this experience exists to the extent to which the needs or desires to recreate are gratified. Thus, *recreation itself is a state of mind.* This explains why it is so easy for us to engage in certain forms of recreation by doing nothing more than thinking. The level of the experience is determined by many variables which are influenced by factors both under the control of the recreationist and not under his control. Therefore, although recreation is highly personal, it can be significantly affected by the actions of others. Being highly personal, the level of the recreational experience will vary from person to person even though they might be subjected to the same external conditions. Further, the level of the experience can vary from goal-state to goal-state. Some people may "peak" during anticipation, others at the point of goal-object attainment, and others during recall. Or the level of the experience may vary at essentially the same goal-states for the same person during different but essentially the same type of engagements.

It is realized that this conceptualization, especially the "dynamics" of the recreational experience continuum at the bottom of Figure 1, is an over-simplification of several aspects of human behavior as it is currently understood. Problems associated with the pursuits of sub-goals and the complex and more dynamic nature of reinforcement-responses emitted have not been adequately considered. For example, the importance of feed-back has not been covered sufficiently. Also, the notion of net utility, at any point in time, does an injustice to the cumulative effects of memory on the level of the experience at that point in time. Although these additional dimensions are important, we feel that for the purposes of this paper they cannot and should not be considered. They would require much time and space to elaborate, would make the structure unreasonably complex and would, thereby, increase the probability of misunderstanding. The structure is reasonably consistent with existing theory and, as an introductory conceptualization, should be both meaningful and applicable as it is presented.

What roles do, or can, the recreation planner play in enhancing the experience of the recreationist? There are many situational contexts within which the planner directly or indirectly enters the "experience continuum" of the recreationists. He enters at the *antecedent condition level* in several ways. Studies of user responses show that recreationists generally have at least partial information about the nature of the experience expected. Frequently this information comes either from prior on-site experiences of the recreationist or of his friends. The recreation planner also strongly influences other decision makers responsible for the design and provision of facilities, for educational programs, and so forth. Thus, they indirectly affect the ·amount of information conveyed and received, and concomitantly, the expectations of the potential users of these landscapes and facilities. Further, if outdoor recreation planners could work more closely with other environmental planners in the creation and/or maintenance of more *harmonious and compatible everyday* life spaces and in the development of such programs as environmental education, these interactions might alter antecedent conditions in a manner which is favorable both to the planners and to the recreationists. Perhaps we would then create and maintain environments which are more liveable and from which certain people would not need to escape temporarily to the degree postulated. Recreation for these citizens, especially those in the inner cities, would not be offered as a mono-functional band-aid but instead as part of an integrated multi-functional program. If this is too Utopian we should at least attempt to provide readily available opportunities for meeting basic recreation needs — opportunities within or near those environmental settings which have superordinate influence on the antecedent conditions.

In addition to the recreation planners' effects on the *antecedent conditions,* many examples can be given of how the recreation planner and developer *intervene* during the recreationists' goal pursuits. For example, the type of on-site information provided affects the extent to which a goal can be realized. So do the type and arrangement of facilities; the restrictions, such as rules and regulations; and the learning environment within which the recreationist is "placed" by the designer. Each of these are significantly influenced by recommendations of the planners. As a specific example, what recommendations should the planner make with respect to the emerging programs which afe developing tò bus city children to the parks? Should recommendations be made that programs be established to provide learning or orientation sessions prior to the journey to the park, at the park, on the bus back to the city or all three? Or, as another specific example, does the planner always recognize the constraints he might be indirectly imposing on certain age groups, especially the elderly? His studies of use rates should disclose that many of our trails are too steep or otherwise inaccessible to our older adults. These constraints are significant intervening variables.

The above discussion of recreation as an experience includes the fundamental elements of the conceptualization. The remaining discussion of the other four descriptors is geared primarily toward differentiating recreational behavior from other types of human responses.

Recreation Requires a Commitment

Our proposition that recreation behavior is goal-directed implies that psychological commitments are present. We pointed out earlier that they may be .at the sub-conscious level. Most of them, however, appear to be more overt.

It is difficult to give an explicit definition of commitment. The one offered is that commitment is an assignment of energy, time, and other personal resources, including money. An assignment means a decision and, as with all decision situations, this implies a course or even a program of action. Energy, as used here, includes both psychic and physical energy. Psychic energy means a personal identity or association with a cause, object or event, such as one's identity with a team in the world series. Physical energy is self-explanatory and is related to an assignment of time. Time means personal cost, either in real or opportunity terms. For example, the time allocated to recreation could be allocated to the acquisition of additional income. The commitment will vary by type of activity engaged in, will relate to the goal-objects being pursued and will be reflected in the expenditures made on equipment, the level of skill development and other factors. The recreationist can be committed as an active participant or as a spectator. It is difficult to be more explicit because there are gradations in intensities and/or magnitudes of commitments.

The notion of commitment has some interesting implications for recreation analyses. For example, would comparative degrees of commitment provide rough measures of the ordinal values placed on different recreational experiences? Do commitments to week-end engagements differ from those for vacations? Are commitments to "disengagement" (to temporary escape) different from those to active engagement, and do responses vary accordingly? Are commitments to wilderness engagements stronger than those to swimming locally? Can the recreation planner expect the wilderness user to expend more energy than the user of a national recreation area? Can he expect the user to walk some distance for certain services? Do some users find the quality of their experience to be increased if they expend a little additional energy? If so, how willing are they to do so? Also, are there identifiable constraints (information, income, etc.) which need to be removed before certain commitments can be made?

Recreational Engagements Are Self-Rewarding

Two criteria are offered in this descriptor. First, the gratifications received from attainment of recreational goal-objects are of such a nature that these objects are pursued for their own sake and not primarily for their effects on or contributions to the attainment of other goal-objects. Contrasted with work, which is pursued for income to be used to meet other goals, *recreation is an end in itself.* Second, recreational experiences are rewarding, not punishing. The experiences have net positive values: utility exceeds disutility. Together the criteria state that recreational engagements find utility in and of themselves. This does not mean that we *cannot* recreate with secondary pay-offs in mind. It only means that we *need* not do so, if we are recreating as defined.

Recreation Involves Personal and Free Choice

This descriptor is closely related to the one above and should be relatively self-explanatory. Several brief comments are: it is difficult to conceive of recreational engagements as *self*-rewarding if not made as a free choice, and recreational activities might best present the opportunity for man to be free. By our definition, engaging in recreational pursuits (especially with respect to obligations of time) is the only opportunity for many people to be completely free, if pure or complete freedom is defined as existing when an individual's action reflects his personal intentions, and his intentions are self-determined (Hampshire, 1965). Obviously, the problem of determinism enters, and man as a social entity with all his roles, expectations, identities and ambiguities is seldom — if ever — free to determine personally his intentions. As with commitments, there is a gradation or continuum of freedom going from complete constraint to pure freedom. It is suggested that recreation lies at the end of the continuum where constraints are minimal and opportunities for spontaneity are the greatest.

Again, the implied question is whether environmental designs are constraining or facilitating. Implied in the descriptors are these three criteria of importance to recreation planners: (1) that an array of *opportunities exists* from which to make a choice, (2) that the individual is *free* and able *to choose,* and (3) that he is *free* and able *to do.* There is a difference between available and real opportunities. Many individuals can *choose* to do something, but their plan of action associated with this commitment and decision cannot be implemented because the individuals are somehow constrained from following through on their choice. These constraints could exist because of low income levels, racial discrimination, information deficiencies, or other factors which make available opportunities unreal.

Recreation Occurs During Non-Obligated Time

It is difficult to define the word obligation. The task becomes even more difficult when the temporal dimension is added — when obligated time is being defined. Oblige stems from the Latin meaning "to bind," which gives one a feeling for the concept of obligated time. Another way to explain the concept is that obligated time refers to time spent during which the allocation is accompanied by a sense of urgency. We are temporally obligated to the extent which we are not free now and in the future to do something other than that which we are doing. The problem of definition is made difficult because we experience gradations in the degree to which we feel obligated with respect to time. We do because we vary in our commitments to those things which bind us temporally. These things in turn require different amounts and scheduling of time. Some are highly structured and require relatively large blocks of time while others permit more discretionary scheduling in small blocks. For example, we feel a greater temporal obligation to our work and to our school activities than we do to our household chores (such as painting the house). There is a greater sense of *urgency* with fewer opportunities for discretionary scheduling. Further, we feel less obligated to certain social commitments and to engagements in non-play type of recreation such as a hobby activity. Finally, we feel less and perhaps no temporal obligations, in true play type activities in which there are fewer rigid structures, greater personal freedom of choice and few (or no) feelings of being time-bound. The point is that during recreational engagements we feel a reduced obligation or no sense of obligation, urgency or boundness, with respect to time. All parents have experienced this "unconsciousness of time" of children playing before dinner — "will they never learn to get to the table on time?" Based on a limited sample, these feelings of the parents are not as intense (or even present) when they too are playing, such as on a camping trip.

It was stated that time allocated to recreation is unobligated. This allocation can occur during time which is alloted to means and ends other than recreation but is not being fully used for these other ends and means. Examples could be reflecting on a happy event while driving, enjoying the roadside amenities while enroute to work or mentally developing a hobby while performing a routine work task. However, in most cases the time during which recreation is pursued would appear to be time allocated to recreation.

Much information is needed on personal time budgets before many prescriptive statements can be made about the significance of this descriptor to recreation planning. However, it can safely be said that in our society time is a resource, perhaps a unique resource, and should be considered as such in planning studies.

In most planning reports time is considered to be an independent variable and is generally quantified in terms of the length of the work-week, the work-day or the vacation. If we really desire ours to be a leisure society defined in terms of creative and self-fulfilling uses of non-work time (and all the psychological and sociological implications associated with the possible demise of the Protestant Ethic), should we as planners not give serious consideration to viewing time allocated to recreational engagements as a dependent variable? By viewing time as an independent variable, we tend to accept the idea that recreation is a *residual* rather than the important social input it is. Recreation planners have much to learn about the facilitating and constraining effects of uses and psychological perceptions of time on recreational behavior and about the effects of this behavior on general welfare.

It appears that a structuring of time is necessary before recreation takes on social significance. This structuring, which became more discernable after the Industrial Revolution, makes words like non-obligated, leisure and discretionary time more meaningful. Recreation planners must question their role in resolving any social problems being created by increasing "structured" leisure time. Viewing leisure time as a residual hardly seems like the best approach. Perhaps we should encourage more social rewards for leisure behavior to balance those for work.

At first commitments and allocations of time seem to be one and the same. But this is not the case. Allocations of time can help define the extent of a commitment, but we can be committed to a goal without feeling "time bound" while pursuing it. Both of these dimensions (postulates) offer interesting possibilities for gaining a better understanding of what recreation is.

Conclusion

Certain implications of the behavioral interpretation of recreation planning have been considered above. At this stage of the development of the "science of recreation," recreation planners will adopt those approaches which are useful in getting the job done. Hopefully, the behavioral interpretation will be a useful supplement to the conventional activity approach. Perhaps the primary usefulness is the raising of specific questions in a slightly different manner within a different comparative structure. Perhaps we can now find a little more meaning in such frequently asked questions as, "are we providing appropriate opportunities to recreate?" The question can now be reworded to ask, "Are we providing those recreational opportunities which will elicit those responses in the user that are most instrumental in satisfactorily meeting his needs and desires? These responses (the engagements in activities), the needs of the recreationist (reflected in his goal-objects), and his satisfaction (the level of the experience) can all be associated within the conceptual structure presented. Admittedly, we need greater objectivity and better quantification, but progress is being made in that area too. Perhaps someday we will have a general theory of recreation behavior.

Recreation Behavior and Recreation Demand

Another possible way in which the conceptualization might be useful to recreation planning is that it requires us to go beyond the four conventional causal factors of demand (mobility, leisure time, population and income).

24

What are the positive (and negative) forces (the antecedent conditions) which shape our needs and desires? What causes and gives vigor and direction to our motivations to recreate?

Ours has been called the age of anxiety. If true, could this be a causal factor in rapidly increasing demand for recreation? Also, is this demand of a type that will best be met through the provision of particular types of opportunities, say for jogging? If an increasing number of people are recreating as a form of stress mediation or reduction (as there is strong evidence to support), are we providing appropriate opportunities for the venting of the frustrations and anxieties which accompany high stress levels? Perhaps we should have punching bags, more do-it-yourself wood piles or other modes of creative destruction in our parks and recreation areas.

The authors are convinced that many of our recreational engagements are underlaid in large part (and others to a lesser degree) by our desires to escape temporarily — to disengage, to leave the structured and the non-random. These recreationists are "pushed" from their everyday life-space, by that life-space, at least temporarily, into a restorative ecological behavioral setting — into an environment that is less demanding, into one that is remedial and one that is in many ways, more predictable and less threatening.

Studies of user attitudes, especially reasons for recreating, support the argument that disengagement from the routine is an important reason for engagement in certain forms of outdoor recreation. The high frequencies of answers like "tranquility," "peace and quiet," "leave the city," and so on, suggest that escape is an important motivation and that replenishment of adaptive energies is an important goal.

Researchers in physiological and psychological stress (actually the two cannot be separated because of complex feed-back mechanisms, especially endocrinal activity)[7] agree that the human organism, (including his "psyche"), seeks diversion, escape, locomotion, isolation, disengagement (the terms vary from writer to writer) as modes of coping with stress, frustration or other threats to the biological or psychological integrity of the individual.[8] Although it is tenuous to postulate relations between recreation as a form of stress mediation and reductions in conflict, hostility and aggression, the existence of such relationships is just as difficult to disprove.

The frequently heard argument that recreation, generically conceived, is *not necessary* for mental health is misleading. What is mental health? It is appraised differently by each individual. It is not an absolute and appears to have few definitive requirements before complete breakdown. Are sexual relations (one of our most important forms of recreation) *necessary* for "mental health"? Probably not, but most adults find such relations satisfying, plan to continue to engage in them and would be somewhat disturbed if they were told they could not. The point is that many people find certain forms of outdoor recreation to be personally satisfying and useful to them for normal functioning. This is mental-health-reason enough without giving too much concern to the spillovers to society (which in the judgment of the authors are, at the margin, frequently equal to or greater than the external effects of other forms of social capital, including education and national defense). We are not advocating that the recreationists should not ever pay to engage. Rather, we are saying that before specific recommendations can be made we need to consider which types of recreation needs are being met. Opportunities for temporary escape, which we conjecture have marginal utility curves with non-negative slopes, would logically provide more spin-off benefits to society than would opportunities for skill development, the maintenance of a self-image, or the collection of status symbols.

Recreation Planners as Innovators

Another question being raised is: are recreation planners weather vanes of current styles of life, social conditions and tastes, or are they reflectors of past conditions? Using only the activity approach recreation planning must, by necessity, be based on past responses, which unfortunately might not satisfy current or future needs or tastes. The reader might ask "is it being suggested that the recreation planner become an innovator as well as a provider?" The answer offered is, "are the risks really much different?" Certainly we can afford the risks of recommending more experimentation and innovation in design and management. If the *primary* task of the recreation planner is to plan to provide an appropriate array of real choice opportunities, should we not know more about the latent demands not being supplied? Are the opportunities provided as rewarding as would be alternative opportunities, and how can those opportunities which are provided lead to more rewarding experiences? Lastly, with regard to the function of recreation planners, are we concerned with large blocks or with marginal (incremental) units of utility? It would seem that, in a relatively affluent society, our concern is increasingly being devoted to enhancing welfare in small bits rather than in a lump-sum manner. If so, the questions being raised have even greater relevance.

Based on the previous comments, it is submitted that the demand for or supply of recreation, as defined in this paper, can never be predicted or projected. Can we project the demand for love, the supply of hostility, the future magnitude of society's greed or happiness? It is realized that we need measures of the extent to which recreational goals are being satisfied, but are we using the most appropriate measures? Certainly surrogates, such as rates of use (including numbers of visitors and visitor days), willingness to pay, resource supply and capacity, and other conventional measures must be used. But these measures tell us little about the output of recreation systems. We have better measures of the productivity of other social service systems like health and education. Few of us would accept counts of users of schools and hospitals as sufficient indicators of the effectiveness of investments in these facilities.

26

We make estimates of short-run participation rates in selected recreational *activities*, and these are too frequently taken as demand projections. But should we not attempt to measure also the meanings that people attach to their recreational experiences? Should we not know what types of constraints are being imposed on the application or development of user skills, and will participation rates give us the answer? Since most human behavior is learned behavior, can we as planners in our data acquisition gather any information on what is desired to be learned, explored, or escaped into, what status symbols are collected, why, and with what personal and social benefits?

Recreation as a Social Service

Finally, it is suggested that through a behavioral approach to recreation, the provision of recreation services will be more appropriately viewed as a social service system or sub-system (like education and health services), which provides *important and necessary inputs* to the total social system. These inputs can help *maintain the integrity* or homostasis and/or *promote the growth and development* of individual members of society.

The inputs to any system consist of matter, energy and information — with matter being defined as anything having mass, such as picnic tables, energy being defined as the ability to do work, and information, in general systems theory, being defined as messages, signals or symbols containing meaning which enhance the operants of the system to discriminate and to make decisions. It would seem a fruitful area of inquiry for recreation planners to attempt to appraise the informational value of recreation. The authors are convinced that the degree to which an experience is recreational or not is *best* reflected in the information transformations which occur from the time the user "enters" any recreation system to the time he "leaves" such a system. It is doubtful if he ever really enters and leaves, but the conceptualization is useful. What is being suggested is that the recreationist, with all his learned behavioral patterns, including his norms, values and expectations, enters a recreation system and during the throughput process of the system's operation experiences information changes.

These information transformations occur when the participant interacts with other components of the recreation system, such as the producers or suppliers, other participants, the facilities and the landscape, within this different ecological behavioral setting. The transformations could be of a learning nature and enhance the ability of the recreationist to discriminate. They may be of a buffering type and enhance his adaptive capacities through a change in stimuli orientation (such as would be the case when there is a motivation to escape temporarily information overload). It is contended that these changes in the information of the participant *best* measure the extent to which his experience is recreational or not.

27

Admittedly, there are important energy transformations which occur in many highly active forms of recreation. Part of the experience from these engagements is feeling better physiologically. But the feeling is still based on information processing, either strictly in a physiological sense or including cognition. Accompanying the relaxed physiological state, following the burning up of excessive hormones and other bio-chemical constituents, is our knowledge that we feel better. The conceptualization does not permit that exercising in and of itself is recreation. Rather, exercise is a response which is instrumental to experiencing a recreational state.

In conclusion, it is suggested that the above conceptualization helps make more apparent the types of information necessary for successful recreation planning. Admittedly, much of this information is difficult to obtain, but current progress is encouraging.

Finally, it is hoped that the discussion in this paper has helped establish a psychological set in the mind of the reader which he will find useful in the on-going process of pursuing a better understanding of recreation phenomena — a goal pursuit that is not always recreational!

Footnotes

1) Recreationist in this paper refers to the person seeking a recreational experience and not to the recreation planner, developer or administrator as the word is sometimes used.

2) Several authors have pointed out these broader implications of recreation, but they have all tended to emphasize activities in their analyses and discussions. Cf. Neumeyer and Neumeyer (1958) and Clawson and Knetsch (1966).

3) Elements of the ideas expressed in these postulates are found in several works. Cf. Larrebee and Meyersohn (1958) and Huizinga (1966).

4) These criteria can be combined to define recreation as a human experience which finds its source in voluntary engagements which are motivated by the inherent satisfactions derived therefrom and which occur during non-obligated time. This definition is similar to the one adopted by Gray (1961).

5) The exceptions to goal-directed behavior would be expressive behavior, such as the way we carry ourselves when we walk.

6) As an aside, the authors would advocate that the *ultimate* objective of recreation planning is to promote self-actualization. But we have a way to go before even the more simple forms of recreational behavior are readily and easily experienced. This is especially true for the poor and for certain minority groups.

7) See reference number 7.

8) See references numbers 3, 8, 15, 17, 21, and 22.

References

1. Atkinson, J.W., *An Introduction to Motivation.* Princeton, N.J.: D. Van Nostrand (1968).

2. Berlyne, D.E., *Conflict, Arousal and Curiosity.* N.Y.: McGraw-Hill (1960).

3. Biddle, B.J. and J. Thomas (Eds.), *Role Theory: Concepts and Research..* N.Y.: Wiley (1966).

4. Bloom, B.S., *Stability and Change in Human Characteristics.* N.Y.: Wiley (1965).

5. Bruner, J.S., "On Perceptual Readiness", *Psychological Review.* 64 (1957), 123-52.

6. Clawson, M. and J. Knetsch, *Economics of Outdoor Recreation.* Baltimore: Johns Hopkins Press (1966).

7. Christian, J.J. and D.E. Davis, "Endocrines, Behavior and Population", *Science.* 146 (1964), pp. 1550-60.

8. Festinger, L., "The Motivating Effects of Cognitive Dissonance". In G. Lindsley (Ed.), *Assessment of Human Motives.* N.Y.: Grove Press (1958).

9. Gray, D.E., "Identification of User-Groups in Forest Recreation and Determination of the Characteristics of Such Groups". Unpublished doctoral dissertation, School of Public Administration, University of California (June, 1961).

10. Gutman, H., "The Biological Roots of Creativity". In. R. Mooney and T. Razik (Eds.), *Explorations in Creativity.* N.Y.: Harper and Row (1967).

11. Hampshire, S., *Freedom of the Individual.* N.Y.: Harper and Row (1965).

12. Huizinga, J., *Homo Ludens: A Study of the Play Element of Culture.* Boston: Beacon Press (1966).

13. Laing, R.D., *The Politics of Experience.* N.Y.: Random House (1967).

14. Larrabee, E. and R. Meyersohn (Eds.), *Mass Leisure.* Glencoe, Ill.: Free Press (1958).

15. Lazarus, R.S., *Psychological Stress and the Coping Process.* N.Y.: McGraw-Hill. (1966).

16. Maslow, A.H., *Motivation and Personality.* N.Y.: Harper and Row (1954).

17. Mayer, W. and R. Van Gelder (Eds.), *Physiological Mammalogy.* Vol. I, N.Y.: Academic Press (1963).

18. McClelland, D.C., *The Achieving Society*. N.Y.: D. Van Nostrand Co., Inc. (1961).

19. Morgan, C.T. and R.A. King, *Introduction to Psychology*. N.Y.: McGraw Hill (1966).

20. Neumeyer, M.H. and E.S. Neumeyer, *Leisure and Recreation*. N.Y.: Ronald Press (1958).

21. Selye, H., *The Stress of Life*. N.Y.: McGraw-Hill (1956).

22. Speilberger, C.D., *Anxiety and Behavior*. N.Y.: Academic Press (1966).

STATEWIDE OUTDOOR RECREATION PLANNING
by
Robert L. Pierce

Chief, State Planning and Technical Assistance Section
Lake Central Region, Bureau of Outdoor Recreation
Ann Arbor, Michigan

A need for the training of planners to develop statewide outdoor recreation plans was expressed at a meeting of the National Association of State Outdoor Recreation Liaison Officers (NASORLO) in Denver in May, 1967. These state liaison officers were appointed by the respective governors to administer the Land and Water Conservation Fund program within the states. They requested the Bureau of Outdoor Recreation to work with the states and universities to help train statewide outdoor recreation planners. Subsequently, the Lake Central Region of the BOR contacted the School of Natural Resources of the University of Michigan to develop and present a short course in outdoor recreation planning. The short course reported in these proceedings is an outgrowth of that request.

In developing the course, it was apparent that the differing problems between BOR regions and between states within regions made it impossible to orient the course toward solving specific problems. Therefore, the course was aimed at presenting planning concepts which can be generally applied across the country. Outdoor recreation planners directly involved in developing state outdoor recreation plans may feel this is not the answer to the problems facing them. They may want to know, specifically, how to develop a workable and economical method for conducting an inventory of private facilities, or how to best determine space standards for various recreation activities or types of recreational areas. I do not think a short course on a national level could hope to resolve all such problems for each individual planner. What it all boils down to is that the major purpose of this course was to present ideas and concepts for consideration. Hopefully, these ideas and general concepts will be useful in performing these related but separate planning functions.

Authors of the papers in these proceedings will emphasize the need to obtain and present information which is the best available and pertinent to the purpose to be served. Also emphasized is the need to coordinate ideas and programs and to communicate adequately such ideas. These and the other subjects discussed must be considered in the development of a statewide outdoor recreation plan. Care must be taken to obtain the best information on current and planned recreation programs at all levels of government and for private enterprise. To do this requires adequate coordination with all agencies and organizations providing recreation facilities within a state's boundaries. Only with such coordination and proper information can objectives be established for best meeting the recreation needs within a state. Having established the objectives, they must then be set forth in an action program aimed at alleviating the priority needs over a period of time. So you can see that planning, as an activity, is only part of your total effort. You must also become immersed in the total planning process, which includes decision making and consideration of political implications. These broad responsibilities of state outdoor recreation planners are reflected throughout the Land and Water Conservation Fund (LWCF) Act of 1965. It might be appropriate to give a brief resume of the relationship of statewide outdoor recreation planning to the LWCF program.

Very briefly, the BOR administers a grants-in-aid program under the LWCF. The Fund is administered through a state liaison officer designated by the Governor and is available to a state and its political subdivisions on a 50-50 matching basis. The monies from the Fund can be used for the planning, acquisition, or development of recreation projects by the state and for acquisition and for development of projects by local units of government. I will not go into the source of the Fund.

A state must have an outdoor recreation plan to be eligible for assistance in acquisition and development. All 55 states and territories have completed at least one statewide outdoor recreation plan to date, and many are being revised or updated at this time. We stress that this updating should be done on a continuing basis. As of April 1 of this year, $150.3 million had been awarded under the LWCF. About 2 percent of this total, or over 3.2 million, was awarded for some 71 planning projects. The largest amount of federal assistance for a single planning project was $322,500.

Six states and four territories have chosen not to use LWCF monies for planning purposes. Some of these states are developing outdoor recreation plans as an integral part of overall statewide comprehensive plans with money made available through HUD under Section 701. Others have selected to expend only state monies for the development of the required state plan and thus reserve the monies allocated to them under the LWCF for acquisition and development only.

We do not stress any particular method for financing the outdoor recreation plan, but the use of Section 701 planning money from HUD would help insure that the outdoor recreation plan is closely coordinated with the overall state comprehensive plan. It would also leave more LWCF money for acquisition and development.

We do stress that the outdoor recreation plan should *not* be developed solely for the purpose of meeting a BOR requirement for obtaining LWCF monies, but, rather, as a usable guide for implementing a total outdoor recreation acquisition and development program within a state. To do this requires a coordination of the programs of all appropriate agencies and organizations as pointed out earlier. We have emphasized that the programs of all federal agencies should be adequately considered in a state plan. This requires the *mutual* cooperation of state and federal agencies. In line with this, the bureau has agreements with HUD and the NPS wherein all state outdoor recreation plans submitted to the bureau for LWCF eligibility are transmitted to HUD and the NPS for review. If any conflicts with federal programs are discovered through such review, the conflicts must be resolved.

The Bureau also asks that each state strive to maintain a certain in-house capability to carry on a continuing planning program. We do not necessarily mean to say that a state should be staffed to accomplish the total planning effort, but the state's planning staff should be adequate to provide guidance and leadership for consultants and universities, which are often contracted to do portions of the plan. Speaking of consultants and their role in state out-door recreation planning, I ran across an interesting definition of a consultant the other day: "A consultant is a well-paid expert who is called in at the last minute to help share the blame." I know that definition does not apply to consultants used in statewide outdoor recreation planning!

To get back to some of the items which we like to have considered in a state plan, I think the basic subjects for consideration have been (1) a deter-mination of the demand for outdoor recreation opportunities, (2) an in-ventory of the supply of recreation facilities, (3) an analysis of demand and supply to establish objectives, and (4) an action program aimed at meeting the objectives. Recognition should be given to the quality of the outdoor recreation experiences of the public. All of these subjects are covered to varying degrees in the papers presented. It will be up to you to relate the concepts to your own individual planning situations.

HIERARCHY OF RESPONSIBILITIES
IN OUTDOOR RECREATION PLANNING
by

A. Heaton Underhill

Assistant Director for State Grants and
Resource Studies, Bureau of Outdoor Recreation
U. S. Department of the Interior, Washington, D. C.

Introduction

Since World War II, the desires of Americans for outdoor recreation opportunities have affected all levels of government. Use pressures on federal, state, and local facilities have resulted in increased governmental programs to provide quality outdoor recreation experiences. Comprehensive long-range planning to guide governmental investments and to formulate sound programs has become a standard requirement.

Awareness of these pressures by Congress resulted in the creation of the Outdoor Recreation Resources Review Commission (ORRRC). Its landmark report surveyed our country's outdoor recreation resources, measured present and likely demands upon them to the year 2000, and recommended action to ensure their availability to present and future generations of Americans. I am certain that the conclusions and recommendations of this report are familiar to you, but I would like to highlight a few of them.

Across the country, considerable public land is available for outdoor recreation, but it does not meet the need. In most cases, land available for public recreation is not where the people are. Few places are near enough to metropolitan centers for a day's outing. By the turn of the century, three-quarters of the people will live in metropolitan areas. These urban dwellers will have the greatest need for outdoor recreation, and their need will be the most difficult to satisfy. Urban centers have the fewest facilities per capita and the sharpest competition for land use.

ORRRC felt that the keys to making outdoor recreation opportunities more available were private enterprise, the states, and local government. It felt that the role of federal agencies should be one of cooperation and assistance. Thus, ORRRC reaffirmed the obvious fact that all levels of government have an interest in and responsibility for meeting the nation's outdoor recreation needs. It was concluded, however, that the state governments have the dominant public responsibility and should play the pivotal role.

ORRRC identified the roles of the different levels of government and the private sector in the following manner:

The role of the federal government should be:

1. Preservation of scenic areas, natural wonders, primitive areas, and historic sites of national significance.

2. Management of federal lands for the broadest possible recreation benefit consistent with other essential uses.

3. Cooperation with the states through technical and financial assistance.

4. Promotion of interstate arrangements, including federal participation where necessary.

5. Assumption of vigorous, cooperative leadership in a nationwide recreation effort.

The states should play a pivotal role in making outdoor recreation opportunities available by:

1. Acquisition of land, development of sites, and provision and maintenance of facilities of state or regional significance.

2. Assistance to local governments.

3. Provision of leadership and planning.

Local governments should expand their efforts to provide outdoor recreation opportunities, with particular emphasis upon securing open space and developing recreation areas in and around metropolitan and other urban areas.

Individual initiative and private enterprise should continue to be the most important force in outdoor recreation, providing many and varied opportunities for a vast number of people, as well as the goods and services used by people in their recreation activities. Government should encourage the work of nonprofit groups wherever possible. It should also stimulate desirable commercial development, which can be particularly effective in providing facilities and services where demand is sufficient to return a profit.

Two rather obvious considerations respecting the private sector should be noted. First, it cannot be expected to perform any welfare functions that outdoor recreation may be asked to provide for society. Second, private areas or facilities have no permanent dedication. If it is important that a particular private facility be perpetuated, public action of some kind may be necessary.

From time to time there have been moves to classify certain types of recreation services as the exclusive domain of the private entrepreneur in order to eliminate or prevent unfair governmental competition. Golf courses, boat liveries, ski slopes, and recently campgrounds are most often mentioned in this category. I disagree with such classification. Certainly, the provision of facilities of this kind by private investment should be encouraged and unfair or unneeded governmental competition prevented. However, there are many instances where a public facility can greatly broaden the use base or can better fulfill an unmet need. Each case must be judged on its merits.

Responsibilities of Federal Government

To fulfill the respective roles that it had assigned the various sectors, ORRRC recommended that:

1. A federal program of grants-in-aid should be established promptly to provide matching grants to the states to stimulate recreation planning and to assist in acquiring lands and developing facilities for public outdoor recreation.

36

2. Each state, through a central agency, should develop a long-range plan for outdoor recreation to provide adequate opportunities for the public, to acquire additional areas where necessary, and to preserve outstanding natural sites.

3. Local governments should give great emphasis to the needs of their citizens for outdoor recreation by considering them in all land-use planning, by opening existing areas with recreation potential to use, and where necessary, by acquiring new areas.

Thus, for the first time, a national outdoor recreation policy was suggested, and the roles of the different levels of government were identified. An understanding of these roles gives us useful insight into the hierarchy of responsibilities in outdoor recreation planning.

Another ORRRC recommendation was the establishment of a new federal agency for outdoor recreation planning and coordination. Both the administration and Congress responded. The Bureau of Outdoor Recreation (BOR) was established in 1962 to promote coordination of federal plans and activities generally relating to outdoor recreation and to formulate and maintain a comprehensive nationwide outdoor recreation plan, taking into consideration the plans of the various federal agencies and those of the states and their political subdivisions.

The nationwide plan will be presented to Congress and the President late in 1968. It will be a policy document to guide actions that will help assure that the variety of outdoor recreation opportunities desired by the American people will be available in sufficient quantity and quality in the general locations needed. Within the context of outdoor recreation, consideration will be given to the preservation of natural beauty and to related means of maintaining and enhancing the quality of the environment. The plan will address itself to urban and rural programs and efforts of public agencies, private organizations, and individuals. It will recognize the major recreation land and water in relation to the demand for outdoor recreation opportunities. It will highlight trends in activities and the socio-economic factors affecting them.

The plan will deal with nationwide and multi-state needs but will not indicate specific state, county, or local needs; i.e., numbers of campsites, playgrounds, picnic tables, etc. . . .From all of this will be developed policy recommendations and broad priorities for programs and actions applicable to all levels of government, the private recreation sector and individuals. Included will be legislative proposals and an indication of the general measure of aggregate expenditures required at the federal level.

Coordination of federal recreation planning and the development of the nationwide outdoor recreation plan has been a challenging assignment, to put it mildly. There are 21 agencies at the federal level *directly* involved in developing recreation plans. They are:

Department of Agriculture
Forest Service

Rural Community Development Service
Soil Conservation Service

Department of Commerce
Economic Development Administration

Department of Defense
Corps of Engineers (Civil Functions)

Department of Housing and Urban Development
Land and Facilities Development Administration
Office of Planning Standards and Coordination

Department of the Interior
Bureau of Indian Affairs
Bureau of Land Management
Bureau of Outdoor Recreation
Bureau of Reclamation
Bureau of Sport Fisheries and Wildlife
Federal Water Pollution Control Administration
National Park Service

Department of Transportation
Bureau of Public Roads

Interdependent agencies, boards, commissions, committees, and councils
Appalachian Regional Commission
Delaware River Basin Commission
Federal Power Commission
President's Council on Recreation and Natural Beauty
Tennessee Valley Authority
Water Resources Council and Regional River Basin Commissions

The planning functions of these agencies are nationwide to local in scope. In addition, there are many other agencies that are concerned with outdoor recreation in the administration of technical and financial assistance programs, the management of land and water resources, or in research.

The primary federal responsibilities in outdoor recreation planning would then appear to be threefold. First, there is the nationwide outdoor recreation plan. It is being prepared by the Bureau of Outdoor Recreation; it will be broad in scope — a coordinating vehicle for action programs by all levels of government and by private agencies and entrepreneurs. Second, there is the planning function of each action agency such as the National Park Service, the Forest Service, the Army Corps of Engineers, the Bureau of Sport Fisheries and Wildlife, the Tennessee Valley Authority, and so forth, all of which must develop long-range plans for performing their particular responsibility in the outdoor recreation field. They must also prepare shorter, more specific action plans. Which area will be bought this year? How much for operation and management on each forest? How many new campgrounds or tent sites at "X" reservoir? These and a thousand similar questions must be answered by the plans of the action agencies. The third federal responsibility

38

is to assist other levels of government in their recreation planning. This is being accomplished to a considerable degree with the grants-in-aid, technical assistance, basic research, and other assistance to state and local planning agencies.

In addition to its planning and coordinating functions, the Bureau of Outdoor Recreation administers the Land and Water Conservation Fund Act of 1965, which has had an immeasurable effect in stimulating comprehensive statewide outdoor recreation planning. Prior to implementation of the Act, most states were very weak in statewide recreation planning. There were notable exceptions. California, New York, Massachusetts, New Jersey, Pennsylvania, Michigan, Wisconsin, Utah, Nevada, and Washington, to name a few, had made advances in this direction. But, for the most part, there had been no overall, long-range planning on a continuous basis. Most states did not even have a unit within state government to provide for coordinated recreation planning.

Ideally, the Nationwide Outdoor Recreation Plan should have come first to provide a broad framework for the state plans. This, unfortunately, was not the case. The states have had to find their own way.

Responsibilities of State Governments

Since the Land and Water Conservation Fund Program began in 1965, each state, to qualify for grants under the Act, has designated an agency responsible for outdoor recreation planning and has set up an on-going planning program. To date, all of the states have submitted qualified initial outdoor recreation plans to the Bureau, and most have completed their first revisions. The Land and Water Conservation Fund has assisted these planning efforts with grants totaling over $3.2 million. In addition, the "701" Planning Program, administered by the Department of Housing and Urban Development, has been an important stimulus to recreation planning as a part of the comprehensive urban development plans of states, metropolitan areas, and small communities.

The statewide comprehensive outdoor recreation plans submitted to BOR have shown a variety of approaches and levels of refinement in their analysis of outdoor recreation requirements. These variations have been recognized by the Bureau in its attempt to be flexible in the review and acceptance of the plans. Emphasis has been placed on how comprehensive the plan is and how realistic has been the programming to meet needs.

It is difficult to generalize about the present status of state recreation planning because of the enormous variations in population characteristics, resources, organizations, and current capabilities of the states. In a few states there is a state planning agency that has responsibility for all planning including outdoor recreation planning. In others, the recreation planning function is performed by the state departments of conservation, by the state highway departments, the fish and game departments, or by the parks and recreation departments. Sometimes the function is assigned to state units responsible for industrial and economic development. There are at the present time 13 different types of agencies performing this function.

By and large, the responsibility for long-range recreation planning, at the state level has not been clearly established. In most cases, the function has been assigned to an existing unit of state government, usually a line agency such as the State Parks Department. Often the special interest of the agency is reflected in the plan at the expense of a comprehensive consideration or analysis of all the state's recreation problems.

There is evidence, however, that the states are moving toward a broader approach to planning. This trend may be further assisted by current reorganization of state government. In California, for example, seven separate resource departments have been combined into a single resource agency. This type of consolidation will further coordinate planning and will assist in reducing conflicts in recreation programs. One of the major problems at all levels of government has been the great number of different agencies involved in providing outdoor recreation.

Recreation planning, of course, has been influenced by the traditional functions of governments. Historically, federal and state agencies have been the suppliers of non-urban natural areas, scenic attractions, forest preserves, and fish and wildlife refuges or hunting grounds. Recently, however, more emphasis has been placed on user-oriented, more intensively developed recreation sites within reasonable travel distances from metropolitan areas.

Congress, for example, has authorized the addition of more than 2.2 million acres to the National Park System in the past few years. Thirty-two of the 34 areas set aside — seashores, lakeshores, and parks — are located near large urban centers. They are within easy driving distance of 120 million people, and include: Fire Island National Seashore, Indiana Dunes National Lakeshore, Delaware Water Gap National Recreation Area, Cape Lookout National Seashore, the "Land Between The Lakes," and many more. This is the thrust of what the President refers to as the "new conservation" — the promise to bring the parks to the people.

While these efforts are definite steps forward in reaching our national goals, there still remains the level of outdoor recreation opportunity that is most critically deficient — the availability of near-at-hand parks and recreation areas, and neighborhood and community facilities, traditionally viewed as the problem and responsibility of local government. By and large, states have not adequately considered urban recreation needs in their state plans or budgets. There are all too few examples of aggressive state action or leadership in meeting urban deficiencies.

State recreation expenditures have, for the most part, been directed to the state park systems, state forest systems, and state fish and wildlife areas. Lands bought have been the cheaper lands, more remote from population centers. State agencies administering recreation areas numbered over 200 in 1964, and had a total expenditure in excess of $247 million. This represents a 61 percent increase over the comparable figure for 1960 reported by 165 agencies. Total expenditure reported in 1955 was $87 million, and in 1960, $152 million.[1]

Since the enactment of the Land and Water Conservation Fund Act, states have stepped up their expenditures considerably. They also have shown an increased willingness to share funds with their political subdivisions. A few states are showing special initiative in the consideration of urban recreation problems. The recent Supreme Court decisions resulting in reapportionment of the rural-oriented state legislatures is another factor helping to focus state attention on urban needs.

The state of New York, for example, has helped to finance a study of New York City's outdoor recreation needs and is now in the process of acquiring lands for state parks within the city. One of the first will be the Harlem River Bronx State Park, which will comprise over 50 acres, and will be developed and operated by the state. I am not suggesting this as the solution to urban problems, but to point out the necessity for new approaches that may break with the traditional role of our levels of government in planning and providing recreation opportunities.

States and their localities have taken advantage of federal funds for acquisition and development, through the Land and Water Conservation Fund Act, the Open Space Program, the Small Watershed Act, and others. Thirty-three percent of the cities reporting their source of public funds for city recreation and park expenditures were assisted through federal programs.[2] As of the middle of April 1968, grants from the Land and Water Conservation Fund Act to states and localities total $153,826,362 for planning, acquisition, and development.

Since 1960, almost half of the states have passed bond issues for outdoor recreation programs, primarily for acquisition and development. The total of special state bond issues for outdoor recreation has already passed the $1 billion mark. Generally, the funds from bonds have been used for direct state programs and for grants-in-aid to cities and counties to assist them in acquiring and/or developing recreation areas. This sharing can be justified on the basis that local facilities help to relieve pressure on state facilities. It is also good politics; without it, passage of the bond issues might have been difficult, if not impossible. Quite obviously, state voters and taxpayers are also all local voters and taxpayers, so in the long run it boils down to what level of government is in the best position to meet particular recreation needs.

Numerous interrelationships between governments at different levels have been mentioned. In providing outdoor recreation there is some measure of responsibility at every level, with no clear-cut lines between them. Clearly, if a hierarchy exists, it is a very flexible one in which there are diversity and over-lapping activities that may continue to grow. Within this hierarchy the states have the major role and an unusual opportunity to exercise leadership in the field of outdoor recreation, if they desire to do so. They are closer to their citizens and to local problems and opportunities than are federal agencies. They include larger areas, and usually have more authority and resources than either their political subdivisions or private groups. States can provide leadership and initiative in cooperative planning for outdoor recreation within their borders. The opportunity is there. Communities and regional authorities can do the detailed planning to develop local action programs; in fact, these are the only levels of government that can do it well, but they are too restricted in outlook to do the comprehensive planning needed at the state level.

Responsibilities of Local Governments

Each state's involvement in urban recreation problems will have to depend on its capability to respond to conditions within the state. In spite of these considerations, however, the states should provide the basis for coordinated planning. The state outdoor recreation plan should be the framework for local plans and programs, and should provide guidance for the effective allocation of funds from all sources.

There is probably no state that can readily afford to take over direct provision of urban recreation. Present federal assistance programs may also be inadequate to provide the finances required. It will only be through concerted efforts of all levels of government that these deficiencies can be overcome.

It is our political heritage that wherever possible problems should be solved at the lowest level of government. When this becomes impossible, or a lower level of government is unwilling to fulfill its role, then it has been customary for other governmental units to assume the responsibility. Sometimes this has been accomplished through federal programs of grants-in-aid, technical assistance, credit, and other measures to assist states and localities in meeting their needs. These programs have been based on a philosophy of "creative federalism," a partnership of governments.

States are urged to provide the same assistance to the subdivisions within their jurisdiction. Efforts can be made to encourage local initiative through the planning process. Whereas the state outdoor recreation plan cannot and should not be a collection of local plans, it should provide guidance for programs covering all activities of the public and private sector that affect the supply of recreation within the state. Effective local planning is required to insure proper location and development of recreation areas within the locality.

In addition, outdoor recreation is difficult to isolate from other aspects of comprehensive planning, especially at the local level. It should be integrated with planning for schools, roads, and water supplies. A major objective of the state planning process, therefore, should be to stimulate planning by local government, and where necessary to provide assistance in preparation of local plans.

As is the case with other levels of government, there is a diversity of local agencies providing outdoor recreation. Sine 1960, however, there has been a noticable trend toward combined local park and recreation agencies, which more than tripled in number during the five-year period from 1960 to 1965, and in 1965 had the following composition:

Local Public Agencies Providing Outdoor Recreation
by Type of Managing Authority[3]

Type of Agency	No.	Percent of Total
Combined park and recreation	1304	41.8
Separate recreation	818	26.2
Separate park	428	13.7
School	142	4.6
Other public	425	13.7
Total	3117	100.0

All types of recreation expenditures by local agencies have been increasing. Since 1940, the money spent by local park and recreation agencies increased from $31 million annually to more than $905 million in 1965. Many local recreation agencies also are utilizing school areas to a greater extent in expanding their recreation programs. School recreation areas used in community recreation programs total over 16,000 and comprise 116,706 acres. In 1960, 1,559 agencies reported use of school areas for general public recreation purposes; in 1965, 2,856 agencies reported such use.[4]

Some communities, like Arlington, Virginia, have used their school grounds as an integral part of their community recreation program and have installed many more facilities than are required just for the school. To encourage this type of community planning, the Bureau of Outdoor Recreation has ruled that the acquisition of land and the development of facilities over the basic needs of the particular school are eligible for assistance from the Land and Water Conservation Fund. As with other Fund projects, the need must be established in the statewide comprehensive outdoor recreation plan and the priority established by the state.

There are still a significant number of school sites, however, that are open only during school hours. These and other potential recreation resources should be explored during the planning process to supplement existing recreation facilities, especially in urban areas. Mobile facilities, rooftop playgrounds, and other new approaches should be considered also. The key element is the willingness to explore outside the traditional bounds of our own particular bailiwicks and to seek imaginative solutions through new measures.

There are two important aspects of recreation planning at the community level. First, there is a need for planning for required facilities and areas and fitting them into overall community needs; and second, the need for outdoor activity and education programs for all age groups. I call this program planning. The latter depends heavily on qualified leadership. In 1965 there were 24,298 playgrounds operated by 2,227 agencies. This was the highest number of playgrounds, and agencies reporting playgrounds, recorded in any of the National Recreation and Park Association's yearbooks. But only one-fourth of these areas were open under leadership the year round, and most of the others were provided with leaders only during the summer months.

The manpower shortage of recreation personnel at the federal, state and local level is being studied in detail by the National Recreation and Park Association for the Department of Health, Education and Welfare. Results of this study will be of considerable value to agencies responsible for providing sufficient, well-rounded recreation programs. It is in this area that we also need to encourage the private sector's contribution to local programs through volunteer work, sponsorships, and donations, especially in urban areas.

As previously shown, states and localities have increased expenditures for outdoor recreation acquisition and development. But these efforts have not kept pace with demand. By the year 2000, our participation in the major forms of summertime outdoor recreation activities will be four times greater than it was in 1960. In 1965, we enjoyed 51 percent more outdoor recreation experiences than we did in 1960. At the same time the cost of land for inclusion in new parks rose at a rate greater than the price escalation of either farm or suburban subdivision land.[5]

In large measure, municipal recreation areas are designed to meet day-to-day needs for active recreation within walking distance of where people live. From the use figures that have been supplied by city after city, it is obvious that the supply is woefully inadequate to meet the demand. The county recreation areas, as might be expected, appear to bridge a gap between municipal and state areas. They tend to be larger than municipal areas, but many are as intensively developed.

This is not the place for a discussion of the role of county government in American democracy; however, the diverse positions of counties in this regard leads to great variation in recreation programs. Smith Point County Park on Fire Island rivals Jones Beach in use intensity. Some of the parks of Los Angeles County, California, or Essex County, New Jersey, are indistinguishable from the better municipal parks in our larger cities and are certainly as heavily used. The Wisconsin county forests, on the other hand, are about as wild and as non-urban as can be found anywhere. The Illinois county forests create a green belt around Chicago that greatly enhances the recreation opportunities of citizens of the Windy City.

Among the more successful county systems providing outdoor recreation are the county conservation boards in Iowa. Much of the success in that state can be attributed to the leadership and assistance provided by the state government. The State Conservation Commission took a leading part in promoting passage of enabling legislation authorizing establishment of county conservation boards. After passage of the act, the state continued its interest by establishing an Office of Director of County Conservation Activities within the Commission. This office, manned by veteran personnel with extensive and varied experience, offered leadership to county conservation boards during and after their formative years. The success of this leadership is shown by the accomplishments made within a short span of ten years. Ninety-one of 99 counties in the state have established county conservation boards. By January 1968, these boards had acquired 546 areas totaling 27,375 acres.

There is every indication that county governments will assume an increasingly important role in providing recreational opportunities. In the past five years county authorities have shown a marked acceleration of interest; this obviously reflects the pressures they are receiving from the citizens they represent. The National Association of County Officials has, in recent years, explored steps that counties can take in this area and has urged its members to assume greater responsibility in the recreation field. In urban areas counties can often assume a regional role in planning for and providing recreation opportunities. In the suburban and rural areas into which the major population centers are expanding, the counties share with the state the opportunity to set aside open space and recreation land before it is pre-empted for other uses or priced out of the market.

In recreation planning, the counties have proved to be the most convenient units for various types of studies. They can be used as the building blocks to form river basins, metropolitan dominated regions, political units such as states, or in other ways be of value for planning purposes. Statistics are available on a county basis, and the counties represent a level of government that can be either urban, suburban, or rural. It appears logical that the county role in outdoor recreation will increase.

The deficiencies of open space and recreation opportunity within walking distance of where people live already have been stressed. It is the major problem facing recreation planners and administrators today. Every community has some unused recreation potential if carefully explored.

Each state is in a good position to assign roles for meeting recreation needs to all the pertinent public and private agencies within its jurisdiction. While most federal agencies do not want the states dictating what their role should be, they have already shown a willingness to work with both the state planners and the state and local action agencies to assure coordination of information and of progress and to work out the federal role.

In planning for as well as providing outdoor recreation, the states are in a pivotal position. Basic information on supply, demand, and need should be shared so that all levels of planners are using the same base.

Research

No discussion of the hierarchy of responsibility for outdoor recreation planning would be complete without some mention of research. The lines of demarcation between planning, research, and technical assistance are indistinct. A number of our most pressing research needs are in the field of planning. In fact, most of the badly needed research in the social science area might well be called planning studies.

The projection of demand for outdoor recreation into the future and the translation of that demand into areas, facilities, and programs is the most difficult problem facing recreation planners at all levels today. The solution to this problem will require an almost endless host of studies covering motivation, social patterns, economic trade-offs, travel habits, substitution tolerance, impact on resources, and demographic variables, to mention just a few. If usable demand models are to be constructed, teams of our most brilliant psychologists, sociologists, economists, and political scientists must be formed to work with the best of our resource scientists.

As I said in Logan, Utah, two weeks ago, I am delighted to report that the National Academy of Sciences has formed a committee of about 25 scientists, representing a wide range of disciplines but with a heavy social science flavor, to convene at Woods Hole, Massachusetts, early in June for a week-long workshop. Their aim will be to formulate a suggested national outdoor recreation research program, to stimulate greater research effort in the social science aspects of the problem and to recommend steps that can be taken to close the gaps in our current knowledge.

Summary

My subject has been the "Hierarchy of Responsibilities in Outdoor Recreation Planning." I fear I have wandered considerably beyond the confines of the title. My only excuse is my firm conviction that plans are worthless unless they are implemented. Unfortunately, most planners refuse to recognize this. I firmly believe that planners should not only devise plans that can be implemented but also assume some responsibility for seeing that the plans they have formulated *are* implemented.

Now, let me briefly summarize. At the local or regional level, planning for recreation cannot, or at least should not, be separated from other kinds of community planning. It should be part of an overall comprehensive planning effort. In my opinion, federal financial assistance for this kind of planning should be consolidated under one agency. The Department of Housing and Urban Development is probably the logical agency to administer such a program.

At the state level, it is possible to develop a statewide comprehensive outdoor recreation plan. However, recreation planning cannot be carried on in a vacuum; and here, too, it is preferable that the outdoor recreation plan be a part of a comprehensive state plan covering all phases of governmental responsibility for orderly development. If there is no comprehensive state planning, then the outdoor recreation planning must be closely coordinated with any planning that is being done. Here again it would appear desirable to center any federal support in a single agency. Since the Department of Housing and Urban Development has supported comprehensive state planning under its "701" Program, I think again it is the logical place for such consolidation. However, the functional agencies should be in a position to specify what is to be included in the plans covering its area of responsibility and should review the plans for adequacy and should follow up to see that plans are implemented. Under the Land and Water Conservation Fund grant program, for example, the Bureau of Outdoor Recreation should continue to set plan requirements, review plans for adequacy, and evaluate project proposals against the plan even though the Department of Housing and Urban Development has financed the recreation planning effort under its "701" Program.

All of the federal agencies that administer public lands or waters must develop plans for both the long-range and the day-to-day management of these systems. It is imperative, however, that such planning be coordinated with state and local efforts. Local, state, and federal planners share the responsibility for seeing that such coordination is accomplished.

The Bureau of Outdoor Recreation is charged by law with being the federal focal point for outdoor recreation planning and coordination. The first Nationwide Outdoor Recreation Plan will be a broad policy guide, establishing the roles and responsibilities of the various levels of government. It will point up needs and will recommend actions to meet those needs. It will be a coordinating document which provides a framework within which the federal action agencies, the states, and local communities can formulate more detailed plans to provide outdoor recreation opportunities to all Americans both for today and for tomorrow.

Planning responsibility will fall into place without too much difficulty if information is freely exchanged. The greatest problem facing both planners and related operants is to devise methods for keeping each other informed. In fact, as our bureaucracy increases in complexity, this may well be the most pressing problem facing public administration. If hierarchy can be defined as a company of angels, it may well be that we will need just that to achieve a final solution.

References

1. National Park and Recreation Association, *1966 Recreation and Park Yearbook,* p. 27.

2. *Ibid.,* Table 38.

3. *Ibid.,* Table 22.

4. *Ibid.,* pg. 49.

5. Bureau of Outdoor Recreation, *Recreation Land Price Escalation,* (1967), pg. 4.

VARIABLES WHICH MUST BE CONSIDERED IN OUTDOOR RECREATION PLANNING

by

Frederick G. Styles

Chief, Division of State Plans, Bureau of Outdoor Recreation
U.S. Department of the Interior, Washington, D.C.

This short course helps answer a continuing need to pull together the various disciplines and the people who are engaged in recreation planning. We in the Bureau of Outdoor Recreation believe that one of our most important functions lies in promoting seminars such as these. We administer a grant program to federal, state, and local agencies of over $100 million annually. However, the impact of this expenditure is slight in comparison to the total public expenditure for recreation at all levels. Our most important contribution, therefore, might best be measured by the extent to which we can point up gaps in knowledge and approaches to recreation problems and, using our own resources as well as those of universities and other public and private institutions, assist in filling the gaps.

The title of my presentation is "Variables Which Must be Considered in Outdoor Recreation Planning." I propose to keep my remarks at a fairly broad level — first, because aspects of the subject appear to be covered in depth in other papers. Secondly, I would like to take this opportunity, based on our experience with state recreation planning over the past four years, to make some general observations about the direction in which we seem to be heading.

Professor Brazer will present a paper on "public goods." I am not sure in what context the term is being used, but I do believe it is a consideration of vital importance to recreation planning in the public sector. To my knowledge, there is no compelling evidence which indicates that a lack of recreation opportunities leads to physical or social ills. This, of course, should not deter us from identifying the public interest in outdoor recreation. The same sort of statement could be made about public education, for example, but we have established a high school education for every child as a social goal within our society. At the same time, recreation does present some social problems. I want to steer clear of entrapment in semantic difficulties regarding the definition of recreation. However, when recreation is defined solely in the light of the immediate pleasure to be derived from it — and in no other terms — it is difficult to view it seriously as a matter of public concern. This is particularly true today when the weight of other social problems is presenting a staggering burden to public bodies at all levels. Therefore, we should make a concerted effort to determine the real values which accrue to society as a result of opportunities to participate in outdoor recreation. At the same time, we must avoid making extravagant claims for the benefits and values of these opportunities.

I believe that the people working in the field of outdoor recreation are among the most dedicated and hard-working to be found in government.

Admittedly, they have a rough battle — recreation and conservation seem to be the first things to go when budgets get tight, and many a park and recreation area has proved irresistible to the highway planner. However, I am afraid that a number of people in the recreation field have developed martyr complexes. They equate recreation with God and motherhood, and if you attack their assumptions or proposals you are attacking the very foundations of our society. We should not be forced to take this extreme position. Our acceptance of the fact that there is nothing mystical and even terribly scientific about our goals can help us get on with the job of asserting a proper role for recreation within our society. Recreation is a legitimate interest of government, if for no other reason than the fact that a society which has achieved the highest standard of living the world has ever known ought to be committed to the provision of a wide range of amenities for its citizens — including meaningful outdoor recreation opportunities.

At this point, I should perhaps make it clear that I do not believe that our planning requirements in recreation are necessarily any less sophisticated or complex than other fields in the public sector. Nor do I cavalierly dismiss the fact that recreation must compete for funds and support in the public arena where aggressive demands are also being made for housing, health services, transportation, education, and a host of other services and facilities. Even in this regard, however, it might well be that we have taken a competitive posture where, in reality, we do not need to. If our efforts to ensure adequate outdoor recreation opportunities, to preserve scenic resources, and to enhance the quality of the environment generally are to be effective, they must become integral considerations in every public program. Recreation cannot operate in a fully independent way in the public sector; it must be an integral part of a total effort to provide all needed services.

There are many of us, I am sure, who believe that we need more central planning and coordination in the recreation field. At the same time opportunities for outdoor recreation and a concern for environmental quality should guide the actions of the highway engineer, the urban planner, the public housing expert, the health services planner, and any number of other disciplines which are shaping our physical and social environment. Our task, therefore, is to provide some sense of direction and a framework within which the recreation potential of other public and private programs can be exploited. We cannot hope to make recreation our own exclusive province and, to the extent that we attempt to do so, we will be doing a real disservice to the public.

The use of the term "variables" is perfectly valid in the context of explaining the factors which influence participation in outdoor recreation. At the same time, I believe we have perhaps over-emphasized the sort of descriptive analysis which the term may imply. One of my biases in recreation planning is that we seem to be too preoccupied with what people do now as a basis for predicting what they will do in the future. This has been the history of most of our outdoor recreation plans. Of course, like the highway engineers, we come out smelling like roses because our predictions become self-fulfilling — the more we provide areas and facilities for certain types or uses at certain locations, the more they are used in predictable fashion. And, in any case, the sheer volume of demand relative to developed recreation resources will continue to save our face for some time to come.

I would certainly concede that to construct a model which explained why people participated in certain recreation activities would be extremely useful. It would be even more useful as a way of testing how they might react under alternative arrangements. It is in this latter area where I believe we need to place greater emphasis. As I stated earlier, we do not have any clear guidelines regarding the necessity of recreation as a condition of modern life. I suspect that most of us are pragmatists in that we concede that the best we can do is to provide areas and facilities which permit the maximum range of choice for individual tastes and pursuits. However, it seems to me that we should not assume that all types of recreation are equally worthwhile, or that somehow government has a responsibility to provide unlimited opportunity for all types of recreation activity, regardless of cost.

In commenting upon the direction of contemporary American society, historian Arthur Schlesinger, Jr. poses the following question: "Will it be an epoch when the American people, seeking mass distraction and mass surcease through mass media, will continue to grow more and more indistinguishable from one another? Or will it be an epoch when people will use leisure creatively to develop their own infinitely diverse individualism?" This question, it seems to me, is quite germane to our discussion here. What are our goals in recreation and how do they relate to the broader goals of our society? Are we to react to fads, are we to relate recreation opportunities to the lowest common denominator in terms of desires, or are we to provide some positive direction in our programs? Presumably, we have the technological know-how to create an artificial surf at every beach to satisfy the growing demand for surfing, or to construct indoor ski-runs within our cities for year-round skiing, but is this investment in the public interest, and how do we decide? There is undoubtedly a number of us who will balk at posing alternatives in this light; it smacks, perhaps, of deciding what people ought to do, of artifically creating desires. However, as Marion Clawson points out, the continuation of past trends in recreation use leads, in a few decades, to total recreation figures which are improbable, even absurd.[1] It is obvious that the public sector cannot continue to provide areas and facilities at the present rate, and it is equally obvious that due to population pressures, the quality of the outdoor recreation experience in many areas will be reduced unless some action is taken. If any of you have ever observed the floor of Yosemite Valley on a mid-summer weekend, you know what I mean. Therefore, we have to make choices whether we like it or not.

I would like to suggest that we experiment in outdoor recreation, that we draw upon other disciplines in this process, and finally that we seek positive and creative ways of influencing participation. There is nothing un-American about this, and we might even take a few lessons from Madison Avenue. Furthermore, the development of more adequate price and costing techniques should help us in selecting the most promising areas for investment. In this process some new concepts of outdoor recreation will undoubtedly evolve. Certainly the continued growth of our urban population would seem to indicate this.

At least 70 percent of our population is now urbanized; our metropolitan area population is growing at a faster rate than the urban population as a whole; and our larger metropolitan areas are growing at a faster rate than our smaller metropolitan areas. Larger and larger proportions of the American people are being removed from immediate or relatively easy access to the non-urban outdoors. Some observers have suggested that increasing generations of American people who have been exposed to urban life only may conceivably lose, rather than increase, interest in outdoor recreation. The findings of the Outdoor Recreation Resources Review Commission tend to support this hypothesis. It was found that non-whites and those in lower income brackets have lower participation rates in outdoor recreation, and that in general, urbanism as a way of life reduces outdoor recreation activity.[2] If we follow this line, it becomes clear that traditional outdoor recreation activities — such as hunting, camping, backpacking, and even fishing — may soon involve such a small proportion of the total population as to raise serious questions regarding the validity of public expenditures for these purposes.

The ORRRC Report poses the policy question in this way: "Should it be made public policy to increase the outdoor recreation activity of the urban population by some combination of programs designed to modify taste, to make outdoor recreation facilities more accessible and to increase effective demand for outdoor recreation facilities?" I think most of us would answer this question in the affirmative. At the very least we are realizing that many groups within our society — teenagers, the aged, the disadvantaged — need encouragement, transportation, special equipment or instructions, and a number of other incentive-building and guidance programs if they are to find constructive uses of their leisure time.

Assuming that we have identified positive values for certain outdoor recreation activities, how can participation be stimulated? The answer to this question may call for a new definition of leisure, and there is some evidence that our concepts may already be changing in this regard. Margaret Mead points out that within our society leisure has been viewed traditionally as the reward for hard work.[3] In our present day culture, leisure assumes much greater importance as a reflection of the direction of our culture. For many individuals, it has replaced work as the central force in providing satisfaction and fulfillment. It is significant, for example, that labor unions are increasingly becoming concerned with what their members can do with their growing leisure time. Recently, Walter Reuther, President of the United Auto Workers, announced the establishment of a U.A.W. Department of Recreation and Leisure Time Activities.

In revising our approach to outdoor recreation, it seems to me there are at least two courses of action which appear immediately promising. The first involves adoption of a positive role by government in education and promotion of outdoor recreation. In this regard our public schools offer a very real potential. Professional educators will undoubtedly resist any attempts to expand further an already overloaded curriculum in our post-Sputnik era. However, there are alternatives, and in the long run they are probably more useful — we can incorporate into our social studies, science, and arts and literature courses certain elements of appreciation and understanding of the outdoors. We can stress respect for land, water, and wildlife resources, and an understanding of man's place in the natural world. And we can teach certain outdoor skills, knowledge, and attitudes which will result in maximum satisfaction. We can also use the outdoors as a laboratory for subject matter courses. Further, we should exploit the potential of mass media communication such as movies, radio, and television. Our objectives should be to instill certain values which will result in life-long habits in terms of the productive use and enjoyment of the nation's outdoor recreation resources.

The second course of action which I would suggest is that we find new forms of outdoor recreation which reflect the realities of urban life. We need to increase the accessibility of existing resource areas to urban populations and to build in appropriate outdoor areas as part of the urban environment. If necessary, we may have to physically transport people, in an organized way, out into the open countryside. If our air pollution problems become any more severe, such "R&R" periods for urban dwellers may become a necessity, rather than a luxury. There are a number of exciting experiments in recreation which are being carried on in urban areas throughout the country. I note that Mr. Heckscher of the New York City Parks Department recently announced that New Yorkers would be permitted to plant flower and vegetable gardens in city parks.

For a number of reasons, we in the recreation field tend to be traditionalists. Hopefully we have laid to rest the struggle between the "petunia pluckers" and the "tee shirt and whistle boys," but a number of other cherished notions seem to persist. Even in the face of enormous demands and rising lands costs, we have been slow to use innovative devices such as development rights and scenic easements. It is true that in our urban areas we are now looking to vacant lots, roof-tops, parking lots, and a whole range of other unoccupied space which may be suitable for outdoor recreation. But we have been hampered by the view that "if you don't own it, you can't control it." And the same point can be made about our recreation programs. You may not consider a "wed in" at Prospect Park to be a contribution to outdoor recreation, but if such activity gets people out, if it gets them to use the parks, we are ahead. There is no reason that we must be purists in this day and age.

Another of our major problems in outdoor recreation is that we in the recreation business have never really been part of the urban planning or, for that matter, the rural planning team. The requirements for recreation, for open space, and scenic conservation are pretty much after-thoughts, if they are considered at all. Why can't we build reservoirs primarily for outdoor recreation purposes, and why is it that our urban renewal projects appear to be so inhuman in scale and function? I believe we must assert our own legitimate interest in the planning of our environment — after all, we presumably have as much knowledge and expertise about spatial arrangements and group behavior in our own field as the highway engineers, the urban planners, and the water resource managers do in theirs. It should be clear now that planning for social services must take account of recreation and leisure time; the same point should be stressed in terms of the physical development of our cities and rural areas. The major complaint about the central cities — one of the major reasons for the flight of the middle class to the suburbs — is that the cities do not provide the amenities and the full range of opportunities for children and family life. And recently there has been expressed an additional concern for the quality of life in our rural areas. Secretary of Agriculture Freeman has recently pointed out that these areas have special requirements which may call for new responses on the part of government.

It might be useful to review some of the major trends which are shaping our environment, and that we, as recreation planners, ought to be sensitive to.

Our pattern of urban development, particularly that which has come about since World War II, is unique, and peculiarly American. It is less an expression of any historical tradition or conscious ideal as it is a concomitant of our advanced technology, our transportation systems, and our economic development. It has even been necessary to coin a new term "megalopolis" to describe the phenomenon of the vast northeastern urbanized area which extends along the eastern seaboard from Boston to Baltimore, and inland from the Atlantic to the Appalachian foothills. Several other areas within the United States are undergoing a similar coalescence of metropolitan centers, and it may well be that megalopolis is the city of the future.

A direct result of our post-war urban pattern has been the dramatic change in the functions and relative importance of our core cities. Between 1950 and 1960, the total population of urbanized areas increased by almost 39 percent; the bulk of this increase, however, was in the fringe areas around the central cities, rather than in the cities themselves. While the central cities grew by almost 20 percent, the fringe areas gained over 80 percent in population. Nine of the core cities in the nation's ten largest urbanized areas lost population between 1950 and 1960. The drop ranged from 1.4 percent in New York City to 13 percent in Boston.

Our core cities are victims of obsolescence — both in terms of function and of age. They represent an enormous fixed investment in land, structure, and utilities. Modernizing and modifying the existing pattern to fit present day requirements are extremely costly, particularly when weighed against opportunities to be found in the suburbs.

By circumstance, those who can live in the core area are narrowed to single adults and young married couples without children — those who are not concerned with obsolete schools. Added to this are the vastly larger number of minority groups, lower income people, and the aged who lack the financial resources and the mobility to live in the suburbs. To be sure, some of the wealthy have remained in their urban townhouses or in luxury high-rise apartments, safely insulated against unwelcome intrusions. As William H. Whyte has expressed it, "the city is becoming a place of extremes - a place for the very poor or the very rich or the very old." [4]

Suburbia — residential, commercial, and industrial — has become a permanent characteristic of urban life in the United States. By far the most dramatic aspect of our suburban pattern is its scale and its emergence in such a short time span. In the face of our population surge and mass movement of people, we have accomplished a tour de force in accomodating our suburban growth — at least by quantitative standards. We have constructed millions of new homes and have provided the schools, roads, water, and other basic services necessary to serve the new residents of suburbia. And all this has been accomplished without any major changes in our basic institutions.

In spite of rising taxes, long commuting distances, and detachment from the variety and excitement of central city life, the dwellers of suburbia apparently believe that they are better off than the in-city residents, and, on the whole, they probably are. They do not live in crowded conditions and are not confronted with the noise, dirt, and congestion of the city. They have access to open space, if not in extensive suburban park systems, at least within the grounds of their own homes. And they can enjoy certain leisure time activities which are denied to the central city dwellers.

Many urban planners and private developers have put forward the idea of the "new town" as an answer to our urban ills. A number of suburban developers have acquired large blocks of land on the fringe of metropolitan areas and are proposing the development of complete communities of up to 100,000 population. Among those now underway are Reston, Virginia; Clear Lake City, outside of Houston; Columbia, Maryland; and the Irvine Ranch, 50 miles south of Los Angeles.

It is still too early to evaluate the impact that the new town movement may have on the form of our urban environment. It may be that they will simply become self-contained enclaves for the upper middle class and thus result in yet further drain of the more prosperous residents and industries of the central cities and older suburbs.

At an earlier period in the development of our country, one could use the term "rural" to describe a physical pattern and a whole agrarian way of life which existed outside the cities. Today, except in the more remote and economically depressed sections of the country, those distinctions which made meaningful comparisons possible have largely disappeared. The urban fringe has blurred the former sharp demarcation which existed between the city and the countryside. The Federal Interstate Highway System, supplemented by extensive state and local highway networks, have linked together all parts of the country. And there have been major shifts in agricultural production and in the farm population which have altered the physical and social pattern of rural areas.

In analyzing the uses of land in the United States, Resources for the Future has estimated that further increases in agricultural land use and intensity and output per acre will equal or outrun increases in total populations. While farm land will be absorbed in the future for urban development, transportation, and other uses, this will tend to be offset by other land capable of being cleared, drained, or irrigated.[5]

The ORRRC Report points out that our frontier has changed from an extensive to an intensive margin, in economic terms. Farms and ranches that are too small, too unproductive, or too poorly managed to produce adequate returns under existing conditions now provide the new frontier in land use.[6] While serving the tourist and the vacationist is now becoming an important economic activity in many rural areas, the potential for further development of private lands and waters is largely untapped. With the single exception of hunting, most of which is done on private farms and woodland, the traditional place for outdoor recreation has been on public land at commercial resorts. However, many of the less productive forest and farm lands, in the New England and southeast regions for example, might be developed into satisfactory and, in some cases, outstanding recreation areas. Dams can be constructed, ponds and lakes developed, trees can be planted, and facilities for public use constructed. The greatest opportunities for meeting future recreation demands exist in our intermediate rural areas — that is, in the areas between the urban concentrations and the purely re-source-based areas, such as mountains and seashores.

With agricultural use fairly stablized and future urban growth largely confined to the fringes of existing metropolitan areas, we are presented with the opportunity to adopt and to implement policies to preserve and enhance the quality of our rural landscape. The challenge which faces us is to identify and to conserve strategically located open and scenic resource areas, to set aside prime agricultural and other lands important to our natural resource base, and to design and locate highways, water projects, and other public and private developments in a manner which sensitively considers their total impact on the rural environment. Both in the cities and in the rural areas, there is currently a planning vacuum from the point of view of recreation and conservation, which we should be prepared to fill.

There are those in the recreation and conservation fields who would argue that we cannot afford to acquire and preserve our resource base areas, and, at the same time, build more open space and outdoor recreation into our urban areas. I think it is clear that we must do both. To the extent the facilities and opportunities are not provided within our metropolitan areas, our more fragile resource areas are overused. I would not argue that there is complete substitution — that visiting a regional park in a metropolitan area provides the same experience as a visit to a state or national park. Nevertheless, to the extent that we provide a full range of areas and facilities, we stand a much better chance of limiting the use of our resource areas to that amount which is required to preserve the resources themselves and to guarantee a certain quality of experience for the visitor. It seems to me that we must think in terms of a balanced recreation system which extends from the small neighborhood park all the way out to the remote wilderness area. Where there are gaps in this system, there will be dislocations, overuse, and unmet demands.

While we are on the subject of spatial arrangements, I would like to say a word or two about standards. While there is some reaction against them, space and facility standards are commonly used in local and state recreation plans. Despite the pitfalls involved, the stereotyped approaches and so forth, I fail to see how we can avoid the use of standards, particularly space standards. I do not know how we can set up the necessary dialogue with the urban planners, for example, without some quantification of our requirements. I also fail to see how we can consider alternatives meaningfully if we do not have standards which can be costed out. Increasingly, the economics of recreation will be a critical factor in recreation planning determinations. It is clear that we will need much more adequate pricing and costing policies as a way of allocating the provision of recreation opportunities among the private and public sectors.

My remarks have largely been directed to urban recreation problems. It might be useful to review briefly the status of state planning.

Few states have developed long-range projections of population, economic, and other growth factors as a guide to state plans; few, if any, have requirements that all planning activity proceed from such common projections in order to ensure consistent growth policies. And the states, as a whole, are only now beginning to come to grips with the policies regarding urban development.

State recreation planning is, of course, strongly influenced by the role of state government in the provision of recreation opportunities. The state's role in recreation has traditionally been that of a direct supplier, or perhaps more accurately, conservator, of areas of outstanding scenic attractions, of forest preserves, and of fish and wildlife resources. The provision of opportunities for various types of active recreation, particularly in urban areas, has been viewed as the responsibility of lower levels of government and the private sector.

A few states provide technical assistance to local units, and more recently, several states have shared state recreation bond funds with local jurisdictions. However, the state's role with respect to urban recreation needs appears to present a major dilemma for most state recreation planners. By and large, the state plans do not contain an analysis of urban recreation, and there are few examples of actions or leadership in meeting urban needs.

Admittedly, there is probably no state which can afford to take over directly the provision of urban recreation needs. The provision of recreation facilities has lagged far behind urban population growth and recent state bond issues for recreation — in the hundreds of millions of dollars — have been directed to only the most pressing needs. Decisions about the state's involvement in urban recreation undoubtedly will be made in response to conditions in each state, but regardless of what accomodations are made, the state should move aggressively into the present vacuum to provide central planning and coordination.

Throughout the nation, the states are going through a period of reorganization and reappraisal of their role in our federal system, and this trend has been assisted and supported at the federal level through President Johnson's emphasis on "creative federalism." The reapportionment of state legislatures and the current reorganization of many state governments is bound to have a very real impact on the recreation function. From these changes will come, I feel sure, a broader view of recreation and the state's responsibility, particularly in terms of the provision of urban recreation opportunities.

In the course of describing the changes which are taking place in our physical environment, I have touched upon some of the accompanying social changes. At this point, I would like to elaborate briefly on the broad leisure time trends which appear to have major implications for outdoor recreation.

While leisure time is growing, all groups within our society do not share equally in advances. Among certain groups — managers, executives, college professors, physicians, lawyers — leisure time has not materially increased and, in some instances, may actually be decreasing. Where leisure time has become available to other groups such as policemen, firemen, teachers, and clerks — it is increasingly common to find individuals taking a second job. And among industrial workers there is a tendency to accept overtime where it is made available.

Another trend affecting the gross amount of leisure time is the growing number of working wives. It has been estimated that if families were counted by the husband's income only, the number of families with incomes of over $10,000 would be cut by almost one-half.[7]

Projections indicate that the shift to occupations requiring higher levels of education, training, and skill will continue. This trend, combined with the growth of the trimester system and summer schools, is also making inroads into the amount of leisure available to youth within our population.

For all groups commuting is taking a larger and larger bite out of the leisure time. Someone has characterized the suburban housewife, for example as a modern centaur — half woman and half station wagon.

While we hear a great deal about the shorter work day, there is a great deal of evidence to suggest that in the future there will be increasingly a "bunching" of leisure time. There will be more paid holidays, and longer weekend and vacation periods. Most American workers seem to prefer this, and this pattern appears to best fit the requirements of many employers.

One result of the growth of leisure time has been that the average worker has free time to expose himself to all of the stimuli for acquiring new consumer tastes; thus, in turn, requiring new sources of income. Recreation equipment such as power boats, campers, snowmobiles, and ski equipment is becoming increasingly more elaborate and costly. This reinforces the tendency, described earlier, for many workers to have a second job and for wives to work. Within certain limits, additional income appears to be preferred over additional leisure time.

While the number of jobs on the service side of our economy continues to increase, there is an increasing emphasis on special skills, education, and training as a prerequisite for employment. Therefore, enforced leisure and chronic unemployment are major problems among the unskilled. Among these groups there is a maximum of leisure time, but less money to spend on leisure time pursuits. In our approach to leisure time activity for these groups, we immediately run head on into our ethic to which I referred earlier, that leisure is the reward for work. And this is going to call for major adjustments in our recreation programs.

In conclusion, I would like to suggest that the two major sets of variables which affect outdoor recreation are those connected with our social forces and our pattern of physical development. Neither of these are immutable or unchangeable; they are independent variables only to the extent that we, as recreation planners, do not try creatively to influence them.

Footnotes

1. Clawson, Marion, *Land for America; Trends, Prospects, and Problems.*

2. Mueller, Eva and Gurin, Gerald; *Participation in Outdoor Recreation: Factors Affecting Demand Among American Adults.* (ORRRC Study Report 20).

3. Mead, Margaret; *Outdoor Recreation in the Context of Emerging American Cultural Values: Background Considerations.* (ORRRC Study Report 22).

4. Whyte, William H., *Open Space Action* (ORRRC Study Report 15).

5. Clawson, *op. cit.*

6. Staff, Outdoor Recreation Resources Review Commission: *Public Outdoor Recreation Areas-Acreage, Use, Potential.* (ORRRC Study Report 1).

7. Carter, Genevieve W., *Changing Social Trends and Recreation Planning.* Presented at the American Association of Health, Physical Education and Recreation Convention, May 1964, Washington, D.C.

RECREATION PREFERENCES AS
CULTURALLY DETERMINED PHENOMENA
by
William R. Burch, Jr.

Sociologist, Forest Management
State College of Forestry at Syracuse University *

The topic on which I was requested to write this paper is impossible. There is no simple, short-cut way to social science knowledge, nor is our data more substantial than that of the physicist. You may recall that physicists now talk of indeterminancy rather than causality. Certainly, the very mention of "cultural determinism" is enough to raise passionately aggressive tendencies among even the most placid and well-mannered gathering of social scientists.

If the planner has found that his drama is so complicated and entangled that plot resolution escapes him, he cannot really expect the social scientist to be the *dues ex machina* which resolves the mess and gets the boy and girl living happily ever after. The drama of real life *is* complicated and entangled. It is ever-becoming and never-resolving. The wonder is that so many do live happily ever after; so many commuters do get somewhere and back; so many parks do survive to face another season.

The wonder is that in a world of complicated confusion so many of our expectations are fulfilled. Seldom do we compliment that nasty fellow, the other driver, when he stops for a red light. Nor do we count the thousands of times we have walked down the streets of our city without being mugged, knifed or fire-bombed. Nor do we keep a running account of the pleasant greetings given by our spouse. But we certainly do notice her sour look, the nasty fellow's failure to stop, and what happened to the "fellow down the street" last week.

We only note behavioral consistency when it is inconsistent. And being Americans we like to raise the inconsistency to the status of a major crisis representing the total breakdown of all we cherish. This is really the subject of our discussion — the great consistency of human behavior which seems confounded by the great diversity of social groups. A summary term for both this consistency and this diversity is "culture." Culture specifies for the members of a social group what is, what ought to be, and how one gets there. Each culture is a distinctive language which shapes the perceptions and behavior of its members. Acquisition of a culture's language marks the difference between being an animal and being a human being.

Aldous Huxley stated it more elegantly when he said:

> Our souls are so little 'us' that we cannot even form the remotest conception of how 'we' should react to the universe, if we were ignorant of language in general, or even of our own particular language. The nature of our souls and of the world they inhabit

*Now at Yale University

would be entirely different from what it is, if we had learnt to talk Eskimo instead of English. Madness consists, among other things, in imagining that our soul exists apart from the language our nurses happen to have taught us.[1]

Whorf stated it more technically when he said:

> We dissect nature along the lines laid down by our native languages. The categories and types that we isolate from the world of phenomena we do not find there because they stare every observer in the face; on the contrary, the world is presented in a kaleidoscopic flux of impressions which has to be organized in our minds — and this means largely by the linguistic systems in our minds. We cut nature up, organize it into concepts, and ascribe significancies as we do, largely because we are parties to an agreement to organize it this way. . . .[2]

Thus, each culture's distinctive vocabulary programs the capacities and incapacities of its members, and there are as many distinctive vocabularies as there are organized social groups. This is often a source of confusion because each culture compels its participants to be ethnocentric, to believe that only its answers are appropriate while all others are false. This is why our weapons of destruction travel easier than our constructive ideals. This is why the American tourist is first surprised that other peoples do things quite differently, and then is outraged when they insist that their way is much superior to the American way. If the President's campaign for tourism to America succeeds we can well anticipate that some equally ethnocentric surprises and outrages about American culture will be expressed by our visitors.

Closer to our interest, most recreation planners share the cultural expectations of white middle class America, and most often they will have a difficult time understanding and including in their plans the different recreational interests of other cultures such as that of Afro-Americans. And without such understanding recreation planners, like educators, may find that their best intentions to equally serve all will have essentially unequal consequences. Culture as a sensitizing perspective may help the planner to recognize where these similar but fundamentally different linguistic lines intersect. This means we cannot remain in the realm of higher social science abstraction, but must work through some specific data on a specific cultural dimension. Perhaps, in this way we will learn to expose our biases to the differences we share with others.

I will do this in three ways. First we will explore some cultural variations in time conceptions to understand why modern man may have problems with his free time. Next, we will look at some cultural variations and social trends in American life which have consequences for recreation planning. And, finally, we will speculate about some possible trained incapacities in the culture of recreation planners.

Cultural Variations in Conceptions of Time

The recreation planner should be interested in understanding cultural variations in time conceptions as the nature of such conceptions largely shape the nature of "free time" behavior. Further, the planner, by his activity, expresses a faith that history can be pulled within the control of men. Yet often we treat history as if it always lies ahead rather than emerging from what went before. Seldom do we recognize that mass leisure is not new, but rather viewing it as a problem is new. Our real question is not "why do we have so much leisure," but rather "why is our leisure apparently problematic."

Perhaps a look at some comparative data will move us in the direction of answering the second question. These data come from ethnographic studies which roughly run the continuum from tribal to post-industrial societies. Let us realize these are merely handy empirical points around which we can group our thinking; there is no intention to indicate a hierarchy of social progress.

As you will note from the highly imaginative graph (Figure 1) there is a tendency for available leisure to follow a U-shaped curve as we move from subsistence societies to the post-industrial affluence of present day America. A few details may be useful.

At one end of the continuum is Tikopia,[3] a culture relatively untouched by industrial thought except for some unpleasant encounters with missionaries, some metal tools, and an occasional trading ship. It is a barter rather than a moneyed economy. The primary organizational feature is the extended kinship system. The division of labor is based upon sex and age grades.

Raymond Firth's study of the New Zealand Maori[4] represents a group on the way to accepting the industrial mode. In their pre-Western contact period the Maori had a further division of labor based upon craft specialization. Also, in many ways the Maori people of today spread over the entire continuum from subsistence to post-industrial consumption.

Firth indicates that the Tikopia were engaged in productive work around six to eight hours a day, and this time had many elements of play. As he indicates, subsistence is the goal, but it is approached somewhat casually. The number of holidays based on seasonal changes, weddings, puberty and other celebrations, indicates that the amount of leisure time is somewhat greater than in the present United States. The Maori had around an eight-hour day, with two months set aside for rest and many holidays to celebrate accomplishments and special events. "A few days hard work was succeeded by a time of leisure and feasting."

Other studies of tribal societies in varied parts of the world indicate similar patterns of work and play. A. I. Richards, in her study of the Bemba of Northern Rhodesia, found that:

> The whole bodily rhythm of the Bemba differs completely from
> that of a peasant in Western Europe, let alone an industrial

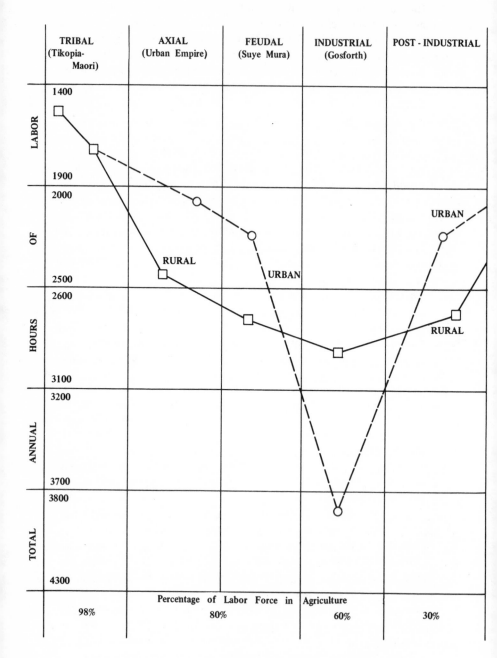

Figure 1

AVAILABLE LEISURE, SUBSISTENCE TO POST-INDUSTRIAL SOCIETIES

worker. For instance, at Kasaka, in a slack season, the old men worked 14 days out of 20 and the young men, 7; while at Kamamba, in a busier season, the men of all ages worked on an average 8 out of 9 working days. The average working day in the first instance was 2-3/4 hours for men and 2 hours gardening, plus 4 hours domestic work for the women, but the figure varied from 0 to 6 hours a day. In the second case the average was 4 hours for the men and 6 for the women, and the figures showed the same daily variation.[5]

J. H. Provinse's study of the Siang Dyak of Borneo indicates that though there was considerable individual variation, approximately one-third of the time was spent on non-productive activities.[6] Hogbin's study of the people of Wogeo Island indicates a workload similiar to that of Tikopia.[7] So much for the subsistence societies.

The next point on our continuum is John Embree's prewar study of Suye Mura.[8] The study is concerned with a Japanese village surrounded by a society determined to move toward industrialism. It is a mixed barter and moneyed economy with production shifting from a family as the major productive unit to other broader associations. William's study of Gosforth,[9] an English village, represents a step closer to accepting not only the artifacts of industrialization, but many of the thought patterns. It is a moneyed economy with mechanized agriculture.

Both Suye Mura and Gosforth note a marked decline in leisure time, and, more importantly, a changed orientation to the social meaning of time. Though both societies have more leisure than did 19th Century industrial society, they have considerably less leisure than Tikopia or the "proles" of imperial Rome.

In the axial period, as Harold Wilensky reminds us:

> ... among the citizens of antiquity, as well as among primitive agriculturalists, the number of days of leisure often approached half of every year. The transformation of tabooed or unlucky days into holy days, and the latter into holidays. . .occurred long before the Middle Ages.
>
> . . . in the old Roman calendar, out of 355 days, nearly one-third (109) were marked as . . . unlawful for judicial and political business. In the last two centuries of the republic, festival days were stretched to accomodate more spectacles and public games. The Roman passion for holidays reached its climax in the middle of the fourth century when days off numbered 175. If we assume a 12-hour day, which is probably on the high side, total working time would be only about 2,160 hours a year. Whatever the work schedules of slaves and women, leisure for the ruling classes, for administrative and professional men, was never again so abundant. Hours of work for comparable populations in subsequent centuries seem to have increased sharply.[10]

In sum: If we begin with either antiquity or Europe before the Reformation, average hours of work per year, if not per week, moved upward into the nineteenth century. The twentieth century decline in work has been grossly exaggerated by selective comparison with the shocking schedules of early English textile mills — an episode which dominates historical discussion of the evils of industrialism.[11]

If the amount of leisure time available in these cultures is not unlike that of the average present-day American, the question then becomes — what makes leisure problematic for us and not for these societies?

Though time was set aside for holidays and special events, Firth cautions us that the Maori life was not characterized " . . .by sporadic labour broken by long seasons of idleness."[12] He does suggest that " . . .the correlation of time measurement with economic activity is an interesting phenomen in native culture."[13] He tells us that the " . . .Maori . . followed a closely determined sequence of operations in accordance with seasonal change and the movements of the animal and plant life around him."[14] The Maori observed a twelve-month lunar calendar containing ten of work and two for resting. And "from this calendar one can easily see how each task had its place in a definite scheme of work; how the coming of each season, and indeed of each month, brought forward its fresh need of work to be done."[15] However, he finds that the calendar varied under different environmental and economic conditions. Thus, "Agriculture gave one calendar of work to the Northern Tribes, seafishing another to people of the coast, reliance on birds, rats and forest food a third to the dwellers of the bush-clad ranges of the Urewera, eels and freshwater fish yet another. . . ."[16]

The Tikopia have no calendar, no measure of time and divisions of time; their activity is governed by their intrinsic requirements. In fact, "the whole atmosphere is one of labor diversified by recreation at will, and exhibits what even the cold-blooded objective scientist may be allowed to call touches of essential humanity."[17] However, the Maori with his lunar calendar has a schedule of work and leisure more closely assigned than the Tikopia. As Firth notes: "It must be remembered that in former times feasts, games, carnivals and even war expeditions were not indiscriminately arranged affairs, but were planned to fit in with the gaps in the working seasons of the year."[18]

These attitudes toward time seem characteristic of most subsistence societies. In his study of the Nuer, Evans-Pritchard says:

> Though I have spoken of time and units of time the Nuer have no expression equivalent to 'time' in our language, and they cannot, therefore, as we can, speak of time as though it were something actual, which passed, can be wasted, can be saved, and so forth. I do not think that they ever experienced the same feeling of fighting against time or of having to coordinate activities with an abstract passage of time, because their points of reference are mainly the activities themselves, which are generally of a leisurely

character. Events follow a logical order, but they are not controlled by an abstract system; there being no autonomous points of reference to which activities have to conform with precision. . . .[19]

Dorothy Lee notes that present day rural "Greeks 'pass' the time: they do not save or accumulate or use it. And they are intent on passing the time, not on budgeting it. Although city people say that this picture is changing, that they are now made aware of the need to use time, the attitude is still widely prevalent, even in the area of private life among the urban groups."[20]

Much as the Greek villagers, the life rhythm for residents of Suye Mura was tied to the seasons; however, the national government was imposing the rationality of the Gregorian calendar. As Embree indicates a large share of the older residents continued to operate by the lunar calendar. However, under the impact of modern methods of agriculture and new conceptions of time there is gradual attrition occurring and many of the festivals centering on the seasons have been dropped. As Embree notes, "The yearly festivals were more generally observed in the old days than they are today. Increased work demanded by the money wheat crop and other side work encouraged by the prefectural government have tended to reduce these celebrations and encourage people to do work and more work."[21]

Thus, in Suye Mura with time assigned a rational money value there is a constriction in both the amount of leisure and its social value as a celebration of communal accomplishment. Work, not leisure, is beginning to take on positive values in a non-Western culture. Leisure becomes only a means of refreshment or re-creation to aid production.

In Gosforth the seasons, though playing an important role in rural life, are seen as facts of life — much as the machinist sees an imperfect piece of metal. The work continues on a rational basis and the seasons are only slightly more important events than are heavier clothing and snow tires to the urban dweller. The pubs are empty as the farmer no longer acts upon the occasional whim to spend a day drinking beer with his friends. Farmer and friends alike have an investment in their equipment and a mortgage on their farms.[22] Time is money. Gosforth's dominant religion is Catholic, though its values are those which have been ascribed to Protestants.

Here time has almost reached the exaggerated urban meaning described by Georg Simmel:

If all clocks and watches in Berlin would suddenly go wrong in different ways, even if only by one hour, all economic life and communication of the city would be disrupted for a long time. . . . Thus, the technique of metropolitan life is unimaginable without the most punctual integration of all activities and mutual relations into a stable and impersonal time schedule. Punctuality, calculability, exactness are forced upon life by the complexity and extension of metropolitan existence and are most intimately connected with its money, economy, and intellectualistic character. These traits must also color the contents of life and favor the exclusion of those irrational, instinctive, sovereign traits and impulses which aim at determining the mode of life from within, instead of receiving the general and precisely schematized form of life from without.[23]

In sum, our data indicate that subsistence man has his leisure activity and time blocs shaped by the shift of seasons rather than the ticking of a clock or the rationality of the Gregorian calendar. His time is measured by seasons rather than seconds and minutes; the passion for speed and efficiency are sporadic rather than ever-present. It makes a good deal of difference in one's orientation to life if one has a conception of minute divisions ever dribbling away, or whether one sees life divided into the broad time span of seasons with their attendant problems and ritualized celebrations. One is concerned with the leavings of time, the other with tasks to be done and the great value of time gaps between the tasks.

We should resist the charming tendency to draw noble savage conclusions from our ethnographic data. Subsistence societies are neither noble nor savage; they simply persist with a distinctive way of life. None of these societies represents high intellectual and material standards. While most of their leisure is collectively organized and seldom at the discretion of the individual, we will have less error if we draw our conclusions from the modern Maori where youth, when given the option, readily leave the traditional patterns for the freedoms, confusions, and hopes of urban-industrial society.

I hope it is equally clear that I completely reject de Grazia's aristocratic polemic on time and leisure.[24] I am more interested in understanding imperfect human societies than charting arcadian illusions. Our ethnographic flashbacks to pre-literate societies suggest that time is not simply a function of planetary movement, but of social meaning. As we vary the nature of the culture we vary the nature of time and leisure. And, if we are wise, our understanding of pre-literate societies may permit framing a rhythm for our culture which gets leisure out of the problem class. Therefore, it may be useful to further trace some distinctive features of industrial culture.

In the embryonic and middle forms of industrialization, valued time was time spent on labor. The factory whistle became as eloquent a voice as the peal of medieval church bells. To social scientists of this period a work ethic with a theological underpinning seemed a possible explanation of man's behavior. Though there is no need to go into detailed discussion of Weber's Protestant ethic theory, it is worthy to note those ideas of his which have a bearing on recreation.

In discussing the struggle between the King and the Puritans over the *Book of Sports,* Weber links the ethic to the new middle classes. "The feudal and monarchial forces protected the pleasure seekers against the rising middle-class morality and the anti-authoritarian ascetic conventicles, just as today capitalistic society tends to protect those willing to work against the class morality of the proletariat and the anti-authoritarian trade union."[25]

Weber says that for the Puritans:

> Sport was accepted if it served a rational purpose, that of recreation necessary for physical efficiency. But as a means for spontaneous expression of undisciplined impulses, it was under suspicion; and in so far as it became purely a means of enjoyment, or awakened pride, raw instincts or the irrational gambling instinct, it was of course strictly condemned. Impulsive enjoyment of life, which leads away both from work in a calling and from religion, was such the enemy of rational asceticism, in the form of seigneurial sports, or the enjoyment of the dance-hall or the public-house of the common man.[26]

Weber, though believing that puritan values may have been instrumental in forming the spirit of capitalism, suggests that such ethical rewards are no longer available. The modern industrial order has secularized such values so that now they are part of existence for all persons, regardless of their religious affiliation.

Weber argues:

> The Puritan wanted to work in a calling; we are forced to do so. For when asceticism was carried out of monastic cells into everyday life, and began to dominate worldly morality, it did its part in building the tremendous cosmos of the modern economic conditions of machine production which today determine the lives of all individuals who are born into this mechanism, not only those directly concerned with economic acquisition. Perhaps it will so determine them until the last ton of fossilized coal is burnt. In Baxter's view the care for external goods should only lie on the shoulders of the 'saint like a light cloak, which can be thrown aside at any moment.' But fate decreed that the cloak should become an iron cage.[27]

Whether we accept Weber's analysis or not, we should be aware that the productive mentality is still with us. To maintain order in an industrial society a rational division of time seems essential, as sacred ritual seems essential for order in subsistence society. These orientations do not cease when leaving one activity but continue to exert their influence where it is not essential. Interesting data on the consequences of this transfer comes from studies of assembly line workers by Chinoy,[28] Walker and Guest,[29] Swados,[30] and others. Patricia Sexton Cayo seems to summarize the findings when she says ". . .The Fisher worker is paced by Chaplin's 'modern times' metronome; he can't unwind or slow down and his leisure is as taxing as his work day."[31] Thus, normative requirements for one context become a trained incapacity when transferred to other contexts.

Sex for the Tikopia or the Maori are play forms, not involving the seriousness with which industrial man approaches these events. Birth, marriage, and death are serious matters. . . sex, however, is enjoyable; hence, the unmarried are kept segregated from the more serious marrieds. For the early industrial bourgeoise, sexual behavior was a productive act, and dangerous women were those who evidenced pleasure in sexual acts. Repression of impulse was the guideline. Woman was a machine for producing future men of property, and man was the starter of this machine. In our time sex seems to be primarily a consumer good, and the frigid woman the dangerous one. Meanwhile, the mass media play their ubiquitous role of guidance as to proper size and shape, and breathlessly announce the season's new standardized model. All of this complete with a philosophy. Yet, in both the Victorian and consumption eras, time directs the "when." It is a virtually certain prediction that the vast majority of copulations in the United States yesterday occurred in the evening after work: for marrieds it was somewhere between electrically brushing the teeth and sleeping, and for singles about the same time. An afternoon love-in is really not the time for most Americans.

Let me briefly identify some of the cumulative human inventions whose convergence trains our peculiar incapacity with leisure.

1) *Abstract conception of time:* the calendar and clock.

2) *Money:* a standardized measure of goods and services.

3) *Urbanism:* population density generates complicated social relations requiring synochronization of many individual actions.

4) *Industrialism:* increased productivity with the machine determining work routines.

5) *Work Ethic:* both cause and rationalization of rising bourgeois; removing dignity from play — placing all emphasis upon productivity overcoming scarcity.

6) *Bureaucracy:* a rationalized system of rules, hierarchy of roles, extensive division of labor, and centralization.

7) *Assembly line:* one-way flow of communication — complex grouping in single plant — routinization, intense simplification with standard replaceable part — and laborer.

8) *Taylorism:* which married the metrics of time and money to rigidly quantify and to control work behavior.

Cultural Variations Within American Society

The human inventions listed above are such significant features of our culture that we hardly notice their influence. And for the masses of men the rhythms of industrial time are their unavoidable personal rhythms. Yet some modern occupations have managed to transcend this limited frame. Curiously, those who have the most enriched and perhaps dignified leisure voluntarily have the least off-work time. Wilensky has presented national sample data which indicates that men who control their own time work longer hours. Wilensky comments:

70

...With economic growth the upper strata have probably lost leisure. Professionals, executives, officials, and proprietors have long workweeks, year-round employment. Their longer vacations and shorter worklives (delayed entry and often earlier retirement) do not offset this edge in working hours. Although lifetime leisure decreases with increased status, the picture is one of bunched, predictable leisure for elites whose worklives are shorter; and intermittent, unpredictable, unstable leisure for the masses, whose worklives are longer.[32]

Other studies of professional groups tend to corroborate Wilensky's findings. Gerstl, in a study of admen, dentists, and professors found that they all work long hours. However, the professors have the most difficulty in telling when their work ends and leisure begins, and even their small bits of leisure are spent on activities similar to work. As Gerstl suggests:

> For many of the professors of Sauk College, the separation of work from the rest of their lives is virtually impossible if it is thought desirable. Their work is their life; their vocation is their avocation. The extremity of role convergence is evidenced in their work orientation as well as in their social life. Their occupational community and geographical community are one.[33]

Why do these professional and administrative groups work so hard? Cynically we could say they are preserving their image or, having limited the market of practitioners, they are compelled to work twice as hard to keep even with the demand for their services. Perhaps there is a less cynical and more realistic explanation. The professional has large rather than minute rhythms of work, he has seasons and duties, not rational time measurements. Second, the professional has a high degree of control over the flow of his work. Within his wide time latitudes he determines the nature of his task and how it will be met. Thirdly, his work is more than a simple means to an end; his work is such a central life purpose that he has a hard time determining what is work and what is leisure.

Those in the industrial order who come closest to the pre-industrial conception of time are those of this "New Leisure Class" — the artist, scholar, philosopher, professional athlete, construction worker. These persons have a rhythm of seasons: the theatre season, the symphony season, the academic season.

However, anti-industrial conceptions of time are no monopoly of these relatively middle-class occupations. Cohen, Fraenkel and Brewer suggest that a small proportion of the poor are:

> . . . an internally organized, often highly resourceful, defiant subculture. . .they have their ideology concerning the middle-class striver, considering him 'sick' and his values inimical. Although other types of slum residents appear to lack integrated social systems for surviving in conditions of economic marginality, the hard-core poor do not. Their neighbors refer to them as "the

self-contained society." They have developed their own adaptive institutional forms, including those for religious expression, economic survival, and social aid. This subculture has its own economic strata (not all of the hard-core group are economically poor), as well as its own elites, its own methods of communication, and highly efficient system maintenance and group insulation mechanisms.[34]

Later they suggest that:

. . . to the hard-core poor, time is a series of discrete moments, each understood in itself, rather than a continuum . . . Such concepts as those of social mobility, infinity, the value of money, group characteristics, improving one's performance, and so forth, which assume a continuous distribution of critical variables are equally strange to the usage. In addition, time appears to be used almost exclusively in a denotative sense, or as a bounded spatial dimension rather than as a continuous resource which can be husbanded. These constructions have similar counterparts in other languages (e.g. Hopi) which do not include a continuum concept. Conflicting assumptions of the discrete in hard-core use and the continuous in standard use then, represent one area of mutual incompatibility.[35]

What does all this mean to the recreation planner? First, it means that though we all share the virtues and limitations of the industrial culture, that culture is not necessarily the only way to organize human life. Secondly, the character of play is intertwined with the other dimensions of life. Where time is seen as a highly metric capital good, then play must have a tangible payoff as in rising production or consumption indexes. Where time is viewed as being seasonally marked, the aesthetic of play may become an end in itself. Further, though recreation may have certain therapeutic qualities, it is no substitute for a meaningful occupational life. Those who direct the behavior of machines and those who avoid machines in their work will seek much different forms of recreation than those who have their work behavior determined by machines.

Finally, no culture is monolithic, but contains many variants which attempt to transcend its *trained* incapacities. In the industrial order the new class of professionals and technical workers represent one sub-culture which not only has different time conceptions but different leisure values. ORRRC and numerous other studies have indicated that the higher the socio-economic status the higher the participation in recreation activities and so forth. However, the ORRRC studies also indicate that when it comes to specific recreation activities only about 30 per cent of the variance is accounted for by the standard social variables.[36]

In my study of camping styles, I found no significant difference between levels of income and style of camping but did find a significant difference between occupational status and style of camping. Table 1 presents those

72

data. As I have reported elsewhere:

> The major contributions to the chi-square indicate that the lower the occupational status the more likely the person is to be found in the easy access style of camping. Easy access campers are underrepresented in the professions (6.63) and upper non-manual occupations (1.09), and overrepresented in the lower manual occupations (5.28). The combination campers are over-represented in the professions (3.97) and underrepresented in lower manual occupations (2.24). While remote campers tend to be distributed as the total sample.[37]

Following Gerstl, I attempted to examine whether specific occupations within the professional group were associated with a particular camping style. Table 2 indicates that a large proportion of remote professionals are technical persons, having a distribution almost identical to that of the state; while combination campers overrepresent those professionals who could be classed as intellectuals. I should note further that there were a considerable number of occupations classed as professional by the Census Bureau which were not uncovered in my sample. In my sample there were no actors, airplane pilots, architects, athletes, chiropractors, designers, entertainers, pharmacists, public relations men, veterinarians, nurses, etc.

These data strongly suggest that we need more refined, rather than more gross, categories if we wish to make better predictions of leisure behavior. Occupational cultures offer considerable variation from the gross trends of national culture. I strongly suspect that humanities professors from the multi-university are more likely to emphasize the aesthetic and abstract qualities of nature while technicians are more likely to emphasize the practical and concrete aspects such as the challenges met, the number of miles traveled and the number of trophies collected. I base my speculation upon the fact that occupational cultures also enforce their own trained capacities and incapacities which spill over into other arenas of life.

Perhaps if recreation planners concentrated upon occupational culture and looked for value associations rather than artifact associations they might be able to avoid some future crises. By this I am suggesting our emphasis upon specific activities and things — "tote gotes," trailers, motor boats, ski-mobiles and so on — keep leaving the planner unprepared. However, if we looked for the value clusters associated with particular groups, we might note consistencies which hold regardless of the latest technological innovation. Persons whose occupations require, instill and reward self-mastery will very likely be persons who minimize television, emphasize arts, walk for pleasure, hike, cross-country ski and sail. While persons whose occupations require, instill and reward conformity to routines established by others, may very likely be persons who emphasize television, minimize the higher arts, avoid walking, dress for downhill skiing, undress for water-skiing and drive power boats for pleasure.

In short, cultural diversity, not homogeneity, is the stuff with which

TABLE 1
HUSBAND'S OCCUPATIONAL STATUS FOR THREE STYLES OF CAMPING AND STATE PERCENTAGES

Occupational Category	Easy Access		Camping Style Combination		Remote		Total		State of Oregon
	N	%	N	%	N	%	N	%	%
Professional, Technical and Kindred Workers	51	21.5	144	35.8	16	27.6	211	30.3	10.6
Upper Non-Manual	18	7.6	42	10.4	7	12.1	67	9.6	14.0
Middle Non-Manual	70	29.5	91	22.6	13	22.4	174	25.0	13.3
Middle Manual	30	21.1	74	18.4	10	17.2	134	19.2	20.2
Lower Manual	45	19.0	43	10.7	6	10.3	94	13.5	34.6
Farmers	3	1.3	8	2.0	6	10.3	17	2.4	7.3
Total	237	100.0	402	99.9	58	99.9	697	100.0	100.0
Student	1		15		3		19		
Unemployed	1		0		0		1		
No Response and Deceased	8		7		1		16		
Retired	7		0		0		7		
Total	254		424		62		740		

$X^2 = 23.60$[a] $.05 > p < .01 > .001$

$\underline{C} = .17$
$\underline{C} = .19$

[a]Chi-square is computed only for the first five rows for a five by three table with eight degrees of freedom.

State data is computed from U. S. Bureau of the Census. U. S. Census of Population: 1960. Detailed Characteristics. Oregon. Final Report PC (1) - 39D, Table 120, pp. 39,

TABLE 2
TYPES OF PROFESSIONALS FOUND IN THREE STYLES OF CAMPING AND SIMILAR STATE DISTRIBUTIONS

Camping Style

Profession	Easy Access		Combination		Remote		Total		State of Oregon[a]
	N	%	N	%	N	%	N	%	%
Intellectual									
Public School Teachers	12	26.7	25	19.8	2	14.3	40	21.1	15.6
College Teachers	4	8.9	20	15.3	1	7.1	25	13.2	4.7
Lawyers	2	4.4	6	4.6	0	0	8	4.2	4.9
Clergymen	1	2.2	4	3.1	0	0	5	2.6	5.1
Journalists, Photographers, Writers	0	0	3	2.3	1	7.1	4	2.1	2.0
Physicists, Chemists	3	6.7	7	5.3	1	7.1	11	5.8	2.2
Total	22	48.9	66	50.4	5	35.6	93	49.0	34.6
Technical									
Other Academic	4	8.9	0	0.0	0	0	4	2.1	N.C.[b]
Medical and Dental	5	11.1	17	13.0	3	21.4	25	13.2	7.8
Foresters, Land Professions	1	2.2	18	13.7	3	21.4	22	11.6	4.0
Engineers	11	24.4	28	21.4	2	14.3	41	21.6	13.8
C.P.A.'s Accountants	2	4.4	2	1.5	1	7.1	5	2.6	9.0
Total	23	51.0	65	49.6	9	64.2	97	51.1	34.5
All Others	0	0	0	0	0	0	0	0	29.9
Grand Total	45	99.9	131	100.0	14	99.8	190	100.1	100

[a]State data is computed from U. S. Bureau of Census. U. S. Census of Population: 1960 Detailed Characteristics, Oregon. Final Report PC (1) – 39D. Table 120, pp. 39 240, and 245.

[b]No comparative data.

recreation planners must work. The professional class has significantly different tastes from other social categories, yet there is considerable variation within this class. However, there are some advantages for the planner as professionals are fitted to occupations which have consistent traditions. Thus, the recreational tastes of professionals are also likely to reflect considerable consistency. And further, there are likely to be both absolutely and proportionally more professionals in the future. Thus, the grave predictions of miniscule annual hours of work are not likely to occur. Prophets of an automated world of ease simply have not looked very closely at the American beginnings of a post-industrial society. They have somehow missed the crowded people in the cities, failed to smell the air and drink of the no-longer shining waters. The task of servicing a society with such an environment is not likely to require less man hours.

The patterns Walter Buckingham notes for our present seem likely to occur in our future:

> Since 1870, productivity in the U.S. has more than quadrupled. The same labor input now produces over four times as much value in goods and services. Yet employment increased over six times — from 10 million to over 65 million — during this period. It can also be shown that most of the jobs held by workers in the U.S. today would not exist if it were not for advanced technology.[38]

However, unless society develops a means of retiming technological changes in factory and clerical occupations, then many persons *will* pay high personal costs for long run social gains. Yet there seems little doubt that many new jobs will emerge. Creative scientific research is no more amenable to total automation than barbering. Nor are executives, transportation engineers, rocketry experts, teachers, students, policemen, social workers, soldiers, janitors and other service workers not yet invented, likely to be replaced, though their efficiency may be improved by automated equipment.

With greater population concentrations there will be greater complexity of regulations and laws which in turn increase the risk of law breaking. Even if better models of control for present problems are developed, it is very likely that the new complexities and new problems will outrun old solutions. Coupled with population increase and concentration, the increasing levels of sophistication and education will reflect greater sensitivity to identifying and treating mental illness and other problems. Professionals with an occupational stake in the deviant and the defective will pressure society to recognize the need for extensive professional care. Thus, it is very likely that our institutionalized population of the mentally and physically ill and the criminally convicted could rise from less than one percent to three percent of the total population, with proportional increases for probationary and preventive work on the outside. The professionals, custodians, technical and administrative personnel, service workers and suppliers will continue to work long hours to meet the needs of this growing industry. And they will be joined by the staff and line workers in the equally growing educational industry.

The growth of a professional, technical and managerial class is not simply a linear projection of their presently large proportional growth, but reflects what will be the new industries of a predominantly tertiary economy. The growth of this class will also reflect continuing pressures by occupations such as morticians, town planners, foresters and recreation directors to claim professional status.

Of course, countervailing forces may seek to routinize and bureaucratize professional and service workers so that their work patterns more closely approximate present clerical routines. However, strong professional guilds would seem some guarantee against such a tendency. And such pressure should continue the attractiveness of the "New Class." As Gailbraith suggests:

> Some of the attractiveness of membership in the New Class, to be sure, derives from a vicarious feeling of superiority — another manifestation of class attitudes. However, membership in the class unquestionably has other and more important rewards. Exemption from manual toil; escape from boredom and confining and severe routine; the chance to spend one's life in clean and physically comfortable surroundings; and some opportunity for applying one's thoughts to the day's work, are regarded as unimportant only by those who take them completely for granted. For these reasons it has been possible to expand the New Class greatly without visibly reducing its attractiveness.[39]

Perhaps of even greater importance to the planner is that the future is likely to have 35-40 per cent of American families continuing to experience, through no fault of their own, improved levels of living. It seems certain they will continue to hold rather strongly to their working and lower middle class culture. Their leisure then and now is likely to continue to upset our social critics such as Mr. de Grazia, however, not because it reflects the final phases of American degeneracy but because it represents real consistency and continuity in an often overlooked style of life. The shape of this life style is already fairly well drawn.

Diaries and autobiographies such as those of Samuel Pepys or Frank Harris indicate that from the 16th Century through the 19th Century and including the present, styles of leisure are little altered by temporal conditions when we remain within a given class culture. Both Pepys and Harris represented new bourgeoisie who mixed traditional low status values with their attempts at emulation of elite values. They flirted, gambled, gossiped, tried learning qualities of wine and food along with foreign languages, moralized about the upper and lower classes, "scored" with women, loved to take drives, were ethnocentric tourists and prided themselves on their clever party conversation. In general, they sought the usual pomp and circumstance that would tell them they had arrived at a satisfactory social position.

Such attempts at announcement and validation of newly won standards of living seem little different from the response of the new middle mass. What is different is their relatively rapid and recent growth in size and thus visibility to elites.

This has been most true of the working class which is now an important segment of the middle mass. However, improved levels of living have not radically changed their cultural values. Richard Hoggart's study of the British working class suggests that "the more we look at working-class life the more we try to reach the core of working-class attitudes, the more surely does it appear that the core is a sense of the personal, the concrete, the local: it is embodied in the idea of, first the family and second, the neighborhood."[40] S.M. Miller and Frank Riessman have summarized a variety of studies on the working-class subculture which seem to substantiate Hoggart.[41] They suggest that the working-class has manufactured from their conditions of existence a successfully adaptive pattern of life. The working-class life style reflects values which are traditional, old-fashioned, religious, and patriarchal. The working-class person likes structure and order, is family centered, has a negative attitude towards leaders and is often stubborn when confronting change. He is concerned with stability and security and believes strongly in an eye for an eye psychology. He engenders considerable excitement over new possessions. He is person centered; that is, he relates to people rather than roles. He has a strong touch of pragmatism and anti-intellectualism — though an exaggerated and vague respect for the learned.

However, new levels of living may somewhat modify traditional life style. Wilmott and Young report that in working-class districts an individual is viewed as a whole person with a multiplicity of statuses.[42] However, when he moves to lower-middle class housing, possessions become significant forms of status placement. As I noted earlier, though this change may somewhat modify recreation behavior it is in a value consistent pattern. That is, an increase in artifacts does not mean a change in values.

Small town lower-middle class culture also seems to have a high degree of persistence. A 1935 study of married young men and women, 15-29 years of age, living in Tompkins County, New York, found that the leisure time activities most frequently engaged in were of the "indoor passive type" such as reading and listening to the radio. "Outing activities" and "household activities" were next in importance. The home was the major center for leisure activity. A later study of unmarried youth in the same area found they had leisure activities similar to the young marrieds. Though both groups of these rural small-town people said reading was their most important leisure activity, this reading was primarily of newspapers and magazines. In a burst of what now seems quaint small-town morality, the authors say "a chief problem with regard to magazines is the character of those read; many are trashy." And of the few who read books, they "read fiction almost exclusively." [43] These people now comfortably settled before the television set in their suburban homes may have simply substituted a higher form of video entertainment for their past lower forms of literary entertainment.

Thirty-two years seems to have made little impact upon this culture. Gans in his study of Levittowners reports that:

> If left to themselves, lower middle class people do what they have always done: put their energies into home and family, seeking to make life as comfortable as possible, and supporting, broadening, and varying it with friends, neighbors, church, and a voluntary association. Because this way of life is much like that of the small-town society or the urban neighborhood in which they grew up, they are able to maintain their optimistic belief that Judeo-Christian morality is a reliable guide to behavior . . . If "blandness" is the word for this quality, it stems from the transition in which the lower middle class finds itself between the familial life of the working class and the cosmopolitanism of the upper middle class. In viewing their homes as the center of life, Levittowners are still using a societal model that fits the rural America of self-sufficient farmers and the feudal Europe of self-isolating extended families.[44]

Gans reports that though there were changes in leisure time and activity in the move to the suburbs, the changes in leisure style were minimal. Of those changes there was a tendency towards more sociability, more work around the house and more organizational participation.[45] Such changes suggest that the "pleasure-seeking" of the new middle mass will continue to emphasize "fixing the home," gardening and family pleasures such as boating and camping.

When members of this culture arrive at the recreation site they will have little interest in Thoreau's self-discovery or Ernest Thompson Seton's individualistic self-testing. They will have more interest in gadgets than unsullied nature. They will be seeking a different setting for continuing the types of social relations they experience in their urban apartments or their suburban horizontal apartments. In this attitude they are little different from the more wealthy who have their Hyannis Ports for continuing their regular social routines in different settings.

And having noted these cultural variations within American society we have not even begun to note the cross-cutting influences of urban and racial life styles. Of interest, given present demographic trends, is the ORRRC findings that in the standard metropolitan areas of the northeast, "woods-oriented activities — fishing, hunting, nature walks, camping, hiking — are significantly lower on the personal activity index than any other form of outdoor recreation."[46]

Gregory Stone's study of the St. Louis metropolitan area suggests that for urbanites, the absolute numbers who are camping may be increasing, but the proportion of outdoor recreationists who camp is decreasing.[47] Though he does report that group or organized camping has both absolute and proportional increases.

Stone also demonstrates that racial influences in state parks can significantly modify patterns of use and types of visitors. Race is often an unspoken but significant variable influencing the behavior of recreation planner and recreationist alike. Perhaps planners should consider their future role if nonwhite participation could be encouraged to equal white rates of participation.

However, if we exclude those lovers of "healthy suntans," the present tendency is for darker skin pigmentation to be negatively associated with outdoor recreation participation. The Michigan Survey Research Center's national study indicated that if nonwhite men participated in outdoor recreation to the same extent as did whites of comparable income levels, their rate of participation would be 50 per cent greater than it is.[48]

Thus, it would seem that both urbanism and race may have a depressing influence upon the participation level of outdoor recreation. As Philip Hauser argues, "it is possible that with the changing way of life being experienced by increasing proportions of the American people and by successive generations who have been exposed only to urban living from birth, the future population may conceiveably lose, rather than increase, interest in outdoor recreation."[49] He then goes on to supply considerable evidence that indeed this is the logical trend in American life.

Later in his report, Hauser notes that "if boating, water skiing, and camping were ignored, the rank orders (of participation) for white and nonwhite population would be almost identical." Furthermore, he notes, the data tend to confirm the hypothesis that urbanization tends to have the same impact on nonwhite as on white outdoor recreation activities."[50] Hauser's study suggests that for participation in fourteen of the major outdoor recreation activities, urbanism, not race, is the significant influence; while boating, water-skiing and camping remain predominantly white activities. But even here we have ignored the some 15 to 20 per cent of the population who share the culture of poverty which Harrington calls the *Other America*.[51] Whatever the criteria for being placed in this culture, recreation planning must seem a cruel joke. Though the proportion of the population in this category may decline from present levels, it seems unlikely to disappear. It seems unlikely because exhortation to personal boot-strap pulling has long been the reward given in plenty to the poor by the wealthy. This was so even when the poor were in a majority; when they are in the minority it may simply mean there are more to tell fewer the same old story. The poor must discover personal enterprise and diligence while the majority righteously search within themselves to find similar attributes that will explain why they deserve the rewards historical fate has awarded them.

At this point let me introduce a personal qualification to the foregoing pessimism. First, I have data which run counter to Hauser's prediction of increasing urbanism joined to a decline in outdoor recreation interest. Secondly, I believe that some of the movement to the West Coast can be partly attributed to the desire for better outdoor recreation opportunity. Third, the growth of the professional class suggests that quality of life will be emphasized by a politically powerful group. Given present occupational trends it is not too surprising that a formerly obscure western outdoor club can challenge a powerful Atlanta-based timber and mining corporation. My fourth qualification is that social science data itself is a source of social change and recreation planners may begin to take to heart such data and seek ways of serving Afro-Americans, the urbanites and the poor. The Reverend Abernathy is presently leading a march which takes place outdoors and aims at re-creating the dignity of individual Americans and the values of their society. Perhaps recreation planners will eventually come to see such a march as well within their responsibility.

The Culture of Recreation Planning

Here it might be useful to speculate how the culture of recreation planning might begin to adjust to its changed responsibilities. I believe there will be an encouraging tendency for recreation planners to shift from reliance upon the forestry model to a reliance upon an educational model for directing their actions. That is, there may be an encouraging shift in interest from things to people. Seldom do recreation and parks people gather without long "can-you-top-this" exchanges of horror stories on vandalism, littering and the general decline of real woodsmanship and morality. The usual tongue-clucking and head-nodding conclusion is that there is something fatalistically malicious and spiteful in human nature which we "goodly souls" must learn to endure. Though shared adversity always makes for a sense of communion, as a way of life, it seldom solves one's problems.

Unfortunately, the foresty model has this tendency to concentrate on things rather than the relation those things may have for people's lives. Such an attitude is not too surprising when we consider the history of wildland recreation in the U.S. Probably at the turn of the century the majority of people managing wildland recreation settings, of necessity, tended more towards a forestry than a humanities orientation. Thus, when the first big boom of auto-influenced recreation came in the 1920's, the response was to try and concentrate the potential blight so that it did not infect the entire forest environment. If anything has changed in the past 40 years I suspect it has been towards fewer poets and more foresters managing these wildlands.

However, the forestry model has its own poetic ambiguities. We are told that a logging operation may be a bit messy but it is only a matter of time and then Nature in her wisdom will clean it up. The pulpwood plant may have some unpleasant side effects but, after all, the jobs, Kleenex and Dixie cups are what keep America going. Do not misunderstand me, I am all in favor of *appropriate* logging and pulpwood operations. But I am confused when the forestry model so easily accepts messy conditions where resources are becoming profitably managed, yet becomes indignant when people consume enjoyment but leave a mess behind. In other situations where we anticipate public use we hire janitors, maintenance men, security officers, garbage collectors and develop depreciation schedules. Apparently Macy's is quite happy to clean-up the daily mess left by their customers. Yet, it seems that in public enterprise or the slums we expect things to take care of themselves while we supply a strong dose of moral rhetoric. Somehow park visitors and slum dwellers are to be more virtuous than the rest of society. They are to keep themselves tidy and proper, and all without the resources and manpower available to the rest of us.

On the other hand, the educational model is only marginally interested in custodial and housekeeping problems. Values, not things, must be conserved, even if it means encouraging radical social change. Education, remains centrally active in an attempt to achieve basic philosophical goals. That is, we believe that public monies directly or indirectly spent on schools, museums and zoological gardens are an investment in people, not things. We believe that people will somehow be better citizens and live fuller lives for having been exposed to the richness of human culture and history and for having seen and understood something about their fellow creatures. Even the urban playground movement has directed its attention to educational goals — playgrounds are to help children develop coordination, to learn about getting along with others and to have a chance to try out their creative individuality in relatively ruleless situations. To be sure, in reality education often lapses in its mission, but its very goals are the means by which we pull it back to being people-centered and to treating resources as expendable means for encouraging the development of people. Such an attitude does not seem characteristic of wildland recreation management.

Even the National Park Service, in spite of its self-guiding nature trails and naturalist programs, seems more committed to the resource than to people. They have responded to clientele pressure by trying to protect the resource for present and future enjoyment. But seldom have they led their clientele into an educational experience. They have simply responded to unanticipated developments and crises. It is as if the educational authorities let the children constantly rewrite the curriculum. The people demand to motorboat and drive and camp — so Yellowstone Lake is zoned, the campgrounds grow, the roadways creep and it becomes hard to tell what is so different about Yellowstone from a thousand other camping spots, country drives and water ski resorts — except that it is more crowded. West Entrance is a clear example of what the Park Service's potential students want — it swings with neon and plastic, squealing Mustangs and psychedelic chicks. West Entrance is an experience, but certainly not an educational one. And market enterprise does a far better job of meeting these tastes than a public bureaucracy could. Yet, in attempting to both preserve and permit enjoyment, the Park Service makes a similar though much slower response to market demands. I am not denying the tremendous pressures park people work under; I am denying the philosophical model which can only lead to the elimination of parks. Suppose the Park Service modeled itself after an educational enterprise. It would run its park as a museum, and no museum lets the public dictate that "tote gotes" should be used for viewing Gauguin. The museum encourages visitors and their loitering, but always on the terms of the museum. All museums lock away certain items from uncontrolled public access, though opening access to appropriately trained persons. Would the political traumas really be so great if Yellowstone left their entertaining and housing to private enterprise on the fringes of the Park? If so it might begin to adopt the notion that education, unlike private enterprise entertainment, costs the individual something more than his dollar and his time, it requires his absorption in the unfamiliar. And because we know that is so, we tell Johnny to shut up and listen to his teacher.

The second factor is that education is cumulative; it moves from lower to higher truths and skills. It takes its clientele as it finds them and attempts to expand their development. From kindergarten to Ph.D. the world grows in even greater complexity, each stage preparing for the next. This seldom occurs in wildland recreation. If we do not begin education in urban parks, our visitors can hardly be expected to arrive at the wildland museum with a vocabulary of understanding. The educational model of outdoor recreation would recognize a hierarchy of experiences where each stage of experience would nuture the next stage. And the design which ensured that each stage meshed with the next would seem to be the prime task of recreation planners. After all planning *is* the application of intelligence to problems of continuity and change.

However, we have generally responded to the lack of integrated experience by continuing to make the wildland experience more and more similar to an ordinary urban experience. This may be partly attributable to the forestry model which assumes that there is something inherently good in the object rather than in its relations to cultural values. We seem to assume you can take a boy from Harlem to the wilderness and he will intuitively appreciate its complexity. This is about as wise as taking a boy from Drain, Oregon, to the middle of Harlem and expecting him to intuitively appreciate its complexity.

In education we are finding, much too late, that ghetto children do not share the same vocabularies (and thus values) of their middle class teachers. We are finding that if these children are to have equal opportunity to expand their minds and to move up the educational ladder they must be approached not by a foreign language but in the tongue of their culture. In those rare cases where ghetto children have been so approached, their "disadvantaged, retarded" qualities soon drop away and the university rather than the reformatory seems a viable alternative. And at this point we are back where we began — the intersection of differing vocabularies.[52]

The forests, nature reserves and parks were established in this country by politically important elites, not by some massive demand of the people. And these elites were well-schooled in vocabularies for appreciating nature. Today the elites are in Switzerland or somewhere equally exotic, and some of the masses are in the parks, often without adequate vocabularies of appreciation. And we wring our hands, build more barriers and more roads, and write more regulations for our retarded clientele. The retarded recreationist is equally certain the planner is demented and he responds in an appropriately negative fashion. Because the planner's mission is action, it is his responsibility to expand his vocabulary so that he may begin to expand the vocabulary of the recreationist. And that is really what this paper has been about.

Footnotes

1) Aldous Huxley, *After Many a Summer Dies the Swan* (New York: Harper & Row, Inc., 1939) pp. 309-310.

2) Benjamin Lee Whorf, "Science and Linguistics," in Theodore M. Newcomb, Eugene L. Hartley *et al.*, *Readings in Social Psychology* (New York: Holt, Rinehart and Winston, Inc., 1947) p. 214.

3) Raymond Firth, *We The Tikopia, A Sociological Study of Kinship in Primitive Polynesia* (London: George Allen and Unwin, Ltd., 1936).

4) Raymond Firth, *Primitive Economics of the New Zealand Maori* (New York: E. P. Dutton and Co., 1929).

5) A. I. Richards, *Land, Labour and Diet in Northern Rhodesia* (London: Oxford Univ. Press, 1939) pp. 392-4.

6) J. H. Provinse, "Cooperative Ricefield Cultivation Among the Siang Dyak of Central Borneo," *Am. Anthro.* Vol. XXXIX (Jan.-Mar., 1939) pp. 77-102.

7) H. I. Hogbin, "Social Advancement in Guadelcanal" *Oceania* (1937-1938) Vol. VIII, pp. 289-305.

8) John Embree, *Suya Mura, A Japanese Village* (Chicago: Univ. of Chicago Press, 1939).

9) W. M. Williams, *Gosforth: The Sociology of an English Village* (Glencoe, Ill.: The Free Press, 1956).

10) Harold Wilensky, "The Uneven Distribution of Leisure: The Impact of Economic Growth on 'Free Time,'" in Erwin O. Smigel (ed.), *Work and Leisure - A Contemporary Social Problem* (New Haven, Conn.: College and Univ. Press, 1963) p. 109.

11) *Ibid.*, p. 112. For an earlier discussion of these patterns of free time see William R. Burch, Jr. and Marvin J. Taves, "Changing Functions of Recreation in Human Society," *Outdoor Recreation in the Upper Great Lakes,* Lake States Exp. Sta. Paper, number 89, 1961.

12) *Op. cit.,* Firth, number four, p. 68.

13) *Ibid.* p. 64.

14) *Ibid.* p. 55.

15) *Ibid.* p. 55.

16) *Ibid.* p. 67.

17) *Op. cit.,* Firth, number three, p. 97.

18) *Op. cit.,* Firth, number four, p. 190.

19) E. A. Evans-Pritchard, *The Nuer* (Oxford: Oxford Univ. Press, 1940) p. 103.

20) Dorothy Lee, *Freedom and Culture* (Englewood Cliffs, N.Y.: Prentice-Hall Inc., 1959) p. 151.

21) *Op. cit.*, Embree, number eight, p. 266. Also see his chart on page 292 which lists the former yearly round of ceremonies.

22) *Op. cit.* Williams, number nine, p. 190.

23) Georg Simmel, *The Sociology of Georg Simmel*, Kurt H. Wolff (Trans. & ed.), (Glencoe, Ill.: The Free Press, 1950) p. 413.

24) Sebastian de Grazia, *Of Time, Work, and Leisure* (Garden City, N.Y.: Doubleday & Co., Inc., 1964).

25) Max Weber, *The Protestant Ethic and the Spirit of Capitalism*, Talcott Parsons (trans.) (New York: Charles Scribners & Sons, 1958) p. 167.

26) *Ibid.* pp. 168-169.

27) *Ibid.* p. 181.

28) Ely Chinoy, *Automobile Workers and the American Dream* (Garden City, New York: Doubleday and Co., Inc., 1955).

29) Charles R. Walker and Robert H. Guest, *The Man on the Assembly Line* (Cambridge, Mass.: Harvard Univ. Press, 1952).

30) Harvey Swados, *On the Line* (New York: Bantam Books, 1967).

31) Patricia Sexton Cayo, "The Auto Assembly Line An Inside View," *Harpers* (June, 1962) p. 56.

32) *Op. cit.,* Wilensky, number ten, p. 113.

33) Joel E. Gerstl, "Determinants of Occupational Community in High Status Occupations," *The Sociological Quarterly*, V. II (January 1961).

34) Rosalie Cohen, Gerd Fraenkel, and John Brewer, "The Language of the Hard-Core Poor: Implications for Culture Conflict," *The Sociological Quarterly* V. 9 (Winter, 1968) p. 19.

35) *Ibid.* pp. 24-25.

36) ORRRC Study Report 20, *Participation in Outdoor Recreation: Factors Affecting Demand Among American Adults* (Washington, D.C.: 1962) p. 69.

37) William R. Burch, Jr., "The Circles of Leisure," Paper presented to Rural Sociological Society annual meeting, San Francisco, 1967.

38) Walter Buckingham, "The Great Employment Controversy" in *Automation*, Charles C. Killingsworth (ed.) (Philadelphia: The Am. Academy of Pol. and Soc. Sci., 1962) p. 47.

39) J. K. Galbraith, *The Affluent Society* (New York: The New American Library of World Literature, Inc., 1958) p. 267.

40) Richard Hoggart, *The Uses of Literacy* (London: Penguin Books, 1963) p. 33.

41) S. M. Miller and Frank Riesman, "The Working-Class Subculture: A New View," *Social Problems*, Vol. 9 (1961) pp. 86-97.

42) Michael Young and Peter Willmott, *Family and Kinship in East London* (London: Penguin Books, 1965) pp. 162-163. Bennet M. Berger's study of an American working class suburb indicates little or no change in leisure behavior though living standards had improved. See his, *Working-Class Suburb: A Study of Auto Workers in Suburbia* (Berkeley, Calif.: Univ. of Calif. Press, 1960) pp. 59-87.

43) W. A. Anderson, "Rural Youth: Activities, Interests, and Problems," (Ithaca, N.Y.: Cornell Univ. Agri. Exp. Sta., Bull. 649, 1936: Bull. 661, 1937) the quotes are from p. 36 of Bull. 661.

44) Herbert J. Gans, *The Levittowners* (New York: Pantheon Books, 1967) pp. 203 and 418.

45) *Ibid.* pp. 267-268.

46) Outdoor Recreation Resources Review Commission Study Report 21, V. 2. *The Future of Outdoor Recreation in Metropolitan Regions of the United States* (Washington, D.C.: 1962)) p. 20.

47) Outdoor Recreation Resources Review Commission Study Report 21, V. 1, *The Future of Outdoor Recreation in Metropolitan Regions of the United States* (Washington, D.C.: 1962 pp. 168-195.

48) Outdoor Recreation Resources Review Commission Study Report 20, *Participation in Outdoor Recreation: Factors Affecting Demand Among American Adults* (Washington, D.C.: 1962) p. 63.

49) Philip M. Hauser, "Demographic and Ecological Changes as Factors in Outdoor Recreation," in Outdoor Recreation Resources Review Commission Study Report 22, *Trends in American Living and Outdoor Recreation* pp. 46-47.

50) *Ibid.* p. 56.

51) Michael Harrington, *The Other America* (Baltimore: Penguin Books, 1963).

52) I hope it is clear that I am not concerned with the specifics of operation but with a general philosophical attitude in public recreational enterprise. Nor am I suggesting we should impose our specific resource standards or our general middle class standards upon an unwilling sector of the public. What I am suggesting is that knowledge is the heritage of all men, though not all men speak in the same tongue. Those concerned with imparting knowledge must learn those different tongues and talk in those terms lest many be denied their heritage. Further, all Americans share a heritage of their land, yet because many have been confused by a foreign tongue they have been denied access to understanding and sharing this heritage. To open such access is not the imposition of alien values, but rather offering the means for the individual to acquire his rightful options.

SOME REFLECTIONS ON THE HISTORY
OF OUTDOOR RECREATION

by

Sebastian de Grazia

Professor of Political Science

The Eagleton Institute of Politics, Rutgers University

Introduction

My primary purpose in this paper will be not so much to present a tidy list of reflections on outdoor recreation — too many puzzles and paradoxes straggle loosely in there — but rather to share with you the queries and doubts that arise in my mind concerning the subject.

The academic locus of my talk may be difficult to place. In part, it could be considered as belonging to the history of ideas, or to politics, to a certain extent sociology, a tiny bit to statistics, and yes, philosophy, though its philosophy may be well hidden. All may be well hidden: so, it may be wiser not to turn the glare to the disciplinary site of discourse. Let me just note that I shall confine my remarks chiefly to high cultures, principally the Mediterranean and the Chinese, and of course the industrial North European. Scientifically, the firmest historical statements I can make are negative ones: I know of no case of this . . .or of that. But even these, though few, may have some importance.

Changes in Recreational Activities Over History

The first queries are these: What have people done in history for their recreation? Where have they done it? When and in what numbers? More pointedly, what is it they have done that we do *not* do? Nothing, really. There may be a different kind of card or dice game, a different juggling act or form of play or story-telling; and who does these various things may differ in class and status, or skin color or religion; their costs of these amusements may range widely. But the activities themselves are no stranger to us. We could find fun in the fun of past peoples and they in ours.

They in ours *for the most part.* For, let me reverse the question. Are there any recreational activities that we engage in in large numbers that people in other times and places have *not* done? The answer here, I think, is yes. We *do* some things they have not done. I am speaking here of an activity engaged in by many persons, either singly or in groups, to the extent that it can be regarded as a cultural trait. For example, flying or air diving may today be a sport that never existed before, yet it is not widespread enough to be called one of our principal national outdoor recreations. Similarly, I should not call polo one of our major recreational activities.

The three activities I am about to mention have all been done before, but never in massive numbers and none before the advent of the industrial or coal, steam and petroleum age.

The first is swimming. By and large, this is a Twentieth Century outdoor recreation. People have swum before, especially in naval countries, but in small numbers and usually to keep off the peril of drowning. Bridge-building Roman military engineers must have had to know how to swim; but, just think, even fishermen typically have not known how to propel themselves on the surface of the water. People in canal cities like Venice or Hang-chow should know how to swim, but you cannot count on it. In the near tropical seas of some island cultures like Polynesia, swimming is a true sport, but I am speaking only of High Cultures. Lord Byron was one of the first in modern times to swim for sport. However, today in summer, the cry is heard on all sides, "To the beach!"

The second activity is usually an association of the first: *sun-bathing*. Westerners have both water-bathing and sun-bathing. Until well past the turn of the century, it was thought to be unhealthy to expose one's fair skin to the sun — ever. A sunburnt skin was also declasse, the occupational hazard of peasants who, incidentially, to avoid it, were always fully clothed and broad-brimmed hatted. People who wanted to go to the country for health went to the hills and mountains to breathe cooly and deeply, but they kept their bodies well-covered.

Rome was a great water-bathing but not swimming world; sun-bathing had little appeal. Even for physicians and spas in the Greco-Roman world, open air yes, but in the shade, if you please. In nineteenth century Europe people sat on the sunny side of beer gardens or cafes only in wintry air — to get warmer. In China, in the Third Century A.D., there was a small nudist movement. However, it was more political than solar.

Nudism as a sun-bathing possibility, which of course it is in the United States, leads to the third great change in recreational activities of our world, a hard one to give a name to. I shall call it *nature-love*.

It is a complicated phenomenon, nature-love, ranging from the naturalistic to the romantic. One important example is Chinese Taoism, an ancient religion of nature spirits, that holds Nature to be the guide to living one's life. But in China, except for hermits and intellectuals, the wild fastnesses as a recreational goal has played no part.

Nature-love seems to be a widespread American phenomenon. Nature poetry, as opposed to the pastoral or bucolic, gained momentum among English poets first with Wordsworth's "The world is too much with us. . . .Little we see in Nature that is ours. We have given our hearts away." Shakespeare himself has the theme of the tonic of nature (a phrase of Thoreau's) running through several of his comedies, especially in *As You Like It*.

Combining nature-love with the love of the wilderness, America is the only land that dotes on the wilderness theme in recreation (Perhaps one should also include the Northern European and Scandinavian countries). The myth of the noble savage started with the image of the American Indian brought back to Europe by Europeans. Rousseau appropriated it and spread his version all over the Western world. The United States linked it to settlers, pioneers, frontiersmen, cowboys, Indians, biologists, naturalists, Boy Scouts, hunting and fishing, camping and wildlife enthusiasts.

There is one thread of the wilderness idea that did not come from the New World but from the north European country of deciduous wilds. Spengler, in his *Decline of the West* makes much of the influence of northern forests on Gothic cathedrals. Undoubtedly, the northern or Teutonic warrior tribe legend, probably coming out of Tacitus, and later embellished by northerners themselves, has had some impact. With the ring of Vikings, Teutons, and Wagnerian opera, it must have played a part in our wilderness ideas. For, unlike Rousseau's notion of the gentleness of simple outdoor folk, our belief is largely in the toughness or toughening power of outdoor life. For us, I should venture, the outdoors produces the strong and hardy, the self-reliant, the uncorrupted, the naturally sane and healthy.

For the rest of the world the wilderness has been something not to be caught out in. William Bradford, in 1620, expressed this sentiment for the first settlers. "What could they see but a hideous and desolate wilderness full of wild beasts and wild men. . . . ? If they looked behind them, there was the mighty ocean which they had passed, and was now the main bar and gulf to separate them for all the civil parts of the world." From Hesiod to Horace to Thoreau, what singers of nature have sung is not the wild winds but the tamed wild, domesticated nature, the bucolic woods and meadows, the fields at sunset, the scents at dawn, the mile and a half walk to the village (Thoreau's).

How strong the wilderness motif is today in the United States is hard to say. Nevertheless, as a motif it easily branches over into the ideal of the small town, which is also part of American heritage, coming in via Greek and Italian models of the polis or small city-state or republic. Before I go into this, I wish to propose that American wilderness worship be distinguished from gentler nature-love, be it Taoist or Rousseauan, and to follow the significance of this distinction later.

Some Great Successes and Failures of Modern Recreation

For each of three great successes there is a corresponding and correspondingly great, failure.

On the success side our indoor environments are cleaner and capable of better temperature control than ever before in history. On the failure side, we have soiled and spoiled our outdoor environments. Never before has a country polluted the great part of its streams, rivers and lakes so that their value as a source of food or recreation almost disappeared.

Nor has any other country in history that I have heard of ever had the means to pollute its air so well. I hear that in Los Angeles the sky is sometimes a lovely brown color. That must be a truly unique sight in all the world. It may even have some tourist attraction. Before industrial towns and cities took over, the summer heat was what people in the cities of temperate zones were bothered by, and perhaps the dust and noise. To get some shade and breeze or height, they went out of the city. Today, for the first time in history, we have made the indoors healthier than the outdoors. If you walk along the streets of New York on a hot summer's night — given you are willing to take the chance — you will have the exquisite sensation of air conditioners on the lower floors spewing their heated discharge into your face. Like the cavemen, we shall be back in neolithic times, when it was healthier to be in a cave than out.

A second great triumph is that we have speeded travel as never before to distant recreational sites, and we have made such travel comfortable by making it indoors. On the negative side, we have less time for and access to the outdoors. The time spent in travel is indoors. Indoors is defined as within or inside a building or enclosure. Travel, though mobile, is indoors — whether by plane, train, or auto. Anything much beyond walking, running, bicycle or horse speed is too fast for unprotected comfort: some protection must be devised, which then impedes open air enjoyment. If our travel were in outdoor vehicles, it would give us more outdoor life — a transatlantic liner, is an example — for we have pushed what we think of as outdoor recreation so far away that travel time to it cannot be attempted on a daily or even a weekend basis.

You don't go for outdoor recreation after dinner. The city average for parks and playgrounds is often at a substandard level of space, not to mention usefulness or attractiveness. County parks are usually not available except by car; they are not within daily reach.

If nature so keeps its distance, it follows that it can be enjoyed generally only on non-working days. The American full-time male worker on the average puts in four hours of work at a job on Saturday.[1] As for non-urban outdoor recreation, what chance does he have for getting to it when out of the whole United States's population, over half has never been to a state or national park in the last five years? What does the American worker, and the rest of the United States urban population, too, do for the 49 or 50 other weeks of the year in which they have no vacation? Fortunately for outdoor recreation, there are still a few national holidays left.

Let me stay with holidays a moment. In ancient Rome and Greece, in Europe in medieval times, and in most of the world up to the Reformation, the work week was not shortened as we have tried to do, by shortening the numbers of hours worked daily; it was shortened instead by holidays and festivals. As a kind of rough average these holidays worked out so that in the Middle Ages the work week was about 45 to 50 hours a week. And this is about the highest limit. In Hellenistic Greece and Imperial Rome the work week was much lower. These figures must be compared with the American male full-time worker who in 1960 was working an average of 47 hours a week, or nearly eight hours a day, six days a week. These figures do not

[1] This was the figure in 1960; it may have changed since then, but I doubt it. The two-day American weekend is a hope, not a reality.

include the hour and a half each worker spends on the average traveling to-and-fro. When I said we have failed not only in pushing outdoor recreation further away, but in providing less time for outdoor recreation, I had figures such as these in mind.

The third pair of success and failure falls in the area of personal budgets or costs. On the positive side we have invented a marvelous, interesting, almost hypnotic form of cheap daily recreation — the telly. But it is indoors. Other cultures have developed cheap, daily recreation for the outdoors or simply out-of-home. The beer or wine garden and the cafe or open tea-houses were places where one can go evening after evening without involving disastrous inroads on one's pocketbook, and there find company, movement, light-heartedness, and variety, all out-of-doors. But we, in our cities, have architecturally discouraged outdoor recreation by leaving sidewalks unprotected from sun and rain, by providing almost no inviting squares, arcades, galleries or promenades. Today, if we had them we could not use them for in the city outdoors you will soon find yourself breathing shallowly, for fear of breathing normally. Automatically, you cease to sniff and smell for fear of breathing deeply; you cease to walk normally for fear of traffic; you cannot talk normally for the noise of traffic, still less can you look up and around to admire the view for the speed of traffic! This has less to do with architecture than with the automobile, which has driven people off the streets and sidewalks and indoors, and made the cities seem more crowded than they are. How much more room there would be in cities, if you could get automobiles out of them. The cars are more fortunate than the people in cities: they discharge their people indoors while they remain outdoors. The car is king of the city.

In sum, our success with indoors has taken the outdoors from us. I doubt very much that any civilization has ever been so indoors. At 6:00 p.m. of any weekday evening, three-fourths of the male population from 20-59 years has arrived safely home and does not leave the hearthside or T.V. screen for the rest of the evening. And the picture for the weekend is not much different. Indoor recreation dominates the scene.

This is curious when you reflect how much we are supposed to love the outdoors and to be an outdoor people. Perhaps, as I hinted before, we have exaggerated the strength and tenaciousness of the outdoor ideal, or have a mistaken idea of its nature. Etymologically, the words *forest* and *park* and *preserve* have politics in their background. The kind of politics they are associated with is royalist politics. In China of the Third Century B.C., you can hear the great Confucian philosopher Mencius trying to persuade the ruler that he ought to let people share in the royal parks: the king would get greater enjoyment if he shared his pleasures with the people.

The history of England's royal and aristocratic preserves are well-known to you from the exploits of Robin Hood and other poachers.

In the United States the great outdoor movement got its impetus from presidential sanction. "Leave it as it is," said Theodore Roosevelt. "The ages have been at work on it and only man can mar it." In an unavoidable way, conservation has both an anti-democratic and a statist tinge to it. The common man destroys the beautiful wilds; the state can save them for the common man's own good, letting him, like the Chinese commoner, share in the pleasures. In the United States much of the conservationist movement from the beginning to the present day has been spurred by our equivalent of good families of wealth, by public-spirited men, we say. The elitist hint in conservation is not merely to be noted and passed over. Sooner or later one must ask, who does and who would and who should use the preserved wilds, and whether planning for outdoor recreation ought to be concentrated on them.

American Ideals of Outdoor Recreation

I suggested earlier that the ideal of the tamed wilderness branches off at some point and becomes the small town ideal, similar in some ways to concepts of garden towns where the green is always nearby. Politically, the ideals of these sparsely populated utopias are as nearly anarchist as one can get. Thoreau put it correctly in his essay on *Civil Disobedience*, "That government is best which governs not at all."

There is another ideal that has greatly affected American thought — it is not unrelated to the small town — and that is the model of the polis or the small city-state or republic I mentioned before. This ideal reaches us through the founding father's traditional education in things Greek and Roman. In the Mediterranean, the wilderness referred to where barbarians lived or where the crazed Dionysians abandoned themselves to orgies; it was the land of the irrational, the uncivilized, the border over which barbarian invasions poured. The tamed countryside, instead, had all the gentle virtues: life was simple and pure, and close to the gods of trees, soil, and sky. It was perfect for the quiet meditation and conversation the Greeks sometimes sought. It was perfect too for the retreat that the Romans needed to balance their busy lives of war and commerce. But it was no substitute for the city. Socrates made this point so that there would be no mistake. ". . . the men who dwell in the city are my teachers, and not the trees or the country." Plato showed a deep appreciation of untouched nature in the *Phaedrus;* at the same time, he held to the city as the only place for the full life.

In the Mediterranean ideal, the city was where there was recreation; and recreation was outdoors in the streets, markets, squares, and porticos. Greek and Italian squares were often built without a trace of green; the cities were small enough that the green was within eyeshot.

The political ideal of these small cities was typically republican, built on the strength of yeoman or sailors. It was not anarchical, for unlike Thoreau's village (the Concord of his day), these towns had walls built for defense and the townsmen knew that a common defense was a government enterprise. Furthermore, they believed that the good life was to be had in society, not in isolation. The streets and squares provided not only the spatial perspective and background for drama, but also the cheap facilities for easy congregation. Here was where something happens, where happenings take place, organized or not, where you went whether you had an errand or not.

So much then for some of the ideals that have entered our history. They have all failed. The wilderness no longer holds any danger. (Sometimes it seems to me like a poor wild beast in captivity, attended by guards who, for a fee, let you in to look at it in comfort and safety.) The wilderness has been tamed; the small town has become the strip; the polis has become megapolis: the city turned into the sprawl. The streets of the city are more dangerous than any wilds of these United States. We venture out onto them only to get our bread and butter from work or to stalk the shopping center for our larder. The dangerous wilderness is now in the very air we breathe outdoors. For our recreation, to be safe and comfortable, we stay indoors. Can this be called recreation?

The Meaning of Recreation

Should the telly be called recreation? Should anything indoors be called recreation? According to Webster, recreation is first, the act of recreating or the state of being recreated: *"refreshment of the strength and spirits after toil";* second, it is a means of getting diversion or entertainment. The *re* in recreation makes it a pendulum: work/recreation, work/play; for children, school/play. For the Romans it was called *optium/negotium.*

If recreation is the foil for work, what are some of the characteristics of work today? Most, but not all, work in America is sedentary, non-muscular, piecemeal, unimaginative, and indoors. I am not objecting to this now; it would be nice were it different, but all work, even the best, requires constraint or restriction of some sort. As long as there is work there will need to be recreation to relieve it.

Recreation's need is based on necessity, the necessity in life for doing things we would not be doing if we still lived in the Garden of Eden, that Paradise of outdoor recreation. All jobs are in some way compulsory; all require the balance of recreation.

Now, if work is muscularly confined and indoors, recreation preferably should be unconfining and outdoors. One can have a relatively unconfined space indoors — but men have a need to get outdoors too. My contention is that no matter how sweet and clean and spacious we make the interiors of enclosures, we will *want* out, we will *get* out, for the sake both of our bodies (there will be something psychologically lacking in any enclosure, even a transparent one).

Television can be put outdoors; it then becomes an outdoor movie. In the end, while it is imaginative, it is not stimulating muscularly. It can serve as part of recreation, but the body has to move around more than to the refrigerator and back to keep its muscle tone. The body should at least do some walking. Moreover, the telly like all other mass media, provides no opportunity for direct and full social intercourse. The spirit needs more than an exchange with the boss or with fellow workers or the wife and kiddies. The eyes need to see more and the brain to wonder more, and yet not get over-stimulated so that one gets over-tired. Daily recreation must have the element of repose. This is the telly's great advantage. It is easy to turn on.

What I see as recreation has two forms 1) recreation daily and outdoors, in the midst of whatever congregation of people we live and work with, that is, in village, city or town; and 2) recreation to restore us to the city. This is for special occasions, more often than we now have time for, in which to have easy and cheap access to the country — not necessarily the wilderness — but country in its many varieties.

If you have the first, your pressure on the resources of the second will be greatly reduced. Indeed, only if you have the first, only if you make the city a place its inhabitants do not wish to flee, only if you give the city a pleasant and healthy outdoor environment, can you slacken the expensive, wasteful and self-destroying drive for the wilderness. *Only the city can save the wilderness* — or what's left of it. What we need to save the countryside is a champion, a Teddy Roosevelt to take on the cause of the fair and bright city.

The Future of Work

For the recreationist, the city and country are linked complementarily, and likewise linked are recreation and work. The recreationist cannot shirk the study of work in his culture.

You may think it a strange idea — "the future of work." Work will always be with us, will it not? Perhaps, but the degrees and variations of work are so different that its future should be looked at, if possible. I want to emphasize this because it may seem that I am deviating from my title now in considering not the history but the future of work and recreation. It so happens that in considering the future of anything, our basis has to be the past. Statisticians in seeking to know how many hours we shall work in the future, make a projection based on the past. It may be a recent past — five, ten, or twenty years — but it nevertheless is part of the past.

Not so long ago I had occasion to examine existing projections on the amount of free time the American worker will have in coming decades. The work week is to get shorter by about an hour and a half each decade. By the year 2000, the overall average of hours worked is projected at 31 per week. It may go down as far as 21 per week. In the year 2020 on-the-job hours are to average about 26 per week or as low as 16 per week. With such figures at hand, it is not surprising that many wonder what people will do with their time.

I have serious reservations about these projections. The past from which these figures were launched was not studied carefully enough. They are based on bad history. Yet, they are important, if only because plans for the future are being drawn up from such projections. And they may be useful if taken with emendations and provisos. So, before discarding the chance of a world without too much work, I want to examine at least two possibilities. *First,* a world of work more or less much as it is, with free time rapidly increasing for youth and age (that is, for the 14-22 and for the 55-65 brackets). I favor this possibility because, first of all, the projections based on it would be more trustworthy; second, the middle group 22-55 is strongly resisting all attempts to cut down its working hours; and because third, whereas we have always exalted the machine as a potential slave-labor force that would relieve people of work, the actual results have always been that more people went to work longer hours with machines than they ever did without them. The *second* possibility is for the projected world without much work – to wit, 2020 A.D. at 16 hours or two days a week. What a world that will be! It should be the heyday of the recreationist; 70-80 percent recreation time.

But does recreation in such a setting truly exist? Where is the work it is supposed to balance? As work decreases, the need for balance to it decreases. That part of free-time that needs no compensation, what is it? What can we say or predict about it? It is difficult to plan for; it has no foil like work to balance. Is it all recreation, and shall we say we live for recreation? Is it play, and shall we say, we live for play? Will we indeed be the playboys of the western world?

The less work there will be for men to do, the more what they do will approach entertainment, and even the arts and culture. One thing we shall have to worry less about – and that is that man's activities may be too fatiguing. There will be little work to tire them out for the evening, and no work in the morning for which he will have to arise early. Recreation, if such it can be called, will become wildly unguided, will settle in spectacular entertainment channels, will shoot off in creative paths.

Whether the first possibility I mentioned endures, or the second possibility bursts forth, the job of the recreationist will not be much different. He will have to think of the whole of man's life outdoors. And, unless man is going to remain indoors, some effort must be devoted to the study of social and cultural life in the city and towns. For that is where the American will be spending his time and that is what will be affecting his desire for the country. When there will be no need for recreation to restore men to work, there will still be need of the outdoors to restore men to the indoors, and for the country to restore men to city and town. For the city is where man's trace is heaviest; the country, where it is lightest. The city is noise; the country quiet. The city is new ideas and exhilaration; the country is peace and reflection. Both the city and country are outdoors; the country is more so.

ELEMENTS OF MASS DEMAND
FOR OUTDOOR RECREATION RESOURCES
by
Francis T. Christy, Jr.
Resources for the Future, Washington, D.C.

Over the past two decades there have been marked changes in the patterns of outdoor recreation activity. Certain sports, such as skiing and surfing, have increased at dramatic rates, while others, like hunting and fishing, have shown only moderate increases. Additional significant shifts can be expected in the future. And, the problems of providing for these shifts are among the most important problems for the recreation planner.

But, this raises difficult questions. We cannot provide for the shifts unless we can anticipate them. And to do this, we must understand — far better than we do now — the factors that underlie the changes. We must begin to understand why people choose the recreation activity they do, and what is likely to influence their choice.

It is these questions that have prompted me to speculate about some of the reasons for the popularity of certain recreation activities and to attempt to describe some that might be important in determining the choices that are made. My approach is quite narrow. It focuses on a few, admittedly superficial, elements of choice. It is restricted to those elements that may be important in stimulating *mass* recreation activities — in stimulating those activities that may grow rapidly in the future and create large demands for recreational resources. My approach says nothing about desirable forms of recreation — whatever those may be; nothing about the quality of the recreation experience; and not much about those activities that will be enjoyed by a relatively small number of people.

I discuss five elements that I think are important in influencing the choice of an individual. It is my hypothesis that if a particular form of recreation activity scores high marks in all of the five elements, then that type of activity is likely to become very popular. The elements are neither mutually exclusive nor exhaustive. Now, with all those caveats and attempts to disarm critics, I will proceed with the speculations.

The five elements are as follows: (1) ease of participation — of developing the ability to participate; (2) a desirable image associated with the activity; (3) characteristics that permit a strong identification with the image — the proof that one belongs; (4) opportunities for demonstrating skills — an audience to appreciate the image; and (5) a comfortable and efficient use of leisure time.

The *ease* of participating in a particular form of recreation activity is clearly an important element in an individual's choice. The penetration of the wilderness requires an investment in the skills of living far from the conveniences of civilization. And, it may be associated with the physical discomfort of arduous physical labor; with insects, snakes, grizzlies, and other fancied and real pests; and with sleeping on the cold, bare ground and

99

cooking over an open fire. Similarly, skiing requires an initial investment in specialized equipment, the acquisition of certain skills, the time required to get to the ski area, and the costs of up-hill transportation.

When an individual considers taking part in an activity with which he has had no experience, his decision will be influenced by his understanding of the difficulties and costs associated with that activity. And, of course, his understanding may be grossly in error — as, for example, when he is seduced by a popular outdoor sports magazine into making his own sailboat, or into taking a wilderness fishing trip on the basis of an article that failed to mention blackflies. Or, to the contrary, he may refrain from experimenting because he thinks the costs are too high or the difficulties too great — as in the case of those who will not swim in the Potomac above tidewater because they think the whole Potomac is polluted. Thus, it is not only the actual ease of participation that is important, but also the degree to which the individual understands the facts — a degree that can be readily affected by the communications media.

Assuming that the individual has accurate knowledge of the problems, and that he actually experiments with the recreation activity, his continued participation in the activity may be affected by the satisfactions that accompany the learning process. If he can overcome the difficulties — develop his skills and acquire his equipment — gradually, and at the same time, get increasing satisfaction, then he is likely to continue. The difficulties of camping, for example, can be overcome by gradual refinements in skill, practice, and equipment. However, for other activities, such as sail-planing (soaring), the apprenticeship is difficult and costly and may deter many from reaching the final objective. Thus, the activity, in order to be popular, must allow for a gradual development of skills in such a way that the participants can enjoy the process.

The ease of participation can be greatly reduced by technological innovations. Indeed, some activities now rapidly becoming popular were virtually unknown prior to the development of the new gear and equipment. The Self-Contained Underwater Breathing Apparatus (SCUBA) has opened up a vast new recreational resource — the underwater areas of our coasts. There is currently a proposal before Florida's Commission on Marine Science and Technology to add more underwater parks and trails to accomodate the booming skindiving hobby. Similarly, the development of inexpensive self-propelled snow sleds is opening up large wilderness areas for wintertime use. The Sport Fishing Institute Bulletin, has pointed out that there are more than 30,000 snowmobiles registered with the Conservation Department in Minnesota. It also stated that at a lake that can only be reached by canoe and portage in the summer there were 67 snowmobiles and 120 anglers on January 20, 1968; they took 257 splake averaging 2.2 pounds. At another "wilderness" lake that can only be reached in summer by six hours of canoe travel, there were 115 snowmobiles that had gotten there in 45 minutes.

And there are many other innovations that have reduced the ease of participating in a recreation activity. New kinds of ski-lifts, fiberglass for boats and surfboards, spinning reels, and dozens of others have all helped to make participation a lot easier and have had significant influence on the popularity of certain activities.

For some people, of course, the ease of participation is not an attraction but a deterrent. They may deliberately seek out the hardships that provide them a feeling of conquering nature or the image of pioneer strength and self-sufficiency. And they may abhor the use of mechanical equipment and of techniques that anyone can acquire with ease. While their feelings may have much value, the fact remains that the popularity and mass enjoyment of an activity will depend upon the ease, not the difficulty, of participation.

The second element that may be important in influencing an individual's choice of a particular recreation activity is that of the individual's image. The desire to enhance our image is, of course, but one of many needs and motivations that determine what we do and how we do it. But it is a motivation that is particularly important for outdoor recreation. As Mr. Davis points out in his paper, the kinds of jobs that many people have are not as rewarding as they once were. And the images associated with these jobs are not as attractive. But our leisure time provides ample opportunities to express to our friends and colleagues the kind of person we like to think we are. When Monday comes around, we can talk about the trophy fish, tell our colleagues about the camping or skiing experience, or show off our sun tan. The importance of this element of image can be demonstrated by the many millions of dollars spent by Madison Avenue in helping us determine what image we want to adopt — and how to project it by buying soap.

The image we choose depends in part upon our cultural surroundings and in part upon our own values. That there are wide differences in cultural surroundings is evident in our pathetic misunderstanding of minority groups. But these cultural differences, while important to the solution of our major social ills, are relatively unimportant to the task of projecting *mass* demands on recreational resources. For the majority of the people — the great white middle class — the cultural environment is relatively uniform, and it is this uniformity that narrows the concepts of desirable images. Thus, along with the increasing size of the middle class, there is a decreasing range in the kinds of images that are appropriate to and acceptable within our society.

Within this range the individual's choice will depend upon his own personal needs and motivations. Certain individuals may reject the popular kinds of recreation activity because of their popularity, and seek to go it alone, demonstrating to all and sundry that they are different. If the activity they choose scores high in the four other elements I have mentioned, then they may find it becoming uncomfortably popular in the future and turn to new kinds of recreation. In these cases, they might be considered the leaders or avant-garde. But most individuals choose to follow, rather than lead, and their choice of image will be restricted to those that are shared by large numbers of people.

The result is that larger numbers of people are seeking more similar kinds of images, and this, in turn, tends to lead to greater demands on those recreational activities that are associated with the desirable images. The mass communications media can have significant effect on both the kind of image that is desired and on the choice of recreation activity. Monitoring of the mass media may be helpful, therefore, in anticipating those activities that will become increasingly popular.

The third element important in anticipating future demand follows the second. It is not only important that the activity be associated with a desirable image, but also that there be the means for expressing one's identity with that image. There must be some paraphernalia, costume, badge, or trophy that identifies its holder as a participant in that particular activity. And the fourth element rises from this — and that is that there must be ample opportunity for demonstrating one's membership or showing off one's skills. That is, there must be an audience to appreciate the fact that one is a member of a certain group.

Skiing scores high on both elements. The ski clothes, ski rack on the car, and other paraphernalia provide ample evidence that one is a skier. And the concentration of skiers on the lifts, on the runs, and in the warming huts provides a large and satisfying audience. For fishing, the score would appear to be lower. Except for certain particular kinds of fishing, there is no uniform (other than the rod and equipment) and the audience has to be generated when the experience is recounted. A trophy on the wall helps, but its visibility is limited. It is significant that surf fishing is growing rapidly in popularity. Here, there is an identifiable uniform — the waders and "sou'wester" gear. The car top rack for rods and the beach used by large numbers of people give the surf fisherman ample opportunity to demonstrate his skill. But most fishermen do not have such opportunities.

In some activities where an audience is difficult to come by except by button-holing one's friends, there is the tendency to generate an audience through promotional activities. These promotional tendencies are common among the participants of a new and slightly developed activity. They include membership drives and publicity ventures such as races or meets or contests of one sort or another. Those pioneers in the activity who say, "we've got a good thing going, let's keep it to ourselves" are inevitably outvoted by those who want to promote the activity primarily in order to show off their skills and demonstrate their membership in an image-enhancing recreation. Thus, we have the snowmobile rallies, the canoe slaloms, the conventions of falconers, etc. . . .

Some activities, in spite of the promotional ventures, do not lend themselves naturally to audience development. And these, like wilderness hiking, cross-country skiing, mountain climbing, are not likely to become *mass* recreation activities.

The final element of importance is that the activity must provide for an efficient use of leisure time. It must give the user a feeling that he is doing something; that during the whole experience — the getting there, the waiting in lines, the evenings – his time is being consumed comfortably and satisfactorily. In down river canoeing, for example, much time is spent in shuttling automobiles and people from starting point to ending point and while many may find driving satisfying in itself, others may resent the time lost in transportation. In skiing, on the other hand, once at the resort, the actual skiing is only part of the many activities that the user may find satisfying and diverting. Or in surfing, the sunning and talking on the beach can be as enjoyable as the actual surfing on the waves.

Certain recreation activities score high on each of the above five elements. Skiing is an excellent example. It is not difficult to learn how to participate in skiing – the experience can be acquired gradually and the initial costs of the equipment are not large. The image associated with skiing is very popular. The paraphernalia and costumes provide clear identification, and there is ample opportunity to show off the identification both at the ski area and while traveling. And finally, there is little lost time in the whole experience.

Trailer camping at national parks also scores highly on all five points, as do surfing and a number of other recreation activities. White-water canoeing, however, is weak on several points and is not likely to become a mass activity unless there is some change. The image associated with white-water canoeing is popular – similar to that of the skiier. The uniform and paraphernalia – the wet suit and crash helmet, the special car rack, and the canoes and kayaks themselves – provide clear identification. However, the necessity for shuttling or getting the canoes upstream makes participation difficult, and in addition there are few good white-water areas that also permit large audiences.

But changes might be made – similar to the changes made in the early development of skiing – and the changes might have similar effects on demand. It is not difficult, for example, to conceive of a man-made white-water canoe course which, by intricate turns and bends, could be quite long but cover only a small area. This would permit large audiences to appreciate the activity and permit the drying (as against warming) huts. A canoe lift could be built to provide up-stream (up-hill) transportation and thereby, reduce the difficulties of participation. With such developments, I would anticipate a rapid and dramatic increase in this activity, and an illustration of how technology might affect future patterns of demand.

Communications media can also have significant effects. They serve to enlarge the perception of opportunities for recreation; introducing the readers or television watchers to new kinds of activities. They can change, even though gradually, the cultural environment of the great white middle class. And they can identify the image leaders and the activities associated with these leaders.

The future patterns of demand for recreation activity are difficult to predict. But it may be that, by watching certain signs and enlarging our understanding of motivations, we can come close to forecasting those recreation activities that will be used by large numbers of people.

SOME FUNCTIONS RECREATION WILL PLAY
FOR THE INDIVIDUAL IN THE FUTURE
by
Ann Satterthwaite

Senior Associate, The Conservation Foundation
Washington, D.C.

Mr. Davis states in the conclusion of his paper, "we cannot really plan the future; we can only imagine it. But we must imagine it in terms of the present, not the past."

Well, we have to more than imagine the future. Whether we feel confident of our decisions or not, we are making capital investments, and we are building facilities which will have a direct bearing on the future as well as the present. And these actions, as they relate to recreation, must be geared to what we can foresee as needed by people, and as Mr. Burch says, by a great range of people with a range of values. Mr. Christy describes some of the impacts of technology, equipment, communication, and transportation on this recreation demand. His five categories apply to mass recreation, especially trend-setting recreation.

I would like to take his image-identification categories a step further to see if we can understand the whys and wherefores — to see if we can understand better the function recreation will play for the individual in the future. Although our emphasis is on outdoor recreation we cannot separate it from indoor recreation any more than we can discuss recreation without an understanding of work.

First of all, let us try to forget our activity orientation. So much of our recreation planning has been bogged down by our clinging to outdated quantitative and static standards; i.e., so many picnic benches for so many people, so many ballfields for so many people. It is not that we should not be thinking of ballfields and picnic benches and how many people can use them. But the problem is that these concerns, this activity allocation, should not be the end product of the recreation planning process. Instead, recreation planning should focus on the functions of recreation. Recreation is more than mere trips and activities; it has become, in fact, an integral part of everyday living for the mainstream of Americans. As the Outdoor Recreation Resources Review Commission found:

> Parks and other recreation areas are only part of the answer. The most important recreation of all is the kind that people find in their everyday life. Do they find enough of it now? Do the children have to be driven to school — or can they walk or cycle to it safely over wooded paths? Are the streams left for an afternoon's fishing — or have they all been buried under concrete culverts? Are the stands of woods all gone — or are a few left for a picnic or a stroll? What this means, in short, is an environment.

Thus our challenge: can we shape future growth so that recreation becomes an integral part of it?

This is what is meant by a recreation environment. An environment where parks and open space are woven into the total fabric of social and economic programming, where corporations will seek locations for plants with recreation benefits for employees, and where private developers will build subdivisions and new communities with recreation as a dominant feature. In short, an environment which blends amenities and recreation opportunities into the urban pattern of living.

The recent new towns and new communities have well demonstrated the popularity of recreation and open space within a community. Assuming good location, design, floor plans, and services, the Leisure Worlds, Restons, El Dorado Hills, and New Seaburys have found recreation a major selling point.

The new trend toward a recreation environment reflects new attitudes toward the role and function of recreation and work. Recreation has come to serve for the individual many functions which work has previously served. While the world of Cotton Mather was dominated by God and work, the world ahead will find *self and leisure* assuming new importance. Basically the focus of the anthropocentric world, so characteristically American, has been shifting from a world where the individual sought Divine approval to one where the individual strives to identify and fulfill himself for his own sake, so he can be a more complete and effective human being. This is what Mr. Christy is talking about: the question is how does recreation fit in this ethos of self-fulfillment. This is more than image seeking. It is a very real and deep personal quest for self-identification.

We cannot divorce the work world from the recreation world. They are obviously intertwined in the complicated process of self-fulfillment. As Mr. Davis points out, there will be vast chunks of our population having an "increase in free time off the job and an increase of dull time on the job," as an AFL-CIO official put it. Aside from the actual numbers of hours worked and free hours, the whole problem of the type of work, the types of demands and pressures and lack of them is critical in any forecast of recreation. Other papers discuss the work environment, so I will add only that recreation planning must consider carefully the impact of that environment.

I want to discuss what I see as some of the functions of recreation resulting from work and related socio-cultural pressures. This is not to say that the image and identification factor is not important, but rather that there is another level of factors, what I shall call the *functional level,* which has not yet been adequately examined. If we can look at the functions of recreation it may be easier for us to imagine future activities. In any case, it should provide us with a more flexible way of projecting demand than multiplying existing activity participation.

I should like to discuss just three functions of recreation which I think will become increasingly important to individuals in the future. These are self-fulfillment, including self-expression; self-testing including skill challenge; and forgetting, including temporary escape.

Self-fulfillment:

Striving for identity and fulfillment of oneself is a burden of the individual. There is no God to blame or look to. Psychology and psychiatry have shown how it is the individual's responsibility to a large extent to determine his destiny. Thus, recreation must be geared to this quest for individual development, self-improvement, and basically self-fulfillment. This will be more on the order of continuing learning and adult education than physical health programs.

Aside from structured and systematic education courses, the future will find more people taking advantage of cultural opportunities, such as museums, concerts, theaters. These non-participating activities have already become popular. The Andrew Wyeth show at the Baltimore Museum of Art had people queued up for two and one half hours in January 1967. The same holds for outdoor culture; band and orchestra concerts and art shows need not be indoors.

Such purposeful utilization of spare time is going to increase for urban populations. It is going to present challenges to educational and cultural institutions. The way that these institutions meet these challenges will have a direct bearing on other recreational suppliers. Recreation has been too often conceived merely as outdoor recreation and merely as active or muscle-flexing recreation. The inter-relationships between indoor and outdoor/physical and mental recreation must be borne in mind by all recreation planners and land use planners. The accommodation of vast numbers of people at peak hours is as much a problem with the Metropolitan Museum of Art as it is with Yosemite National Park. Also the problem of financing these non-self-supporting activities is similar.

As leisure increases, as education levels rise, and as the rationalized work world blossoms, the need for this type of recreation function will undoubtedly increase. More than cultural picnicking is involved. Direct participation and means of self-expression are involved in this need for fulfillment. This does not bear merely on the creative or artistic person, but rather on a wide range of people seeking self-expression, involvement, accomplishment, or results of individual action. These are activities where the individual input makes some visible change on every product.

Certainly important forms of self-expressive activities are the arts. The increase in group and individual activities undoubtedly is going to increase. For paint-by-number sets, for art school classes, or for just Sunday afternoon sketching, both the quantity of people and varieties of ages, income, and training has been expanding. The craze of do-it-yourself crafts attests to the popularity of this form of self-expression.

The impact for recreation of this interest in self-expression goes far beyond planning recreation programs — including more art and craft classes and programs. It gets at the very basic philosophy behind a great deal of recreation planning and programming and certainly challenges traditional facility design. The need for people to participate and express themselves to the point where some impact of themselves can be seen or felt is something all too often forgotten by recreation planners.

Playground design perhaps best illustrates the need for recreation planning to take better account of these desires for self-expression. The traditional easy-to-care-for playground has asphalt surface, sandboxes, swings, and maybe a jungle gym or seesaw. Except for the sand, each piece of equipment is a fixed object to be played on or with. The same can be said of the molded concrete turtles, horses, ducks which adorn "better designed" playgrounds. What can you do but climb on them or sit on them? These objects have been presented to children to play with, yet, is this what they want? The Washington Post recently photographed in Washington's well-designed Southwest renewal area a fallen tree covered with children. Adjacent to it were the concrete horses — empty. This points to the need for playground play equipment to be designed so there is some sense of exploration, of discovery, of doing something on one's own. This is all a part of self-expression.

Recently in publicized park programs like New York's, attempts have been made to better orient playground equipment and design to the immediate needs of the particular children served by playgrounds. But these parks are still designed by designers or architects or landscape architects. They are good to look at — but are they good to play with? Even parks like the publicized one in the Jacob Riis housing project has a formal and fixed quality to it. Except for sand there are no opportunities to change or move things. Where can a child get the feeling that he is doing something, that he is building, moving or configurating?

Future opportunities for more self-expression, more discovery, adventure, and exploration will be designed into recreational facilities, be they neighborhood playgrounds, scenic highways, or wilderness areas.

Several types of recreation or new playground programs point to future directions in recreation design. Examples are neighborhood commons and adventure playgrounds. Both involve self-expression of many different sorts.

Self-testing and Skill Challenging:

As Mr. Christy has pointed out, active sports and sports requiring skill often with an element of risk and/or exploration, will loom important in the future. Activities like scuba diving, gliding, drag racing, may seem like passing fads for a small element of challenge-seeking Americans. Yet numbers of these people are increasing and will increase. As work becomes more routinized, many an individual will seek the rugged challenge of skill-requiring recreation activities. The motivations for these activities are too complicated for any non-medically trained observer, but there appears to be many needs for such individual testing and skill displays in this soft and affluent society which engulfs us. In many instances these motivations do not appear to be of a lasting nature. Elaborate equipment is acquired, complicated skills are learned and then the kick is over — and off to the next activity.

Aside from these restless fadists, there is a growth in the number of people dedicated to individual recreational activities like mountain and rock climbing, hiking, bicycling, pack tripping, cross-country skiing, wilderness exploring, canoeing. Some of these activities like rock climbing, spelunking, and white-water canoeing involve risks and skills, while others like cross-country skiing and bicycling require skills and few risks. Pack-tripping, float-tripping, and wilderness-exploring despite whatever commercial trappings, basically contain a challenge of survival or testing of endurance or exposure to primitive elements.

For many there has been a deep-seated need for such physically challenging activities. For others there is a restlessness and curiosity which moves them from challenge to challenge. Others have turned to these activities as regular active sports like downhill-skiing got crowded, became status activities and lost the stress of skill performance.

These activities depend on physical resources usually of a unique nature. Thus, to ensure the possibility of future use of such activities it is necessary to see that resources for these activities are planned and programmed in regional and state resource and recreation plans. These areas are often at considerable distances from urban coves, so threats to them do not seem immediate. However, action to secure them must be taken now not only to ensure their existence but also to keep down their acquisition or control cost.

Although the percentage of total population participating for this function of recreation may not now seem impressive, the percentage increase of *growth* in activities providing this service makes them a significant consideration for future recreation.

Self-forgetting and Escape:

Another recreational function which will become more and more significant is escape, the random, the non-participating pursuits. Despite the purposefulness inherent in most recreational activities, there would appear to be a growing trend to just distractions. Activities may be enjoyed for their own sake and they need not necessarily be purposeful.

The routinized and rationalized everyday world with its excessive organization is bound to elevate the function of sheer random. Many of these activities will not be provided by burdening public agencies. Government controls may be involved, but government investment will be low.

Many of these self-forgetting activities are simply distractions or time fillers. Spectatorship would rank high among them. In the future the vicarious involvement and pleasure from watching spectator sports may be found to take the place of some direct participation in sports like skiing which involves complicated arrangements, expensive equipment, long waits and questionable conditions.

The role of perception-affecting chemicals or drugs as a legitimate concern must be considered for recreation of the future. Controlled use of drugs may provide a non-habit-forming, inexpensive and safe way to take "trips." For those interested in self-forgetting, drugs can either intensify or modify emotions and produce new experiences and novelties. This type of tripping has its place in a discussion on recreation activities, if for no other reason than its effect on total recreation demand.

The purposefulness that has permeated American life may find itself nudged in the future by more hedonistic prods than in the past. Certainly the functions of self-forgetting activities, which need not be solely hedonistic will demand attention of the recreation policy makers. They will have an effect on both demand and supply. Options for these activities must be planned into the urban environments.

When planning ahead for recreation we must bear in mind the needs and demands of the mainstream of America. This is what we usually concern ourselves with. Yet one of our greatest information gaps is sound knowledge of the great variety of publics, many of whom do not fit into this mainstream. I would like to discuss a couple of these overlooked publics, for they deserve special attention and study. They represent social priorities.

The Poor: The poor — the ghetto dwellers, the unemployed, the economic misfits — will find themselves more and more out of tune with the mainstream of the affluent society. The significance of leisure and recreation depends on a relationship to the work environment, and when these people are not full participants in the work environment, the counterpart of leisure and recreation is relatively meaningless. They need critical economic and social assistance, like a guaranteed annual income, income supplements or some other form of assured minimal income level as well as housing, education, and health programs. Yet this does not mean that recreation should overlook the poor. All too often public agencies have provided just middle class opportunities and private charitable organizations have stepped in with elitist and patronizing attitudes. Public and private recreation plans and programs must try to reach these people with programs and activities geared to their values and needs.

Accessibility, both physical, pyschological, and financial, as well as imaginative programming will be critical components of any plan to assure adequate recreation opportunities for the poor. It may be hard for some of us to understand how the crowded beach at Coney Island throbbing with transistor radio music can be more inviting than the glories of the Tetons, yet for someone who has not ventured beyond a block or two-block radius of his Bedford-Stuyvesant tenement, those Tetons are distant, alien and terrifying.

Closer-in facilities and programs atuned to needs as well as subsidized transportation to outlying recreation areas will be needed. Imaginative design and programming of close-in facilities mounts as a pressing problem as urban densities swell. Technology such as mobile, flexible recreation units like portable swimming pools and temporary equipment can help to meet recreation needs of immediate neighborhoods short of parks and playgrounds. And city and metropolitan park systems must find ways of allowing greater participation by the carless ghetto dwellers.

Recreation may be seen as a democratization tool. Integration of use of facilities in all parts of the country must be completed. The Jackson,

Mississippi's and Cambridge, Maryland's, must open up their closed swimming pools so the Negroes as well as the poor whites, unable to build their own pools or join a private club can enjoy already constructed facilities. Whites swim twice as much as Negroes, according to the 1965 Bureau of Outdoor Recreation Study of summertime activities. Psychological factors like fears of inadequate skills and new territories are often as important in these low activity figures as absence of facilities. More aggressive steps and overt policies must be taken to assure not just that facilities are integrated, but that facilities and programs are made inviting to these alienated groups. Location and programming must be geared to their needs.

Women: Women make another group for whom recreation policy makers must make special efforts. Predictions of great home automation, of longer school programs from nurseries on, and younger grandparents all point to more leisure for the housewife. Coupled with more free hours are the isolation and loneliness of the professional man's wife from his all-consuming, self-fulfilling and self-propelling career involvements. Much of his entertainment and recreation is with business associates. These groups of women find themselves looking for useful ways to fill their empty hours and lives.

Continuing education and re-entry or just entry into the work world are two means of meeting this problem of women. The contribution which women can make just in local recreation planning and programming cannot be overlooked. Recent Head Start volunteer work has proven the high quality of abilities that can be put to serious tasks.

So far I have been concerned primarily with the impact of technology and its socio-economic effects on demand. I should like to close with two comments on the utility of technology in outdoor recreation planning.

First, as Mr. Davis states, technology can assist in the planning process. Systematic thinking and computer analysis make it possible for the planner to consider a myriad of social, economic, physical, and political factors never before possible. We have the tools to help us understand the different publics and the means to program a system of recreation, relating background, neighborhood, local, regional, state, and federal involvements.

Second, technology can expand the supply base. The overwhelming interest, for instance, in water-based recreation will call for new man-made lakes, rivers, offshore islands, portable pools, etc. While respecting the intrinsic natural beauty of existing areas, it will be possible to expand and create totally new facilities. Desalinization will probably make it possible for many shoreline states to use inland fresh water reservoirs for far more extensive recreation purposes than are now possible. Why not artificial mountains; we already have artificial snow. The values of innovation and the possibilities from technological advances should not be overlooked by outdoor recreation planners.

TECHNOLOGICAL CHANGE
AND RECREATION PLANNING
by
Hugh C. Davis

Associate Professor, Resource Planning

Department of Landscape Architecture, University of Massachusetts

It has been customary to base the causes of the so-called "recreation explosion" on four changes in our society. These have been described by Clawson as an increase in population, a greater amount of leisure time, more disposable or discretionary income and better transportation.[1] Once these four changes have been identified, the recreation planners then usually start collecting masses of data which, in fact, appear to prove the validity of Clawson's original insight. Not so very long ago, when 701 money was more readily obtainable, countless man-hours were devoted to establishing sophisticated sampling techniques to obtain these data. Fascinating new computer programs were produced by equally fascinated computer programmers. Magnetic tapes charged with all sorts of reliable sample data were zipped into ever-increasingly complicated machines. Then, in almost no time at all, the "print-out" appeared at the other end of the computer in long folds of neatly typed paper.

The amount of data that can be and is being processed in this fashion is truly staggering. The total dollar costs can be relatively high in the initial stage, but the per unit cost of this information is extremely low. Properly programmed, the extra cost for each additional bit of information, once the system is operating efficiently, is practically nil. Under these circumstances the urge to ask the machine more questions is almost irresistible. Perhaps, however, the time to ask the questions is before the whole process gets under way.

For example, is the growth in population, leisure time, disposable income and transportation the real cause for the growth in the popularity of outdoor recreation as Clawson has said it is and as ORRRC has implied it is?[2] There are some indications that we may have put all our eggs in the wrong basket − or the wrong data into the computer.

In a study published in 1961, Wilensky states that:

> The average man's gain in leisure with economic growth has been exaggerated. . . skilled urban worker may have gained the position of his thirteenth century counterpart. Upper strata [workers] have, in fact, lost out. . .these men work many steady hours week after week − sometimes reaching a truly startling lifetime total.[3]

DeGrazia comes to very much the same conclusion in his extensive study of leisure time:

> Comparisons in our favor are delusive. Since 1850, free time has not appreciably increased and compared with medieval Europe or

113

ancient Rome, free time today suffers by comparison and leisure even more.[4]

But assume for the moment that these men, for one reason or another, are incorrect in their assessment and that more free time *really* is available. Then ask, why has such a heavy proportion of it been used for outdoor recreation? Why have we chosen to use this discretionary time in such large chunks for recreation? Why hasn't it been used for continuing education, civic work, or any number of other possible options available?

Has population increased? One can hardly argue this fact. There *are* more people today in the United States than there were in 1945. Yet perhaps we should consider the *rate* of increase rather than the total number. The rate of increase in the use of outdoor recreation facilities has been many times that of the population growth rate. However, let us assume we do not use the rates but we work with whole numbers and that the rate of change in population growth is unimportant in this instance. Then ask: Why is it that several states experiencing a decline in population between 1950 and 1960 have also shown an increase in the use of recreation facilities within the state by *residents of that state*? In other words, there was a declining population but a greater use of recreation facilities.

When it comes to income, almost any valid way one wishes to judge the gross statistics, the country does seem to be better off in terms of disposable income than it was in 1945. However, Mueller, in her study for the Recreation Commission, did find that:

> Many people desire to engage in more recreation activities but are prevented from doing so primarily by a lack of *time* and in some cases a lack of *money*.[5]

This is undoubtedly true. There are some 32.6 million people in this country classified by the Social Security Administration as "poor" and one must assume that these people can ill afford much time or money for recreation. It may also be so that some people have the money but decide to use it in other ways, in effect saying "we don't have enough money for everything so outdoor recreation has to be by-passed."

And finally, on the matter of better transportation facilities, it is again quite obvious that there are more and better cars being driven on more and better roads than there were even two decades ago. Certainly, long distance auto travel (anything greater than a hundred miles) is far superior to what it was even a few years ago. For short distance auto travel, however, the situation may be somewhat different. Anyone trying to drive into or out of some of the major cities in this country on a summer week-end, may conclude that the family on the way for a swim at the state park is going in spite of the transportation facilities, not because of them.

My point in talking about all this is not an attempt to say that Clawson, ORRRC, and many others are incorrect in regard to these four changes in society. This is neither the time nor the place to do that. My reason for raising these questions now is to suggest that this approach may be too superficial for current and future planning needs.

114

It seems to me rather self-evident that Clawson's original thoughts on this matter are correct — as far as they go. What I am suggesting here is that there are other things changing in the society that are more basic, that lie behind these four variables, and it is these more fundamental social and cultural changes that we as recreation planners should be analyzing.

The remainder of this paper focuses on five of these changes which I have selected as being important. There may well be others.

I. **A shifting philosophy in our cultural viewpoint towards work**: There is clear evidence that the strong Calvinist doctrine concerning the goodness of work, work for its own sake, is changing.[6] The idea that work is somehow more valuable than play is slowly shifting (and perhaps not quite as slowly as some of the hard-working, hard-driving professionals and executives may think). This notion is giving way to such statements as:

> . . .it is essential to recognize that traditional links between jobs and income are being broken. The economy of abundance can sustain all citizens in comfort and economic security, whether or not they engage in what is commonly reckoned as work. Wealth produced by machines rather than by man is still wealth.[7]

This line of reasoning forms part of the basic justification for proposals of a guaranteed annual income. Only a few years ago many believed such an idea to be little short of ridiculous, but today even a major presidential candidate has pointed to the need for a guaranteed income for all citizens. And, indeed, we already have what might be called the forerunner in the Social Security system established in the 1930's. The possibility of the nation having a guaranteed annual income is, in the minds of some highly competent and responsible men, both essential and desirable.[8] This will not happen tomorrow, but there seems to me to be sufficient growing support for such a national policy that we, as recreation planners, will be well advised to ponder its possible influence upon the future recreation market.

II. **There is an upward change in the man-hour production capacities in all major facets of our economy**: This shift is leading to a growing realization that all the fruits of technology are not so sweet. Consider for example, the prediction put forth by Kahn and Wiener:

> By the year 2000, computers are likely to match, simulate or surpass some of man's most human-like intellectual abilities, including perhaps some of his aesthetic and creative capacities, in addition to having some new kinds of capacities that human beings do not have.[9]

Or consider the findings of a study by Rand Corporation which reported that by 1984 (an interesting year to choose):

> Automation will span the gamut from many service operations to some types of decision-making at the managerial level and that by the year 2000 it will have advanced much farther — from many menial robot services to sophisticated, high I.Q. machines.[10]

The implications here are painfully clear. Automation and its offspring, cybernetics, are replacing the man on the job. It is now almost universally accepted by students of the subject, that the wishful dreams of the mid-fifties of automation merely causing a shift in employment and not sustained unemployment have been shattered. Instead we are faced with the harsh reality of an irreversible and perhaps inadvertent new trend which is leading us to a society where work will no longer be a necessity but a privilege.

The speed with which the computer and automation are being adopted by industry is remarkable. In 1951, when the changeover began in earnest, there were seven general-purpose digital machines in use by the manufacturing world. Ten years later there were 7,500 far more efficient and vastly more versatile systems in operation. By 1966 there were 22,000. The advantage of the computer controlled production line is far too great for any competitive industry to ignore. The computers permit greater capacity, higher productivity, less time in production, increased time of pure machine operation, and decrease in man-machine time, reduced inventories, high standards of uniform products, less floor space, and far lower cost per unit of output.[11] An automated system never calls in sick, does not take or require a coffee-break, does not ask for paid vacations, never goes out on strike, can work long hours at peak efficiency and can learn an extremely complicated task after one set of simple instructions.

It is impossible here to treat the implications of this form of new technology in the detail that it deserves, but I would like to call your attention to one of several recent books on this subject. Its title is *Most Notorious Victory* by Ben Seligman, published by the Free Press in 1966. This book is both fascinating and extremely disturbing reading.

III. **There are major changes in the nature of the individual's work**: These changes are also an outgrowth of the new technology. It seems to me that since 1945 they may have emerged as a major force behind the growing popularity of outdoor recreation. I am referring to changes in the nature of an individual's work. In 1964 Charlesworthy put it in these words:

> Before the industrial revolution transformed the work pattern and the family life of people in the western world, the working day was long and labor was more arduous than they are now, but occupations were vastly more interesting.[12]

Technology has made an increasing number of jobs just plain boring and monotonous. It has led one British labor union to demand "lonesome pay" for certain kinds of work where the employee is forced to be by himself for eight hours a day with no opportunity for social intercourse with his fellow workers.

In countless numbers of jobs, the worker no longer has any decisions to make and his working habits on the job are not regulated by a human supervisor, but by an invisible electronic circuit that conditions every working operation he makes hour after hour. The computer not only decides how fast and how hard he will work, but it decides what specific duties will be performed and in what sequence they will be undertaken.

The effect upon the worker's intellect and psyche of these new computer controlled production lines will be great indeed! The new electronic revolution is far more profound than that of the industrial revolution of the 18th and 19th century, if for no other reason than the speed with which it is occurring. The time lag between the development of a new device and its adoption by industry is diminishing. The time required for social adjustment, however, to these new changes is remaining relatively constant.

What I am suggesting here is that in the past most jobs required a certain amount of mental ability, though obviously there was great variation from one job to another. Many occupations offered some degree of personal challenge, of skills, coordination, strength, or judgment and even aesthetic choice. As these qualities of work are lost, perhaps the individual turns to some form of recreation to seek his fulfillment. As recreation planners we should be considering the possibility that outdoor recreation is becoming a substitute for work *whether or not the individual has a job.*

IV. The difficulty of changing with change: Marshall McLuhan, commenting on our time of electronic technology, says:

> . . . .it is reshaping and restructing patterns of social interdependence and every aspect of our personal life. It is forcing us to reconsider and reevaluate practically every thought, every action, and every institution formerly taken for granted. Everything is changing, you, your family, your neighborhood, your education, your job, your government, your relation to others. And they are changing dramatically. . . .Innumerable confusions and a profound feeling of despair inevitably emerge in periods of great technological and cultural transformation. Our age of anxiety is in great part, the result of trying to do today's job with yesterday's tools. . .with yesterday's concepts.[13]

As mentioned above, the rate at which change is taking place is rapid indeed. It took almost fifty years for the telephone to be widely used. It was about 15 years before television was generally adopted. Transistors required only five years for general use, and the lasers, though still far from being completely exploited, became an industrial tool in a little over one year.[14]

The significance of this change rate lies in the apparent difficulty of our society to adjust at anything like the same speed. We are indeed, as McLuhan says, still trying to work with yesterday's concepts.

Ten or fifteen years ago, it was probably all right to delve no deeper into the causes of outdoor recreation explosion than did Clawson or the Recreation Commission. I do not believe this will suffice today. This is especially the case for recreation planning.

An example of an old concept still in use is the 40-hour work week as a major variable considered in anticipating future recreation participation rates. If we reduce this to a 34-hour week or even a 15-hour week, we are still not catching up with technological change. What we should be doing is giving deep analysis to the "no-hour work week" and how *this* may affect the outdoor recreation facilities. To quote from Norbert Weiner:

There is no rate of pay at which a pick and shovel laborer can live which is low enough to compete with the work of a steam shovel as an excavator. The modern industrial revolution is similarly bound to devaluate the human mind. . .the average human being of mediocre attainment or less, has nothing to sell that is worth anyone's money to buy.[15]

Virtually all authorities agree in general terms with this point of view.[16] As our productive capacity continues to rise, more and more people will find that their traditional work abilities are simply unneeded. The fact of "forced leisure" for large segments of the population is already upon us. It will grow in importance and size.

There is only very spotty evidence to indicate that recreation planning across the country is changing its concepts with anything like the flexibility and innovation required to cope with the new social environment being formed all around us by the use of electronic technology. We have not come very far from the basic thinking originally put forward by Olmsted, Murie or Albright.

It seems to me that many of the innovative approaches and services offered to the residents of New York City by its past commissioner of parks and recreation come very close to the kind of new thinking required. It is unfortunate, it seems to me, that Mr. Hoving is more often thought of as a controversial public servant, rather than as a man coping with contemporary needs with contemporary concepts.

V. Urbanization: The fifth and last point I wish to mention also stems from technology. It is the matter of urbanization. This is not new to any of us. All of us have been thinking about it now for some years. I simply want to mention that the new technology will further intensify this national problem:

> Once we realize that by the year 2000 urban environments will have to be provided for as many additional people as are now living in our cities, the possibilities appear in their true dimensions.[17]

The mechanization of agriculture is one of the major contributing factors to urbanization. This mechanization has not run its full course. Within the past few years, machines have been developed that now pick 85 per cent of the State of California's one hundred and twenty-eight million dollar tomato crop. Cucumber harvesters are now replacing manual labor and within two or three years it seems extremely probable that all but a fraction of California's grape crop will be harvested by machine.[18]

If past trends are any indication, the field worker of the 1960's will be an urban slum dweller in the 1970's. He will be added to the swelling numbers of men and women being replaced by technology as it continues to replace the farm, factory and office worker.[19]

118

In summary, this is what I am saying. Today, in order to obtain any sort of realistic comprehension of what is likely to happen in the future of outdoor recreation, we must go far beyond where Clawson went a decade ago. It is all too apparent that changes are taking place. But in order to adequately understand these and then to project future patterns and needs in recreation, we must grasp why and how the shifts are occurring. The mores of the past are not and will not be the mores of the future. Technology, particularly electronic technology, is changing everything.

We can not, in fact, really plan the future; we can only imagine it. But we must imagine in terms of the present not the past. We must face reality.

In the words of McLuhan: "There is absolutely no inevitability as long as there is a willingness to contemplate what is happening."[20]

Footnotes

1) Clawson, Marion, "The Crisis in Outdoor Recreation," in *American Forests,* March and April 1959.

2) The Outdoor Recreation Resources Review Commission, *Recreation for America,* p. 1, Wash., D.C., 1962.

3) Wilensky, Harold L., "The Uneven Distribution of Leisure," in *Social Problems.* Vol. 9, No. 1 p. 55, Spring 1961.

4) DeGrazia, Sebastian, "Of Time, Work and Leisure," *The Twentieth Century Fund.* p. 90, N.Y.C., 1962.

5) Outdoor Recreation Resources Review Commission, Special Study Report No. 20, *Participation in Outdoor Recreation: Factors Affecting Demand Among American Adults,* Wash. D.C., p. 9, 1962.

6) Fabu, Don, *The Dynamics of Change,* Chapter 6, Prentice-Hall, 1967.

7) *The Triple Revolution:* mimeographed and distributed by Students for a Democratic Society. N.Y.C. 1964.

8) *Ibid.* Note the 32 signatures of individuals agreeing with the philosophy of this document.

9) Kahn, Herman and Wiener, Anthony, *The Year 2000,* p. 89. MacMillan Co., N.Y.C. 1967.

10) Helmer, Olaf, *Social Technology,* p. 78-79. Basic Books, N.Y.C.

11) Seligman, Ben B., *Most Notorious Victory,* p. 117-118, The Free Press, N.Y.C. 1966.

12) American Academy of Political & Social Science, *Leisure in America; Blessing or Curse,* "A Comprehensive Plan for the Wise Use of Leisure" Charlesworthy, James C., Monograph 4, April 1964.

13) McLuhan, Marshall, *The Medium is the Message,* Bantam Books N.Y.C. 1967.

14) *Op. Cit.* Seligman, p. 163.

15) Wiener, Norbert, *Cybernetics,* 2nd ed. Cambridge, Mass. p. 28, 1966.

16) The American Academy of Arts and Science, *Daedalus,* various authors, Summer, 1967.

17) Perloff, Harvey S. in *Daedalus,* p. 790, American Academy of Arts and Science, Summer 1967.

18) *The New Republic,* April 13, 1968, p. 11.

19) For an interesting discussion of the possible implications of urbanization to outdoor recreation see: ORRRC, Special Study Report, No. 22, pp. 27-59, Wash. D.C. 1962.

20) *Op. Cit.* McLuhan, Marshall, 1967.

OUTDOOR RECREATION AS A PUBLIC GOOD
AND SOME PROBLEMS OF FINANCING [1]

by

Harvey E. Brazer

Chairman, Department of Economics

The University of Michigan

I

Total expenditures in 1967 by federal, state, and local governments on outdoor recreation amounted to less than $2 billion, well below one percent of total governmental expenditures. Outdoor recreation may be broadly defined, however, to encompass everything from swinging in a hammock in one's own back yard to canoeing in a wilderness area. Moreover, outdoor recreation may require complementary expenditures in widely varying amounts for equipment and other consumer goods and services, ranging up to elaborate camping equipment or a sea-going yacht costing hundreds of thousands of dollars. Thus, the total annual outlay for outdoor recreation is many times the amount spent on current and capital accounts by public authorities.

In this paper I shall explore two principal issues. They are the question of why or whether there is justification for viewing outdoor recreation as a public good and the question of how expenditures in the public sector should be financed. In order to pursue these questions rationally we need, first, to examine the question of what is meant by the term "public good."

II

In the literature "public good," "social good," and "collective good" are all used to mean essentially the same thing, and I shall use these terms interchangeably. In the Samuelson-Musgrave tradition they refer to a good which, once supplied, is equally available to all; it is impossible to exclude anyone from its enjoyment; and one man's consumption does not detract from another's ability to consume. Units of the good cannot be assigned among individuals and the value of the individual's enjoyment of it is subjectively perceived. Thus, a public good may be contrasted with a private good, units of which may be parcelled out among individuals who can be granted and can realize exclusive rights of enjoyment of such units.

From these definitions it follows that national defense or mosquito spraying of an area are public goods and that artichokes and apples are private goods. But while it is easy to extend our list of private goods, it is not at all easy to think of any large number of pure public goods. If we examine the

[1] I am grateful to my colleagues, F. M. Scherer and G. R. Wilensky and to Jack L. Knetsch for their useful comments on an earlier draft of this paper.

array of goods and services supplied by governments – things like police and fire protection, health and hospital services, education, and the like – we find, on reflection, that almost all of them fail to meet our public good criteria. They fail, generally, either because they are goods which in fact lend themselves at small cost to the application of the exclusion principle, or because consumption by some does impinge upon the opportunity of others to consume at the same time. Similarly, many goods that are supplied and purchased in private markets and consumed at the discretion of individuals throw off benefits that are not and cannot be captured by their immediate consumers. These "external economies" or unappropriable benefits may be positive or negative – negative, for example, in the consumption of narcotics or alcohol, positive with respect to education or the planting of trees on private property.

Viewed in these terms, it becomes possible to set up an array which includes all goods ranged in a continuum from pure public goods at one end to pure private goods at the other. The polar private goods are those with respect to which all consumption benefits are appropriable, where the ratio of unappropriable to total consumption benefits is zero or near enough to zero so that the difference does not matter. On the other hand polar public goods (e.g., defense) exhibit an unappropriable to total benefit ratio of 1.0. Clearly a large number of goods fall into the range of something less than 1.0 to substantially greater than zero, including most of the goods and services supplied by governments in the U.S.

Unappropriable or public benefits of goods consumed, rather than broad categories of goods themselves, fit the now commonly accepted criteria for a public, social, or collective good. These benefits should be paid for by the public at large through the general tax system (ignoring here the appropriate shape of the tax structure). On the other hand, private or appropriable benefits lend themselves readily to being paid for by means of a system of prices. These rules follow provided that the costs of exclusion of those not willing to pay for private benefits are zero or "small." Where these costs are prohibitively high the good becomes, in effect, a pure public good. The principle of financing assumes that the existing distribution of income is socially acceptable or that it is to be adjusted by means other than what amounts to distribution or transfers in kind in the form of "free" public services.

Efficiency, in the sense of resource allocation in accordance with consumer preferences and maximization of output and consumer satisfaction, requires that the prices charged equal marginal costs of supplying the private benefits in question (this holds strictly only when all goods are so priced); provided it be understood that costs at the margin include congestion costs that may be imposed by additional consumers. But when cost per unit is declining, as may be expected through the relevant range of output or consumption of many, if not most, goods supplied in the public sector, marginal-cost pricing will not cover full or average costs. Financing the deficit then requires a two-part pricing system, one part consisting of price=marginal cost, and the other part consisting of a lump-sum charge that is invariant with use or consumption but which reflects the value to people of the existence of the supply of the good.

The total cost of supplying the good is then made up of three parts: (a) a general-tax financed portion equal to the ratio of unappropriable to total benefits; (b) a price equal to marginal cost; and (c) a lump-sum charge to actual or potential consumers of private benefits associated with the good in question.

Neither the definition nor the suggested scheme of financing public good elements of consumption, however, provide useful guidelines or answers to the question as to whether the goods in question should be supplied publicly or privately. The alternatives are subsidies to either consumers or private suppliers in amounts equal to the proportion of total costs given by the ratio of unappropriable to total benefits and no public production, or public production of supply with the general taxpayer meeting that same proportion of costs. There would appear to be a clear presumption in favor of public supply where the good is purely or predominantly public in nature. In this case government is the sole purchaser. If declining costs prevail through the relevant range we have a natural monopoly, and a government monopoly of supply may be preferred to a bi-lateral monopoly with the government on one side and one private firm on the other. Thus, it would not seem to make sense for the government to contract with a private firm for defense services, for example. But as we depart from the case of the pure public good toward the private good end of our spectrum, it is by no means easy to establish rules. Public supply seems indicated by such considerations as whether or not elements of natural monopoly exist and how important they are, whether or not the coercive powers of government are needed, as in the assemblage of large tracts of land, and whether or not standardization of the good and methods of production are appropriate or even inevitable. In a predominantly private capitalist enterprise economy there may always be said to be a presumption in favor of private supply, simply as part of the ideological ethos. Public supply may be the choice primarily where competitive private market forces fail, or a public-private mix may be preferred as a means of ensuring effective competition or establishing minimum standards of performance.

III

Given the suggested approach to the definition of public goods, how does outdoor recreation fit into the picture? One of the difficulties we encounter in the effort to answer this question stems from the wide diversity of facilities and services that fit anyone's conception of "outdoor recreation." It is all too easy to fall into the trap of definition by observation of the kinds of facilities governments now in fact provide. But this, clearly, will not do. Nor does it seem appropriate in the present context to attempt to list all of the kinds of outdoor recreation that people indulge in. Rather, we can only hope to develop our principles by examining some illustrative kinds of facilities or activities.

In order to view outdoor recreation as a "public good" we must be able to identify externalities in consumption or benefits unappropriable directly by consumers. It has been alleged that the availability of opportunities to enjoy the out-of-doors somehow makes for a healthier, happier, more productive citizenry. But no one has succeeded in demonstrating quite how this result comes about, or if it comes about, much less in even beginning to quantify the benefits to the community at large. Surely the case for associating elements of public goods with outdoor recreation must be made to rest on firmer foundations. Thus, it seems to me that if justification for public subsidy and/or public supply of outdoor recreation is to be established it must be sought elsewhere.

Our earlier analysis suggests, in my view, a promising approach, one that can and should be buttressed by consideration of factors more or less specific to outdoor recreation. As with all goods in an economy of relative scarcity we must recognize at the outset that we operate within a system of constraints. Neither resources nor budget funds are free; their costs are properly measurable in terms of the values attaching to the alternatives foregone. But granted that demand for outdoor recreation exists, in the sense that the community at large prefers more of it at the margin to more of other things, whether or not we are dealing with a good that is public or collective in nature depends upon whether or not consumption benefits are perceived as accruing exclusively to direct consumers or in part or in whole to all or segments of the community, direct consumers as well as others. Another way to put the question at issue is by asking whether or not and to what extent the exclusion principle can be applied. That is, can non-users be excluded from sharing in the benefits flowing from the particular outdoor recreation facility?

One specific aspect of outdoor recreation that requires attention is the fact that in most instances decisions with respect to land use are involved, and these decisions are not reversible in the future except, possibly, at very high cost. Thus to a far greater extent than in the case of most other goods and services, the decision to allocate resources (land in particular) to outdoor recreation involves the interests of future generations as well as those of the current generation. Since the preferences of unborn generations obviously cannot be expressed in the market place of today, their interests can and probably should be subsumed under the heading of public benefits, thus justifying collective participation in meeting at least the land acquisition costs of outdoor recreation facilities.

A second specific feature of outdoor recreation related directly to its land intensity characteristic, especially in urban areas, is the fact that recreational use of land provides aesthetic values to neighborhoods that may ordinarily be expected to be more pleasing than alternative uses. Since such values accrue to the community at large, they justify general (but local) tax-payer support of the recreational facility. By the same token, however, account should be taken of such added auto and pedestrian traffic as the facility may impose upon the area and the negative benefits associated with it.

Before turning to an examination of the public or collective aspects of some selected types of outdoor recreation, the issues relating to the assignment of responsibility for outdoor recreation among the federal, state, and local units of government should be noted. The guiding principle here derives from the spatial distribution of collective benefits. Where these benefits may be expected to be primarily local, it seems obvious that allocation considerations require that the provision and/or subsidy of the facilities should be the responsibility of local government. And while state political boundaries are likely to prove substantially less than ideal for our purposes, the states' responsibilities extend to those facilities that throw off collective benefits primarily accruing to residents of a region that is larger than a local community but not appreciably larger than the state. In the abstract one may assume that border crossings more or less wash out. But in practice the state's role in outdoor recreation is likely to be very difficult to define because some states, for geographic as well as other reasons, are bound to be substantial "net exporters" of outdoor recreation. Thus, for example, can the State of Michigan be justified in providing or subsidizing outdoor recreation facilities in the western counties of the Upper Peninsula when these areas are more readily accessible to residents of Milwaukee, Minneapolis, or Chicago than they are to the people of the Detroit area? What appears to be suggested, therefore, is that local governments, both separately and in cooperation in metropolitan areas, together with the national government should bear the bulk of the responsibility for outdoor recreation insofar as it is a public good, but that a major role for the states cannot be justified.

The latter conclusion will be sharply challenged by the champions of expansion of the states' outdoor recreation function. They see state parks, for example, as attracting out-of-state tourists whose spending in the state contributes to tax dollars directly and indirectly and to employment and income of residents of the state. As an argument in the kind of advocatory proceeding that is involved in the budgetary process this view is understandable when offered by an expansionist-oriented bureaucracy or by private interest groups. Until and unless, however, it can be shown that the non-resident in fact contributes not just some positive sum, but in an amount such that his use of the facilities in question is not being subsidized by the taxpayer of the state, the argument remains unconvincing. But it is at this juncture that federal aid to the states may enter to play a major role. Federal conditional grants-in-aid, under which the federal and state governments' shares are determined by the proportions of collective benefits accruing to out-of-state and in-state residents, respectively, would seem appropriate.

Outdoor recreation facilities for which local units of government are appropriately responsible may, of course, take a wide variety of forms. The neighborhood park that provides primarily play space for youngsters with little investment other than in the acquisition of land is one prototype. Is it in some intrinsic sense a public good? My answer is a somewhat hesitant "yes." It is possible to exclude individuals, but the cost of doing so and the structural means necessary would be high relative to charges that might be imposed for its use and might be destructive of much of its value. Moreover, in the absence of congestion, marginal costs associated with use would ordinarily be small, if not negligible, so that user charges would not be justifiable.

A second kind of local outdoor recreation facility may be seen in the swimming pool, golf courses, tennis courts, and so forth. In these cases the costs of exclusion are likely to be small, and some control of access may be necessary, particularly at peak use periods, to permit anyone's enjoyment of the facilities. That is to say, in effect, that congestion costs enter and may readily become extremely high. Furthermore, apart from the aesthetic values that may attach to the area in use and concern for future generations, there do not appear to be substantial benefits accruing to those other than the direct consumers. I should regard facilities of this kind, therefore, as supplying essentially private goods, the subsidy of which may be no more nor less justifiable than subsidies for thousands of other private consumer goods and services. Their subsidy would involve redistribution of income, an objective that we may view favorably in and of itself, but which hardly seems likely to lend itself to efficient achievement through the combination of taxes and transfers in kind in the form of subsidized tennis, golf, or swimming. In fact, given regressive local tax structures, the income redistribution achieved may well involve net transfers from poor to rich.

In any rational allocation of responsibilites within our federal-state-local governmental structure it seems inevitable that the federal and state governments would be concerned with outdoor recreation that involves rather massive inputs of land or "open space." Here the matter of concern for the preferences of future generations assumes major importance, but barring excessive exclusion costs, there would appear to remain a major element of private benefit. The latter probably increases relative to public benefit as "improvements" specific to the needs of visitors assume increasing importance. I should say, for example, that the archtype outdoor recreation public good may be found in the wilderness area, whereas the highly developed campsite, complete with electricity, running water, sanitary facilities, bathhouse, and so forth, brings us close to the private good end of our spectrum.

Thus we may all agree, perhaps, that the Grand Canyon or Mount Washington in their "unimproved" states are public goods, appropriately acquired and maintained by the taxpayers of the nation as a whole. But "publicness" of outdoor recreation appears to me to be rather narrowly limited and confined to a small proportion of the total of all facilities we are accustomed to thinking of as being encompassed in its scope. This is not to say, however, that there is or is not a "need" for more space and facilities for outdoor recreation. It is merely suggestive of the appropriate approach to the question of financing. And to this issue we now turn.

IV

The question of financing outdoor recreation is most effectively viewed in two parts. The first relates to the matter of financing the operation of existing recreation resources while the second involves decisions with respect to the acquisition or putting in place of new ones.

With respect to existing facilities our objectives in financing are twofold. The first is to ensure efficient use of resources and the second is to provide the means of meeting costs of operation.

Efficiency in resource use requires that users pay prices equal to the marginal cost that their use or consumption imposes. Prices that exceed marginal cost involve economic waste in the sense that those to whom the use of the facility is worth an amount equal to marginal cost, but not more than that, are denied that use and opportunities for gaining satisfaction at no net cost to the remainder of the community are foregone. On the other hand, a price less than marginal cost means that some users derive satisfaction that is worth less to them than it costs the community to provide it.

It should be made clear that marginal cost includes not only the out-of-pocket cost involved in operation of the recreation facility, but also the "congestion cost" imposed upon other users. This congestion cost may be seen in the reduction in the quality of the service provided by the facility or in the opportunity to enjoy it that is experienced by other users. In the case of some kinds of facilities congestion cost may be far larger than any other cost. The problem is essentially one of "peak-load" pricing where the intensity of use of the outdoor recreation facility varies substantially according to the season, the day of the week, or the hour of the day.

Thus a rational system of pricing should reflect marginal cost in the comprehensive sense suggested and this will mean not a fixed system of prices but, rather, a system under which the price or user charge varies with the degree of congestion expected. For example, the price charged for the use of a public beach might be zero or very low on weekdays off-season, highest on summer weekends and so on.

An appropriate price system, moreover, may be employed not only as a means of achieving a better time-spread of use, but also to shift use of outdoor recreation facilities from those with high to those with low marginal costs.

Marginal-cost pricing (assuming no congestion costs), however, will cover total costs only if average costs are constant or rising. But the nature of the production function in virtually any conceivable outdoor recreation enterprise is very likely to be such that average costs will decline with increasing output or use. This means that marginal cost and, hence, price will be less than average or total unit cost, leaving a gap between total revenue and total cost. To the extent that there are external economies in consumption or unappropriable benefits there is justification for financing this deficit out of general tax funds. Any remaining deficit, however, should be met by users, but not in amounts determined by use. What is suggested, rather, is that a kind of "club principle" or two-part pricing system be used. One part is the price (equal marginal cost) per unit of use, and the other is a fixed or lump-sum charge which entitles the payor access to the facilities. The latter represents essentially, a readiness-to-serve charge. This approach is roughly approximated in highway financing, where the gasoline tax is a proxy for a price charged according to use, while the motor vehicle license fee is the fixed charge paid for the privilege of having access to the highway system.

Obviously if congestion costs are high and admission prices that are in fact paid yield more than enough revenue to cover total (including capital) costs we have a clear-cut indication that there is justification for expansion of facilities.

All of the foregoing assumes that exclusion costs are minimal. The difficult question is the one that asks "at what point are exclusion costs too high?" "Too high" in this context means so high that we would be better off simply to permit free access to unlimited numbers. This level is reached when exclusion costs exceed the addition to total cost that would be imposed by those who would use the facility at all prices below marginal cost, less the value to them of that use, plus the congestion costs, if any, that these additional users would bring. As long as exclusion costs are less than this sum, however, the community or society at large is better off to incur them.

This then is the case the economist may make for marginal-cost pricing in a system of rational or efficient financing of outdoor recreation. Although nothing I have said will be regarded as anything but well known to economists, I doubt that my prescription will be accepted widely and immediately by people in the field of outdoor recreation, either as members of organized bodies of users, as people working in the field, or as interested legislators. Certainly, I can hear the objections to a pricing system such as I have proposed coming from those who would and do argue that access prices tend to exclude low-income people and are therefore discriminatory. My answer to this objection is that low-income people suffer from deficiencies in consumption of many things — food, clothing, shelter among them — and I do not believe that the best way to redistribute income in their favor is through free access to outdoor recreation. The argument is particularly spurious when it is applied to non-urban type facilities that require heavy outlays for complementary goods like automobiles, camping equipment, and so forth, or even in urban areas to golf clubs or tennis rackets. In fact, free access coupled with full tax finance is most likely to prove to be an engine for transfering income from the poor to the relatively rich.

Some hold as a matter of faith that parks and other outdoor recreation facilities should be free to all, simply as part of our democratic credo. But one cannot effectively argue with faith, and I have no intention of doing so.

Is it feasible to charge prices? My discussion of exclusion costs, I believe, answers this question.

The one major problem that cannot be dismissed out of hand is the problem of measurement or accounting. Can we, in fact, ascertain marginal out-of-pocket costs and can we place a value on congestion costs? These, I suppose, are questions of fact. I should argue that precision is not essential and that even rough approximations will do. I am not prepared to throw away the principle because of doubt as to our ability to apply it with precision.

The investment decision, I think, presents the more troublesome problems. All that is perfectly clear is that the notion that the more public outdoor recreation resources the better is not acceptable, nor can we look to mechanical rules that give us such objectives as "X acres of park per 1,000 of population." As I noted earlier, outdoor recreation resources are not costless, and in our world of relative scarcity, resource use in this area must be justified in competition with the use of resources elsewhere in the public sector as well as in the private sector.

Thus, public investment in additional outdoor recreation should be undertaken when, and only when, it can be shown that the discounted value of the expected stream of benefits less costs is greater with respect to the project in question than with respect to the relevant mutually exclusive alternatives. This of course is easily enough said. Practical difficulties, particularly in the measurement of benefits, abound and are well known. I can only plead that this is not the occasion on which we can expect to point to easy means of overcoming them. But until or unless they can be overcome we will continue to lack adequate guidelines, however appealing the rule of maximizing B-C may appear in principle.

Unfortunately, however, our problems do not end here, for thus far our discussion of financing has focused primarily on variable rather than fixed or capital costs. In referring to the gap between marginal and average cost, however, I have, at least by implication, alluded to these fixed costs. And here, I would reiterate only that capital costs, like variable costs not covered by prices charged, should be financed out of general taxes and fixed access fees in accordance with estimates of the relative weights to be assigned to unappropriable as compared with appropriable or private benefits.

V

In concluding I have no fundamental truths to summarize. If I have a "message" it is the reminder that however praiseworthy one's objectives may be they are rarely, if ever, achieved without cost, and resources and budget funds are never so plentiful that considerations of economic efficiency can ever be ignored with impunity.

I have observed administrative officials of the federal government and of the states desperately seeking means of financing the acquisition of outdoor recreation resources they were convinced were "needed" and would be provided if only niggardly legislative bodies could be made to see the light. And one is hard put to find the Secretary of the Interior or the state parks commissioner who has not advocated "painless" taxes earmarked to recreational land acquisition and other recreational ends.

The earmarking for such purposes of taxes on goods that are closely complementary to the enjoyment of specific outdoor recreation facilities has much to commend it. Examples of such earmarking that seem commendable would include the assignment of fuel taxes paid by motor boat users to state waterways commissions (even if one questions the absence of a contribution by sail boats), excise taxes on fishing equipment going to improvement of sport fishing, and so on. But there appear to be rather narrow limits to the scope and dimensions of such financing. At best it may be thought of as a substitute for user charges or prices in connection with the financing of facilities that entail excessively high exclusion costs or where exclusion is simply not feasible.

Least commendable are such suggestions as the one that was offered in recent years that would have levied an excise tax on soft drinks with the proceeds to be used to purchase national park lands. It all too readily conjures up the picture of the deprived, unemployed teenager of our urban ghettos paying an extra penny for his "coke" so that his affluent fellow citizen may enjoy the great outdoors!

In fact, of course, there are no easy answers — only hard questions.

ASSESSING THE DEMANDS FOR OUTDOOR RECREATION
by
Jack L. Knetsch

Director, Natural Resources Policy Center and
Professor of Economics, George Washington University

To do any sort of reasonable planning it is not enough to know that the demand for outdoor recreation is increasing. There is sufficient evidence to make this growth abundantly clear to all. This is no longer a valid issue. What we do about it is. And for this we need to know far more about the nature of recreation demands.

In the face of increased use pressures, large investments are now and will continue to be made in recreation facilities. It is, furthermore, fairly well accepted that planning efforts are needed to improve the allocation of these investments. This is commendable. What is less commendable is the way in which many studies designed to guide these planning efforts are being carried out and the links being forged between the results and recreation investment, management, and policy.

In our fairly new-found enthusiasm for recreation planning, we are making great use and apparently increasing use of the notions of recreation demand, recreation supply, and recreation needs. In particular, outdoor recreation demand is judged to be a useful notion in planning the provision of facilities and recreation developments. With this I could not agree more. However, the ways in which this is done are inappropriate and by-and-large incorrect, and almost completely miss the opportunity provided by even fairly rough, but meaningful, estimates of demand. The myths persist that somehow we are able to multiply population figures by recreation activity participation rates and call the product "demand" and that such figures justify doing just about anything we care to in the name of satisfying recreation needs. While much of such number manipulation occurs, it is economic and planning nonsense to treat resulting magnitudes seriously as guides for improving the provision of recreation opportunities.

There is first a need to seriously question this ambiguous procedure and the public policy decisions that presumably stem from it. There is then the need to define demand in a way which will provide more appropriate guidance.

Public bodies — at national, state, and local levels — and private firms need to have the nature of demand for activities and facilities defined in such a way that they can make rational policy and investment decisions to meet the expressed desires of their various publics. Too many of the current efforts do not provide this.

Recreation demand has often been used in a somewhat special, and in terms of planning guidance, a fairly disasterously misleading way. This in large part stems from confusion of recreation demand terminology given wide currency by the Outdoor Recreation Resources Review Commission studies. Many have unfortunately and uncritically read into this early work and subsequently propagated erroneous concepts of demand. This no doubt finds its sharpest focus in many state and river basin planning efforts.

Ambiguity enters principally at two points and makes many so-called demand studies nearly useless as guides to planning recreation investments.

The first is that the basic premise of price-quantity relationships which lie behind the concepts of demand and supply are ignored. Although recreation participation entails costs which influence numbers of visits to recreation areas, most areas, especially those provided publicly, are customarily available at zero or nominal charges. The millions of days of outdoor recreation currently being consumed are those demanded at these prevailing near zero prices for those resources. If these prices were raised substantially by the imposition of entrance fees or by some other means, a far different quantity would be demanded or consumed.

A second difficulty, and one really more to the current point, is that which is usually called "demand" is not demand at all. The participation rate figures which are observed are the quantities taken at prevailing recreation opportunity conditions. This use or attendance is determined or influenced by both demand and the availability of supply. That is, the data we commonly call "demand" are consumption figures for existing facilities.

It is common to use participation rates such as obtained from the Outdoor Recreation Resources Review Commission studies to project the number of visitor-days for certain types of recreation activities which would be expected from a population of given characteristics. However, these participation rates are again consumption data, not demand data, for they reflect both the characteristics of the population and the facilities that were available to them.

We should expect that the availability of opportunities would have much — and probably more — to do with rates of participation among populations of different areas than differences in the characteristics of the populations. It should not surprise us, for example, that people in Colorado or Montreal ski in far greater numbers than people in Washington, D.C. This difference does not by itself indicate differences in demand for skiing. The figures are the result of the interaction between demand and supply factors and are the measurement of the consequent consumption of quantities taken by recreationists given these supplies and demands.

This is more than a semantic quibble, it is an ambiguity which can increasingly cause mischief to well-intentioned planning efforts. What we have in effect is an extremely arbitrary determination of what outdoor recreation demands really exist and their relative importance. Improper accounting of supply considerations leads, for instance, to the assumption that people demand only increasing quantities of what they now have, and therefore can perpetuate present imbalances. For example, if some areas of the country show far greater participation rates on the part of the population for swimming and if this were taken as a demand statement without consideration of availability of opportunities, it could lead to decisions to build even more facilities in areas most adequately served, rather than attempting to provide opportunities in deficient areas.

An equally serious error is that we may miss completely many important demands for recreation and related amenity values. These are indeed critical if we are at all serious about the business of outdoor recreation and serious about a concern for the environment in which we find ourselves.

Judging from the large funds that go into them and the reports that result, the participation rate studies do have continuing appeal or at least popularity. This seems to be due to such attractions of the method as:

1. It appears right.

2. It is straightforward — easily institutionalized.

3. It gives large numbers.

However, the reality seems to be that:

1. It is wrong.

2. It gives erroneous planning guides.

3. It is a waste of effort that pre-empts the opportunity to undertake something useful.

The major trouble which has plagued many — no doubt well enough intentioned — efforts remains the confusion over the difference between demand and consumption. Without an explicit account taken of the dependence of use on facilities, "demand" studies can direct planning efforts to wrong conclusions or to irrelevancies and blunt plans and investment policy in outdoor recreation.

As Professor Wantrup has warned:

> Existing projections of land and water use are neither conceptually nor empirically identical with projections of land and water demand. In the first place, use projections do not separate demand and supply conceptually nor statistically. If demand is to serve as a principal of orientation for public land and water policy — that is to help in planning on the supply side — problems of demand and supply need to be separated conceptually and in empirical investigation, variables pertaining to demand must be differentiated from those pertaining to supply.[1]

The warning has been repeated in the technical literature, and empirical evidence has amply demonstrated the importance of the distinction between consumption and demand. Consumption data refer to and are measures of participation.

The extent to which the standardized methods and an improper notion and interpretation of demand can go astray is illustrated by many of the "demand" analyses in state comprehensive outdoor recreation plans and river

---

[1] S.V. Ciriacy-Wantrup, "Conceptual Problems in Projecting the Demand for Land and Water," in Land Economic Institute, *Modern Land Policy.* Urbana: University of Illinois Press (1960), pp. 41-68.

basin planning efforts. In one of these, for example, the evaluation of the user statistics and subtraction of supply numbers led to the conclusion that some $93,000,000 was needed in additional recreation facilities to catch up with "demand." If these added facilities were put in place and the same study repeated, it would, however, unfortunately show that instead of having met the demand with the expenditure, as would have been expected, the gap between supply and demand would be even greater! This would occur because the added facility supply would have brought about increased visitor numbers which would then be mistakenly read as even greater "demand." Another study led to the startling conclusion that the future needs for recreation water were so overwhelmingly great that all of the numerous water impoundment projects proposed by four federal agencies in a region were required.

A methodology which mistakes consumption – or in the case of recreation, visits or use – not only must dampen our enthusiasm on principle, but will indicate more "demand" for the same type of facilities in those areas where more of the facilities are located. This can have the important consequence of perpetuating the kind of facilities already in place in the areas already best served. Thus, as facilities are developed and used, new studies would report that more of the same should be built in these same places. Nearly any manner or amount of investment can be "justified" and investment decisions will be severely warped.

Furthermore, some of the most important recreation demands of the population are never brought to light. It says, in effect, that if only white bread is available for purchase, the subsequent buying of white bread by people shows that there exists a demand for white bread but none for brown and only more white should be supplied.

The standardization of methodology, the bulk of the reports, the mass of machine-derived numbers, and the dollar costs involved do not lessen the inherent weakness of these procedures. The concepts underlining the methods are simply inadequate for the intended purpose, making the subsequent collection of facts and figures almost worthless. They may show that a demand for recreation opportunities does in fact exist, but this is generally well known.

The chief need to overcome current problems is a better definition and examination of the demand for recreation activities and facilities that vary by type, location, and management. Information is required on the future demand for present facilities and for alternative areas and facilities that might be added.

Demand studies have a very practical purpose. Their objective is to yield estimates or forecasts for improving or adjusting the supply of recreation opportunities and to estimate the probable effects of alternative programs and policies. Recreation planners at any jurisdictional level remain at a loss without some notion of how recreation use will respond to alternative recreation opportunities that might be provided.

What is needed is not a collection of miscellaneous facts, but an understanding of the relationships inherent in recreation behavior and the ability to forecast the effects of proposed alternative actions. A more efficient and equitable provision of recreation opportunities is dependent upon the recognition of the wide spectrum of outdoor recreation possibilities in all regions of the country. It is also dependent on an assessment of the relative demands for different segments of this spectrum — for these are tangible expressions of personal values that are most significant as guides to what people want.

The single most serious and most fundamental deficiency in most demand surveys and studies is that they do not provide any means of determining how recreation use will respond to changes in supply — and that, after all, is the portion on which guidance is needed. The studies, consequently, are of little value as an aid to planning or to policy decisions.

Recreation demand studies, to be useful for planning purposes, must consider the effect of both supply and demand factors on recreation use or participation. Use data in the form of participation rates of population segments or visits to recreation areas must be obtained, but the interpretation must consider that both demand and supply variables explain or determine these rates. That is, the emphasis should be placed on determining and explaining patterns of use which emerge given an availability of opportunities and the characteristics of the using populations. Data should be collected and analyzed in such a way that predictions can be made of how the use patterns would be expected to change given changes in supply, that is, changes in the availability of recreation opportunities. This would allow estimates to be made of the consequences of varying recreation investments or varying recreational policies. For example, it would then be possible to make a forecast of the use that might be expected of a proposed reservoir or recreation area, taking explicitly into account such things as its location, size, facilities, and the existence of other recreation areas in proximity to it.

Park and recreation area attendance statistics are collected by nearly all public park and recreation agencies. While there are difficulties associated with the accuracy and comparability of these figures, the major weakness is that more data and better analysis are required before explanations can be offered for the patterns of use that occur. If the statistics from different areas are to be meaningful, and if much is to be learned from them, they must be related to economic, social, and physical environments.

We look at what people do, but we must interpret this as being determined by what they want to do — demand — and the opportunities available to them — supply.

The important implication of this for the design of recreation demand investigations is that it is quite impossible to carry out studies in a meaningful way by only asking people how many times they participated in various kinds of outdoor recreation activities. The supply of opportunities is ignored; consequently, very little of the differences in participation rates among different individuals or even groups of individuals can be explained.

Statements can be made of the demand for any commodity — automobiles, houses, or beef — but these must be taken to mean the quantity demanded at the prevailing prices, incomes, and given levels of other factors. If these prices or other factors were different, the amount demanded would differ. The demand for outdoor recreation similarly depends on various factors. One of the most important of these is the availability of opportunities. As the amount of participation in any recreation activity is directly dependent on the availability of opportunities, there can be no set quantity of recreation demanded by a population. Any prediction of recreation demand must, therefore, consider supply elements. We need to carry on demand studies for recreation as we have for many years for all manner of other goods and services. The principles and basic procedures are the same for each.

SUPPLY OF OUTDOOR RECREATION
by
Robert H. Twiss

Pacific Southwest Forest and Range Experiment Station
Forest Service, U.S. Department of Agriculture, Berkeley and
Lecturer in Landscape Architeccture
University of California, Berkeley*

Many decisions in outdoor recreation concern the supply of recreation facilities and environments: What is available for use? What different types of resources are needed? How much pressure will available resources withstand? In what areas should investments be located?

Sound guidance in supply planning is hard to find. Most writings in economics of outdoor recreation have emphasized the demand side of the equation, although Clawson and Knetsch do discuss the nature of the supply problem.[1] They identify such variables as: use requirements and standards, location, temporal patterns of use, multiple-use of resources, preservation of quality environments, and descriptions of area ownership and administration. In practical recreation planning the emphasis has been just the reverse, with a preponderance of the planning effort going into the description and inventory of the supply of recreation areas and facilities.

The purpose of this brief paper is to merely review some major supply issues in outdoor recreation planning by taking a practical approach but offering some critique of the techniques and methodologies used. Seven problem areas are raised as being critical in the consideration of supply: inventory, capacity estimation, classification, location, information handling, goal setting, and analysis.

Inventory

Inventory is a basic part of virtually all considerations in supply. Usually, inventories include existing and potential areas of land directly significant to recreation use. There is, however, great difficulty in deciding on the boundaries of lands to be included. For example, a particular national forest might have only one thousand acres of designated campground space and over a million acres of public land open to recreation activity of one kind or another.

The problem of what to inventory is usually solved by reference to standard recreation activities, such as auto-camping, picnicking, deer hunting, swimming, and from these activities referring back to specific types of facilities and chosen environments. Thus, the chosen set of activities becomes the key to the identification of resources. Care must be taken to be sufficiently farsighted and broad in scope so as not to bias the selection in favor of traditional but declining activities (such as tent-camping or duck hunting) or in favor of the tastes of any particular class of people. The

*Now associate professor in Landscape Architecture

activity-oriented approach to inventory is also open to question because of the danger of thinking in terms of purely leisure-oriented recreation, a concept currently being re-examined in recreation planning circles. A significant portion of so-called recreation activity may well become increasingly work-related in nature: management of the forest around the second home or cabin; community building in rural areas; running a camp or boat yard; owning marginally profitable mines or ranches; learning Indian cultures first hand; traveling with, say, a geologist or other professional guide (as opposed to a "fun" oriented tour guide), and so on.

Thus, it is not too surprising that studies and plans vary widely as to what is to be included as a recreation resource. The California Public Outdoor Recreation Plan for example, focused on resources needed for camping, winter sports, fishing, hunting, swimming, boating, picnicking, riding, hiking, golf, and community activities.[2]

In contrast, the California Urban-Metropolitan Open Space Study inventoried not only potential facility locations but all sorts of open spaces regardless of function. Examples are areas managed for forestry, agriculture, mineral production, water supply, wildlife habitat, geological features and hazard areas, historical and cultural sites, waste disposal areas, air shed quality control areas, travel rights of way, flood control reservoirs, flood plains and drainage channels, unstable soil areas, airport flight path zones, fire hazard zones, power transmission lines, canals, conduit and aquaduct ways.[3]

The essential point here is that there is no standard list of activities and concomitant resources which will meet the needs of each plan. Inventory must be based on a clear understanding of the purposes and expectations for outdoor recreation in the broadest sense of the word.

Classification

Classification of lands and facilities may take any of several forms. The Outdoor Recreation Resources Review Commission suggested a six-fold paradigm based essentially on intensity of use. Class I, High Density; II, General; III, Natural Environment; IV, Unique Natural Areas; V, Primitive; and VI, Historical and Cultural.[4]

Aside from administrative classifications (into federal, state, local, private), emphasis is often placed on the difference between user-oriented and resource-oriented activities and areas. The Boundary Waters Canoe Area is zoned concentrically by distance from road heads and high-use nodes — a zoning established by observing and surveying human activity (auto-camping, power boating, wilderness canoeing), and by determining the user's perceptions of the relative wildness of various parts of the area.

In contrast, some planners have used the ecological "life zone" concept as a guide. The multiple-use management guid for the Forest Service's Intermountain Region uses such definitions as a high mountain Crest Zone, a mid-elevation Intermediate Zone and arid Lower Zone.[5]

Each of these concepts is no doubt useful as a guide, but no one concept should be interpreted too strictly, as is often the case. For example, part of the appeal of a vacation in Europe is that one can camp in downtown Marseilles, France, and/or find luxury accomodations high in the Alps. Recognizing that one man's hometown is another's vacation end-point, we must insist on a flexible view of recreation resources to meet not only the statistical average of standard activity demands, but a broadening array of expectations and possibilities.

Moreover, classification systems can lead to an over-separation of activities, which could in fact be complementary. City planners are now seeing some detrimental effects of strict partition of the city into heavy industry, light industry, commercial, and residential. Each zone suffers from an internal sameness and a loss of the interest, contrast, diversity, and richness which can add to city life.

Capacity

Capacity estimates are key coefficients in comparing available land to projected demand. We usually would like to know the number of people per acre per day that can be accomodated without deterioration of the resource or the recreation activity. The difficulty here is in reaching some agreement on capacity standards, for small variations in levels of capacity can make great differences in the amount and number of facilities "needed." A common procedure is to set standards through consensus of professional planners and resource managers. The bias would be expected to be in the direction of standards which would assure easy administration and protection of the resource.

Another approach is to seek to identify the "natural" carrying capacity of the environment. The prime example here is the density standards set for forest service campgrounds based on estimates of the average site's capacities to withstand trampling, soil compaction, destructive vandalism, and related human impacts.[6] A merit of this approach was its reference to verifiable attributes of the natural environment; but nonetheless, firm estimates of impact are difficult to prove through research. Furthermore, the natural capacities of a site can be simulated or augmented by horticultural techniques and thus greatly vary the carrying capacity.[7]

In some types of recreation activities, the natural capacity of a site may be less significant than the attitudes of recreationists toward crowding. Robert Lucas's work in the Boundary Waters Canoe Area illustrates an extreme case of low density requirements.[8]

Still another criterion is that of health and safety, which is increasingly applied not only in terms of water pollution and sanitation but in other safety aspects of recreation sites.[9]

It is clear that all capacity standards are a function of user-site interaction, and capacity varies according to personal taste, the nature of the recreational activity, the quality of facility design, the natural features of the site, and the levels of investment in cultural treatments, supervision, and education.

Location

The location of lands and facilities in relation to population centers and travel routes presents another complex set of tasks for the planner. Most frequently we find the use of the basic gravity model and its attendant application into use zones, such as day use, over-night, and vacation. These are valuable concepts as initial steps, and help to forecast the intensity and type of use as a function of proximity to population centers, relative accessibility, and the expected attractiveness of the area. A number of studies throughout the United States have shown rather uniform correlation between distance and use. Still there is a problem, that with the increasing mobility of populations, any particular site may be potentially useful to many user groups. City and county parks tend to be used by travelers as well as local residents. On the other hand Yosemite National Park not only serves as a vacation end-point for Easterners but as a sort of regional park for residents of California's Central Valley.

Quite often decisions to locate recreation facilities are based strongly on expected impact upon local economic development. A sizeable portion of federal expenditures in recreation is primarily or secondarily for just this purpose. In this situation, the concepts of central place theory and areal functional organization should give deeper insight into economic impact and yield more accurate estimates of the economic multiplier effects.[10]

Handling of Information

Informational handling inevitably becomes a major problem in inventory and analysis. Of note here is the Forest Service's Recreation Information Management (RIM) System. This computer based administrative system keeps track of use estimates, investments in facilities, and site characteristics for virtually all developed recreation sites in the United States.[11] Included among other items, is information on the size of the area, ownership, designated purpose, and the type and condition of the facilities and improvements. Reports can be made not only according to Forest Service region, forest, and district, but by states, counties, congressional districts, or census divisions, by river basin, or by related planning units.

Frequently the planner is interested not in tabular statistics but in map-oriented data and storage and presentation. Fortunately, several computer mapping systems are now available.[12] In general, however, these automated methods are justified and feasible only when there is a continuing, high level use of stored information. While it is accepted that planning should be a continuing and recurring operation and that there should be continuing use of planning information at the highest level, there are few examples of planning which can now justify the high cost in acquisition, coding, and computation that the above systems entail.

Program Goals

The question of program goals is important not only at the outset of recreation planning but recurs at many points throughout the planning process. What should be included in the inventory? What activities constitute public outdoor recreation? Should we consider only camping, picnicking and hiking, or should we also include skydiving, dog-running, transcendental meditation, experimental community building and so on?

Some recreation agencies define rather particular spheres of influence; others are now becoming the public's advocate for all types of environmental quality. For example, the California Recreation and Parks Department is now involved in highway route alignment not only in non-park scenic areas, but through sensitive urban core areas such as Watts.

A somewhat trivial but persistent manifestation of such goal identification is what can be termed the "hot showers dilemma." Here the agency is forced to decide between considerations of comfort and public health and its image of the primitiveness of facilities appropriate to the agency's mission and clientele. The myriad of questions such as these can be answered best through considering the functions of all agencies and firms providing lands and services. Thus it is understandable why state recreation plans deal heavily in organization, function, and coordination between government levels and between the public and private sectors.

Analyses of Data

Analysis of supply and demand data is certainly a weak link in recreation planning today. Most take a rationalistic approach of demand minus supply equals unmet needs, with supply standards acting as key coefficients. For example, if the inventory shows 2500 feet of shoreline suitable for swimming and the planners accept a standard of 25 frontage feet per 150 people per day [13] and the demand study forecasts a population of 20,000 swimmers per design day, then 3,333 frontage feet will be "demanded" and the planners are 833 feet short. Simple, but potentially misleading. The swimming example is perhaps the most favorable to the standards approach because the activity is concentrated and easily studied and because administrators have had a considerable practical experience. But even here standards become tenuous if swimming is expanded to include related activities such as surfing, scuba diving, or collecting shells. Yet, we see attempts at setting exact standards for upland game hunting, trout fishing, scenic driving, and the like. One can only comment that this approach must be based on more valid research than we can find available today.

An alternative method might be termed the "black box approach." It attempts only to statistically describe the recreation resources, travel routes, and user populations in terms of a network or system. Neither supply nor demand need be forecast as such, but if relationships are assumed to be stable, one can postulate the effects on the system of changes made in population, cost of travel, or the availability of recreation sites.[14] Since various analytical approaches have yet to be fully described and compared it seems at this point that we should favor a variety of exploratory and developmental exercises as opposed to the sometimes slavish dependence on a supply-demand-standards methodology.

In conclusion, it must be stated that there are many other aspects of planning which deserve mention. However, the discussion of the foregoing factors perhaps will serve to illustrate the nature of supply planning and the problems to be faced. It is difficult to criticize planning efforts to date, given the paucity of reliable data. At best, one can but caution against over-rationalization and urge a frank reporting of both objective and subjective aspects of supply evaluation. For example, a broad survey and mapping of environmental and landscape attributes may be of more use to planners than calculations based on tabular data about gross acreage and standards. Comprehensive inventories can serve as a continuing basis for supply decisions even though recreation activities and tastes change somewhat over time. The techniques of such work are still being evolved, but guidelines and reviews of existing inventory procedures are already available.[15] We must remember that plans are needed not only for initial program guidance, but to serve as a cumulative bases for ever more objective and precise decisions.

Footnotes

1) Clawson, Marion and Knetsch, Jack L., *Economics of Outdoor Recreation.* 328 pp., 1966.

2) California Public Outdoor Recreation Plan, Part I., Sacramento, Calif., 81 pp., 1960.

3) Western Center for Community Education and Development., Univ. of Calif., Extension, Los Angeles, "Open Space in California: Issues and Options," 73 pp., 1968.

4) Outdoor Recreation Resources Commission, *Outdoor Recreation for America.* 73 pp., 1962.

5) U.S.D.A., Forest Service, "Multiple Use Management Guide Intermountain Region," *Forest Service Handbook,* R-4, December 1965.

6) Meinecke, P., A Campground Policy: A report to the Calif. Dept. of Natural Resources, 1928; and "Recreation Planning: A Discussion," *J. Forestry,* Vol. XXXV, No. 12, December 1937.

7) Magill, Arthur W. and Leiser, Andrew T., "New Help for Worn Out Campgrounds," *Family Camping Leader,* 4(4): 16-18, illus. 1967.

8) Lucas, Robert C., "Wilderness Preception and Use: The Example of the Boundary Waters Canoe Area." *Natural Resources J.* 3(3), 394-411.

9) Paine, Lee A., Accidents Caused by Hazardous Trees on California Forest Recreation Sites, U.S.D.A. Forest Service Research Note PSW-133, 1966.

10) Berry, J.J.L. and Garrison, W.L., Functional Bases of the Central Place Hierarchy, *Economic Geography,* 34, 145-54, 1958-B.

11) U.S.D.A., Forest Service, "Recreation Information Management," In-Service Training Guide, 127 pp., (no date).

12) Amidon, Elliot L. "MIADS2 An Alphanumeric Map Information Assembly and Display System for a Large Computer," U.S.D.A., Forest Service Research Paper PSW-38, 1966.

13) California Public Outdoor Recreation Plan, *loc. cit.*

14) Ellis, Jack B. and Van Doren, Carlten S. "A Comparitive Evaluation of Gravity and System Theory Models for Statewide Recreational Traffic Flows," *J. of Regional Science,* Vol. 6, No. 2, pp. 57-70, 1966.

15) Belknap, R.K. and Furtado, J.G. "Three Approaches to Environmental Resource Analysis," Landscape Architecture Research Office, Graduate School of Design, Harvard University, 102 pp., 1967.

THE ROLE OF THE PRIVATE SECTOR
IN PROVIDING RECREATIONAL OPPORTUNITIES

by

Joseph C. Horvath

Senior Recreation Economist, Midwest Research Institute

Kansas City, Missouri*

In this article, we will consider the present and future role of the private sector in providing recreation opportunities for the public. We will also analyze the present character of the private sector, what it is trying to assume in the future, and the functions of the private sector within the environment of a changing economic base.

Before going into these concepts, we must first consider several basic principles that make recreation considerably different now from what it was in the immediate past:

First, there is a growing national awareness that recreation — especially outdoor recreation — is a necessity for modern man.

Second, changes in the economic base have provided modern man with more leisure time, income, and mobility, thus enabling him to satisfy his need for recreation. And it is more than likely that leisure time and income will continue to increase in the future.

Third, research has given us a better understanding of the principles underlying recreation and tourism. Much of this research has been made possible by the Land and Water Conservation Fund Act which has provided research and planning funds for state comprehensive plans.

Market Frame of Reference

Because private industry is very much a part of our growing research and planning projects, we must consider its following theoretical frame of reference:

1. The tourism and recreation industry is service oriented. It does not yet have a clearly defined place among the other kinds of industries; it needs time to achieve maturity and to take its proper place. Recreation is now not even included as an industry in the statistical reports issued by the United States government.

2. Recreation is a two-headed phenomenon — it may take place either indoors or outdoors. Recreation is also a direct function of the amount of leisure time available. Most leisure time is spent indoors, a smaller portion outdoors. In many cases, however, the dual nature of

---

*Now with Adley Associates, Inc., Atlanta, Georgia.

recreation is not recognized, and the industry is still primarily oriented to only one side — the smaller portion — of the potential leisure time market. If the industry is to strengthen its position, it must cater to the whole spectrum of the market.

3. The outdoor recreation and tourism industry is a transfer industry. Money made in more highly industrial regions of the United States and the world is transferred to regions of less economic wealth.

4. The so-called tourist dollar is an export dollar. The local economy exports its goods and services for money earned elsewhere.

5. These export dollars have a multiplier effect on the local economy. The money circulates and recirculates. While doing so it creates additional wealth in the local economy. The more developed the area in which the money is spent, the greater the effect. For example, $1.00 from California spent in Bemidji, Minnesota, creates about an additional $1.50. The same dollar spent in the Minneapolis-St. Paul region creates $2.50 or more for the local economy.

6. The greatest economic significance of the tourist dollar is that it helps provide a base for the economic growth of the area in which it is spent. That tourist dollar is especially significant in the local economy, as it not only provides more jobs but also acts as a repopulator or as a preventive force against depopulation.

These six basic characteristics enable us to analyze the role of the private industry in providing recreation opportunities. The first characteristic, the service oriented nature of the industry, can be met better by the private sector than by the public sector.[1] People want recreation opportunities both en route to their vacation destinations and at their destination. Other major industries such as transportation (railroads, airlines, and the like) also provide opportunities for recreationists. Again, the population is demanding more and better services at vacation and weekend locations and these demands can be fulfilled more satisfactorily by the private, rather than by the public, sector.

With the increasing amount of leisure time, the private sector will have a longer season on which to base its business. The longer season will enable the industry to play a more than proportionate role in providing outdoor recreation opportunities. Recent studies[2] indicate that financial institutions lack information about the profitability of recreation enterprises.

The recreation industry in this country is still at the "kindergarten" level when compared with Europe. Historically, Europe's leisure classes have had more than 1,000 years to develop ways of utilizing leisure time. In addition, urbanization took place earlier in Europe than in the United States. Perhaps as a result, the United States and Europe are very different in their recreation and leisure time orientation. In this country we almost have to plan and institutionalize recreation, while recreation is an accepted, natural way of life in the urban societies of Europe. This gap is constantly being filled, and in many aspects the United States is more advanced than Europe. (Incidentally, no other country in the world has sponsored such comprehensive studies as those by our Outdoor Recreation Resources Review Commission, or ORRRC.)

Present Use of Leisure Time

It was stated earlier that recreation is a two-headed phenomenon and a function of leisure time. We have undertaken recreation demand and tourism impact surveys, inventories of recreation areas, analyses of available and desired leisure time by categories, and other related studies in more than a dozen states. One of the major items in all of the demand surveys was the availability of leisure time. We wanted to determine the saturation point of leisure time, in comparison with the present economic base, and the distribution of leisure time by its categories for outdoor and indoor recreation. Table 1 lists the definitions of the various categories of leisure time: vacation, holidays, weekends, and weekdays. Some of the results of the Colorado and Minnesota surveys, which are highly comparable, are presented here.

The theoretically available leisure time was calculated as 2,590 hours or 29.56 per cent of the annual of 8,760 hours (See Table 2). We asked each member of the household (husband, wife, children 6 years and older, single male, and single female) about their leisure time on weekdays, weekends, holidays, and vacation. If we exclude vacation time for the time being, Colorado adults had 1,745 hours of leisure time, about 20 per cent of their total annual hours. Minnesota adults had somewhat less, 18.40 per cent of the annual total. Again excluding vacation time, actually available leisure time as a per cent of theoretically available leisure time is 67 per cent for Colorado adults and 62 per cent for Minnesota adults. Children have a higher percentage of available leisure time — 90.66 per cent for Colorado children and 89.81 per cent for Minnesota children.

When vacation time is added to available leisure and outdoor participation is measured as 3 hours per activity occasion, we find that Colorado adults spent 17.90 per cent of their actual leisure time on outdoor recreation. The figure is almost double for Minnesota adults — 35.93 per cent. Colorado children report 21.09 per cent, and Minnesota children report 63.17 per cent.

Economic Trends and Opportunities

In comparing recreation demand (measured in recreation participation rates) with length of vacation, we find absolute unity of correlation; therefore, future vacation trends are of crucial importance to recreation planning. Because the private recreation and tourism industry is a transfer industry, it is dependent upon the level of the economy in the highly industrialized parts of the nation and other nations overseas. In this sense, the tourist industry is a marginal one. (Even so, some leading recreation economists report that the number of visits to national parks and forests is almost recession-proof.)

TABLE 1

<u>SUMMARY TABLE FOR LEISURE TIME DEFINITIONS USED IN</u>
<u>THE COLORADO & MINNESOTA RECREATION DEMAND & TOURISM IMPACT SURVEYS</u>

A.   <u>Theoretical Leisure Time Definitions</u>

1.	Vacation	Measured in working days only
2.	Holidays	Measured in working days only, there were eight in the study period
3.	Weekday	Maximum 4 hours — 6:00 through 10:00 p.m. Monday through Thursday
4.	Weekend	Maximum 32 hours — Friday, 6:00 p.m. through 10:00 p.m.
		Saturday, 8:00 a.m. through 10:00 p.m.
		Sunday, 8:00 a.m. through 10:00 p.m.

B.   <u>Theoretically Available Leisure Time by Category (vacation time excluded)</u>

	Leisure Time Category	Number of Days	Subtotal	Total Hr.
1.	Weekdays	201 (times 4 hrs.)	804	804 <u>Weekday</u>
2.	Weekends (45)	90 (times 14 hrs.)	1,260	-----
	Friday nights	45 (times 4 hrs.)	180	1,440 <u>Weekend</u>
3.	Holidays	8 (times 14 hrs.)	112	-----
	Associated days	15 (times 14 hrs,)	210	----
	Friday nights	6 (times 4 hrs.)	24	346 <u>Holidays</u>
Total Days and Hours		365 days	2,590 Hrs.	2,590 Hrs.
		10 days x 8 hrs.	80	
		11 days x 8 hrs.	88	88 <u>Vacation</u>
				2,678

Source: Colorado and Minnesota Recreation Demand and Tourism Impact Surveys, 1967, Published in the Respectiv
State Outdoor Recreation Comprehensive Plan, 1968, by Midwest Research Institute, Kansas City, Missouri, 6411(

Adley Associates, Inc.,
1968

148

TABLE 2

COMPARISON OF THEORETICALLY AVAILABLE & ACTUALLY REPORTED LEISURE TIME WITH OUTDOOR RECREATION PARTICIPATION, COLORADO & MINNESOTA

(Theoretically available 2,590 hrs. without vacation)

A. **Actually Available Leisure Time with Vacation Time Added**

	Colorado	Minnesota
Adults	Vacation sample average 13.008 days = 1,849 hrs.	Vacation sample average 10.2 days = 2,672 hrs.
Children	Vacation sample average 82.900 days = 3,011 hrs.	Vacation sample average 69.2 days = 3,004 hrs.

B. **Actual Leisure Time Expressed in Annual Totals in Hours and Percentages**

	Actual Leisure Time Reported (vacation time excluded)	% of Total Annual Hrs. of 8,760 (2,590 Hrs. = 29.56%)	Actually Available Leisure Time as % of Theoretically Available Leisure Time (Base = 2,590 Hrs.)	
			With Vacation Time Added (see Item A for resp. state & categ.)	Without Vacation Time
1. Colorado				
Adults	1,745 Hrs.	19.92	71.39%	67.37%
Children	2,348 Hrs.	26.80	116.25%	90.66%
2. Minnesota				
Adults	1,612 Hrs.	18.40	103.17%	62.24%
Children	2,326 Hrs.	26.55	117.53%	89.81%

C. **Outdoor Recreation Participation Within Actually Available Leisure Time (vacation included) as Percent of Total**

1. Colorado				
Adults	110.41 activity occasions,	times 3 hrs. = 331 hrs.	17.90% of the annual total
Children	211.66 activity occasions,	times 3 hrs. = 635 hrs.	21.09% of the annual total
2. Minnesota				
Adults	320.21 activity occasions,	times 3 hrs. = 960 hrs.	35.93% of the annual total
Children	649.99 activity occasions,	times 3 hrs. = 1,923 hrs.	63.17% of the annual total

Source: Colorado and Minnesota Recreation Demand and Tourism Impact Surveys, Midwest Research Institute, Kansas City, Missouri, (1967).

Adley Associates, Inc.
1968

The basic question is: *Is there going to be a shorter work week or a longer paid vacation?* This question has fascinated me ever since I began my research of the leisure time market. The opportunity to answer this question came with the Minnesota Recreation and Tourism Impact Survey, conducted in 1967. We found a trend to a 40- to 43-hour work week. Although the general population does not want this work week to be reduced, it wants very much to have a longer paid vacation. At present, vacations average 11.4 days; they want 16 days — a 40 percent increase — which is considered a reasonable amount of vacation even now. What does this trend toward a longer paid vacation mean to the private sector?

We know that there is a significant degree of association between the amount of vacation time and the demand for outdoor recreation and tourism. If within a short time, let us assume five years, annual paid vacation time increases by 40 percent, there could be a 40 percent additional demand for recreation. In addition, we think that vacation time demand for recreation opportunities and tourist facilities is elastic, so that the increase in vacation time could amount to a more than proportionate increase in the demand for opportunities and services — perhaps as much as 80 percent. This would represent an annual increase of 16 percent over the next five years. Presently many owners of private recreation enterprises are at the marginal level — they are barely able to stay in business. If the amount of paid vacation increases, not only could these enterprises stay in business and improve facilities, but new firms could also enter the market and provide more jobs and income for the rural population.

Public and private agencies will have to shift their policies to accommodate these changes. In general, there will be a trend toward developing recreation opportunities away from populated centers as longer paid vacations become common.

In the constant competition between indoor and outdoor recreation for leisure time, the quality of recreation opportunities will be the decisive factor. The contest will be decided in favor of those opportunities that best relieve the pressures of modern society on the individual. Development of the recreation and tourism industry should be encouraged in concentrated areas in particular scenic locations. Large, unpopulated areas should be left intact for recreation, scenery, and agriculture.

When many marginal industries are clustered together in one resort town, the tourist dollar — for which local services and products are exported — goes further than if it is scattered over many smaller towns. By recognizing this multiplier effect, the private sector in tourism can be helped, and major scenic areas will not have to be controlled by individual recreation and tourism enterprises. In this way, the private tourist industry could provide a base for a permanent, year-round core of population, and visitors might also find the area attractive for an out-of-season vacation. Prime examples of such developments already exist in the U.S. — Estes Park, Colorado; Bemidji, Minnesota; Hot Springs, Arkansas; Gatlinburg, Tennessee. Nearby federal and state natural resource areas could provide the "hinterland" for recreation and tourism, while tourism-resort towns could provide the "bedroom and dining room" for the vacationers.

Analysis of Demand for Recreation

The main concern of this article is the role of private industry. In the course of our research, we have conducted complete inventories of public and private recreation areas, facilities, and carrying capacities in various states. Table 3 lists the possible private recreation enterprises by types of services offered that were included in these studies. For each recreation area we collected data on the leading recreation opportunities provided for the visitors. Tables 4 and 5 list these opportunities by activities for the states of Kansas, Missouri, and Colorado. By weighting the top ten opportunities offered by the private sector in each state, we find that swimming, picnicking, and warm-water fishing are the top three activities. Horseback riding, sight-seeing, golfing, playing outdoor games, trout fishing, boating, and waterfowl hunting are the remainder of the top ten activities. Tables 6 and 7 list the opportunities provided by the public sector for comparison with those of the private sector. The public areas offered playgrounds, picnic areas, and viewing outdoor games as their first three leading recreation opportunities. The roles played by these two segments of the recreation industry are clearly seen from those comparisons.

Further research showed the distribution of day visits and overnight visits to all private and public recreation areas in Kansas, Missouri, and Colorado. For day visits the private sector in Kansas had 2.8 percent, in Missouri had 19.7 percent, and in Colorado had 7.23 percent of the total visits reported. Overnight stays in private areas show a complete turnabout in favor of the private sector: in Kansas, 82.59 percent; in Missouri, 49.54 percent; and in Colorado, 41.06 percent of the total visits reported. Table 8 illustrates our point here, that while private recreation areas constitute between 30 to 46 percent of the total areas in these three states, day visits to private areas are low, but overnight visits are significantly higher.

Major recreation facilities were measured and comparisons were made between the private and public sectors in Kansas, Missouri, and Colorado. The most common opportunity was found to be swimming, provided mostly by the private sector. The small table below illustrates the relative standing in each state.

Swimming Pool and Beach Facilities Privately Owned/Administered, as Percent of State Total

Recreation Facility	Kansas	Missouri	Colorado
Swimming and wading pool	11.13%	39.20%	47.09%
Swimming beach	66.48%	35.60%	24.70%

TABLE 3

POSSIBLE PRIVATELY OWNED AND/OR ADMINISTERED RECREATION ENTERPRISES

Wildlife societies owned or leased lands
Private owned forest lands
Railroad owned lands
Private hunting preserves
Private owned country clubs and golf courses
Lands of non-public schools, churches, and colleges
Youth organization camps
Fish farms, game farms
Historical sites
Archeological sites
Service organization camps and recreation areas
Resorts
Sport and playfields
Swimming beach or pool
Picnic area with tables and/or outdoor cooking facilities
Boat access
Tent camp
Trailer camp and "camper" parking area
Cabin and motel ⎫ ⎧ only if resort; not transient facility, unless located near
Hotel and lodge ⎬ ⎨ major recreation resource (i.e., Gatlinburg)
Parking facility
Group camping grounds
Ice skating facility
Ski slope facility
Vista point
Marina
Golf and putting course
Golf driving range
Fishing areas
Hiking trails and horse trails
Stables
Shooting preserve
Shooting range
Archery range
Camps: youth and adult, profit and nonprofit
Sledding or toboganning facilities
Vacation farm (dude ranch)
Nature study areas
Stadium and related outdoor facilities for group activities
Fairgrounds
Airports for pleasure flying
Zoo
Deer camps and clubs
Duck camps and clubs

Source: Midwest Research Institute, Kansas City, Missouri

Adley Associa
1

152

TABLE 4

THE MAJOR RECREATION FACILITIES (OPPORTUNITIES) PROVIDED BY
THE PRIVATE SECTOR IN KANSAS, MISSOURI, & COLORADO
(measured in outdoor recreation activities)

Kansas[1]	Missouri[2]	Colorado[3]
Fishing, Warm Water	Other Boating	Fishing, Cold Water
Picnicking	Swimming	Horseback Riding
Playing Golf	Playing Outdoor Games	Swimming
Hunting, Waterfowl	Fishing, Warm Water	Sightseeing
Swimming	Picnicking	Snow Skiing
Hunting, Small Game	Sightseeing	Picnicking
Horseback Riding	Water Skiing	Trailer Camping
Group Camping	Attend. Concerts, Plays	Tent Camping
Playing Outdoor Games	Tent Camping	Playing Golf
Viewing Outdoor Games	Trailer Camping	Hiking

---

nsas State Recreation Plan 1966, Vol. 2, Final Report, Midwest Research Institute (MRI), Kansas City, Missouri (1966)

souri State Comprehensive Outdoor Recreation Plan 1967, Vol. 2, pp. 44-45, (MRI), 1967

lorado Outdoor Recreation Comprehensive Plan 1967, Vol. 3, p. 978, (MRI), 1968

e: The above rankings were derived from the list of the three most popular activities provided by the existing
private sector in the respective state recreation plans.

Adley Associates, Inc.
1968

153

TABLE 5

THE LEADING OUTDOOR RECREATION ACTIVITIES (OPPORTUNITIES) PROVIDED BY THE PRIVATE SECTOR IN KANSAS, COLORADO, & MISSOURI
(measured in weighted-ranked values)

Weighted Value	Activity	Number of Times Appearing in Top
23	Swimming	3
20	Picnicking	3
17	Fish, Warm Water	2
13	Horseback Riding	2
12	Sightseeing	2
10	Golf	2
10	Playing Outdoor Games	2
10	Fishing, Cold Water	1
10	Other Boating	1
7	Hunting Waterfowl	1
6	Snow Skiing	1
5	Hunting Small Game	1
5	Tent Camping	2
5	Trailer Camping	2
4	Water Skiing	1
3	Group Camping	1
3	Attending Concerts and Plays	1
1	Viewing Outdoor Games	1
1	Hiking	1

Source: Comprehensive Recreation Plans of Kansas, Missouri, and Colorado. Ranking by weights calculated by Mid Research Institute, Kansas City, Missouri.

Adley Associa
196

TABLE 6

THE MAJOR RECREATION FACILITIES (OPPORTUNITIES) PROVIDED BY THE PUBLIC SECTOR IN KANSAS, MISSOURI, & COLORADO
(measured in outdoor recreation activities)

Rank	Kansas [1]	Missouri [2]	Colorado [3]
1.	Playing Outdoor Games	Playing Outdoor Games	Playing Outdoor Games
2.	Viewing Outdoor Games	Picnicking	Picnicking
3.	Picnicking	Viewing Outdoor Games	Viewing Outdoor Games
4.	Swimming	Fishing, Warm Water	Fishing, Cold Water
5.	Fishing, Warm Water	Swimming	Hunting Big Game
6.	Driving and Sightseeing	Driving for Pleasure	Sightseeing
7.	Nature Study	Sightseeing	Swimming
8.	Hiking and Walking	Walking for Pleasure	Driving for Pleasure
9.	Playing Golf	Hunting Small Game	Playing Tennis
10.	Attending Concerts and Plays	Other Boating	Fishing, Warm Water

[1] Kansas State Recreation Plan 1966, Vol. 2, Final Report, Midwest Research Institute (MRI), Kansas City, Missouri (1966)

[2] Missouri State Comprehensive Outdoor Recreation Plan 1967, Vol. 2, p. 31, (MRI) (1967)

[3] Colorado Outdoor Recreation Comprehensive Plan 1967, Vol. 3, p. 910, (MRI) (1968)

Note: The above rankings were derived from the list of the three most popular activities provided by the existing public sector in the respective state recreation plans.

Adley Associates, Inc.
1968

TABLE 7

THE LEADING OUTDOOR RECREATION ACTIVITIES (OPPORTUNITIES) PROVIDED BY THE PUBLIC SECTOR IN KANSAS, COLORADO & MISSOURI
(Measured in weighted-ranked values)

Weighted Value	Activity	Number of Times Appearing in Top Ten
30	Playing Outdoor Games	3
26	Picnicking	3
25	Viewing Outdoor Games	3
22	*Driving and Sightseeing	5
17	Swimming	3
14	Fishing, Warm Water	3
7	Fishing, Cold Water	1
6	Hiking and Walking	2
6	Hunting Big Game	1
4	Nature Study	1
2	Playing Golf	1
2	Hunting Small Game	1
2	Playing Tennis	1
1	Attending Concerts and Plays	1
1	Other Boating	1

---

* Driving for pleasure and sightseeing were combined into one classification for this ranking purpose.

Source: Comprehensive Recreation Plans of Kansas, Missouri and Colorado. Ranking weights calculated by Midwest Research Institute, Kansas City, Missouri (1968)

Adley Associates, Inc.
1968

TABLE 8

COMPARISON OF TOTAL PUBLIC & PRIVATE SECTOR VISITATION TO THEIR RESPECTIVE RECREATION AREAS IN KANSAS, MISSOURI, & MINNESOTA

Kansas

	State Total	Private Total	Private as Percent of Total
y Visits	46,948,557	1,303,808	2.777%
ernight Visits	1,107,016	91,424	82.586
mber of Areas	2,146	632	29.450

urce: Kansas State Recreation Plan, 1966, Vol. 2, Final Report

Missouri

	State Total	Private Total	Private as Percent of Total
y Visits	88,314,017	17,441,511	19.749%
ernight Visits	5,871,012	2,908,500	49.540
mber of Areas	3,026	1,418	46.861

urce: Missouri State Comprehensive Outdoor Recreation Plan, 1967, Vol. 2, pp. 30, 31, 44, 45

Colorado

	State Total	Private Total	Private as Percent of Total
y Visits	78,094,526	5,643,129	7.226%
ernight Visits	4,916,057	2,018,358	41.056
mber of Areas	2,189	671	30.653

urce: Colorado Outdoor Recreation Comprehensive Plan, 1967, Vol. 3, pp. 908, 909, 977, 978, Midwest Research Institute, Kansas City, Missouri (1968)

Adley Associates, Inc.
1968

157

In Kansas the most common private facility is the swimming beach; the least common private facility is playgrounds. In Missouri, 55.97 percent of the ice skating areas are privately owned or administered. Only 26.86 percent of campground facilities in Missouri are privately owned.

In Colorado, most of the ski slopes – 78.58 percent – are privately owned or administered, while the lowest relative percentage of facilities in private hands was tent campgrounds with 6.64 percent of the total. Tables 9, 10 and 11 further define the role played by the private sector in those three states.

In the research studies for the outdoor recreation plans of Minnesota, Arkansas, and Tennessee, we have gone one step further and measured the major recreation facilities by capacities. However, only the Colorado data are presently available – the other are under study. It is interesting to note in Table 12 that 91.18 percent of the hotel, motel, lodge, and cabin facilities – measured in number of bed units – are privately owned or administered. Group camping areas also show 91.18 percent private ownership or administration. However, the highest percentage of private ownership and administration is the ski lift capacities with 96.11 percent. Golf courses, putting courses, and driving ranges also show a high percentage of private ownership – 68.73 percent, 82.35 percent, and 70.83 percent, respectively. The lowest private ownership in Colorado is tennis courts, with only 14.54 percent of the state total. By looking at these opportunities offered by the private sector we see the service industry aspect – the high concentration of capital investment, and seasonality. These private businesses are also usually located near large federal and state landholdings where they can provide food, shelter, and amusement for the visitors in these areas. When a complete inventory of the public and private sectors of the recreation and tourism industry is available for each state, we will then be able to define more accurately the role of the private sector. However, present trends in leisure time and changes in the economic base indicate that there is a brilliant future for both the private and public sectors in this industry.

The silent competition between the private and public sector is going to increase; however, the distinction between these two will become clearer as more and better recreation areas are established. To discover public opinion on this subject, we asked the Colorado and Minnesota population whether they preferred private or public recreation areas and facilities, and we received the following answers:

	Colorado	Minnesota
Preference for public areas	76.8%	46.3%
Preference for private areas	12.9%	36.1%
No opinion or both	7.6%	17.3%
Not reported	2.7%	0.3%
Total:	100.0%	100.0%

MAJOR RECREATION FACILITIES COMPARED BY TYPE OF ADMINISTRATION:

STATE OF KANSAS, 1966

Recreation Facility	Unit of Measurement [1]	Existing Areas State Total No. [2]	Percent	Private Adm. as Percent of State Total No. [3]	Percent
A. Measured in Size of Area					
Swimming and Wading Pool	Sq. Ft.	1,400,529	100.000	155,835	11.126
Swimming Beach	Acres	489	100.000	325	66.482
Picnic Area	Acres	11,594	100.000	1,978	17.060
Tent Camping	Acres	3,051	100.000	548	17.961
Trailer Camping	Acres	682	100.000	201	29.472
Ski Slope	Acres	N.R.			
Golf Course	Acres	N.R.			
Ice Skating Area	Acres	N.R.			
Playfield	Acres	14,323	100.000	1,299	9.069

---

[1] Kansas Final Report, Statistical Summary, Vol. II, Need and/or Idle Capacity Calculation for Kansas, Midwest Research Institute, Kansas City, Missouri (1966)

[2] Same as Footnote 1

[3] Kansas Final Report, Statistical Summary, Vol. II, Recreation Carrying Capacity for Areas administered by private interests.

NOTE: N.R. = not reported.

Adley Associates, Inc.
1968

159

TABLE 10

MAJOR RECREATION FACILITIES COMPARED BY TYPE OF ADMINISTRATION: STATE OF MISSOURI, 1965 AND 1966

Recreation Facility	Unit of Measurement[1]	Existing Areas State Total No.[2]	Percent	Private Adm. as Percent of State Total No.[3]	Percent
A. Measured in Size of Area					
Swimming and Wading Pool	Sq. Ft.	1,452,255	100.000	569,362	39.205
Swimming Beach	Acres	2,730	100.000	972	35.604
Picnic Area	Acres	11,102	100.000	33,642	32.804
Tent Camping	Acres	3,291	100.000	884	26.861
Trailer Camping	Acres	1,351	100.000	494	36.565
Golf Course	Acres	5,960	100.000	3,025	50.755
Ice Skating Area	Acres	1,306	100.000	731	55.972
Playfield	Acres	8,305	100.000	1,703	20.505

[1] Missouri State Comprehensive Outdoor Recreation Plan, Vol. II, pp. 18, 19, Midwest Research Institute, Kansas City, Missouri (1967)

[2] Missouri State Comprehensive Outdoor Recreation Plan, Vol. II, pp. 30

[3] Missouri State Comprehensive Outdoor Recreation Plan, Vol. II, pp. 44

Adley Associates, Inc.

MAJOR RECREATION FACILITIES COMPARED BY TYPE OF ADMINISTRATION; STATE OF COLORADO, 1967

Recreation Facility	Unit of Measurement	Existing Areas State Total No.	Percent	Private Adm. as Percent of State Total No.	Areas Reporting Percent
A. Measured in Size of Area					
Swimming and Wading Pool	Sq. Ft.	956,740	100.000	450,584	47.095
Swimming Beach	Sq. Ft.	6,594,176	100.000	1,626,752	24.669
Picnic Area	Acres	14,414	100.000	4,751	32.961
Tent Camping	Acres	15,978	100.000	1,061	6.640
Trailer Camping	Acres	13,193	100.000	1,891	14.333
Ski Slope	Acres	30,098	100.000	23,652	78.583
Golf Course	Acres	7,781	100.000	4,361	56.046
Ice Skating Area	Acres	498	100.000	141	28.313
Playfield	Acres	7,639	100.000	588	7.697

Note: Private administrative breakdowns include both existing and potential facilities. There are 2,189 existing and 213 potential recreation areas in the State of Colorado, January 1, 1967. Forest Service areas and school board administered areas (especially Denver Metro. area, Grand Junction and Montrose) are mostly summary figures.

Source: Colorado Recreation Survey, Midwest Research Institute, Kansas City, Missouri (1968)

Adley Associates, Inc.
1968

TABLE 12

MAJOR RECREATION FACILITIES COMPARED BY TYPE OF ADMINISTRATION: STATE OF COLORADO

Recreation Facility	Unit of Measurement	Existing Areas State Total No.	Percent	Private Administration State Total No.	Percent
B. Measured in Capacity					
Hotel, Motel, Lodge, and Cabin	No. Units	8,924	100.000	8,199	91.875
Organized Camps	No. Beds	10,719	100.000	9,774	91.183
Boat Access	Loadings/Hr.	2,546	100.000	522	20.502
Ski Lifts	Persons/Hr.	58,861	100.000	56,570	96.107
Marina	Docking Cap.	2,831	100.000	870	30.731
Tennis Courts	Number	454	100.000	66	14.537
Golf Course	No. Holes	1,097	100.000	754	68.732
Putting Golf Course	Number	34	100.000	28	82.352
Driving Range	Number	24	100.000	17	70.833
Car Parking	Number	232,630	100.000	71,824	30.874
Picnic Areas	Sites	37,396	100.000	18,514	49.507

Note: Private administrative breakdowns include both existing and potential facilities. There are 2,189 existing and 213 potential recreation areas in the State of Colorado, January 1, 1967. Forest Service areas and school board administered areas (especially Denver Metro. area, Grand Junction and Montrose) are mostly summary figures.

Source: Colorado Recreation Survey, Midwest Research Institute, Kansas City, Missouri (1967)　　　　Adley Associates, Inc. 1968

We believe that these answers were very much influenced by the availability of private and public areas. In Colorado, 69.3 percent of all the recreation areas are in public hands, including Rocky Mountain National Park, Mesa Verde National Park, Curecanti-Gunnison River National Recreation Area, and many national forests. In Minnesota at least half of the recreation areas are privately owned. We will know more about the situation in Arkansas and Tennessee within a year. However, further research is needed on this subject throughout the country.

The demand for outdoor recreation is a function not only of population, the availability of funds, and leisure time, but also of geographical location. Table 13 compares the average annual outdoor recreation participation rates for the populations of Colorado and Minnesota. The rates are significantly different, due to climatic and ethnic differences, as well as availability of opportunities.

Further analysis of the ten most popular activities in Minnesota is given in Table 14, which compares adult participation rates in various categories: vacations, weekends, preferred activities on weekends within a 90-minute driving range, weekday participation, and preference for day use activities. These activities were converted from average annual activity occasions into percentages for each leisure time category, which enables us to compare them. It is significant that the demand for each recreation opportunity differs with each category of leisure time. On an annual basis the top ten activities for adults amount to 82.44 percent of their total participation. For the children this figure is 57.04 percent. Within each leisure time category, the top ten activities take up from 41.95 percent to 67.80 percent of the total activity for that category. The difference is due to structural differences within demand for each leisure time category.

What the Private Sector Can Do

One can raise the question, why are we devoting so much time to analyzing the demand for outdoor recreation activities by categories when we are basically discussing the role of the private sector in outdoor recreation? This detailed knowledge of the structure of demand is necessary because the private sector can and should cater to the demand. The demand is expressed in major outdoor recreation activities, each requiring different resources and a wide range of facilities. We also know that the leading activities — the ten major ones out of forty-four — take up at least 80 percent of the total annual demand. Just listing these ten activities for each of the nine leisure time categories, for both adults and children, is a significant step toward identification of those opportunities to which the recreation industry should cater. Any recreation area owner who provides opportunities for these top ten activities in the proper geographical location will be appealing to at least 80 percent of the total demand, assuming similar price and other demand variables.

TABLE 13

COMPARISON OF AVERAGE ANNUAL RATES OF PARTICIPATION IN
DIFFERENT RECREATION ACTIVITIES BY THE RESIDENTS OF MINNESOTA & COLORADO
(Expressed in Activity Occasions per Person)

	Minnesota		Colorado	
	Adults	Children	Adults	Children
Activities Sample Persons:	6,279	4,555	6,323	3,721
Fishing, Cold Water	0.54	0.47	5.42	4.19
Fishing, Warm Water	7.26	7.41	1.53	1.77
Swimming	7.70	45.44	3.89	17.76
Water Skiing	0.99	3.58	0.65	0.92
Canoeing	0.49	1.07	0.09	0.13
Sailing	0.18	0.29	0.24	0.18
Boating	7.78	9.48	1.69	1.56
Waterfowl Hunting	0.77	0.38	0.60	0.40
Biking	5.97	128.27	2.61	48.35
Horseback Riding	0.45	3.16	1.98	5.21
Hiking with Gear	0.15	0.82	2.19	3.83
Nature Walking	7.33	10.25	4.32	4.77
Walking - Urban	38.57	60.02	14.10	9.28
Bird Watching	21.96	10.42	4.22	1.25
Wildlife Photography	0.59	0.45	0.53	0.50
Playing Games	12.54	128.53	5.05	46.21
View Outdoor Games	8.37	15.65	4.42	7.91
Attending Concerts, etc.	1.61	1.92	0.38	0.33
Playing Golf	4.10	2.19	2.32	0.85
Playing Tennis	0.57	2.94	0.87	1.83
Mountain Climbing	0.08	0.08	0.62	0.72
Picnicking	12.56	15.38	8.47	10.03
Camping: Trailer	1.48	1.69	2.27	1.87
Camping: Tent	0.87	1.99	1.25	1.30
Camping: Organized	0.22	1.19	0.26	0.87
Sightseeing	22.00	19.89	12.20	9.78
Driving for Pleasure	47.18	38.55	17.82	13.80
Driving, 4-Wheel Drive, etc.	1.05	3.11	3.15	2.80
Shooting, Trap & Target	0.76	0.79	0.97	0.98
Hunting Small Game	1.15	1.32	1.14	1.56
Hunting Big Game	0.75	0.24	0.85	0.41
Visiting Zoo	2.64	2.93	1.07	1.46
Wild Berry Picking	0.71	0.86	Not Considered	
Snow Skiing & Shoeing	0.45	2.36	1.16	2.07
Sledding & Tob.	1.84	23.70	0.45	2.68
Snow Mobiling	1.62	2.61	0.32	0.23
Ice Skating & Hockey	1.39	20.55	0.50	1.88
Ice Fishing	1.70	1.05	1.16	0.06
Ice Sailing	0.00	0.02	Not Considered	
Flying for Pleasure	0.41	0.12	0.42	0.18
Sail Plane	0.00	0.01	0.05	0.13
Model Plane & Kite	0.38	1.99	0.21	1.62
Relax Outdoors	67.42	63.62	Not Considered	
Gardening for Pleasure	25.63	4.20	Not Considered	
Grand Totals:	320.21	640.99	110.41	211.66
Total, Less Four Items:	226.45	572.29	110.41	211.66

Source: Midwest Research Institute, Kansas City, Missouri (1968)

Adley Associates, In

COMPARATIVE RECREATION DEMAND FOR 10 MAJOR ACTIVITIES BY ANNUAL TOTAL BY VACATION, BY WEEKEND AND BY WEEKDAY IN PERCENTAGES: MINNESOTA

(rates based on percentages of average annual activity occasions)

Activities	Total Annual Participation Rates as % of Total		Vacation Rates as Percent of Total		Weekend, 3 Most Popular Activities[1]	Preferred Activities Within 1½ Hr. Drive Zone	Weekday Demand for the 3 Most Popular Activities[1]		Weekday Preference (day use)
	Adult	Children	Adult	Children			Summer	Winter	
Relax outdoors	21.054	9.925	9.114	2.809	6.970	2.400	21.300	1.339	7.932
Driving for pleasure	14.734	6.014	14.582	7.363	17.170	15.900	8.318	17.121	0.891
Walking – Urban	12.045	9.363	2.402	1.643	5.450	0.800	6.674	13.511	5.128
Gardening for Pleasure	8.004	0.655	1.039	0.010	4.120	0.300	10.205	0.058	0.596
Sight-seeing	6.870	3.103	19.323	12.450	9.310	13.500	1.874	6.745	0.920
Bird Watching	6.857	1.620	0.359	0.081	1.450	0.400	1.237	2.680	0.647
Picnicking	3.922	2.399	4.548	4.050	4.470	8.700	3.626	0.063	7.666
Playing games	3.916	20.041	1.182	7.462	4.930	1.400	10.246	6.832	15.896
View outdoor games	2.613	2.441	1.149	1.012	2.750	4.000	2.777	2.436	3.406
Boating	2.428	1.478	5.306	5.072	2.640	5.100	1.539	0.016	1.010
Grand Totals:	100.000	100.000	100.000	100.000	100.000	100.000	100.000	100.000	100.000
Totals of ten Activities:	82.443	57.039	59.004	41.952	59.260	52.500	67.796	50.801	44.092

[1] Percentages based on frequency of occurrence of top ten most popular activities selected from forty-four activities.

Source: Minnesota Recreation and Tourism Survey, Midwest Research Institute, Kansas City, Missouri (1967)

Adley Associates, Inc. 1968

As in any other industry, product differentiation is a major necessity. Therefore, if a private recreation area provides facilities for more than the top ten recreation activities for adults and children, its business will be even better. Table 15 lists the top ten activities in each leisure time category and may be compared with Table 14. The summary *percentages* for the top ten activities in each category of leisure time, based on the Minnesota Recreation Demand and Tourism Survey, are:

	Percent
Total annual participation rates, adults	82.44
Total annual participation rates, children	85.16
Vacation rates, adults	83.01
Vacation rates, children	81.00
Weekend, all family	69.67
Preferred activities within 90-minute driving zone, weekend	79.00
Weekday demand for summer day use activities	87.51
Weekday demand for winter day use activities	91.54
Weekday preference for day use activities	84.33

What are the basic requirements for the success of a private business in the recreation and tourism field? Along with the other characteristics that are essential to all businesses, the following are predominant:

1. A private business must know the segment of the recreation-tourism market for which the business is going to be built. Upper class, the "average" tourist, or any other segment of the potential clientele must be correctly identified, and then the business must be built specifically for that segment.

2. The business must have a unique design for product identification.

3. Ideally, the business should cater to the whole spectrum of the leisure time market and if possible in all seasons.

4. The business should be large enough to take advantage of the economics of scale and be able to provide at least ten activity opportunities in every season for each family member.

5. The business should be attractive to the convention market.

The recreation industry should receive more recognition from the United States statistical reporting system as an industry, which would also simplify data collection. The private sector of the recreation industry is trying to develop more leisure oriented opportunities and to lead the way in providing more recreation services for the public. The function of the private sector of the recreation industry may be summarized as providing the best leisure time market opportunities at the least cost for the ever-increasing recreating public in conjunction with the assistance of public agencies.

TABLE 15

COMPARATIVE RECREATION DEMAND FOR 10 MOST POPULAR ACTIVITIES BY ANNUAL TOTAL, BY VACATION, AND BY WEEKDAY; MINNESOTA

	Total Annual Participation Rates		Vacation Rates		Weekend 3 Most Popular Activities [1]	Weekday Preference (Day Use)
	Adults	Children	Adults	Children		
1.	Relax Outdoors	Playing Games	Sightseeing	Swimming	Driving for Pleasure	Swimming
2.	Driving for Pleasure	Biking	Driving for Pleasure	Sightseeing	Sightseeing	Playing Games
3.	Walking – Urban	Relax Outdoors	Fishing, Warm Water	Fishing, Warm Water	Fishing, Warm Water	Relax Outdoors
4.	Gardening for Pleasure	Walking – Urban	Relax Outdoors	Playing Games	Relax Outdoors	Picnicking
5.	Sightseeing	Swimming	Swimming	Driving for Pleasure	Walking – Urban	Playing Tennis
6.	Bird Watching	Driving for Pleasure	Boating	Boating	Playing Games	Walking – Urban
7.	Picnicking	Sledding and Tob.	Picnicking	Picnicking	Swimming	Ice Skating and Hockey
8.	Playing Games	Ice Skating and Hockey	Nature Walking	Biking	Picnicking	View Outdoor Games
9.	Viewing Outdoor Games	Sightseeing	Walking – Urban	Relax Outdoors	Gardening for Pleasure	Playing Golf
10.	Boating	Viewing Outdoor Games	Camping: Trailer	Nature Walking	Sledding and Tob.	Biking

	Preferred Activities within 1-1½ Dr. Zone	Weekday Demand for the 3 Most Popular Activities [1]	
		Summer	Winter
1.	Driving for Pleasure	Relax Outdoors	Sledding and Tob.
2.	Fishing, Warm Water	Swimming	Driving for Pleasure
3.	Sightseeing	Playing Games	Ice Skating and Hockey
4.	Swimming	Gardening for Pleasure	Walking – Urban
5.	Picnicking	Biking	Playing Games
6.	Boating	Driving for Pleasure	Sightseeing
7.	Viewing Outdoor Games	Walking – Urban	Ice Fishing
8.	Visiting Zoo	Picnicking	Snowmobiling
9.	Relax Outdoors	Playing Golf	Snow Skiing and Shoeing
10.	Camping: Tent	Fishing, Warm Water	Bird Watching

[1] Ranking based on frequency of occurrence of top 3 most popular activities selected from a list of 44 activities.

Source: Midwest Research Institute, Kansas City, Missouri (1968)   Adley Associates, Inc.   1968

The state recreation planner in the outdoor recreation field is in the unique position of being able to assist the private sector of the recreation industry in at least the following ways:

1. He can maintain and permit easy access to a data bank on all public and private recreation business. Preferably, the data bank should be computerized.

2. He should maintain the data banks on both supply and demand by keeping a constant watch on trends in demand and on potential areas for future development. The data bank should be completely updated every three to five years.

3. He should encourage, as much as possible, the operation of service-oriented indoor-outdoor recreation facilities by private business.

4. He should keep in constant touch with leaders in the private recreation industry and hold at least an annual conference on recreation.

We have attempted to look at the role of the private sector of the recreation industry in the United States. If I may repeat, we are still at the "kindergarten level" in this field. We, the research and planning personnel, must realize that we are dealing with a potential giant who is just about to enter the "first grade." We need constant research on the underlying principles to help us to understand and plan for the future. Certainly, there is plenty of room for discussion and more knowledge. In the meantime, we must encourage private businessmen to enter this field and offer them any knowledge we have.

The leisure time industry may well be the industry of the future. We have solved many of the problems in manufacturing, agriculture, and transportation, but we have paid little attention to the problems inherent in how we spend our leisure time. The private sector of the recreation industry should relieve the pressure from the areas administered by the public agencies, which up to now have carried, and are still carrying, most of the burden. We – the research and planning professionals – foresee a great future for the private recreation and tourism industry.

Footnotes

1) According to ORRRC Study No. 11 *Private Outdoor Recreation Facilities* p. xvii: "Owners of a number of facilities open to the public for recreation activities in effect subsidize such recreation by providing outstanding opportunities for public enjoyment at less than actual cost. Such situations should be recognized and further encouraged. The remnants of our national antipathy toward play needs to be overcome, and many problems typical of the growing pains of new types of enterprise need to be alleviated. The variety of mass-produced, economy-packaged recreation demanded today by vacationers was almost unknown a generation ago. Even government — national, state, and local — often looks askance at this rapidly growing business. Many people want a variety of recreation experiences that are incompatible with the practical limitations of public facilities. Many of the expressed desires for recreation services are outside the traditional realm of public service. For maximum development, public recreation programs should complement rather than compete with private recreation enterprise; should be compatible rather than combatant; and each should operate in its own area of responsibility."

2) *Financing of Private Outdoor Recreation* and *Federal Credit for Recreation Enterprises,* both published by the Bureau of Outdoor Recreation, USDI, Washington, D.C., May, 1967. See also Kansas and Missouri Bank Surveys in their respective State Outdoor Recreation Plans by Midwest Research Institute, Kansas City, Missouri 64110.

THE PRIVATE ROLE IN THE PROVISION OF
LARGE-SCALE OUTDOOR RECREATION

by

Henry L. Diamond

Vice-President, American Conservation
Association, Inc., New York, New York

The national policy toward private recreation development is clear enough. The Outdoor Recreation Resources Review Commission said, "the most important single force in outdoor recreation is private endeavor — individual initiative, voluntary groups of many kinds and commercial enterprise." ORRRC went on to say that private development should be encouraged and stimulated.

This approach has been reinforced by subsequent pronouncements from the Bureau of Outdoor Recreation, the Department of the Interior and the Administration. The states, for the most part, have taken the same attitude.

Booklets and guides on private recreation development have been issued. The states are required to give due consideration to private operations in their comprehensive recreation plans.

In short, *laissez-faire* capitalism in outdoor recreation has the official stamp of approval.

However, the point I wish to make is that we may be making too much of the potentials of private development in outdoor recreation planning. The official policies, the attitudes, the incorporation of the private role in statewide plans are fine, but these are not what makes private development succeed.

The force that generates private development is the opportunity for profit. Nobody goes into business because the government says its good policy. People risk capital and labor because they think they can make a buck.

The basic problem with private recreation development is that there are considerably better ways to make a buck. Put into more academic terms, the alternative uses of capital are more attractive. A number of factors reduce the lure of recreation as an investment. Some of the most significant ones are:

1. Recreational enterprises are generally seasonal. Too often the cost of fulltime capital must be amortized in a ninety-day season.

2. Initial capital investment is generally high.

3. Recreation is a consumer expenditure which can be foregone rather easily so it is among the first items in a family budget to be trimmed when times get tougher.

4. In many cases recreation requires a high labor input.

5. Recreation is often subject to capricious and unpredictable changes in public taste; witness the empty bowling alleys in many areas.

Perhaps the basic constraint on the public policy favoring private outdoor recreation development is an earlier policy decision. In the last century when the citizens of Boston set aside the Common, when Bryant and Olmsted created Central Park in New York, and when the United States Congress set aside Yellowstone as a public pleasuring ground, we as a nation decided to spend public money to provide outdoor recreation. This decision has been expanded and reinforced over the years.

Indeed, it has been a long and difficult fight to assure that outdoor recreation achieved a share of governmental expenditures. But today, although we still need more, government — state, local and federal — is spending about $1.5 billion annually on outdoor recreation. This is a hard won battle of which we should be proud. But we must recognize the economic consequences of that decision. If government is going to provide outdoor recreation free or on a subsidized basis, the role of private enterprise is necessarily limited. We cannot give away cake and expect people to rush into the bakery business at the same time.

There are basic limitations — government action and economic reality are central to consideration of the private role as a means of providing major outdoor recreation opportunities. But given these limitations, there remains a substantial private role.

At this point an important distinction should be made. The official jargon on recreation development is filled with references to something called "the private sector." Now in economic terms that generally means the part of the gross national product which is non-government. In the recreation field, however, perhaps the most important part of the "private sector" is not based on economics but rather on the human impulse to provide pleasure for oneself.

People spend a lot of money on recreation which does not flow into commercial recreation enterprises. They join golf clubs, they build beach homes or mountain homes, they build swimming pools in the backyard. They hang a tire on the tree in the backyard for the kids to swing on.

This and kindred activity is private action for outdoor recreation. It reduces the demand for public facilities; yet in the strict economic sense it does not involve recreation development by the private sector.

Frankly, I am not quite sure how all the country clubs, private swimming pools, and second homes get cranked into the outdoor recreation planning process. They certainly serve as an alternative source of supply which reduces pressure on public facilities and thus will be a continuing important factor. It is clear that we need far better methods of measuring the impact of private activities. As an indication of its importance, private expenditures for all recreation exceeded $28 billion in 1966 — about five percent of disposable income.

In passing, I would note one highly interesting development. At a recent meeting of the President's Council on Youth Opportunity (this is a group headed by the Vice President which plans for long hot summer programs), it was announced that the Council was going to ask private clubs to set aside some time each week for the use of disadvantaged children.

The social and political problems in this idea seem immense. It is hard to imagine the New York Athletic Club welcoming buses from Bedford-Stuyvesant. But perhaps the national need is so great that it will transpire. If it does, then private recreation facilities may become a more real part of our recreation resources.

Having postulated (1) that recreation is not basically a good business, (2) that government has to some extent pre-empted the field, and (3) that one of the major roles of the private sector is private expenditure and not business development at all, let me turn to a more positive approach and explore examples where private investment can provide recreation with some hope of success.

Since outdoor recreation is such a complex mix of activities, it would seem best to take up a series of general situations where private development can work. Exploring each activity would take far more time than we have here. The following, then, are special situations which I would suggest are important exceptions to the rather gloomy general picture I have painted:

1. Special High Quality and High Cost Recreation:

The resort business is an old one in this country. Early in the last century people were packing their trunks for Saratoga or their appetites for boarding houses in the Catskills. These resorts provide outdoor recreation. The fact is, however, that their costs are high and they must necessarily cater to the upper income market. I am talking here about resorts which offer their own facilities — golf, swimming, tennis, riding, and so on.

These facilities require large investments in plant. Many resorts which are operating profitably today were built in an earlier day at lower costs. If the same facilities were to be duplicated today at present prices, the rates necessarily would soar out of sight. Nonetheless, resort operations will continue to be a specialized part of our total recreation resource.

2. Provision of Outdoor Recreation with Hopes of Making Money on Associated Land Values:

This is one of the more promising areas of private investment. Many developers have found that if they take a tract of raw land and create a central recreation attraction, the land values around the attraction will rise sufficiently to make the investment pay off.

A number of new housing developments are being built with golf courses, and the smart, well-financed developer always builds the golf course first.

This technique accounts for the real money that is being made in the ski business. If the snow holds out and the whim of skiers does not stray, a ski operation can survive, but the real money is made in selling the home sites adjacent to the ski area. What was once cheap, hillside land becomes $5,000 an acre chalet sites if the ski area becomes popular.

The same technique is true of marina related development where the intricate cutting of canals can give waterfront footage to the most remote lot in the development.

173

3. Provision of Supplemental Facilities:

Where public investment has created the basic attraction — an outstanding park, a lake or access to the seashore — there is a possibility for private capital to provide supplemental food, overnight facilities and some recreation opportunities. The point is that private capital can build a marina on the lake the Corps of Engineers has created, but it cannot really create the lake and then build the facilities.

The National Park Service is more and more turning to the concept that visitor service facilities should be outside of the parks and this creates opportunities for private investment. The distinction here, of course, is that the private sector is providing *supplemental* services — *not* basic outdoor recreation resources.

4. Concessions on Publicly Owned Land:

This is a large and rather complicated area of private investment. The problems of concessions on federally owned areas have been under almost constant review by committees of Congress and the executive branch since 1948. A new study is before the President at the present time.

The federal concessionaire system grew up almost by accident, but it is now established and confirmed by the Congress. Concessionaires build facilities and operate them. They are usually the exclusive source of service within the National Park System and on some other federal areas.

Basically, federal concessionaires have most of the problems of any other private resort developer and in addition they must operate under federal regulation. Unfortunately, the legal status of their rights in the structures they build is so vague that until recently most lenders would not go near them.

Rather paradoxically, the states have, for the most part, assumed a policy of *greater* government participation in the operation of facilities within parks. Some states build and operate facilities directly. Many build them and lease them out to private concessionaires for operation. Few follow the federal pattern of having the concessionaire doing the building.

In 1965, Congress affirmed the long standing policies and recommendations of the National Park Service and gave the concessionaires some assurances which they sought. On the signing of the legislation the President directed a further review of the subject. Since then there have been two reviews, one by the Bureau of the Budget and one by the President's Council on Recreation and Natural Beauty.

There are a number of long standing problems in the relationship between the concessionaires and the government, but the basic issue is this: Having made the decision to rely upon concessionaires to provide facilities, how do you give them sufficient rights in the park land they operate to convince bankers to lend them the *long term* capital they need to provide facilities to meet growing demand?

Let me recapitulate and try to frame what I have said in terms of its implications for recreation planning and policy.

174

First, while we pay a great deal of lip service to the role of the private sector, realistically we cannot expect too much of it. Government is in competition and recreation just is not a very good business.

Second, the role of the private sector is perhaps most important in the sense of people providing their own recreation opportunities and not placing demands upon publicly owned facilities. There are not now sufficient tools available for measuring the significance of this important factor in planning for total recreation resources.

Third, pure commercialism does have a role to play but under the constraints I have noted, it is specialized and supplemental. High quality resorts, facilities associated with land development, supplemental facilities to public areas and concessions appear to have the highest potentiality. Recent federal policy statements are clearly encouraging for concessionaires, particularly those located where the tourist season is long. Contracts extending over a more adequate number of years will surely help to attract investment capital. Some agencies may now extend contracts to 30 years where the private investment is substantial.

Discussion of points raised by the participants of the short course after the presentation of this paper focused largely on the importance of recreation facilities in urban areas and the greatly improved opportunities for private investment in connection with such facilities. Other than large stadiums and arenas, which offer only an opportunity for passive recreation, private investment in urban areas must necessarily be limited to relatively small scale endeavors, or again, to concessions within public park areas because of the tremendous land costs. Indeed, in some of our larger urban concentrations, the municipal governments are experiencing considerable difficulties in their attempts to create more park and outdoor recreation areas. They are, of course, being assisted by federal and, in some cases, state cost-sharing programs.

I do not view this somewhat limited role for the private sector with alarm. I only urge that we be realistic in planning for what the private sector can do. There sometimes seems to be an inclination on the part of some government officials to be more royal than the king in extolling private enterprise.

To be sure, capitalism is great and as every government employee is often reminded, it provides the money to pay his salary and fund his programs. But it is now time that recreation and parks people assume a measure of self-confidence. The country has made the determination that it is in the public interest to provide outdoor recreation opportunities with public money. The task is to provide a basic outdoor recreation system within the reach of every citizen. There *is* an important role for private initiative but it is *not* a dominant role.

The role of the private sector in recreation must be similar to its role in other areas where government provides the basics, like education for example. There are private schools at every level to offer specialized education for one purpose or another or for the highest quality education possible. Private schools are extremely important and must be encouraged and considered in the overall education resource, but they provide a supplemental and specialized function. The basic resource is still the public school system. The same, I suggest, applies in providing outdoor recreation opportunities.

TOURIST ACCOMMODATIONS
by
I. V. Fine

Professor of Business, School of Business,
The University of Wisconsin, Madison

The provision of accommodations for tourists is basically a responsibility of the private sector of our economy. One must recognize that there may be occasions when governmental agencies become involved. However, such involvement should be restricted to needs that private enterprise is either incapable of or unwilling to provide. An isolated outdoor recreational development, in its formative stages, may not provide sufficient volume to justify private investment; the design or control requirements of a development may have to be protected; or policies of governmental agencies may dictate initial development as a public interest responsibility. However, even in these cases, the ultimate goal should be the operation of tourist accommodations as private enterprises.

The provision of tourist accommodations in an economically efficient and effective matter is not different from the provision of any other type of economic good or service in terms of the principles and concepts of business management. The resort operator, hotel keeper, or motel operator is engaged in the retailing of a service. He should operate as a retailer does. He should study his product and his customers and bend every effort to match the product to the customers' needs and desires. Such matching is the only sure route to successful operations.

Let us look at the *product*. Over the past twenty years there has been a proliferation of tourist studies in the various states. I have spent some time perusing these research reports prior to the preparation of this paper and am impressed by the remarkable degree of uniformity of findings that exist by way of describing the tourist accommodations which are available. This is especially true of the several states comprising the upper midwest. What do we find?

1. The vast majority of accommodations are seasonal operations. In Wisconsin approximately 75 percent of all tourist accommodations are open for six months or less each year. The percentage is even higher when one restricts the survey to resort-type operations.

2. Most of these resort establishments are of a small size. In Wisconsin our year-round operators average 17 bedroom units per firm, whereas, seasonal operators have an average of 8.3 rooms per unit. If one eliminates the few large hotels and motels, the average size decreases markedly.

3. Only about 10 percent of the accommodations in Wisconsin provide complete food service for all guests at the resort. Another 10 percent are roadside businesses catering to transients. Thus we have 80 percent of our establishments — usually located on water and catering to

177

vacationers — referred to as housekeeping-cottage resorts in which guests have facilities to prepare their own food. (Incidentally there is a growing antipathy to this designation since the term "housekeeping" suggests work to the lady of the house. Some operators are suggesting and using such terms as "efficiency units" or "self-service cottages" to describe their tourist accommodations.)

4. Resort business in Wisconsin, like much of the upper-midwest, is a resource-based enterprise. It is directly related to the geography and distribution of certain natural resources, notably water—lakes and rivers—and good quality shoreline. The more than 4,000 such establishments located on water in Wisconsin utilize an estimated 450 miles of shoreline and approximately 45,000 acres of choice waterfront real estate.

There are five major classes of lake shoreline in Wisconsin as follows:
Soft Shorelines

  A. Bog
  B. Marsh

Hard Shorelines

  C. Beach
  D. Bank
  E. Bluff

Virtually all of the present resort establishments utilize either Class C (Beach) or Class D (Bank) shorelines, which are the most desirable and valuable types available. Most resort developers prefer at least some sandy beach area, and this class of shoreline is pretty largely confined to the 1,920 *named lakes* that are over 50 acres in surface area (Wisconsin has about 8,700 lakes, of which 4,138 are named). As a consequence only a small percentage of the resort establishments are to be found on Wisconsin lakes that are less than 50 acres in size. And certain large lakes with predominately "soft" shorelines will have relatively few resort operations on their margins.

5. One last characteristic of the tourist accommodations that is available which must be called to your attention is the age of the establishments. This is a characteristic which is common to all long established areas of outdoor recreational opportunity. In Wisconsin 61 percent of all accommodations are more than twenty years old. In the tourist business we are still selling high-button ladies' shoes This is intolerable.

To summarize considerations regarding the *product* (accomodations):

1. It is not a year-round product.
2. It is a small type enterprise.
3. It cannot be completely separated from food enterprises.
4. It is water resource based.
5. It is an aged product.

Now let us turn to a consideration of the *customer.*

1. He spends the bulk of his recreational dollars on accommodations, food, and drink. A brief summary derived from a few of the state studies shows:

Percentage Expenditures

	Food and Drink	*Accommodations*	*Both Combined*
Connecticut[1]	34%	37%	71%
Indiana[2]	------	------	66%
Wisconsin[3]	------	------	65%
Georgia[4]	13%	18%	31%
West Virginia[5]	20%	31%	51%

The foregoing is but a sample. However, a more lengthy list would show the same pattern being repeated. Areas which are end-points for vacation and recreation will show higher expenditures for accommodations, but even in those states which are primarily transit routes, the expenditures for accommodations are significant.

2. Studies indicate that he is spending less time at any one recreation-vacation location. Touring types of vacations are on the rise.

3. The average recreation party is approximately threee people. However, more than one-third of all recreation parties contain no children.

4. Income levels of vacationers are significantly higher. In the Connecticut study, 70 percent of all vacationers had incomes in excess of $7,000. Twenty percent had incomes in excess of $15,000.

5. In most studies the occupational class most commonly found among vacationers is the professional, technical, managerial group. Retired individuals and couples account for approximately 10 percent of vacation travelers.

To summarize pertinent considerations regarding the *customer* (tourist-vacationer):

1. Most of his recreation money is spent on accommodations and food.
2. His vacation patterns are changing.
3. His vacation party frequently contains no children.
4. He has money to spend.
5. He is predominantly of the upper middle class.

Now let us look at the problems facing private enterprise providers of tourist accommodations. We can discuss them only briefly here. Before doing so, however, we would like to emphasize the close similarity between the resort business and agriculture. In many ways a cottage-resort is almost like a small farm—with many of the same characteristics and problems. Here are a number of ways in which the two types of business resemble one another rather closely:

179

1. **Short season**: Resort establishments and farms are quite seasonal, and both are subject to a fairly short season in the upper midwest. Cottage-resorts are pretty well limited to a 10—to 14—week vacation season, whereas farms in this same area are limited to a 90-100 day growing season.

2. **Weather**: Both resort and farm operations are dependent to a great extent on weather conditions. A cold summer is not the best for either business. Prolonged drought (summer or winter) can affect both farms and resorts. Storms, unseasonal frost, and insects are other problems which often face both farmers and resorters.

3. **Resource depletion**: Soil erosion and fertility depletion lower farm productivity. Similarly, lakes can be too acid, too infertile (sometimes too fertile), discolored, polluted, weedy, or silted so as to affect their productivity and quality for water users. Thus, both farms and resorts are dependent on basic resources, which must be conserved and properly managed for best results.

4. **High investment**: Both resorts and farms require a heavy initial investment in proportion to the annual gross income. Even on many good farms the annual gross income seldom exceeds 30 percent of the total investment in land, buildings, livestock and machines. Similarly, the annual gross income from a cottage-resort located on a good lake is seldom over 20 percent of the total investment (or replacement cost) of the establishment. Most cottage resorts, like small farms, are part-time enterprises since additional income is needed.

5. **Family business**: Both the cottage-resort and farming business are family-type enterprises. Because of the low income in relation to the money invested, it is difficult to hire much outside help, and thus all members of the family must "pitch in" to operate the business. Small resorts, like small farms, provide very few job opportunities in the community, aside from family employment.

6. **Way of life**: Both cottage resorts and small farms are often a "way of life" for many families. These people would not be happy doing anything else, despite the relatively low income possibilities afforded by the business. Both businesses give ample opportunity for outdoor work and pleasures, with a minimum of restrictions and a maximum of independence. Many people would rather do resort work or farm work more than anything else in the world, and thus they tend to stay in the business despite little or no net income above costs.

Short Season Is Problem

Perhaps the most serious problem of all in the upper midwest is the extremely short guest season for cottage resorts, the bulk of which are not located near winter sports areas. Most of them enjoy only 8—to 12—weeks of fairly good business each summer. It is true that some successful operators are extending the season to 14 and even 16 weeks, but they have had to build up this business by skillful advertising and providing more services for their guests.

The short season is not a matter of climate alone, although 16 weeks is getting pretty close to the limit in terms of good, warm weather. The biggest problem is the school vacation term which is always a factor in the vacation plans of city families. The big city school systems seldom close before June 15 and most families with children like to have a week or two at home before school begins in the late summer. Thus, there are only 75 to 80 days available for vacationing city families with school-age children.

Resources Deteriorate

Another problem that is already troublesome in some areas is lake and stream deterioration. Overcrowding of these waters, as well as misuse and pollution, lead to such problems as siltation, weed growth, fish kills, algae infestation, and loss of esthetic values. For example, one lake of 970 acres in Vilas County in Wisconsin has 38 summer resorts plus more than 200 summer cottages. As a consequence, this lake has only 23 acres of available water surface per resort.

In addition, overcrowding has led to serious conflicts between speed-boaters, water skiers, fishermen, canoeists, swimmers and other users of the water resources. For example, excessive use of speedboats and water skis near shore can lead to destruction of spawning grounds and create other fish management problems.

Obsolete Facilities

Another problem that is plaguing resort operators in certain areas is the matter of obsolete facilities. This is particularly true where the resorts were built from 25 to 50 years ago and still remain on the same sites. Many of the earlier resorts, particularly those built between 1900 and 1940, were designed for sportsmen and were in the nature of fishing camps. Thus the cottages were largely of cabin size (less than 300 usable square feet) and had to be expanded for rental to family groups later on. Since many of the structures were not especially suited to expansion and modernization (installing running water with modern toilets and bath fixtures), the results were often not satisfactory.

Vacationers and other visitors in this modern era insist on a wide range of special services beyond the lodging and usual waterfront activities. Unfortunately, many of our housekeeping-cottage resorts have not kept pace with this demand and still have little to offer the public beyond lodging, a boat, and access to water. Since the visitors of today are much more mobile and can go much farther afield in seeking the guest services and recreational activities they want, many of the older resorts are not getting the percentage of "repeat business" that is necessary to stay in operation.

There is a general lack of professionalism among cottage resort operators, many of whom came to this business after being mechanics or storekeepers or factory workers most of their lives. As a consequence, they have had little or no experience in catering to the traveling public, nor have they had sufficient experience in tourist-business management.

Trends and The Future

There are several rather noticeable trends in the resort business of Wisconsin. One of the most noticeable trends is the decline in numbers of small establishments. This is particularly true in the case of house-keeping-cottage resorts on popular, well-known lakes. These small establishments are being subdivided and sold as individual cottages or as waterfront lots to people who wish to own summer cottages or year-round homes in these areas.

Part of the reason for this decline in small resorts is the increasing land cost, since good lake frontage property has been appreciating in value at the rate of about 10 percent a year since 1946. This means a much higher land cost and higher taxes for housekeeping-cottage resorts which have, in most areas, shown gross incomes of only about $700 per cottage per year. Thus the cottage resort's waterfront land is often sold and goes over to a "higher use"— either residential building or intensive resort operations.

Hand in hand with the decline of small establishments has been the increase of larger resorts and resort hotels in some areas. It appears that approximately 20 average-to-good cottages are needed to provide a reasonable profit to the seasonal operator with 10 to 14 weeks of business (at 80 percent occupancy). Many of the newer resort-type establishments are of the more efficient motel or apartment type, particularly where the season can be extended.

There is also a definite trend toward *complete* resorts which can offer lodging, food service, car service, private airstrips, gift shops, sports apparel and equipment shops, beverage service, entertainment, meeting rooms, swimming pools, marina service, and a variety of personal services—all at one location. Although the number of such establishments is quite small at the present time, at least a dozen have been built or developed since 1960 in Wisconsin. Some of these do not offer the entire range of services yet, but the increase in number of motel-supper club establishments in our resort counties is quite noticeable. Many of these are not located on the water, but instead are situated near a town or on a well-traveled highway within easy driving distance of a dozen or more lakes, rivers, sports areas, and so forth.

Another noticeable trend has been the development of "off-season" activities and facilities which tend to lengthen the visitor-lodging season in many areas. Perhaps the development of winter sports areas has been most noticeable. The first commercial ski area in Wisconsin was started in 1946 with a single rope tow and tarpaper shelter. In 1959-60 there were 37 major ski areas in Wisconsin, and 44,000 ski enthusiasts were contributing about $4 million a year to our economy. By the winter of 1963-64 the number of winter sports areas had increased to 53, and the total gross income from 100,000 or more skiers, and ski followers certainly exceeded $10 million this last season.

There are many other examples of winter, spring and fall activities that have meant more weekend guests and visitors for Wisconsin, even the northern areas. Convention business, contests, festivals, guided tours, nature study, historic sites, factory tours, and many other things have helped the cause. In addition, more and more people, particularly our senior citizens, are taking vacations in the spring and fall months, and this trend will continue. There was a 17 percent increase in the number of people over 65 years of age between 1950 and 1960, and this group can take recreational trips at any season. Additional opportunities for more "off-season" vacation business develop each year.

As far as the future is concerned, I feel that the upper midwest is big enough and has natural resources enough to have both a good volume of tourist business and an abundant supply of natural resources of good quality. However, it will take both individual and organized efforts by progressive operators and communities to guide future developments along proper lines.

Footnotes

1) *Nonresident Vacation Travel in Connecticut*, 1966, Bureau of Business Research, University of Connecticut, 1966.

2) *Indiana Hotel-Motel Lodging Survey*, 1967, Indiana Department of Commerce, 1967.

3) *The Wisconsin Vacationer*, Bureau of Business Research, University of Wisconsin, 1960.

4) *Tourism Developments in the Georgia Mountain Area*, Bureau of Business Research, University of Georgia, 1967.

5) *West Virginia Travel and Tourism Study,* Bureau of Business Research, West Virginia University, 1965.

PART II

A GENERAL VIEW OF OUTDOOR RECREATION
PLANNING, POLICY FORMATION AND
ADMINISTRATION

The papers in this part focus on the general characteristics of planning as an activity and on specific steps of the planning process. The objectives are to distinguish the planning process from related decision processes and to provide criteria by which outdoor recreation planners can better understand their responsibilities and apply their skills. As in Part I, the papers provide information necessary for an integrative and comprehensive approach to outdoor recreation planning.

The General Nature of Planning

Driver   (Some Thoughts on Planning, The Planning Process
            and Related Decision Processes):

In this paper an attempt is made to distinguish planning as an activity from the planning process. The planning process is differentiated from three other important decision processes of which it is a part—the democratic (political) process, the decision process, and the administrative process. This is done by defining each process, explaining what activities occur therein and describing the primary roles and responsibilities of the key actors in each process. Planning is defined as the systematic collection, organization and processing of technical information to facilitate decision making. The importance of information in decision making is considered in some detail and related to the responsibilities of outdoor recreation planners. The discussion of the primary role of planners as providers of technical information is supplemented by a consideration of their secondary roles — including education, innovation, community liaison and strategic involvement in the decision-making process. Different types, scales, orientations and purposes of plans are discussed within the context of the definitions given.

Fox   (The Nature of Planning Decisions in a Democratic Society):

In this paper Mr. Fox considers several criteria for evaluating the responsibilities of outdoor recreation planners in a democracy. He begins by stating that a major component of planning consists of the weighing of values associated with alternative ways of meeting specified goals—of specifying objectives and of weighing the costs and returns of alternative ways of meeting them. Basic principles fundamental to any planning activity in a democratic society are discussed. Mr. Fox identifies these tenets as being: (1) the individual should be the final judge of what is best for him; (2) the individual or his representative will make his decision on the basis of the best information about available alternatives and their consequences which it is practical to obtain; and (3) minority as well as majority preferences should be served. He points out that under a clearly competitive situation these three principles are largely met. But because we seldom, if ever, have a fully competitive situation, government must intervene to complement the private sector. Some of the reasons offered to explain why government has intervened in the field of outdoor recreation are: (1) to redistribute income by making recreational services available to people at no or less than actual cost; (2) to preserve the unique character of certain areas which cannot be allocated competitively because of their scarcity; and (3) to prevent external diseconomies and to capture external economies. Mr. Fox argues that it is essential to distinguish between two different kinds of intervention; intervention to influence private behavior and intervention in which the government acts as an entrepreneur and provides certain types of outdoor recreation services. He further argues that the general objectives of public outdoor recreation planning are related to these two kinds of intervention. These objectives are to help establish a set of guides and influences under which the public and private sectors will act to optimize net social welfare and to design public programs in such a way that they will tend to optimize net welfare. Thus, Mr. Fox distinguishes between policy planning and program planning. In concluding his paper, Mr. Fox relates these above criteria to inherent problems in public outdoor recreation planning. In doing this he emphasizes several additional points, among which are: in a democratic society the public planner is not the one who renders the final judgement because the individual should be the final judge of what is best for him; the public or some representative of the public must have the opportunity to express value judgements on alternative planning proposals; and there is a need to plan on a comprehensive basis to examine the overall demand-supply picture to serve a variety of preferences.

Wise   (The State-Of-The-Art of Comprehensive Planning):

In this paper Mr. Wise describes the general characteristics of comprehensive planning today and traces the history of its changes over the past fifty years. He argues that we are in the middle of a planning epic which is characterized by change and expansion in planning requirements. Five significant changes in planning since 1917 were considered. These are: the change in scale or size of political jurisdictions; changes in techniques and details, including statistical models, electronic data processing facilities and cost-effectiveness testing; expansion of the scope of concern of planning, such as the current emphasis on social systems planning; changes in the means of and concerns with the implementation of plans, including increased federal support through grants-in-aids; better modes of post-auditing or appraising the effectiveness of plans; and changes in attitudes and in the institutional machinery, especially the identification of the elected public official as the person who is responsible for planning decisions and actions. Mr. Wise states that to understand what has and is happening in comprehensive planning, it is necessary to appreciate the broad concern and involvement of the U.S. Congress, especially its many grants-in-aid programs to states and localities. Examples of the programs discussed in the paper are: the Section 701 program of the 1954 Housing Act, as amended; The Highway Act of 1962; water and sewer assistance grants; the Land and Water Conservation Fund Act; the Hill-Burton Act; the Demonstration Cities and Metropolitan Development Act; and the Comprehensive Health Planning Act. It is pointed out that local comprehensive planning is a necessary requirement for qualifying for federal funds under these programs. In concluding his paper, Mr. Wise argues that these increasing needs for comprehensive planning apply to outdoor recreation planning too. He states "...if you plan for outdoor recreation outside of and isolated from the planning activities of other related and concerned functional programs, you do so at your own peril."

Steps of The Planning Process

Marquis   (Steps in the Planning Process):

Mr. Marquis presents a detailed description of the steps of the planning process. He begins his paper by explaining the basic behavioral (tote) unit proposed by Miller, Galanter and Pribram in their *Plans and the Structure of Behavior*. These three psychologists have suggested that an individual's relatively stable (and his adaptive) behavior can meaningfully be analyzed by viewing humans as having built-in images and programs which serve as basic plans for resolving familiar and routine problems, and as being able to execute systematic search patterns and tests to develop new plans of behavior for resolving (adapting to) new problem situations. Starting with the basic tote unit (of test, operate, test and exit), Mr. Marquis systematically develops a model which becomes increasingly complex and inclusive of the activities commonly and not so commonly included in the planning process. After expanding the basic tote unit to a linear sequence of tote units (which he designates the major or primary substantive sequence of the planning process), he develops his model by adding additional (secondary) sequences of units to each step of the preliminary sequence. In turn, these secondary sequences of tote units gain greater specificity about sub-activities involved in the planning process through the addition of tertiary sequences. Through such a model and the accompanying graphics, a better understanding of the planning process is achieved, including the dynamics of image formation, searching, feed-back processing, testing, predicting, and implementing. The proposed model of the planning process is discussed within the context of specific problems encountered in a planning situation. Included are considerations of value handling, goal formulation, image changing, problem definition and redefinition, test criteria selection and application, operationalization of goals, conflict resolution, searching for and evaluation of alternatives, and problems of coordination and cooperation.

Young   (Establishment of Goals and Definitions of Objectives):

Mr. Young concentrates his attention on some of the most, if not the most important activities of the planning process. He begins his paper by emphasizing that planners — for outdoor recreation and other services — must increasingly pay more attention to the "whys" rather than continue to focus on the "hows" of planning. To establish a structure within which goals and objectives can be considered, he lists four universal steps of planning as: (1) establishment of a goal, which states the purpose of the plan; (2) establishment of objectives, which state the targets for the plan; (3) investigation into the dynamics of the subject matter and study of potential controls; and (4) formulation of strategies designed to reach the objectives in a manner consistent with the goals. He defines a goal as that which by stating a value to be pursued gives the purpose of the planning action. A standard is defined as a quantitative unit measurement related to the goal and an objective is defined as a specific target to be reached. These definitions are illustrated by examples and differentiated with respect to their unique characteristics. This differentiation is accomplished by Mr. Young's use of steps or criteria, such as his discussion of four steps of the goal-setting process. He explains how goals are converted into objectives and again establishes and discusses criteria for doing so. Included in this discussion is a consideration of how and why standards are adopted and employed. Specific examples from recreation planning are given.

Policy Making and Plan Implementation

Pressman   (Decision Making and Public Policy:
                 The Perils and Possibilities of Fragmentation):

In this paper Mr. Pressman explains the basic concepts and the relative advantages and disadvantages of the "classical" models of public decision making, including policy formulation. He develops a useful structure within which planners can better understand the dynamic nature of policy making and public administration, especially the limitations and possibilities of our fragmented or decentralized system of decision making. He begins by explaining the rational decision model — that unlikely decision situation in which complete or total information is possessed about all alternatives, their consequences and all values affected. After a necessarily abbreviated, but rather thorough description of this model he points out some of the "chinks in the rationalist armor." This logically leads him to a discussion of the other better known models which have been developed either as replacements for or supplements to the rational model. The first such model to be considered is Lindblom's "disjointed-incremental" model which attempts to explain how decision makers do behave rather than how they should behave. The essential (incremental or marginal, fragmentary, sequential, familiar or status quo and remedial) characteristics of this model, its attractiveness and deficiencies are

190

considered in some detail, including examples of its application. Next, the fundamental features of Simon's "satisficing" model are described, including consideration of: Simon's modification of rationality to provide criteria based on results of rational *action* rather than on characteristics of a rational *thought* process; how decision makers tend not to optimize (as in the rational model) but instead to decide on courses of action that are satisfactory (to satisfice); and within what institutional or organizational context do decision makers operate. As for the disjointed incremental model, the relative advantages and shortcomings and selected practical examples of Simon's model are considered. The last model to be considered is Gore's more complex, less explicit and more dynamic heuristic model, which views the decision process as being as much concerned with an organization's survival in an environmental context as it is with the accomplishment of specific and implied, internally generated, organizational objectives (a general characteristic of the other three models). Gore's complex model of adaptive decision behavior is compared to the other three models, and examples of its application are given. Following his explanation of the models, Mr. Pressman considers the limits and opportunities of leadership in each one. This discussion enables a better appreciation of the models and, through its examples, provides meaningful insights into the dynamics of public policy formulation. Except for the rational model, all of the models discussed imply or require decentralized patterns of decision making. This raises a question to which Mr. Pressman addresses himself. It is: If decision centers are dispersed, how are decisions reached at various places brought together to form broader policies; how are decisions coordinated? This question is answered by Pressman's description of the concept of the partisan mutual adjustment process, which explains why and how partisan decision makers coordinate and adjust their decisions. Next, Mr. Pressman considers a frequently raised objection to fragmented and incremental decision models: How is innovation and change accomplished? Three methods of meeting this objective are considered and illustrated by examples. Mr. Pressman concludes his paper with a discussion of the extent to which the decentralized models provide for equitable and representative public policy and a discussion of the possibilities of fragmented decision making in a republican form of government that is being called upon at all levels to provide an increasing array of public goods and services.

Rettie   (Plans Don't Work; People Do):

In this paper, Mr. Rettie comprehensively describes the importance and roles of communication and coordination in planning and in plan implementation. He begins the paper by considering the relationships between planning and decision making. Although he argues that plans are not decisions, he just as strongly states that the art of planning must contain a large measure of involvement by the planner in the political decision making process. He emphasizes that the effective planner must understand where he is located in an organizational structure, especially in respect to his relationship with the decision maker. He establishes and discusses three organizational criteria that planning must meet. These are: it should be in direct linkage with the decision maker; it should identify and relate to programs and to the end products of the organization; and it should be responsive and responsible to the decision maker. Each emphasizes the need for coordination and points out the importance of good communication. Indirectly, the criteria emphasize a point made by Mr. Rettie that planners need to establish and maintain close communication with program administrators and program staffs. The need for flexible plans and planners is considered. Also considered is the importance of evaluating plan performance or effectiveness, which again points up the need for good communications, especially feed-back. Mr. Rettie elaborates on the nature of coordination by explaining why comprehensive outdoor recreation planning must be done within the context of the total system of planning and development at all levels of government and for all related activities. He concludes his paper by considering some of the new dimensions in outdoor recreation planning, especially those related to coordination of planning activities.

Koenings   (Some Broad Implications of Outdoor Recreation Planning):

In his brief paper (which was presented as a luncheon address) Mr. Koenings cogently iterates and emphasizes several points about planning in general. He begins by stating that it is next to impossible to identify a plan per se because changing conditions make planning a constant and dynamic effort. He then emphasizes the point that the action phase of a plan—the program for implementation—is as important as any other phase of the plan. Lastly, he iterates the statement found several times in Part II of these proceedings that the plan must be presented in such a way that is a usable document to the decision makers—to those employed or elected personnel served by the planners. To these three general statements about planning, Mr. Koenings adds five perspectives on outdoor recreation specifically. First, he states that outdoor recreation planners must continue to move away from the conventional interpretation of outdoor recreation and give greater attention to the total leisure time "problem." Second, he suggests that it might be instructive for recreation planners to view ORRRC's classification scheme as representing three categories of areas—national heritage, natural heritage and activity oriented areas. Third, he emphasizes that outdoor recreation and tourism are big business and that planners should keep in mind the many items that are not commonly included in the accounting of the economic impact of such. Fourth, he states that outdoor recreation planners must accept responsibility for informing decision makers of relevant social and economic factors. He concludes his paper with the fifth perspective that outdoor recreation planners must give due consideration to the quality of the total environment as well as to specific recreational areas.

Cain   (Concluding Remarks):

Although Mr. Cain states that the planner is an adviser without authority, his paper strongly develops the theme that the planner is not an adviser without influence. After making a broad and insightful commentary on physical and social environmental problems facing—and frequently created by—contemporary man, Mr. Cain poses a bold challenge to outdoor recreation planners. He states that planners, along with other decision makers, must be discriminating thinkers who lead and challenge the herd psychology. He does this by systematically developing the idea that "it is somewhere in the interface of three sectors—the political, the administrative, and the technical—that society has lost control of its destiny. The argument is not that the danger to modern man arises from his growing capacity to *induce* change. Rather, Mr. Cain feels the danger lies in man's poor ability to *control* sensibly his new powers. The suggestion is made that planning for humanistic as well as technological goals must not reflect single-mindedness. Instead, the planner must be aware of and sensitive to the many values affected by his actions. Although he must be aware of the group dynamics — especially compromise — involved in defining, clarifying and realizing the public interest, he must also be a discriminating critic.

SOME THOUGHTS ON PLANNING, THE PLANNING PROCESS AND RELATED DECISION PROCESSES

by
B. L. Driver
Assistant Professor, Outdoor Recreation Studies,
Department of Forestry, School of Natural Resources,
The University of Michigan

What is meant by the word planning? Each reader probably has a different and meaningful definition. Equally probable is the existence of wide variation among these definitions. These many interpretations cause confusion about the appropriate roles of planners. Is the planner a decision maker, a policy maker, a program analyst, an adviser, the one who implements and administers, each of these, or what?

This paper considers these questions. A definition of planning will be offered, the planning process will be distinguished from other selected decision processes of which it is a part, and different roles of planners and types of plans will be considered. We shall begin by defining planning.

Planning Defined

To help establish a definition of planning, let us look at how it is commonly defined in the literature:

1. Planning is orderly development (Beyer, 1967).

2. City planning may be regarded as a means for systematically anticipating and achieving adjustment in the physical environment of a city consistent with social and economic trends and sound principles of civic design (Chapin, 1965).

3. The planning process represents the self-conscious attempt by man to order his environment so as to realize common goals and values (Weaver, 1963).

4. The job of the planner is to propose courses of action not to execute them (Altshuler, 1966).

5. Planning is that process of making rational decisions about future goals and future courses of action which relies upon explicit tracings of the repercussions and of the value implications associated with alternative courses of actions, and, in turn, requires explicit evaluation and choice among the alternative matching goal-action sets (Webber, 1963).

6. Planning is a way of defining purposes and of choosing means of obtaining them (Banfield, 1942).

7. Planning is the conscious and deliberate guidance of thinking so as to create logical means for achieving agreed-upon goals (Trecker, 1950).

What, if anything, do these definitions tell us? Most common to the definitions are the notion of doing things right and the idea that planning is equivalent to decision making. No comment is necessary about the conceptual usefulness of the "doing things right" definition. But the idea that planning is equivalent to decision making deserves consideration. To begin, let it be stated emphatically that planning does involve decision making: planners are decision makers and have crucial roles in the decision making process. But just as emphatically, it should be insisted that to equate planning with decision making is a distortion of the primary activity of planning and is practically meaningless for definitional purposes.

The author is of the opinion that it is more useful to define planning in terms of its relationships to decision making, not equivalence to it. Accordingly, planning will be defined as an *activity* concerned with the systematic collection, analysis, organization and processing of technical information to facilitate decision making.

The definition states that the primary role of the planner is to provide technical information. This is somewhat of an overstatement but, in the author's opinion, not a great one. Planners in all areas (whether research, recreation, transportation, economics, social psychology, communications, water resources development, or timber management) do — or should — have special professional and technical competences. When these professional people have responsibilities for planning their primary role is to apply their technical and analytical skills. Certainly they will need integrative and behavioral competences to define relevant questions and to relate to the "human elements" of planning. But these latter competences are no more unique to the planner than they are to other decision makers.

The definition should also be useful in clarifying the purpose of planning. Trecker (1950) has stated:

> The motive of planning is frequently obscured by our feelings about it. It is strange but true that many people have a fear of planning because they envision someone else making the plan for them to obey or execute. The fear is not of planning per se but rather a fear of *how* the planning is done. In the last analysis it is fear of control rather than of planning.

Trecker also states that "we cannot live our lives a single day without planning, for planning is an established fact." The point is that planning, per se, is not a mode of controlling; it is a mode of preparing for decisions. Certainly, information gathered through planning can lead to the imposition of controls, but these are usually consequences, not purposes, of planning. Such controls are generally instituted to protect and insure freedom rather than to reduce or constrain it. It becomes a question of whose freedom and individuality.

Please notice that planning was defined as an activity and not as a process. In much of the literature planning is discussed in terms of its being a process. This causes much confusion. There is a planning process, but many activities other than planning (as defined above) take place in it, and many people other than planners perform crucial steps in the process. Examples would be the *selection* of a course of action, once comparative evaluations have been made of several alternatives, and *implementation* of the plan. These activities are not planning, but they are a part of the planning process. To develop this point, let us briefly consider the planning and related processes. We will then return to the role of planning in decision making.

Planning and Related Decision Processes

The purpose of this section will be to describe some of the distinguishing characteristics which can help in relating the planning process to the other decision processes *of which it is a part.* Through this conceptualization, a better appreciation can be gained of who the *key* actors are in each process and of their *primary* responsibilities (roles) as key actors. Or, put differently, by describing the processes within which the various actors take on their primary responsibilities, we can better understand these responsibilities.

The processes are considered according to their decreasing complexity of organization. They are *the democratic process, the decision process, the administrative process, and the planning process.* The processes are not mutually exclusive. Also, any *one individual* might perform primary roles in *each* process. But it is important to recognize that when they are performing in these different capacities, the actors (whether decision makers, administrators, planners or electorate) will be wearing different hats (perhaps masks would be more appropriate) and have different demands placed upon them. It is even more important to have criteria by which these differences in primary role responsibilities can be identified. These criteria can help establish a vocabulary so badly needed in planning education and practice.

To describe the processes three elements of each will be given. First, the process will be defined in terms of functions performed. Second, the key actor(s) within the process will be described based upon who performs the primary function(s). Third, the primary responsibilities of the key actors will be drawn from the definition. Also, the notion of key activities within the process will be developed. The processes will now be described.

Democratic Process

Definition:
The democratic process is the process by which representation of interests and values are built into the political process of a democracy. According to Appleby (1947), the democratic process (which he calls the political process) consists of the following activities:

1. Presidential nominating.

2. General nominating.

3. Voting.

4. Party maintenance and operation, excluding nominating.

5. Educating (through such activities as petitioning, public comment, lobbying and interest group participation).

6. Legislating.

7. Adjudicating.

8. Administering.

Key Actors:

Activities 1 through 5 are carried out by citizens or interest groups (clientele). Activity 6 is done by officials elected to represent interest groups and citizens. Activity 7 is performed by elected or appointed officials. Activity 8 is done by appointed personnel.

Primary Roles:

In activities 1 through 5, the key actors (i.e., the citizens served) have primary roles of defining and expressing their felt needs, selecting and electing officials to represent their interests, keeping these official representatives informed of the "value states" of the interests represented, providing these representatives with information on means and consequences of alternative "allocations of value mixes,"[1] and providing a test by the ballot of the effectiveness of the official representatives in serving their interests. Key actors in activity 6 have the primary roles of being, and keeping open, input channels for the processing of information on the value mixes of the key actors in activities 1-5, establishing rules to govern conduct of themselves and all other key actors, creating institutional machinery for key actors in activity 8 (discussed below, under the Administrative Process) to operate, approving allocations of public resources, and passing judgement on the degree to which key actors in activity 8 perform their primary roles.

Decision Process

Definition:

The decision process consists of the making of a decision; it is the choosing among alternative means of accomplishing an objective. For the structure being developed, it is conceptually useful to divide the decision making process into two kinds defined by types of decision makers. The usefulness relates to the notions of primary role responsibilities, to those of accountability, and to the assurance of an internal system of checks and balances. These two types of decision makers are:

1. Focal-Point Decision Makers:

Definition: These are decision makers who have legal authority to represent an interest group or clientele. Examples would be a member of a legislative body or an elected executive.

Key Actors: Elected officials and their top-level appointees.

Primary Roles: Compromise conflicting interests (values) through formation of coalitions which are broadly representative of the public interest and regulate activities of administrators, planners and other contributory decision makers.

2. *Contributory Decision Makers:*

Definition: Those decision makers who serve or advise focal-point decision makers are contributory decision makers.

Key Actors: People appointed or hired by focal-point decision makers perform this function. They are not elected and do not have legal authority although they frequently have responsibilities delegated to them from focal-point decision makers.

Primary role: Advise and assist focal-point decision makers.

Administrative Process

Definition:
The administrative process is the one in which agencies (administrative, managerial, comptrolling, planning, etc.) created by focal-point decision makers carry out the functions (policy or program analysis, selection, and implementation; coordination; budgeting; auditing; planning; etc...) assigned or entrusted to them by the focal-point decision makers.[2]

Key Actors:
Personnel appointed or hired by focal-point decision makers to perform these functions carry out this process.

Primary Roles:
Policy and program analysis, selection and implementation and any other function assigned them by focal point decision makers are their primary roles.

In the literature on public administration, many authors prefer to separate administration from policy making. They define administration as the execution of policy. Policy making is defined as formulation of goals and selection of programs to be executed to accomplish these goals. These authors argue that administrators, within our systems of checks and balances, should not be concerned with the formulation of goals, which is a more appropriate function (responsibility) of focal-point decision makers. For the purposes of this paper, administration will be viewed as defined above and will include both the roles of assisting in the formulation and in the execution of policy. As proposed, it will be done within the context of focal-point decision makers assigning the administrators their responsibilities in both of these areas.

Planning Process

Definition:
The planning process has as its objective the accomplishment of premeditated goals and is primarily concerned with providing technical information for decisiom making and for plan implementation and control. Obviously, the planning process is a subpart of the decision making process

since the information is being provided to decision makers. Also, it is a subpart of the administrative process, because plan implementation and control are important parts (steps) of the process.

Key Actors:

The key actors are the people hired or appointed by focal-point decision makers or administrative personnel to perform the tasks of the process.

Primary Roles:

The primary roles will vary according to the task to be performed at each step of the process.

Those who have written on the planning process generally agree that it is a sequential and iterative (recursive or looping-back) process. Also, they usually agree that the sequence of steps goes something as follows: expression of need, establishment of goals and objectives, evaluations of alternative courses of action, adoption of a program, and program implementation and control. I prefer an extended version as follows: anticipation, expression and/or recognition and relative appraisal of need; definition and establishment of goals; creation of a planning agency (if necessary); delineation of the planning unit; identification of planning assumptions; statement of objectives; definition of evaluative criteria and standards; preliminary identification of alternative courses of actions; re-evaluation of objectives; selection of alternative courses of actions to be evaluated; gathering of information on alternatives; evaluation of alternatives; ranking of alternatives; making recommendations to decision makers; support during the decision process; policy articulation (or redefinition) and program (plan) selection; plan implementation and control; and plan evaluation and revision.

The primary roles are indicated by the titles of the steps. Further, the steps of the process show that key actors in each of the decision processes have important roles in the planning process. For example, the electorate (the clientele for which the plan is being made) has the responsibility of expressing its needs. The focal-point decision makers will create the planning agency and establish the goals. The administrators (managers, etc.) will implement the plan. And the planners, using their technical competence, will have primary responsibilities in defining objectives, applying standards, gathering information and selecting and evaluating alternatives. Again, it is pointed out that all this might be done by the same individual, but this is not usually the case.

The general purpose for this conceptualization has been discussed. Let us now expand that discussion and consider five specific reasons for such a structure or vocabulary.

First, when one speaks of a clientele or interest group, a decision maker, an administrator or a planner, the definitions provide some measure of their major activities and primary roles. It points out the need for each key actor to appraise what his responsibilities are. Primary responsibility becomes more explicit, and we have a more common basis for understanding.

Second, and closely related, under the definition of the planner as being a collector, organizer and processor of technical information, this primary role of the planner receives *the importance it should:* by concentrating on the provision of information this responsibility of the planner, including his technical and analytical competences in providing quality information and the effects of information in the decision processes, receives the recognition of importance it should. The author's major criticism of planners is that they too frequently view themselves as occupying chairs which they have not been hired to sit in. Through such discrepant role identifications they lose sight of the *crucial and vital nature* of their actual role or primary responsibility. They frequently fail to realize that the nature and quality of the information provided and the manner in which it is provided plays a significant part in determining what decisions will be made and how they will be implemented.

Third, the structure enables us to emphasize clearly that planners (and administrators) are decision makers. They are "direct" decision makers when they decide what information to process, what alternatives to evaluate and so on. They are "indirect" decision makers through their influence (via the information they provide) on other decision makers.

Fourth, the definition of planning provides a useful measure for the planner to use in gauging the success of his efforts. Instead of becoming discouraged and even unmotivated because his plans are not implemented, he can "get his rewards" from observing the effects he has had on decision making. Frequently, these rewards come to the planner with a time lag, but they are rewards — something appraisals of numbers of plans implemented frequently are not.

The fifth reason is that it makes explicit the need to coordinate activities. It should be apparent that planners as information processors must keep the communications channels open and operative.[3]

Planning and Rational Choice

It has been argued that the above conceptualization, especially the definition of planning, focuses appropriate attention on the importance of providing high quality (sufficient, relevant, reliable, accurate, etc.) information to decision makers. It was also argued that the primary role of planners is to provide this information. Information is important because it enhances the rationality of decision making. Thus, planning can be redefined as an activity concerned with enhancing the rationality of choice.

Outdoor recreation and other types of planners, at least normatively, should not object to this description of their function. It can be objected that the implied assumption that decision makers are rational is open to debate. To avoid this objection, let us make another assumption and state that decision makers are rational with a time lag. That is, they make reasoned responses to additional information after given sufficient time to adjust to the new information. Such an adjustment period might be necessary to protect the integrity of the decision makers, such as their saving face. So the normative proposition that decision makers ought to behave rationally should be an acceptable one.

Before we bog down in a discussion of rationality, let us define rationality as action reasonably directed (supported by logic or empirical evidence) toward the achievement of preferred behavioral alternatives in terms of some system of values whereby the consequences of the behavior can be evaluated (Simon, 1959).[4] This definition avoids the shortcomings of the completely rational (or economic) man, who knows all values, has information on all alternatives and their consequences and operates under no constraints. Also, the definition makes clear the potential roles of information in enhancing the rationality of choice — in making the decisions more effective. It does so by emphasizing the need for information on values, behavioral alternatives and consequences.

A better understanding of the effects of information on decision making can perhaps be gained through examining the expected behavior of decision makers who possess different amounts of information. Amounts of information are generally defined in terms of certainty, risk and uncertainty. Complete certainty exists when the decision maker knows all alternatives, the consequences of these alternatives and all social values associated with the alternatives and their consequences. Risk exists when at least some of the alternatives are known and not all the consequences are known, but the decision maker does have probability distributions of expected consequences based on past experience. Decision under uncertainty exists when at least some of the alternatives are known, but no information is possessed about the consequences, including no information on probabilities of expected occurrences.

The expected behavior of the decision maker under conditions of complete information — or certainty — is that he will act (decide) so as to maximize net benefits. This behavior is expected because all benefits and all costs are known, and a decision will be made to optimize societal returns (maximize *net* benefits). This is equivalent to the behavior of the unlikely economic or rational man. Under conditions of risk, less information is possessed than under conditions of complete certainty. The expected behavior of the decision maker is to maximize *expected net* utility with expectations determined by probability functions of occurrences, payoffs and costs. Under conditions of uncertainty, the expected behavior of the decision maker is to minimize the costs of reaching the goal for which decisions are being made.

As mentioned certainty, risk and uncertainty depict decision situations possessing different amounts of information. Since conditions of complete certainty seldom, if ever exist, the role of the planner as provider of information is to help move the decision situation toward this position. By doing this he enhances the rationality of choice; he increases the probabilities that the consequent actions of the decision will be more effective, efficient and/or appropriate. This is a more limited role than normally perceived by many planners, but it is certainly a vitally important one.

Associated with the primary role of the planner as information provider are several other important roles. We will call them secondary roles because they all complement or are necessary for successful execution of the primary role. These secondary roles should be interpreted as normative statements of responsibilities the planner must assume to be an effective operant within the planning process.

There is very little literature addressed directly to the topic of roles of planners. Daland and Parker (1962) list four roles of the planner. They are institutional, educational, professional and political innovation. Meyerson (1956) states that the functions (from which roles can be interpreted) of planners are central intelligence, pulse-taking, policy clarification, detailed development planning and feedback renewal. Davidoff (1965) has proposed that an important role of the planner is that of being an advocate for his client, similar to an advocate in a legal process. The roles discussed below resulted from a modification and expansion of the works of these authors. These secondary roles are labelled professional or technical, strategic, innovative, community and clientele liaison, educational, and political.

Professional or Technical Role

The importance of this role is stated in the definition of a planner as a provider of technical information, so limited elaboration is necessary.

In addition to being competent in gathering, analyzing, reporting and otherwise processing technical data, the planner also has the responsibility of helping maintain, protect and advance the integrity and capabilities of his profession. He does this in a variety of ways, notably through his personal code of ethics, staying informed in his field and supporting his profession in other ways, such as contributing to its journals and participating in its activities.

It should go without saying that the planner should provide that information which is technically and/or analytically the most *appropriate* and not the information which is the most *acceptable* to the decision maker. Certainly, conflict is to be avoided when possible, but the fact remains that planners function to advise, not placate, those they serve.

Strategic Role

Some confusion might be caused by the word strategic. The definition used is the one given by Luce and Raiffa (1957) as "the development of alternative sets of instructions to pursue a desired course of action to net an expected payoff." All that is being said is that the planner should be competently able to compromise his recommendations (and positions) *in an informed manner* without losing sight of the planning objectives.

One should not expect a competent planner to be a passive agent. He has blood, guts, pride and an ego and needs positive reinforcement like anyone else. So it is a mistake to assume that a technical advisor can be detached, unless he is unmotivated and completely indifferent. Although it is important for those who work with the planner to realize this, it is probably more important that the planner be aware of and take pride in this fact. He should accept the fact that value-free human endeavors are non-existent and that his information will be used to promote and defend that alternative or recommendation with which he, as a competent planner, most closely allies himself—the one that is most appropriate from his professional point of view. Although the system should remain open, this alignment will most probably take place early in the planning process. Once the planner knows the position he is supporting, he should develop the appropriate strategy (the "alternative sets of instructions" he might need to make recourse to) to assure, within the realms of his capacities as an advisor, that the objective will be met in the manner he deems most appropriate. The alternative instructions need not imply a new course of action. They may merely mean modifications in the one proposed.

This role of the planner need not and should not imply rigidities, wheeling and dealing and other undesirable behavior. Counterwise, it changes nothing with respect to the provision of technical information and the role of the planner as a facilitator of decision making. It only takes cognizance of the fact that planners have a personal reward system operating for them too, and that they are frequently the most qualified to help resolve conflict after the plan is submitted for approval. To be sure, the planner will not always be aware of the intricacies of what is happening "upstairs," and he should be able to adapt to new information. But the point remains that since he must support his recommendations in the decision process, he must be prepared to competently propose his alternative set(s) of recommendations.

Innovative Role

Daland and Parker have stated that the innovative role consists of the responsibility of the planner for injecting *new* ideas into the political decision process.

The importance of this role cannot be overemphasized. The planner is frequently in the best position to have special knowledge about certain aspects of a problem under study. This knowledge might not be available to or not recognized by the other operants within the process. Unless it is then introduced into the process by the planner, it will not be considered. Once a decision has been made, it is generally difficult to reconsider or open up the debate to include new considerations. The planner should not shy away from these responsibilities nor should he be discouraged from at least thinking about new methods and approaches.

This role of the planner could be expanded into a very lengthy discourse. However, since the objective of this paper is to provide a conceptual framework against which planning activities can be evaluated and to provide guidelines for planning action, the relative importance of the community liaison role of the planner will be discussed in a more normative manner. Anyone who has participated in a planning activity is quite aware of the interaction of the many interest groups, conflicting opinions, diverse power structures, and different motivations of the many participants. Obviously, the planner needs to be competent in dealing with these factors. But it is extremely difficult to provide a normative structure outlining the degree to which a planner should participate in one activity or another or align himself with one power group or another. Suffice it to say here—and the intention is not to deprecate the importance of the role—that the planner must be aware of the needs and preferences of those for whom the plan is being made, of the community power structures and other relevant value structures of his clientele. He must retain the confidence of his clientele and know where he can bargain within the realm of his role as advisor. Thus, he needs to be a capable applied behavioral scientist. Although the information being processed in these interactions will not always be technical, it is difficult to refute the contention that there is important information to be gathered and processed by the planner during the exercise of this secondary role. The role does relate to the primary role of provision of technical information because the planner's technical skills will be used to provide for the special needs of the clientele served.

Many writers in the field of planning argue that one of the most important roles of the planner is that of advocate of his client's needs. He should serve as the client's representative and defender. Although, the author is in sympathy with the view that everyone — black, ebony, white, yellow, red, pink, old, young, poor, rich, male or female — should be appropriately represented in the decision processes, it is his feeling that this is not a primary or secondary role of the *planner*. Rather, it is the role of a representative advocate to consider the values and interests of his clientele. Over-involvement in conflict, and even its generation, just do not fit into the general structure being developed for planning in a republican form of government. Put differently, advocatory planning is fine, but it is not planning as defined in this paper. In the next section of this paper, several different orientations or end-states of planning will be discussed briefly. Under several of these orientations, such as caretaking or revolutionary planning, the *secondary* role of the planner as advocate is more prominent.

Educational Role

Problems of defining boundaries for the extent of appropriate action exist for this role too. However, the educational role of planners is an important one, either directly or indirectly. Planners may do the educating themselves or the information they provide may be used for that purpose.

Who is to be educated? The answer is the clientele, the planner himself, members of the decision and administrative processes and segments of the public at large.

A frequent criticism leveled against planning is that there are closets full of plans which have not been implemented. But unimplemented plans do not mean that the planning process is a waste of time. Certainly, those who have participated have learned from the experience. Probably the *greatest* benefits obtained from planning are the *educational* ones even if we exclude the education of those for whom the information is being provided. Admittedly, it might not be the most efficient method of obtaining this benefit. But given the fact that planning was undertaken for other reasons, this benefit should not be overlooked.

As discussed in the following section, plans can have education as their goal or purpose. Certain fire prevention and natural history interpretation plans are examples. But generally the educational function is an important though subsidiary one. For example, many wildlife management plans, especially those making recommendations on the harvesting of surplus doe animals, were not effective because of an uneducated clientele. Similarly, many potential recreation resource users are constrained from enjoying the opportunities provided because they lack information.

There are two essential dimensions of the responsibility of the planner as educator. First, there is the need to provide appropriate information to educate while the planning process is going on, such as informing the citizens of their rights to express themselves in public hearings. Second, there is the planner's responsibility to provide instructions and information in the plan itself on how an educational process should be implemented once the plan is approved. Examples are informing the potential user of an available opportunity or educating the user to help protect and preserve the values inherent in a resource which gives it its recreational potential.

Political Role

It is difficult to make generalizations about this role of the planner. The position of the author is that the political role of the planner is primarily manifested through the competence with which he influences focal-point decision making within the bounds of his primary responsibility as provider of technical information. His alignment with an alternative to which he has committed himself and his development of alternative sets of instructions (his strategy) cannot be done strictly within the context of the primary role discussed. However, as discussed above, these should pose little difficulty.

The conceptual structure has been developed in such a manner that focal-point decision makers are accountable to their electorate for the decisions made. It seems logical to assume that they are in a position to exercise the principal political role. By political role is meant the compromising of conflicting interests through the formation of coalitions to arrive at an orderly, reasonable, and acceptable solution to a problem which involves opposing values. Given this position and the conceptual construct being developed, the planner should play a limited political role as defined. His responsibilities are not primarily those of forming coalitions to achieve compromises for the purposes of allocating scarce values. Further, within this conceptual construct, the planner enters the activity of value articulation and defense only through his role as an anticipator of needs of an interest group, which was mentioned as the first step of the planning process and discussed in the community liaison role. It is difficult to build a system of checks and balances into the structure if the planner assumes a political role of greater intensity than that indicated here. Also, the planner who assumes a strong political role is likely to get caught up in the process and lose site of his primary role; the quality of his information can suffer because of these other allocations of time and energy. Lastly, he may not be as detached as he should be to make competent technical recommendations.

In concluding this discussion of the secondary roles of the planner, it should be apparent that all of these roles are subsumed under his primary role as gatherer, processor, and provider of technical information. His strategies are based on this information, his educational activities use this information, his innovations relate to this information, his relationships to his clientele are with regard to this information and his political influences stem from the quality of this information and its direct and indirect effects on the "politician." Further, it can be more clearly emphasized that the planner needs behavioral and integrative skills as well as analytical and professional competence. But again the professional and technical skills are superordinate in importance.

Types of Plans

The types of information provided by planners and how it is processed is determined by the purpose and type of plan being prepared. For this reason, this paper will be concluded with a brief discussion of some different types of plans.

Plans can be classified in many ways. They might be policy (position) plans or program (development) plans, with policy plans being largely concerned with goals and addressed to questions of what and why and program plans focusing on means and questions of how, when and at what cost. Or they may be typed as to scale as could be illustrated by unit (such as a camping unit), site (such as a picnic site including several picnic units), area (such as a recreation area including many sites), regional (such as several areas), and national (including many regional) plans. Such a system of differentiation would be based on some combination of variables describing spatial, institutional, and possibly functional dimensions of the plans.

Another system of classification could be based on the type of resource being considered. Thus, we would have wildlife, recreation, water resource, timber, and so on plans. Alternatively, the taxonomy can be based on functions (services provided), such as recreation, communication, transportation, health, etc. Or several functions can be given detailed attention within one planning framework which has as its purpose the recommendation of *specific courses of action* along functionally integrated lines as would be the case in general or master plans. These plans may be less intensive with respect to specific analyses but more extensive with respect to total coverage and thus become comprehensive plans. Further, they might be short, intermediate or long-range plans.

All of the above are common taxonomies of plans. Let us briefly consider a different system of classification which might be useful for planners to keep in mind when evaluating their responsibilities or when setting plan objectives. The classification will be based on the orientation of the plan and/or its end-purpose. Some non-mutually exclusive orientations or purposes of plans are utopian, remedial, stop-gap, conflict aversion, preventative, catering, caretaking (including clinical and therapeutic), educational, innovative, strategic, advocatory, coercive and revolutionary. Any one plan might have several of these orientations. For example, a plan can be preventative, caretaking, innovative, educational and advocatory in orientation.

Given their titles the orientations or purposes of the plans are more or less self-explanatory. Some brief and general comments will be made. Utopian planners are few and far between. Nevertheless, many accusations are made that planners are Utopians and are attempting to plan for (and control!) human welfare within an all-knowing context. Obviously, these comments are exaggerations and distortions. A relevant point, however, is that there is a difference between Utopians and Utopian thinkers. The latter are people, generally philosophers, who are concerned about improving the state of society. They become Utopian thinkers to the extent that they recommend desirable *steps* to be taken in an *approach* to a more desired state.

Remedial plans are corrective in nature, and the purpose to be served is the correction of an existing situation for which action is needed. Frequently, these types of plans are made under crises situations. Stop-gap plans can be remedial plans but are generally for a shorter duration and are to be followed by more adequate plans to resolve the problem. Preventative planning is self-explanatory.

Catering perhaps should not be referred to as an orientation or purpose of a plan because the word implies that the decision has already been made. Therefore, the planner actually becomes a caterer instead of someone processing information to facilitate decision making. Quite frequently consultants are viewed as caterers and are hired to provide information to justify a previously-made decision. Other uses of consultants as planners, within the context defined before, are more frequent.

Under the notion of caretaking planning, several concepts can be developed to provide more information about the roles and responsibilities of the planner under certain extended conditions. In caretaking planning the planner is viewed as a custodian of societal values. Within this role of stewardship the planner is expected to *take* responsibility not only for identifying the needs of his clientele but also for recommending and even initiating and supervising appropriate actions for its welfare. It is conceptually useful to divide caretaking planning into two types: clinical and psychoanalytic. A rough analogy can be made between the clinical planner and the clinical psychologist and between the psychoanalytic planner and the psychoanalyst. Under clinical planning, the planner in consultation with his client makes a diagnosis, determines appropriate courses of action (remedies) for the clientele, *then lets the clientele decide if and what action will be taken.* In psychoanalytic planning, the planner as psychoanalyst makes a diagnosis, *decides* upon alternative courses of action, *selects one* and then *leads the client through the treatment.*

These are nice abstractions but can analogies to the real world be drawn? An example of clinical planning would be a situation in which the planner alerts the citizen of the potential hazards of air pollution, recommends alternative ways of preventing or abating pollution, and then leaves it up to the clientele to choose whether or not to implement the program. An example of psychoanalytic planning would be the situation in which the landscape architect, through the application of his skills, designs highways in such a manner that highly imageable components of the landscape are exposed to view. Or through design he manipulates the expectations of the user by an incremental exposure to selected components of the landscape. By the time the user (the client) reaches a point of destination, his expectations have been elevated and his response to the situation is different than would have been the case had the landscape architect not intervened and designed in a manner to raise expectations.

The educational type plan is self-explanatory. An example would be Smoky the Bear Fire Prevention Programs. Innovative planning consists of planning that has as its orientation the injection of new ideas into the decision process. Examples would be experimentations in building new towns such as Columbia, near Washington, D.C., especially the preliminary preparations of these endeavors. Strategic planning is best illustrated by the use of war game planning. Also, the development of the planner's alternative sets of instructions for his strategy would be a type of strategic planning. In this case the strategic plan will generally be a subpart of a plan done for another purpose. Advocatory planning is planning under which the planner becomes an advocate for his clientele. All planning within a democracy should be to some degree, advocatory.

Perhaps conflict-aversion is not really a type of planning because it is conducted with no intention on the part of the decision makers to accept or implement its recommendations. The planning is done to buy time. It is the type that occurs when an issue is "relegated to committee" because the debate is too hot. Perhaps coercive planning also should not be called planning if it is the decision makers who are being pressured. But in many instances, some coercion might be necessary to strengthen an argument or to obtain needed information. Certain aspects of labor union negotiations would be coercive planning. Revolutionary planning strictly defined does not have much application within a democracy, but it obviously has had its impact in the world at large.

The above scheme of classification might be useful for several reasons. One of the most difficult problems facing planners is that of clearly defining objectives. The taxonomy can be useful, at least in starting convergence. The relative emphasis for each orientation will determine the amount of attention the planner should give to that end purpose. Finally, the above taxonomy, and the others mentioned, help describe the amounts, types, and even sources of information the planner will need.

This paper began with what appeared to be a rather narrow definition of planning and of the primary role of the planner. Here at the end of the paper the definition and the primary role have remained unchanged. But the discussion has evolved to the point where the planner, as systematic gatherer, organizer, and processor of technical information to facilitate decision making, does not appear to be an insignificant member of the decision team. Is it an over-statement to say (perhaps normatively) that he is the most important member?

Footnotes

1) By "allocation of value mixes" is meant the relative importance that different values are given in public decisions as reflected in the allocation of public resources.

2) Pfiffner and Presthus (1960) offer a useful definition of public administration as "decision making and the direction of individuals to achieve ends that have been determined by political leaders." This would include management which the author distinguishes from administration (especially the policy making aspects of it) in terms of the degree to which specific professional or technical skills are required to accomplish organizational objectives, especially those related to productivity. Thus, as we move down through the decision hierarchy from citizen participation, to policy formation, to administration, to management, to planning the amount of professional or technical expertise required of the key actors increases.

3) Although examples have been drawn from the public sector in the above conceptualization, they just as easily could have been drawn from the private sector. The electorate in the political process would be replaced by the stock holder (or the union member). The elected official would be replaced by the President of the Board (or the president of the labor union). The administrative official would be the manager of the business, and the planner would be the technical advisor or specialist. The dynamics of the process, including the nature of the responsibilities would remain essentially the same.

4) The author is aware of the philosophical problems posed (1) by defining rationality as action rather than a mode of thinking and (2) by discussing enhancing the rationality of choice. Obviously, a decision made with little information can be as rational as one made with more information. But the intention is not to discuss the thought processes of the decision maker. Rather, it is to focus on the results of that process.

References

1. Altshuler, A.A., *The City Planning Process*. Ithaca, N.Y.: Cornell University Press (1966), p. 1.

2. Appleby, P., *Policy and Administration*. University, Alabama: University of Alabama Press (1947), pp. 32-36.

3. Banfield, E.C., "The Field of Planning." Undated. Mimeo, p. 1.

4. Beyer, G.H., *Housing and Society*. N.Y.: MacMillan Co. (1967), pp. 106-111.

5. Chapin, F.S., Jr., *Urban Land Use Planning*. Urbana, Illinois: University of Illinois Press (1965), p. vi.

6. Daland, R.T. and J.A. Parker, "Roles of the Planner in Urban Development." In F. S. Chapin, Jr. and S. E. Weiss (Eds.) *Urban Growth Dynamics in a Regional Cluster of Cities*. (1962), Chapter 7.

7. Davidoff, P., "Advocacy and Pluralism in Planning," *Journal of the American Institute of Planners*, XXXI (Nov. 1965), pp. 331-338.

8. Luce, R.D. and H. Raiffa, *Games and Decisions*. N.Y.: Wiley (1957).

9. Meyerson, M., "Building the Middle Range Bridge for Comprehensive Planning," *Journal of the American Institute of Planners*, XXII (Spring, 1956), pp. 58-64.

10. Pfiffner, J.M. and R.V. Presthus, *Public Administration*. N.Y.: Ronald Press (1960), p. 5.

11. Simon, H.A., *Administrative Behavior*, Second Edition, N.Y.: The Free Press (1965), p. 75.

12. Trecker, H.B., *Group Process in Administration*, Revised Edition, New York: Woman's Press (1950), pp. 232-233.

13. Weaver, Robert C., "Major Factors in Urban Planning," In L.J. Duhl (Ed.), *The Urban Condition*. New York: Basic Books (1963), p. 97.

14. Webber, Melvin M., "The Prospects for Policies Planning," In L.J.Duhl (Ed.), *The Urban Condition*, New York: Basic Books (1963), p. 320.

THE NATURE OF PLANNING DECISIONS
IN A DEMOCRATIC SOCIETY
by
Irving K. Fox

Professor of Regional Planning, Department of Urban and Regional Planning
and Associate Director, Water Resources Center
The University of Wisconsin, Madison.

In my dictionary a plan is defined as a "scheme of action or procedure," "a formulated method of doing something." And it goes on to say that planning "refers to any method of thinking out acts and purposes." In this paper we are concerned, therefore, with a "scheme of action or procedure" for outdoor recreation. My task is to identify the distinctive features of the decision-making processes which we should utilize in a democratic society in arriving at a "scheme of action" or a "formulated method" for providing outdoor recreation services.

This may seem like a relatively simple and straightforward assignment inasmuch as all of us engage in planning of one type or another, even though we may not be members of a formal planning organization. However, we have become increasingly aware of both the technical complexities of planning with the tools we now have available and of some rather perplexing philosophical issues associated with public planning in a democratic society.

The Planning Process

In subsequent sessions of the seminar you will examine in some detail the components of the planning process. Nevertheless, to deal with our assignment in a satisfactory way it is necessary to specify generally what the planning process involves. In particular, it is important to have in mind that plans are made to achieve objectives and that the plans that are adopted should be the "best" ways of meeting specified objectives. What I wish to emphasize is that planning deals on the one hand with goals and on the other hand with the assessment or evaluation of ways of meeting specified goals. In other words, a person who plans, whether in the field of outdoor recreation or in some other field, seeks on the one hand to define what ought to be accomplished, and then evaluates alternative ways of achieving such an accomplishment. A major component of planning, therefore, is that of weighing the values associated with alternative plans. Whatever methodology is applied by the planner, one of the things that he is helping to do is determine what program is best; this entails the weighing of values in some fashion.

In saying that planning involves the specification of objectives and the evaluation of alternative ways of meeting an objective, one should not conclude that these are independent tasks. The specification of objectives and the assessment of opportunities for achieving them are inextricably inter-related in the process of planning. If the cost is low for realizing a given

213

objective, one is likely to raise one's standard and seek a higher objective. If the cost is high, one might lower one's goal. The important point here is that the planning process is not a simple case of specifying an objective and then selecting the best plan for achieving it. Instead, it is what might be called an iterative process. Objectives are specified and alternatives are examined for realizing them. If the cost is more than the individual or the organization can afford, then the objective is changed and new plans are considered. Alternatively, if it is discovered that more can be achieved than was originally contemplated, a higher standard will be sought and other alternatives will be examined. Thus, the planner almost invariably considers a variety of combinations of objectives and programs before selecting what he considers to be the best combination.   This is such an important point, I would like to illustrate it by an example. Let us assume that the Division of Conservation of the State of Wisconsin concludes that it needs about 100 miles of hiking trails in wild areas which are readily accessible to major population centers. Furthermore, the Division concludes that the trails should run through the most scenic wild areas in the region.

The planner who is assigned this task may encounter a number of difficulties. First, he may face a major problem in identifying sufficient wild land for 100 miles of trails close to the population centers. Furthermore, he may discover that the most attractive scenic areas through which trails could go are in private ownership, and acquisition or easements would be extremely costly. Upon making this determination, the planner may compromise his accessibility objective and decide to consider the possibility of locating the trails somewhat farther away from the population centers than he originally intended. On the other hand, if he considers that accessibility is extremely important, he may compromise the objective of running the trails through wild land and decide that substantial portions of them could go along pastures and cultivated lands. If the most attractive areas are too costly, he may decide for less attractive areas. Alternatively, he may conclude that it is better to build fewer miles of trail, let us say 50 miles of trail rather than 100 miles, and have what is built close to the population centers and through very attractive wild lands. The point I wish to emphasize here is that the planner is unlikely to hold firm to his original objective but will move back and forth between objectives and opportunities and by weighing costs and returns arrive at a best plan. I am sure that it is abundantly clear to all of you that one of the most difficult aspects of the task that the planner faces is that of weighing the costs and returns even in such a simple situation as determining where to locate a trail. Yet, we cannot avoid this responsibility and much of the remainder of this paper deals with this problem of weighing costs and returns in a democratic society.

Some Important Premises Underlying the Evaluation of Costs and Returns

Our culture has evolved over the centuries certain basic principles with regard to the relationship between the individual and other members of

214

society. It is not appropriate here to undertake a detailed exploration of these principles. However, some of them are so fundamental to any planning activity that we must have them in mind as we proceed.

First of all, it has long been a basic tenet of our culture that *the individual should be the final judge of what is best for him.* This means that no expert, no matter how well qualified he is — no planner, no matter how well informed or experienced he may be — should have final responsibility for determining what is the best course of action on matters that affect other individuals. The principle is recognized in classical economic theory. There we have the concept of "consumer sovereignty." Under this concept the consumer through his participation in the market decides upon the value of goods and services. This determination is not made by a government, nor is it made by any other individual or body. The individual decides whether he is willing to buy or sell on the basis of the prices that the commodity will command, and prices are determined through competitive forces. This principle is also recognized in our governmental processes. Here, the determination of what is best for individuals is made through what we call "political processes" and judicial procedures designed to protect individual rights and privileges. The final decisions are made by elected representatives, if not by the individual himself, or by judges in accord with carefully proscribed rules of law. When a career civil servant assumes responsibility for decisions without a clear mandate from politically designated representatives or in a manner inconsistent with accepted judicial processes he is operating in a manner contrary to the basic principles of our society.

An associated second basic principle of our culture is that *the individual or his representative will make his decision on the basis of the best information about available alternatives and their consequences that it is practicable to provide.* In accord with classical economic theory, the buyer is expected to have full knowledge of alternative commodities that are available to him and the prices they command. Similarly, it is assumed in a democratic society that the citizen and his representative will have the best information it is practicable to provide on alternative policies and programs as a basis for deciding the course of action to pursue.

A third tenet of our culture is that *minority as well as majority preferences will be served* to the extent that minority preferences do not infringe upon the rights of others. This is an extremely important point and one that is often overlooked. There is a tendency on the part of some to feel that what the majority prefers is necessarily the best preference and the popular preference should be our only concern. This view is contrary to the principles on which our society is based. For example, we assume that, if there is a sufficient demand for a highly abstruse sort of book, it is appropriate for it to be produced, provided the cost of production and marketing can be met by those who value it. Many a book of a scholarly nature may have a market of only a few hundred or a thousand copies. Similarly, we cater to minority preferences in the production of automobiles, in the design of houses, and so on. We encounter certain problems in serving minority preferences through governmental institutions, and I will return to these later in this paper.

The relevance of these principles for planning will become clearer, I hope, as we proceed with our examination. However, at this point we should recognize that the planner does not make the final decision with regard to what is the best plan, but he does play a crucial part in this decision. The final decision is or should be made by the individual or individuals affected by the plan, or their designated representatives will make their decision with regard to what is best on the basis of knowledge of alternatives. Finally, in a democratic society plans are made to serve not only the majority preferences, but the minority preferences as well.

Private Planning and the Competitive Market

Since a very large proportion of the outdoor recreation services provided in the United States are produced by private institutions, it is necessary to make a brief examination of the task of private planning and its relationship to the public sector.

Under fully competitive conditions, economic theory indicates that the entrepreneur will weigh the demand, estimate the cost of providing the service demanded, and determine what combination of services and prices will maximize profit. Under this arrangement the individual decides what recreation service to buy in light of other alternatives that are available. The competitive nature of the market assures the existence of other alternatives, and the assumption is that the user of the recreation service knows about these alternatives. Furthermore, if there is a demand for a unique type of service, such as an extremely expensive golf course or a luxurious beach facility, the entrepreneur will serve this minority demand provided that the minority is willing to pay the cost plus a reasonable profit. Thus, under a clearly competitive situation our three principles are met, inasmuch as the individual decides what service to buy, he has knowledge of alternatives and the system provides services to suit the preferences of the minority. Seldom, if ever, in our present day society do we have a fully competitive situation, and although a substantial portion of recreation services are provided by private institutions, many of these do not function in an environment which approximates the competitive market. Also, there are a number of other reasons why private institutions have been considered incapable by themselves of meeting demands for outdoor recreation services in a fully satisfactory manner. Therefore, government has intervened to complement the private sector in this as well as in many other fields. A few brief comments on the reasons for government intervention in the field of outdoor recreation are in order because they have such an important bearing upon the task of evaluating policies and programs.

One important reason that government is involved is the judgment of our society that outdoor recreation services should be available to people even though they cannot afford the cost of providing such services. In other words, government intervenes to redistribute income (free recreation opportunities are a form of income) by making recreation services available to people at no cost or less than the actual cost. In a sense we recognize an external economy. Not only does the individual benefit from his participation in outdoor recreation; other members of society presumably benefit from the improved health and well-being of the individual. In the case of the national parks and many state and city parks, government action has been taken to preserve certain areas because of their unique character. In other words, the services these facilities provide cannot be provided competitively because there are few or no others of comparable character and quality. In this same connection, it has been suggested that individuals are willing to pay to preserve such areas even though they may never use them. The reasoning is that they are in effect taking an option on these areas so that they can use them if they ever wish to do so. In addition, it is suggested that people generally are interested in preserving such areas as a heritage for future generations. As a final point, government has intervened with regard to outdoor recreation because of the existence of what the economist calls external economies and diseconomies. Pollution of a waterway may have an important adverse effect (external diseconomy) upon the use of a waterway for outdoor recreation purposes. Conversely, the preservation of a scenic area may have a major benefit for the surrounding lands and people who view the area from a distance, even though they do not use it. This is an external economy.

As a consequence of the foregoing factors, we find ourselves with a mixed system of public and private enterprise in the field of outdoor recreation. However, it is essential to distinguish between two different kinds of public intervention. On the one hand, government acts to influence private behavior in the field of outdoor recreation, and on the other hand it acts as an entrepreneur and provides certain categories of outdoor recreation services. Thus, we can say that the general objectives of public planning in the field of outdoor recreation are twofold and as follows:

1. To help establish a set of guides and influences under which the public and private sectors will offer the range of recreation services people demand with a social benefit to social cost relationship that tends to optimize.

2. To design these public programs that serve the portion of the market assigned to government with a social benefit to social cost relationship that tends to optimize.

In other words, government seeks to provide a policy environment which, through the combined efforts of the public and private enterprise systems, fulfills the demands for outdoor recreation services. Also, government undertakes certain public programs to provide outdoor recreation services. This leads to a distinction between two types of public planning in the field of outdoor recreation, namely policy and program planning.

Let us now examine some of the problems confronted by the public planner in the outdoor recreation field.

The planner concerned with policy seeks to understand the operation of the total system which embraces both public and private activities. He seeks to answer such questions as the following:

1. To what extent should private recreation activities be regulated and in what way?

2. To what extent should taxes be utilized to influence the behavior of private enterprise?

3. To what extent should government subsidies be offered to encourage certain patterns of private behavior?

4. To what extent should fees be charged for public services at public outdoor recreation facilities?

5. What portion of the demand for outdoor recreation services should the public system serve, and what portion should be left to the private sector?

Now, a basic problem confronted by the policy planner is that of evaluating the costs and returns from different patterns of results. I propose to leave that issue for the moment and discuss it more fully when I talk about program planning. Another fundamental issue that the policy planner faces is that of estimating the behavior of public and private institutions under different potential policy arrangements. How will the private sector respond to subsidies? What will be the reaction of the public to a given system of fees and charges? How will government agencies cooperate or not cooperate in dealing with certain aspects of outdoor recreation? We know all too little about such matters, and there is no doubt that questions of this nature constitute one of the important areas of research in the field of outdoor recreation.

Program planning, as we have noted above, is concerned with designing a program that seeks to optimize. In other words, we are seeking an outdoor recreation program in a given instance in which the net benefits to society are a maximum. Now this is an ideal and we probably never quite achieve it, but certainly this is the goal that the planner must pursue. Also, as we noted earlier, the planner must go through what I called an iterative process under which he specifies an objective, examines alternative possibilities and their costs and returns, then revises the objective, goes through the process again, and so on. Here the major problem confronting the planner is that of evaluating the costs and returns associated with alternative programs.

A major difficulty in evaluating any proposed program stems from uncertainty about the future. We are not concerned alone with the demand for outdoor recreation services today; we would like to know the demand during some period in the future. As anyone knows who has confronted this task, even the best of projections may prove with time to be unsound.

218

Population may not grow as rapidly as estimated, or it may grow more rapidly than estimated. The preferences of individuals may change. New technologies may make some kinds of facilities out of date in a relatively short period. All of us are familiar with this kind of problem.

The most serious difficulty we face in planning outdoor recreation facilities is that of measuring costs and returns in some reasonably objective fashion. How much should we be willing to pay to provide a given type of outdoor recreation service? How much is it worth to have a higher quality scenic area than the alternative? What is the value of preserving unique areas for the benefit of future generations? With regard to many of these matters, we do not have a system of prices and a market which aids us in establishing these values. And to complicate matters, the value to one individual of a given type of recreation experience may be substantially different than to another. Some excellent work has been done on measuring recreation values, but no one presumes to have precise quantitative measurements of all recreation values.

Finally, the planner faces a difficult problem stemming from minority preferences. To what extent should the public agency feel a responsibility to provide rather unique outdoor recreation opportunities? Should it be assisting people in scaling remote mountain peaks? To what extent should it preserve rushing white water streams for that relatively small minority that engages in white water canoeing? Not only is the question that of whether it is good public policy to provide these services, but how much is it worth to do so?

Unfortunately, the planner does not have the tools to deal with these problems in a totally objective fashion. He has no techniques that will tell him clearly and precisely what program is best. His projections are open to question, and he has relatively precise quantitative measures of value for only a portion of the services and costs with which he is concerned. Thus, we come down to the application of judgment and the issue we face here is whose judgment will be used to measure these values.

The point I wish to emphasize is that in accordance with the premises suggested earlier in this paper, in a democratic society the public planner is not the one who renders the final judgment because the individual is the final judge of what is best for him. In the case of outdoor recreation, it is not the planner who is to be served by the facilities. Instead, the individuals served are among the general public, and taxpayers often bear most of the cost. The final decision should rest with those who use the services and those who pay for them.

Here it is important to differentiate between public and private enterprise. Under private enterprise the private organization estimates what the public will buy and provides services in accord with that estimate. The individual then determines what services he wishes to buy. In theory at least, under a competitive market, he can choose from among a range of alternatives. These conditions do not apply for the public sector. The individual is certainly free to decide whether he will use the services provided by public agencies. However, there is no competitive market, since the government has a virtual monopoly on many of the services, so the individual not only must take what is offered, or go without, but in addition he must as a taxpayer help pay for whatever the government offers. Thus, in the field of outdoor recreation the users and taxpayers are those affected, and in accord with our basic premises, the final decision about what plan is best should rest with them and not with the planner.

Now, let us examine a little more carefully the problems of serving minority preferences. Here, outdoor recreation planning faces a difficult problem. In order to clarify this problem, let us assume that a state has four wild scenic areas which, to be seen and enjoyed, require the user to hike and back-pack into the area. As we all know, suggestions are invariably made that roads be built into such areas in order than more individuals can enjoy their beauty. If the planner considers each such area *individually* and estimates as best he can the value of preserving the area as opposed to opening it up, he will usually find that many, many more people will be served if roads are built into the area than if it is left accessible only to hikers. Moreover, if the public should vote on the matter − a case at a time − one will likely discover that more people would prefer to have the area opened up than to leave it as it is. The same applies to a number of other matters such as the issue of preserving a trout stream for a few trout fishermen versus building a reservoir which will be used by thousands, or preserving habitat for wolves because some feel wolves should be preserved versus preserving deer for the multitude of deer hunters.

Confronted with this kind of situation, what constitutes a best plan? It is clear that if action is taken so that one wild area or one trout stream at a time is considered, majority preferences may gradually wipe out all wild areas and all trout streams unless there happen to be no competing demands. It has been proposed that in this kind of situation the answer is to plan on a more comprehensive basis so as to serve the range of preferences, including the less popular ones. Such planning would examine the overall supply-demand picture and seek to serve a variety of preferences which would mean, for example, setting aside certain wild areas for wilderness type activities and prohibiting the construction of roads into them. Again, we must recognize that the decision should not rest with the planner but with those affected by the decision.

If the planner is not capable of deciding what program is best, what are the implications of this conclusion for the planning process? It means that this iterative process to which we referred earlier must include the public or its designated representative. In other words, the public should have the opportunity to consider alternative plans which will meet alternative objectives with different configurations of costs and returns so that the public or public representatives can have their value judgments reflected in deciding what is the best plan.

This means in short that under an ideal public planning arrangement the following steps might apply:

1. The planner seeks to identify and understand the likely range of preferences of different groups in our society.

2. Planning organizations develop a set of alternative programs which reflect the preferences of these groups. In order to serve minority preferences, the alternative programs would include components that would serve and protect minority as well as the popular preferences.

3. The alternative plans would be debated by the public and/or its political representatives.

4. The planning organization would firm up alternative plans in light of the debate by the public and its representatives so that they may be considered for final action.

5. The political representatives of the public would select the plan for action.

Now this approach sounds relatively simple and easy, but unfortunately it is not. It would appear from this that we could ask a park and recreation agency or a state government, for example, to examine alternative plans, follow the procedure that has been outlined and arrive at what might be considered best plans on the basis of the judgment of political representatives. Unfortunately we cannot be assured of this result. Several difficult problems must be overcome.

One important problem arises because of our capability today of developing tremendous quantities of information about the characteristics and consequences of alternative plans. I was involved in one research study in which, by using a relatively simple approach, it was possible through the use of the computer to develop data on nearly 300 alternatives. In another situation which was more complex it was estimated that the potential alternatives on which data could conceivably be produced ran into the tens of thousands. It certainly is not realistic to suggest that the public or its political representatives can sift through and assess so many different possibilities.

Another important difficulty with the procedure outlined is that all analysts have their own value standards. The value preferences of the analyst are almost invariably reflected in the presentation of the technical data and in the selection of alternatives that are submitted for public consideration. Contrary to what I thought some years ago, there simply does not exist an unbiased engineer, economist, landscape architect, or representative of any other technical field. Thus, if we request the Michigan Department of Natural Resources, or the Division of Conservation in the State of Wisconsin to follow the procedure outlined, it is only reasonable to expect that the alternatives they submit for public consideration and the analyses that they make of alternative plans will reflect the biases and value preferences of these organizations and their employees. Accordingly, we have some distance to travel before we will succeed in establishing a planning environment which will illuminate the range of choice in outdoor recreation so that the public can consider and act intelligently on possible programs.

Unfortunately, I do not have any simple solution to the problems I have outlined. At the same time, it would be unwise to assume that these problems do not exist. The fact that they are real and important problems indicates that we need a deeper understanding of organizational behavior and that special studies are called for dealing with public enterprise systems which are not subject to the kinds of influences that determine the behavior of private organizations operating in competitive situations. We also need to give much more consideration than we have to the problem of illuminating the range of choice so that the public does, in fact, make the final decision. How can we select from among the many thousands of alternatives that might be considered, a few that the public can consider without having the alternatives presented reflect the value preferences of the planner? There are, however, several ways in which we can move to improve planning decisions in the field of outdoor recreation.

For one thing, I would encourage more duplication in planning efforts than we have thought desirable in the past. It has long been accepted doctrine that duplication in the field of government results in waste, whereas duplication and competition in private industry is desirable and conducive to efficiency. Outdoor recreation is one field where we could well afford to encourage duplication of planning efforts. Such duplication need not extend to detailed design and layout of facilities. Let me illustrate this point by an example. The United States Corps of Engineers plans outdoor recreation facilities and has an important effect upon the provision of outdoor recreation services through the construction of reservoirs and other waterway improvements. Park, recreation, and wildlife people have often been sharp critics of the programs of the Corps of Engineers. My view is that instead of merely being critics of the plans of the Corps of Engineers, it would be preferable for park, recreation, and wildlife organizations to be equipped to develop alternative plans. This would mean that these organizations will need engineers, hydrologists, economists, and others capable of developing preliminary but sound water resources plans. By many this would be considered duplication of effort and undesirable. My judgment is that if the recreation organizations had technically qualified people to engage in such planning and developed alternative plans when conflicts arose, we would have an improvement in water resources and outdoor recreation planning that would well justify the cost.

Another suggestion that merits consideration is for private organizations — both foundations and special interest groups — to intensify their studies of program alternatives. Such organizations as the Sierra Club have done yeoman work in illuminating important issues in outdoor recreation programs. All too often, however, the effects of such organizations have suffered from a lack of analytical input. They have opposed and criticized, yet they have lacked the resources to examine the technical aspects of proposed plans and to offer technically sound alternatives. Where they have had the technical staff available to produce solid analytical reports, their efforts have been most useful. I would hope that these organizations might expand their technical capacity to a greater extent than they now do, analyze the plans submitted by public agencies, and come up with their own alternatives. Furthermore, we might well encourage such activity through public policy. Is it possible for us to provide income tax benefits to private organizations when they use their funds for such analytical purposes? I know that this is a difficult question, but I am also convinced that the only way the range of choice can be illuminated, so as to reflect the differing value standards of members of society, is to have competition among ideas and proposals rather than to try to function through single planning and action organizations. It is difficult for me to conceive of any public agency, no matter how idealistic and highly motivated it may be, as being capable of reflecting in its alternative plans the full range of preferences of the people in our relatively complex society.

There is one other idea which I feel merits consideration. This relates to our system of fees and charges for the use of parks and recreation facilities. It has long been our policy to provide public outdoor recreation opportunities at little or no cost to users. I am among those who feel that this policy should certainly continue for certain categories of parks and recreation facilities, and especially those within cities and their environs. On the other hand, for other park and recreation facilities, it would seem timely to reconsider this policy (as we have been doing to some extent) and possibly charge fees for the use of areas on a basis related to cost. I do not believe that this policy can or should be adopted fully and immediately without changes in certain other public policies. One of our reasons for limiting fees for outdoor recreation facilities is that we feel that poor people as well as rich people should have access to such areas. However, in our current consideration of poverty situations in the United States, serious consideration is being given to what I consider to be better techniques of income distribution. If we can achieve a policy which would assure all people of the United States a minimum standard of living above a poverty line, we then would have no justification for trying to redistribute income by subsidizing the provision of parks and outdoor recreation facilities. This, in my judgment, would have two great virtues. It would encourage private entrepreneurs to develop their resources for park and recreation activities where they could compete with public enterprise and thus enlarge the available resources for park and recreation purposes. Of equal or greater importance, such a system of pricing would provide a better basis for measuring the preferences of individuals and their value than we can through existing analytical techniques. In this instance public policy in the field of outdoor recreation is intimately interrelated with other public, social and economic policies.

I trust that this paper has indicated some of the distinguishing features of public planning for outdoor recreation in a democratic society. It is evident that where a fully competitive market functions, the private sector will tend to fulfill the demand for services in accord with the basic premises that underlie our culture. But for reasons which we have indicated, we are unable to rely on a fully competitive market, and therefore, government has had to intervene. It has intervened in two ways. It has adopted policies which influence behavior of private individuals and organizations, and it provides a large portion of the services in the outdoor recreation field. This means that public planning in the field of outdoor recreation has a large responsibility to discharge and a dual role to perform. Public planning involves on the one hand policy planning to arrive at that combination of policies and that division of responsibility between the public and private sector which will tend to optimize in the provision of outdoor recreation services. Public planning also involves the development of programs for the provision of services by our public enterprise system.

A major problem in policy planning is that of estimating public and private reactions to possible public policies and organizational arrangements. This is an area that deserves more research and study than it has received.

In view of the premises of our culture, public planning should be a divided process in which the planner or analyst illuminates the range of choice — the range of objectives, the range of alternative programs and their consequences — and the public or its representatives makes the selection from among the alternative plans presented by the analyst.

Analysts have their own value standards and if we depend upon one planning organization, one group of planners and analysts, their value standards will limit the range of alternatives presented for public consideration. Therefore, we must seek and encourage competitive and countervailing activities, both within government and by private organizations, so that the range of choice will be better revealed for public consideration.

Finally, we have noted that incremental decisions tend to destroy the opportunities for satisfying minority preferences. To remedy this situation it is necessary to deal with certain kinds of demands on a comprehensive basis in order that minority preferences can be related to the provision of services to satisfy the majory and thus avoid the gradual erosion of possibilities for fulfilling the minority demand.

THE STATE-OF-THE-ART OF COMPREHENSIVE PLANNING
by
Harold F. Wise

Planning Consultant, Harold F. Wise, Robert Gladstone and Associates
Washington, D.C.

No little amount of intellectual effort has become a part of history since the Committee on Town Planning of the American Institute of Architects summarized "City Planning Progress in 1917." The report also stated "it is only quite recently that we have realized the urgent need of looking ahead in our planning with intelligent and practical imagination; of preparing our cities and towns to meet, in a logical way, the probable future demands of business, recreation, housing and circulation." In 1917, the architects summarized the previous ten years or so of planning effort with this comment:

> Throughout the book the committe has layed particular stress on the economic and engineering side of city planning, because it believes that that is fundamental to progress, and while, as architects, the members of the committee are necessarily strongly interested in the aesthetic side of city planning, they are firmly convinced that city planning in America has been retarded because the first emphasis has been given to the "city beautiful" instead of "city practical."They insist with vigor that all city planning should start on a foundation of economic practicableness and good business; that it must be something which will appeal to the businessman, and to the manufacturer, as sane and reasonable.

Having touted the importance of practicableness and good business, the architects' report then went on with hundreds of finely and precisely rendered illustrations to indicate the state of city planning throughout the country. Almost all of the illustrations dealt specifically and directly with the city beautiful — with extensive parks, landscaped malls and vast civic centers — in spite of the admonition that planning had to be more practical and economic and engineering oriented so as to appeal to the businessman and the manufacturer.

I wonder if we have learned a great deal during the ensuing fifty years. Do we not too often sell "conservation" today when we really mean recreation? Have we not too often confused "needs" with past behavior and trends and, in turn, confused trends with policy? Have we not, in fact, sought to turn our backs on innovation and creativeness?

Maybe, we planners need some serious lessons in the fine art of semantics and logic. Today in planning there is a crying need for directness, for simplicity, for honesty, for confidence in one's self and in what one does, for exposing sham (particularly intellectual sham), for plugging people into the planning formulization and above all, for recognition of the elected public official as the client and the person who is ultimately and absolutely responsible for our works and the well-functioning of the total environment.

The American Institute of Planners today counts its membership at approximately 5,000, and this does not include the additional thousands who are engaged in planning, programming and budgeting; in the planning for health, for outdoor recreation, for highways and transit, for vocational rehabilitation, for mental health; and so on.

We are, today, in the middle of a planning epic. Planning changes are not breakthroughs to be noted every half decade or so. Rather, change and expansion in planning requirements are almost continuous phenomena of every day which bring on new planning needs and new vistas. Let me briefly comment on some of these significant changes as I see them.

First, from 1917 to 1968, a short fifty years have seen a change in the scale of planning from narrow jurisdictional bound city planning to meaningful metropolitan-wide regional planning and to policy oriented statewide planning.

Second, the same fifty years have seen change in techniques and in detail. No longer is the plan solely expressed as a drawing or a map. Today, our planning is more policy oriented and more concerned with problem-solving. It is looking more and more to the clear establishment of goals and the enunciation of specific targets. Further, today's planning is developing new techniques of measurement, utilizing statistical models and making more and more practical use of electronic data processing and other measurement devices even though when some of these devices were introduced, the "hardware fixation" seemed to far outweigh an understanding of the problems and policies that these exercises should address themselves to.

Third, the last fifty years have seen a considerable change in the expansion of the areas of concern of official governmental planning. We have broadened our scope from the "probable future demands of business, recreation, housing and circulation," mentioned by the American Institute of Architects in its 1917 report, to concerns today for mental and physical health, for education and vocational rehabilitation, for law enforcement and the administration of criminal justice, to say nothing of the current attempts to understand the social systems of the intercore of our major cities as we tackle the problems associated with the war on poverty and model cities programming. In short, our planning today is concerned as much with people-oriented social systems in urban areas as with the means of getting around, as much with how people earn a living as how they recreate, as much with their social status and aspirations as with the width of a side yard.

Fourth, the last fifty years have seen a considerable change also in the means of and concerns with the implementation of plans. With a vast array of federal funds available and increasing participation in the solution of urban problems by the states, the planner of today has at his disposal specific aids in various functional areas that can be mixed to assist in achieving the public policy targets identified by the planning process.

Development programming, too, has emerged as a process for the translation of plans to reality on a regular and recurring basis; we now have greater ability to match the means of accomplishment to the ends desired and to regularly, on an annual basis, post-audit the effectiveness of our planning and programming by asking such questions as did we reach our target, or did we get where we wanted to go?

Fifth and finally (and I believe most significantly of all), the last fifty years, and most particularly the last half dozen years, have seen a considerable change in the identification (clearly and unequivically) of the elected public official as the person who is responsible for the well functioning of the environment in its broadest, most total, physical, economic and social context. Planners are not responsible; they work for elected officials who are.

This responsibility of the elected official has been hidden for some time by the lay planning commissioner. It should be recognized that the device of the city planning commission was initially conceived to provide an institutional framework, basically designed to protect the people from corrput politicians. The planning commission was initially conceived during the muckraking period of Lincoln Stephans and Ida Tarbell. This was the period at the turn of the century when perforce all locally elected officials were corrupt and when Jacob Riis wrote his shocking exposures of the ghettos of New York City.

In today's society, local units of government are increasingly completely staffed with professionally trained and competent people, and the rule and role of corruption is almost a thing of the past. The planning commission today, although extant and ubiquitous at the local city and county level, is on its way out at the metropolitan level and at the state level.

Today, at the metropolitan and state levels planning organizations are, for the most part, directly responsible to those who are elected to govern. I suspect that as we continue to tighten up the administration of cities and counties and as we begin to understand better what it takes to govern these communities that the local planning commission will be finally recognized for what it is — an old fashioned institution, not necessary today, a blocker of communication, an institution that blurs and fuzzes up a straightforward understanding of who is in charge and who is responsible. Under these circumstances we may find that local planning commissions will slowly waste away and none too soon. I am not saying that there are not hard working and honest and courageous people on planning commissions. There are. What I am saying is that, in today's context, this institution is inapppropriate.

The National Governors' Conferences and their committees on state planning over the years have purely, simply and unequivically recommended and urged that the state planning function be placed directly in or directly accessible to the governor and the governor's office. Recent legislation in Georgia, in Minnesota and in many other states recites the fact in the opening and enacting clauses that the governor is the chief planning officer of the state. This follows tradition and pattern in that, in most states, the governor is named by statute as the state's budget officer. Michigan has new legislation, too, as does Colorado and Florida, all in this pattern.

Furthermore, Title II of the 1967 congressionally passed Demonstration Cities and Metropolitan Development Act, which calls for the organization of metropolitan planning agencies in every metropolitan area in this country, requires that to be certified as the agency to review applications for federal grants-in-aid, those agencies must be composed of or be directly responsible to the elected officials of the units of general government within the metropolitan area. In these instances, those who are elected to office are having to wrestle with the essential, the important and the basic policy issues that face every metropolitan area in the country with regard to the growth and development and the well-being of the people of the metropolitan area as a whole. Also, they are wrestling with the problems of intergovernmental relations that have blocked effective action for so long.

I have outlined what I consider to be some of the essential changes in planning that have been occuring at a rapidly accelerated rate every day. We have seen changes in techniques and in detail, changes in areas of planning concern, changes in the scale of planning, expansion in the means of and the understanding of implementation and a clear emergence of the elected political official as the person who bears the prime responsibility for the well-functioning of the environment, and more importantly the people within that environment.

How did all of these changes come about?

I feel that as planning technicians, many of us in this field have learned a few lessons along the line. I am sure also that there has been a growing maturity on the part of the elected local official and a growing desire to meet problems and opportunities that are identified. Contributing undoubtedly to these changes is the nature of our affluent society, in that we are planning today, not in a period of depression, not in a period of war, but in a period of rising expectations and people with rising expectations, whether core-city located or suburbanite, are watching all of this much more closely than in the past.

All of these factors have had a significant influence, and most importantly, they have been welded together by the Congress of the United States in their actions, particularly over the last six years.

To appreciate the significance of what is happening in comprehensive planning today, we must understand fully the extraordinary concern with planning on the part of the Congress of the United States as indicated by the planning requirements they are consistently inserting into new legislation in a variety of fields covering literally hundreds of grants-in-aid programs to states and localities.

Let us start reviewing this congressionally enacted planning onslaught with the passage of the Housing Act of 1954, as amended. That is where a great deal of contemporary comprehensive planning began, especially with Section 701 which deals with local planning assistance.

Section 701 was initially conceived as a "seed money" program to grant to small communities with populations under 25,000 two-thirds of their proposed budgets for comprehensive planning.

Section 701 has been amended some 13 times since its initial enactment and every time that it has been amended the program has expanded. For example, aid was extended to cities of under 50,000 population, then to any county in the United States, then to state planning agencies and finally to metropolitan planning agencies. Section 701 provides assistance in planning to councils of locally elected public officials — to councils of government. It also provides for planning assistance to depressed areas certified by the Economic Development Administration of the Department of Commerce — to Appalachia, to tribal councils in our Indian reservations, and to make surveys of local architectural history.

Amazingly enough, just a few days ago, as the Housing Subcommittee of the House Banking and Currency Committee reported out the Administration's Housing Bill for 1968, there was one significant amendment added to Section 701, this time at the behest of the National Association of Homebuilders. In essence, this amendment and the committee report that goes with it says, and this is now proposed to be part of federal law, that any land-use plan prepared with the assistance of 701 money must include a housing element that analyzes and projects the housing market and the housing need for the jurisdiction or jurisdictions involved.

I welcome this enlightened attitude on the part of the National Association of Homebuilders.

At the metropolitan scale this means that not only should the housing needs for the affluent be projected but certainly the need for middle income and low income public housing must also become a part of the record.

I have dwelt a bit on the 701 program since, undoubtedly, this planning assistance has had a great deal to do with the stabilization and the expansion of planning and the planning profession.

But there is more to the story as far as the Congress is concerned. During the Kennedy administration, Congress enacted the Highway Act of 1962, and here for the first time in a functional program, comprehensive planning requirements were imposed *at the metropolital scale and on an intergovernmental basis.* This act provided that after June of 1965, no more federal highway dollars would be available unless the highways to be assisted were identified and located as a part of a continuous comprehensive metropolitan-wide transportation planning process. These requirements related highways and hopefully, but really not effectively at the outset, transit to projected uses of the land in the 231 standard metropolitan statistical areas of the country.

At first, these fledgling metropolitan planning efforts were often little more than rubber stamp operations designed to approve the preconceived notions of state highway engineers throughout the country. But in an evolutionary fashion, solid and truly comprehensive planning has begun to emerge from these faltering first steps.

When mass transit provisions were made a part of federal law, just after the beginning of the Kennedy Administration, Congress provided that assistance to transit would only become available if there were broadly based metropolitan comprehensive planning, not just transportation planning. Similarly, the water and sewer assistance grants administered by the

Department of Housing and Urban Development carried the same requirements.

We are all familiar with the planning requirements of the Land and Water Conservation Act. These requirements are completely consistent with the Congress's policy in other functional areas.

The Hill-Burton Act, providing assistance for the construction of hospital facilities, required comprehensive planning in that functional area when it was enacted. And in the social field (vocational rehabilitation, mental health and mental retardation, together with health services and a host of others) federal assistance is contingent on the development of long-range planning.

A year or so ago my office, in cooperation with the budget director and the state planning office in the State of Georgia, examined all of the federal programs being utilized in that state. With the exception of federal programs specifically supporting the activities of the state university, we found that there were over 200 federal programs being utilized in the state of Georgia. These programs brought over $300 million dollars into the treasury of that state in 1966. The astounding thing was that, on close examination, we found that over 82 of these federal programs required a long-range plan or a multi-yeared program as a condition precedent to the granting of the aid. The shocking thing was, of course, that putting them all together they did not really mean comprehensive planning. Not only was there no filing cabinet in the state office buildings or in the capitol in the State of Georgia that held more than one of those plans, quite often planning in one functional area was in conflict and in competition with other functional areas, and you can be sure that the governor really did not know what was going on.

Now we come to the next chapter in the role of the federal government in comprehensive planning.

Federal programs have so proliferated that some kind of coordination is absolutely necessary at all levels of government, and the Congress, I believe, is somewhat disparing of the ability to coordinate these programs at the federal level. Furthermore, and perhaps more importantly, the Congress has recognized that the most effective and best coordination is done at the local level — at the level closest to where the action really is. Therefore, Section 204 of the Demonstration Cities and Metropolitan Development Act passed by the 89th Congress provides that:

> All applications made after June 30, 1967, for federal loans or grants to assist in carrying out open space land projects or for the planning or construction of hospitals, airports, libraries, water supply and distribution facilities, sewerage facilities and waste treatment works, highways, transportation facilities, and water development and land conservation projects within any metropolitan area shall be submitted for review to an areawide agency which is designated to perform metropolitan or regional planning for the area within which the assistance is to be used, and which is, to the greatest practicable extent, composed of or responsible

to the elected officials of a unit of areawide government or of the units of general local government within whose jurisdiction such agency is authorized to engage in such planning.

What this means is that all over the United States metropolitan planning agencies must review their application for federal assistance in terms of long-range comprehensive planning. The U.S. Bureau of the Budget in President Circular A-82, revised on December 18, 1967, and addressed to the heads of all executive departments and to establishments of the federal government, defined comprehensive planning as follows:

Comprehensive planning includes the following, to the extent directly related to area needs or needs of a unit of general local government: (1) preparation, as a guide for long range development, of general physical plans with respect to the pattern and intensity of land use and the provision of public facilities, including transportation facilities; (2) programming of capital improvements based on a determination of relative urgency; (3) long range fiscal plans for implementing such plans and programs; and (4) proposed regulatory and administrative measures which aid in achieving coordination of all related plans of the departments or sub-divisions of the governments concerned and intergovernmental coordination of related planned activities among the state and local governmental agencies concerned.

If the Housing Act of 1968 is passed, we can include housing as one of the required elements of comprehensive planning.

Hence, from the federal view, comprehensive planning includes not only the drawing of plans but, most importantly, the programming of the development called for by the plans "based on a determination of relative urgency" and regulatory or administrative coordinative measures.

In general this is the state-of-the-art today.

While many of our metropolitan planning agencies are just getting off the ground, they are beginning to develop, nonetheless, a knowledge about the nature of the metropolitan scene and most particularly they are beginning to identify the needs of the region and to establish clear-cut goals and targets against which development programming can be judged and can have an effect.

A similar surge in comprehensive planning activities is going on at the state level. It is being brought on by the absolute necessity of the chief executive of the respective states to coordinate, to plan and to know what is going on.

State planning today is providing the stuff and the basis for the making of conscious decisions in the real world in spite of the most horrendous organizational structures that characterize almost all of our state governments.

If state governments are to survive, the governors today realize that they must overcome the deeply seated, sweetheart contract arrangements between federal program administrators and their counterparts at the state level. From my studies and research I call this the buddy system of state government organization. Federal and state program administrators all belong to the same club in their respective, functional areas. They have newsletters and regular regional and national meetings. They support and feed on each other, and until some kind of a system is devised at the state level to integrate these individual efforts, to examine them in detail and in depth and to see whether or not individual programs are making a contribution or indeed whether or not they are worth doing at all, there will continue to be chaos and wasteful duplication and even competition among state agencies and state programs at the state level. All of this is being clearly understood today.

Most of the planning I have been talking about to this point, which is aided and abetted and insisted upon by the federal government, relates to the location and development of physical facilities. But today there is an even more important development calling for comprehensive planning in social areas of governmental concern. Perhaps the most important recently enacted legislation is Public Law 89-749, the Comprehensive Health Planning Law, enacted under the partnership in health amendments of 1966.

In effect Public Law 89-749 wipes out a whole bundle of categorical functional aids that had been enacted over a period of many years in various aspects and parts of the health field. Today, rather than applying for one fiftieth of the federal pie, for example, in the field of venereal disease control, the comprehensive health planning legislation indicates that each state must determine what their health needs are, must establish their own sets of priorities; in short, they must plan and then the federal government will fund the plan.

While this law does not completely eliminate planning requirements imposed by the medicare and medicaid programs, by the mental health and mental retardation laws or by the vocational rehabilitation programs or a host of other programs (including the regional medical programs dealing with heart, cancer and stroke), this law does mean that, at the state level and in the metropolitan areas around the country, there is now a massive (and there will be an even more massive and meaningful) coordination of all of these efforts under comprehensive health planning.

If Congress passes the law enforcement and safe streets legislation in the form which passed the last session of the House of Representatives, a similar approach to block grants will be made, and activities will be funded at the state and metropolitan levels for comprehensive law enforcement and the administration of criminal justice in accordance with comprehensive planning in these areas.

There are similar approaches being taken now to the war on poverty and to comprehensive regional planning for model cities at the metropolitan scale. Planning for education at the metropolitan scale is not far behind.

Now, it may seem to you that I have talked about almost everything here today except outdoor recreation. On the contrary, everything I have said concerns outdoor recreation.

If you are going to plan effectively for outdoor recreation you must plan in the context of and as a part of the overall comprehensive planning program at the state or metropolitan level. This does not mean that there should not be strong planning but it does mean that if you plan for outdoor recreation outside of and isolated from the planning activities of other related and concerned functional programs – if you plan for outdoor recreation only in the context of your own private club – you do so at your peril.

Let me illustrate this point. Recently the chairman of the Committee of the Metropolitan Council in the Minneapolis-St. Paul area, which was studying the needs for a zoo at the metropolitan scale there, said that a zoo was worth five miles of freeway. Now, I recognize that the highway boys have so totally locked in and ear-marked the funds for highways, that no metropolitan government agency really has a freedom of choice today to set a series of priorities that would call for the construction of a zoo in any given year rather than the construction of five miles of freeway. But let me say that thoughts of this type are really uppermost in the minds of many local government officials today. They want to set up a series of regional accounts. They want to be able to determine matters of relative urgency and priority. They want to think creatively. And, therefore, the quasi-private system of walls that has been built around many of our special purpose functional programs are being torn down all over the place, and this trend is just beginning.

Let me also comment on the Bureau of Outdoor Recreation's required surveys of needs. We need more today in outdoor recreation than a rote type of need survey which is really an extrapolation of past behavior.

You are asked to justify your programs by comparing recreation supply with demand to arrive at need. Demand is arrived at by measuring participation and preference rates based on household interviews. In our experience such surveys do not begin to answer the real gut questions relating to: What kinds of new recreation? Where do you put it? How big should something be? How should it relate to where people live? Or whose responsibility is it to provide such facilities?

We need to be innovative and creative in this period of rising expectations and in this period of increasing affluence and more leisure time. An extrapolation of past behavior and past demonstrated desires simply is not going to be good enough. The needs for a symphony orchestra, for example in western Kansas would be found to be zero based upon the needs justification techniques required by the Bureau of Outdoor Recreation simply because there never has been one there before.

Furthermore, let me remind you that the solutions to environmental quality do not belong exclusively to outdoor recreation planners. The location of highways and water and sewer facilities have a great effect on environmental quality. All of these things complement or conflict with one another, and only when they are regarded as a part of a whole – comprehensively, if you please – can effective decisions about environmental quality be made.

Most of all we need to have an outdoor recreation planning process that is going to be challenging and innovative. It must meet the needs of the people today and tomorrow and in the years to come.

I recently asked the planning director of the City of Los Angeles what the outdoor recreation needs of that city would be — the leisure time needs and the needs for cultural satisfaction — if we won the war on poverty. We may not win this war this month or next year, but there will come a day when, perhaps, we will have a minimum family income say of $7,500 a year. What will happen to our beaches and our parks, to say nothing of our highways, if everybody in the ghettos of America joins the affluent society and has the opportunity of participating in the kind of society that is demonstrated to them nightly on their television screens?

Comprehensive planning for law enforcement, for the administration of criminal justice and the reduction of crime, comprehensive planning for housing, for the war on poverty, for outdoor recreation, for highways, and for water development are all intertwined and are all part of a total fabric. Furthermore, they are the issues on which people are running for office today.

The plans that we develop today must be an expression of the levels of desired achievement of our society. They must and will be even more people-oriented and must be designed to meet the recognized and felt needs and requirements of this and the next generation.

We can no longer afford the luxury of uncoordinated and isolated special purpose functional planning in any area of governmental concern. Our elected officials simply will not stand for it. So I want to welcome you to the club. I want to encourage you to become a part of an integrative and imaginative and very necessary social experience, wherein our plans are indeed expressions of the highest order of achievement that our society can offer today.

That is the picture as I see it, and in general, that is the state-of-the-art of comprehensive planning today.

STEPS IN THE PLANNING PROCESS
by
Stewart Marquis

Institute for Community Development, Michigan State University*

Planning is generally thought of as a rational, logical, analytical process that goes through some definite sequence of steps. Those steps and sequences vary widely in the many planning fields. I do not intend to review all those variations here. Instead, I want to suggest some different perspectives for taking a fundamental look at what planning involves.

My purpose is to bring some of the hidden parts of the planning process out into the open where we can consider them more fully, along with the connections between them. This focus is consistent with the questioning of *a priori* assumptions nowadays, which explains our self-conscious concern with the planning process. The orientation is part of the same trend that presses for greater explicitness in our statements of goals and other policies.

I assume that the reader will take what I suggest today and build it into his own existing ideas about the planning process. Thus, he will evaluate these ideas aagainst his own experience, keep what seems useful and discard what does not. This is also what happens in planning. A new plan must find a place among existing set of plans. But very few plans are really entirely new. They tend to be made up of old parts we already know about, recombined into different forms. Or they may include parts that are new to us but were developed and tried out somewhere else.

Behavior and the Structures of Plans[1]

Three psychologists (Miller, Galanter, and Pribram, 1960) have provided a useful analysis of individual behavior in terms of images and plans. They offer us a model of behavior based on built-in programs or plans for behavior. These programs are triggered by specific situations as perceived by the individual. Miller *et al.* suggest that while much of our behavior is guided by fairly stable plans, our adaptive behavior requires special plans for forming new behavioral programs.

This psychological model involves search processes in which people follow either systematic search plans (algorithms) or short-cut search plans (heuristics) as they strive for new behavioral plans for coping with new situations. The concept of the image, as used here, refers to the sum total of the individual's accumulated information (including his models for how things work and his plans for changing them) as suggested by Boulding (1956). It implies that while people seek better plans for behavior they also seek to improve their image of the problem situations that confront them.

The most important part of any search plan is the *test* that enables us to identify that for which we are searching when we find it. We need some kind

*Now with School of Natural Resources and Institute of Public Policy Studies, University of Michigan.

of criterion for determining whether or not our behavior has been satisfactory. For example, if we are searching for a needle in a haystack, we have to be able to identify the needle when we locate it. If we plan to meet a friend, we have to be able to recognize him when we see him. We can usually tell when we have had a good day of fishing, though many of us may have other criteria besides the number and size of fish we have caught.

All plans include some tests for determining satisfactory outcomes. But a plan also includes instructions for the behavior needed to achieve the desired outcomes − to satisfy the tests. Our plan to find the needle may include detailed *operations* of looking and feeling. Our plan to meet a friend may involve specific walking and driving and looking *operations*. And our plan for fishing may involve driving, buying bait, getting the boat in the water, casting and trolling, and so on.

Putting tests and operations together, Miller *et al.* suggest a basic behavioral unit. They call this a TOTE unit because it involves the sequence of *T*est, *O*perate, *T*est, and *E*xit. As shown in Figure 1a this basic TOTE unit involves some kind of test of a problem situation, followed by an operation, and then a repetition of the test to determine whether or not the test has been satisfied − the problem solved. If the test is satisfied, that means that the outcome of the operation matches the test criterion. Then, this unit of behavior is completed. But if the test is not satisfied, the outcome does not match the test criterion, and the operation and test must be repeated. Obviously this is a simple feedback loop.

In this very simple form a plan can be seen as a set of instructions for the operations needed if we are to change the situation so that the test will be satisfied. When we go beyond the level of this simple TOTE unit, we find that the plans for complex sets of operations can be built up out of additional TOTE units. This means that the box labelled "operate" in Figure 1a gets filled up with a complex hierarchy of additional tests and operations, as shown in Figure 1b. There will be a set of instructions for each suboperation as well as a test to determine if that suboperation had a satisfactory outcome. Thus, each complex plan will not only include a complex set of instructions for many suboperations but also a complex set of tests for those suboperations. And there will be many more tests than operations.

We might look at the plan for the short course at which this paper was presented as an example. The plan was stated as a schedule of topic lectures, each followed by three, small group discussion sessions and a final group reporting-questioning and lecturer response session. This was the hierarchy of suboperations performed. The plan also had some general guidelines on content for each paper. The tests are not so obvious though they are implied in the instructions, but I am sure that the organizers of this short course have some criteria by which they will evaluate its outcome and you will have added your own.

Another example might be state outdoor recreation plans and the content which the Bureau of Outdoor Recreation specifies for those plans. These specifications set particular criteria which will be used to test the content of

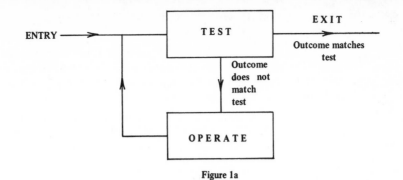

Figure 1a

TOTE UNIT

(from G. A. Miller, E. Galanter and K. H. Pribram,
Plans and the Structure of Behavior. N. Y. : Holt, 1960)

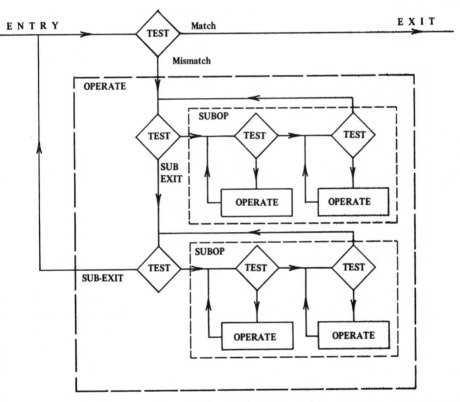

Figure 1b

HIERARCHICAL PLAN OF TOTE UNITS

237

completed plans. Specific operations may not be stated, but the very language of the specifications may imply clearly what particular operations are expected. When state agencies and the Bureau of Outdoor Recreation use these tests in appraising completed plans, they are checking to see if outcomes match test criteria. Where these do not match the agency may have to cycle back through one or more of its operational loops, or even add new ones.

Readers with some exposure to computers will have noticed that our tests are very like the decision points in the flow diagrams of instructions for computers. Miller *et al.* state that their notions of a plan are identical to that of a computer program (though they state carefully that this does not mean that a person is a computer). The test, like the decision point, means that some definite criterion (objective, standards, etc.) must be met before going on to the next TOTE unit. And this test must involve a differentiation that tells us whether to go ahead or to cycle back through any operation again. These cycles are also like "do-loops" in computer programming. Many such tests will also include a "stop rule" that puts some kind of limits on recycling.

Planning, in its most basic sense, can thus be thought of as constructing a *list of tests* to perform, and a *list of instructions* for the operations we must carry out if we are to satisfy those tests. Tests and instructions are readily available in our images (memories) for the many kinds of behavior needed for coping with situations we have dealt with before. When faced with some new situation, we tend first to search through our store of existing plans to see if one of them will probably change as a result of our actions. Usually, we do not begin to search elsewhere unless we find no workable plan stored in our own memory, or any that shows promise of working. Some of you may now be ranging far ahead of me and thinking of how this applies to your agencies. But let us stay with this initial scaffold a little longer before we tackle the complexities of organizational planning.

Whether we talk of using plans already available or of the development of new sets of tests and instructions, both will depend on how we perceive and interpret the problem situation before us. Our image of the situation combines the information we get from our environment with the information stored in our memories. These together determine our image of the problem, and hence the tests and instructions we find appropriate for dealing with it. For example, you individually may have stored information about pro-fessional recreation planners using different orientations to recreation problems. Some of you may be "resource-oriented" while others are "people-oriented." When you meet someone new you tend to match your new information against these categories.

We change our images — including our stored lists of tests for problems and our stored sets of behavioral plans — on the basis of information we get from outside ourselves. The most important source of information is our personal observation of events that affect us directly. But most critical here is what we learn about the results of our own actions — about what follows from enacting our own plans and evaluating them against our own built-in tests. For this is how our information gets converted into knowledge.

Man, as a social animal, also gets information from other people which significantly alters his images and plans. His store of potential problem images, and the behavioral plans to cope with them, are built up as much on the experience of others as they are on his own. He does not even have to get his information by direct verbal communication with others, since he can receive and decode information in written forms. Much of human communications has to do with possible ways to look at problems, possible tests for problems and operations, and possible sets of operational behavior. We might even apply here March and Simon's (1958) suggestion that problem-solving involves short-run adaptive behavior (in which we select plans from an existing repertory of behavioral programs) while learning involves longer-run adaptive behavior (in which we modify existing programs, or add additional programs to the repertory).

In discussing efforts to improve images, Miller *et al.* refer to a "prediction paradigm," in contrast to the "search paradigm" we use in forming plans. The prediction paradigm involves the making of predictions about some external situation, then observing whether or not the predictions are satisfied (as measured against some kind of prediction test), then altering the image to improve its power of prediction. They even suggest that some people tend to focus on improving their images of problem situations as the best way to go about coping with problems. Others, by contrast, tend to concentrate on finding better plans by which to alter the problem situation.

Both of these efforts — toward image-prediction or plan-search — are closely intertwined. When we store plans in our memories we store with them our predictions of their outcomes. We search first in our memories for better images and then search outside for the more complex images we call models. Images are thus central to the tests that get built into our plans. And plans become necessary for the behavior involved in prediction. Nevertheless there is a distinction, and it will play a part in our further consideration of the planning process.

A Simplified Planning Model

To begin with let us say that the major substantive sequence of the planning process is a linear sequence of TOTE units, as shown in Figure 2. Here I have included the goals-plans-outcomes sequence most generally viewed as part of the planning process. After goals I have inserted a problem step, since goals provide the tests for problems. I have added an image step at the beginning, since all other steps depend on what information we have about ourselves and our environment. I have omitted alternative plans, evaluation, and selection. This secondary sequence will be dealt with in the next level of our planning model.

Figure 3 shows the secondary sequence of procedure entailed in *each* of these major planning steps. I will start with the secondary steps for arriving at

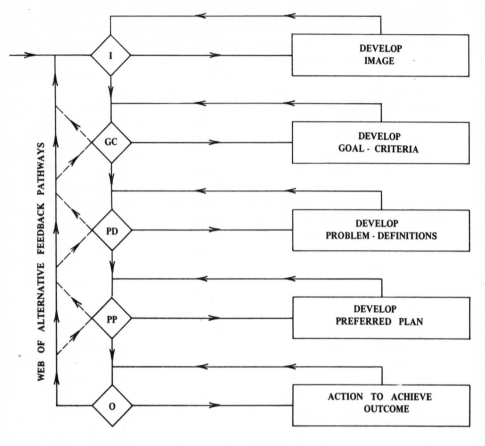

Figure 2

MAJOR SUBSTANTIVE SEQUENCE OF TOTE UNITS IN A SIMPLIFIED PLANNING MODEL

a preferred plan — the one most familiar to us in the planning process. In Figure 3, I have included the usual steps of development of alternatives, evaluation of alternatives, and selection of a preferred alternative. To this I have added a prior step — describe the behavioral plans already in operation. I do this to insure that we will never omit it in our consideration of alternatives. While an existing plan may seem just another alternative I suggest that it is more important than the others and deserves special consideration. It can serve as a datum plane to work from in our search for alternatives.

Let us now move to what I believe is a major departure from familiar models of the planning process. I want to suggest that *each* of the major substantive steps — images, goals, problems, and plans — also involves the secondary set of substeps I have just presented for arriving at a preferred plan. This means, for example, that the image step itself consists of a set of secondary substeps in which we will need to consider existing images, alternative images, evaluation of images, and selection of preferred images. In this context we might think of the emphasis nowadays on mathematical models as providing very precise kinds of images. I believe our development of models is nothing but a searching for alternative images, evaluating them, and selecting the one that best suits our given purpose.

What I say here of images is just as true of goals.[2] I suggest that our current emphasis on the explicit statement of goals means that we are also searching for alternative goals and criteria, evaluating them in some way, then selecting the preferred ones for use in other steps of planning. Likewise we are constantly searching for better problem statements, considering and evaluating alternatives, and selecting those we prefer. And we are searching for better statements of the goals of other individuals and groups.

In short, I am suggesting that each of our major substantive steps (shown in Figure 2) involves a set of secondary procedural substeps (shown in Figure 3) comprising the same basic units as those commonly used in the search for alternative plans. Our expanded planning model will then appear as in Figure 4. We may not be used to considering these extra steps as part of the planning process. But, if I read correctly the current ferment in planning in a variety of fields, I think a great deal of it involves the opening up and breaking apart of the image, goal, and problem steps. I am suggesting here that we consciously and deliberately think of those steps as being broken apart, just as we have already learned to do in the matter of alternative plans.

Our outcome step involves the action or operations of carrying out the tests and suboperations we have listed in our preferred alternative plan. This implies that the outcome is quite different from prior steps and probably not even part of the planning process. Nevertheless, some feedback in evaluating the outcome is part of planning, and I have indicated that by a feedback loop which cycles us back to the image again — for a revision of the plan or to initiate the process for a different plan.

Though I want to suggest some tertiary sequences for each secondary step, I am not nearly as confident of them. First, let us look at a possible set of steps needed to search for or generate worthwhile alternatives. As shown in

241

Figure 3

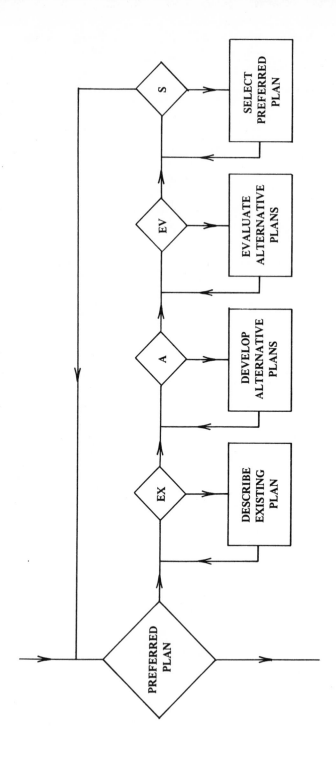

SECONDARY PROCEDURAL SEQUENCE OF TOTE UNITS IN A SIMPLIFIED PLANNING MODEL
(APPLIES TO EACH STEP IN MAJOR SUBSTANTIVE SEQUENCE)

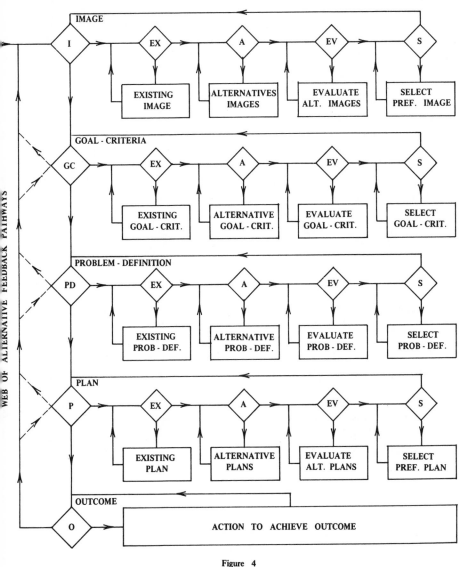

Figure 4

A SIMPLIFIED PLANNING MODEL

(COMBINING FIGURES 2 & 3)

Figure 5a, this might involve an initial step of searching through all information about existing alternatives, stored internally (in the individual or organization). Next might come the effort to generate a new alternative by marginal or incremental variations from the plan already operating. Then might follow some search for alternatives using information stored outside the individual or organization. The next step might be the generation of new alternatives by making major innovations in existing plans. And last, we might include a step of cycling back to change images, goal-criteria, or problem definition. We might prefer instead to follow a suggestion by March and Simon: that we search first for plans involving alterations in controllable factors (primarily internal), next for plans involving alterations of factors not so directly controllable (primarily external), and last that we cycle back and review our criteria for identifying feasible plans. But this set of substeps might also apply to each of the search-and-generate-steps we have suggested for arriving at alternatives worth evaluating.

In the secondary sequence our evaluating and selecting steps seem to call for different tertiary substeps than those for finding or generating alternatives. In Figure 5b, I suggest that the evaluation step might be broken down into two substeps: (1) to project expected outcomes for the various alternatives, and (2) to evaluate those expected outcomes. Figure 5c, suggests that the selection step might include a comparison of expected outcomes with the desired outcome (based on goal criteria), and the use of some kind of satisficing or optimizing criterion in selecting a preferred alternative..

We might consider that something like this set of tertiary steps applies to each of the secondary steps dealing with each of the primary steps (images, goals, problems, and plans). This may also be the point where steps in planning begin to differ for the various substantive fields. In any case we have now built up a fairly complex image of the planning process from a set of basic TOTE units. More important, while these modular building blocks have similar characteristics, they nevertheless deal with different substantive and procedural parts of the planning process.

Some Additional Complexities

I want to turn now to some of the complexities involved in any real planning operation, including the problems that arise when some of the steps are not really included, when more than one person is involved, and when extra feedback loops make the planning process more of a complex network than a linear sequence of steps. This means that we will look a bit closer at what happens in the planning process, for example, when we concentrate our attention on goals, problems, and criteria; alternative plans; and images, information and models.

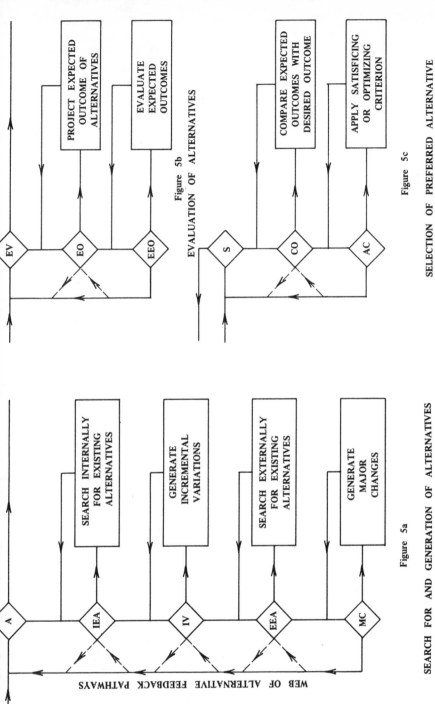

Figure 5b

EVALUATION OF ALTERNATIVES

Figure 5c

SELECTION OF PREFERRED ALTERNATIVE

(TERTIARY STEPS FOR EACH SECONDARY STEP SHOWN IN FIGURES 3 & 4)

Figure 5a

SEARCH FOR AND GENERATION OF ALTERNATIVES

Much of the current ferment in our planning for cities and transportation hinges on the growing uncertainty about problems and goals. I suspect the same is true of outdoor recreation planning. There is much conscious, deliberate attention being focused on goal and problem statements as the starting point in planning.

Planning as a process can be looked at as either a way to find solutions to problems or a way to find plans and actions that will satisfy goals. Many of the most useful ideas we can draw on for a better understanding of the process come from discussions of problem solving. But most discussions of planning focus on goal satisfaction. In our simplified model we have indicated that goals and problems are closely interrelated. But goals remain primary, since it is they which provide the tests we apply to the actual situation to see whether or not it contains problems and to determine our success in resolving problems.

Problems may be considered to exist when the actual situation (or our image of it) and some statement of desired outcome do not match. Any problem statement implies that some goal is not satisfied, that some desired outcome is not achieved. When a goal is satisfied the problem has been solved, at least for the time being. But some goals, especially those based on biological and psychological needs, may only be temporarily satisfied. So I am suggesting that goals are more fundamental than problems. We may start into the planning process with some problem statement, but we should cycle back to goals and images to determine whether or not we actually face a problem. If the actual situation matches our goal-criteria, then there is no problem to be solved.

Often in planning we assume that the goal or the problem is well defined. While this may not be true, the assumption frees us to move on to the search for and generating of plan alternatives without the need to question basic goals. Later, when implemented plans do not accomplish desired outcomes, we are forced to cycle back to reconsider goals and problems. I think each of us can recall many actual planning operations which began by assuming that goals and problems were known. The fact that they were not really known, or that what was known was incorrect, did not often show up because neither plans nor outcomes were evaluated against the assumed goals and problems. If outcomes are evaluated at all, it is often against "planning principles and standards" and not the more fundamental goals. By now, for example, the separation of land uses is traditional as a principle in designing new communities or in redesigning old ones. But then, in evaluating actual outcomes, the criterion is not "How does it work for the people who live there? Or what new problems, if any, does it also generate?" Instead, the conclusion is: "It separates the uses of land and is therefore good."

In some cases an evaluation is made by comparing outcomes and plans which completely short-circuits criteria based on goals and problems. This is especially common where plans have no built-in criteria for testing.

In our simplified planning model we showed images as coming prior to goals. This makes the human goal a special kind of image — the one that directs us in our planning behavior. Goals are used to derive the tests needed for all subsequent stages in the planning process. Just as goals provide tests for problems, so they also lead to tests for alternative plans and actual outcomes.

Vague or general goal statements are not very useful as tests, since they lack any adequate criteria for identifying desired outcomes when achieved. At the same time, general goals are more readily shared by several people, since each can read into them his more specific desired outcome (objective or standard).

Making goals precise enough to serve as tests is often called operationalizing goals. Since quantitative terms are more precise than verbal ones, we find quantitative standards a common type among goal-based criteria. Still, verbal goal statements show a considerable range of precision and to operationalize goals usually requires deriving criteria at several points along a continuum from very general to very specific. For example, we may have a general goal of "adequate recreation space," a more precise verbal statement of "sufficient recreation space of the types required for the full range of age groups," and a still more precise standard of "one acre of active sports space per 100 persons for a given sex and age group."

Operationalized goals are expected to provide criteria for the complex set of tests that I have suggested in my planning model. This means that we must think ahead in the planning process and try to foresee as many of the later tests as we can for which criteria will be needed. When we have a clear image of the desired outcome, that image can provide the specifications for subsequent tests.

Here we might begin to make some distinctions between the different kinds of tests. Some will test *actual* outcomes and these will involve the monitoring and evaluation of the actual execution of some selected plan. I will call these postvaluation tests. Others will test *expected* outcomes of various alternative plans, and I will call these prevaluation tests. Somewhat different kinds of tests will be needed for identifying alternatives worth prevaluating and for selecting a preferred alternative plan.

March and Simon suggest that most of these tests are what they call "satisficing" not "optimizing" tests. It means stating them in terms of some level of satisfaction and not as some criterion for identifying an optimum outcome. Although many sophisticated analytic techniques imply some optimizing criterion, March and Simon believe that we normally test each alternative singly against some test for satisfaction. If we do test alternatives in batches, then our criterion for the preferred plan will have to be suitable for selecting the best or optimum plan in the given batch. But we seldom gather together large sets of alternatives for prevaluation and selection, and we cannot keep searching forever for some optimal plan. Moreover, with satisficing criteria, the search for an acceptable alternative can stop when even one such alternative has been identified.

We can also think of either satisficing or optimizing criteria as applying where we wish to test for an outcome that is better than the one we expect to get by continuing the present plan and operations. So we can use such test criteria to prevaluate and select plans that will bring marginal or incremental improvements compared to the present outcome. As I have indicated in my planning model, we must always remind ourselves that the present course of action is one alternative, so expected results from continuing that plan must also be considered.

So far I have talked as if each goal could be used independently in developing test criteria. Simon suggests (1964) that we are always dealing with complex sets of constraints, and often we choose to regard as goals the constraints to which we give highest priority. These top priority goal-constraints are used not only for prevaluation and postvaluation, but also in the search for and generation of promising alternatives. Our goals must be operationalized so that they become the tests we use for identifying alternatives as well as tests for evaluation and selection. When we are searching for or generating potential alternative plans for outdoor recreation, our primary concern is to uncover or develop the kind of plans whose outcomes will satisfy our outdoor recreation goals. Other constraints, such as limited resources, must come second at this point, since they do not help us find or design a better recreation plan. Once we have identified one or more promising alternatives, we know that we will also have to apply tests for resource constraints in evaluating expected outcomes and in selecting a preferred plan. As a matter of fact, if we find several recreation plan alternatives that satisfy our recreation goals about equally, then resource constraints will probably be primary tests in selecting a preferred plan. What I want to stress here is that the only valid test for identifying a good recreation plan is one derived from our recreational goals. Certainly we cannot find a good recreation plan if our tests derive only from our resource constraints.

I have hinted before at the need for reconciling the goals of different people in the planning process, but I have so far said little about it. March and Simon suggest that the sharing and operationalizing of goals tend to determine whether or not the choosing of alternative plans can occur by rational analysis or must result from bargaining between individuals and groups. If goals are shared and operational, then the selection of preferred plans tends to be made after rational analysis. If shared goals are not operational or if operational subgoals are not shared, then decisions tend to come out of bargaining between individuals and groups. If all of you here were to agree with me on an operational test to use in selecting a plan for developing a state park, we could all proceed to use rational analysis in choosing a plan. We might disagree on the type of rational analysis to use, but that's another matter. But if we all can agree only on some vague, general goal for that park, or if groups of us share different subgoals as to whether it should be developed for camping or picnicking or as a wildlife preserve, then only bargaining will help us arrive at some preferred plan for its development.

One solution, suggested by Cyert and March, is to give sequential attention to the goals of subgroups. Goals of service personnel may get top priority in this year's budget, along with a commitment to shift priority to the goals of a specific support group the next year, and so on. In this way we can proceed to deal with goals without any absolute resolution of priorities among them. Clearly, this will be harder to accomplish where decisions involve long-term commitments of policies and resources, as in selecting preferred plans, say, for land acquisition or capital facilities, or even for major organizational changes or legislation not easily changed.

Still another way to deal with goal conflicts is to divide the planning and action operations up into segments based on subgoals that can be shared — as the more general goals cannot. Then the functional subgroups can proceed in relative independence to develop their own operational goal criteria, preferred plans, operations, and outcomes.

I am fully aware that the complexities of goal conflicts in planning are vast. I can only begin to suggest here how one or two of them might be looked at within the framework of my planning model. Since goals are critical in the derivation of tests for all steps in planning, this suggests the need for some form of continuous reassessment of goals, problems, and criteria. It also suggests that our fairly simplified planning model grows even more complex very quickly.

We must add the feedback loops needed for such goal review. Additional paths will have to be added for cycling back to our goals, even at secondary and tertiary steps in our model. If, for example, we cannot find a plan that satisfies our initially-stated test, we must include some way in which we will cycle back to reconsider our test criteria before proceeding with further search. It is at this point that we have to start talking about a complex network of feedback loops rather than a linear sequence of planning steps. We must allow for a whole set of possible readjustments for changing images and goals. However foresighted we are in stating various tests at the outset, none of us can foresee all the requirements there are. This implies a multitude of pathways through the growing maze of our planning model, as we make it flexible enough to cover the host of uncertainties that may arise. It must even be flexible enough to handle our changing capacities for coping with uncertainty.

This whole planning model is obviously full of feedback. Each individual TOTE unit is a feedback loop which may be passed over or repeated many times. Each tertiary, secondary, and primary step is also a feedback loop. And there is a complex web of alternative feedback pathways for interconnecting the major substantive steps in our planning model. In each actual situation the particular pathway through the model will be determined by whether the specific tests at each decision point are met or not. And that will depend, in part, on whether those tests themselves provide adequate criteria for determining which pathway to follow. As our planning model has gotten more complex, we find that some of these tests involve multiple alternatives, so test criteria must be adequate to determine whether or not to go on to the next step, recycle this step, or cycle back to some earlier step.

We must also add the division of labor represented by different individuals and groups taking on simultaneous assignments in the planning process. We can merely suggest how such divisions add to complexity and also how they lead to certain pathologies in planning which too often go unnoticed. Consider, for example, the freezing of subgroups into internal loops, where their goals and tests, their plans and even their actions and outcomes are never measured against the original set of overall goals set down by the parent organization. Figure 6 suggests how this anomaly might appear as a special version of our planning model.

Alternative Plans

When we search for plan alternatives, we are looking for relevant and feasible ways to satisfy goals or resolve problems. Our tests must therefore specify what we mean by relevance and feasibility, as derived from goals and problems. Having said a good deal by now about alternatives, let us think about the different kinds of plans that must be found or formed.

Some plans are not for "courses of action" (as major alternatives are usually described), but for "arrangements of structure." The blueprint for a house describes a proposed structural outcome, while a construction schedule describes the behavior required to achieve that structural outcome. And neither describes the behavioral outcome in terms of the activities of people living in the finished house. I have become only too aware of the confusion between these different kinds of outcomes and actions in urban planning. There a land use plan describes a structural outcome, which should be clearly differentiated from the action plan required to achieve that land use outcome. And both should be distinguished from the behavioral outcome plans of people who live in the city and "use land."

I suspect that it may be equally useful to make these distinctions in outdoor recreation planning. We may refer to camping facilities in a national park as structural outcomes and the recreational activities of campers as behavioral outcomes. We may develop structural outcome plans for the facilities, but campers will work out their own behavioral outcome plans for using these facilities. But we do have to plan the human behavior involved in constructing, operating, and maintaining the camping facilities and in otherwise serving campers. These are action plans for accomplishing and maintaining structural outcomes (facilities) and for aiding campers to satisfy their desired behavioral outcomes.

Current emphasis on research into recreational behavior implies that we must be concerned about the probable behavioral plans of campers before we start designing and building facilities. We are trying to help them satisfy their goals, so we must consider what their desired outcomes may be. But we are well aware that we do not prepare behavioral plans for the activities of campers. (However, we may prepare alternative behavioral plans for them to choose from, such as supervised nature hikes or special events like pageants.)

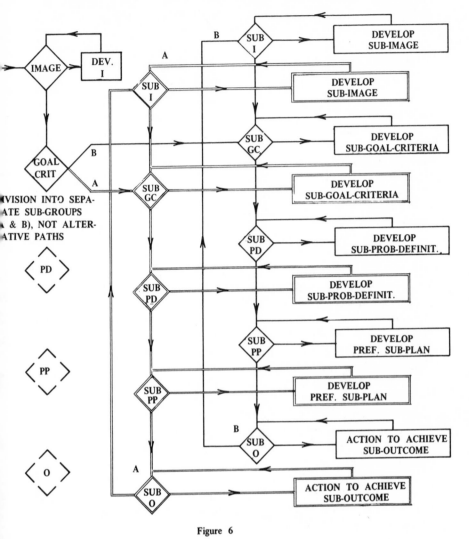

Figure 6

DIVISION INTO SUB-GROUPS WITH SEPARATION
INTO INDEPENDENT PLANNING-ACTION LOOPS

If park planners are anything like urban planners, I suspect that evaluations of camping facilities tend to be circular — couched in terms of how the facilities and improvements measure up to facility standards, instead of to the level of satisfaction among the people who use the facilities, the behavioral outcome. I consider that the ultimate tests for all plans must come down to some kind of measure of human satisfaction, however difficult that is to determine. We have to look at the incidence and distribution of satisfactions among the many different groups in the population — age, sex, race, income — if we are to begin to weigh the satisfactions of different kinds of goals against each other.

When we add to our planning model the distinction between plans for outcome and action, our planning model expands to the form shown in Figure 7. The circular evaluation of structural outcomes (as in land use or camping facilities) in terms of the structural outcome plans themselves would appear as a closed loop from actual outcome to outcome plan, without any reference to other goal-based criteria.

Our expansion of the planning model to include outcome plans only reflects the fact that the kind of planning that involves facilities and service personnel is more complex than the kind that involves only service personnel. For many facilities there is the additional complexity that much of their use is by people who plan their own activities entirely apart from the planning of the agency that provides the campgrounds, highways, trails, or playfields. We can design facilities so that people can use them only in certain ways, or we can otherwise plan to constrain people's activities in the use of facilities. But we cannot insure that the activities for which we provide facilities will even take place. So in large part we must try to project the demand of facilities by acquiring better images, information, and models.

As we search for better alternative plans, we will probably search internally at first, within our own group and organization. We will make marginal adjustments if we can or change one or two controllable factors if we have to. In some cases we may even cycle back to revise our images or goals, revising even our test criteria sooner than taking our hunt outside the organization. But at some point we will extend the search outward, if only by looking through the relevant literature.

We may call in a consultant as a specialized source of information about how other organizations have dealt with similar problems. The consultant will have accumulated experience with this type of problem many times, while we may have experienced it only a few times. Thus, for example, the management of an industrial firm may never have faced the problem of seeking a new location and designing a whole new factory building. But they can call on a locational consultant who has tackled this type of problem many times, so that he has a store of experience in this particular problem. And they can call on a factory design consultant who spends all his time dealing with the layout of new plants.

Equally as important in our context here a consultant will have had experience with many and more different images of problem situations. Hence he may also guide us toward a wholly new definition of images, goals,

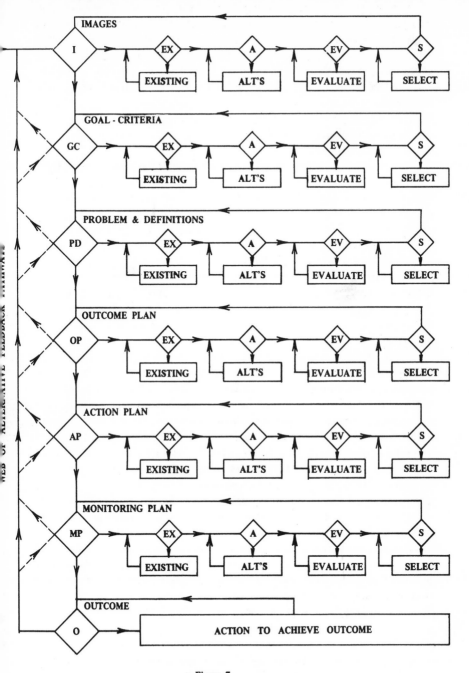

Figure 7

A SIMPLIFIED PLANNING MODEL WITH OUTCOME PLAN
AND MONITORING PLAN STEPS ADDED

253

and problems. Sometimes consultants serve us more by shocking us into a fresh look at old familiar problems than through any help they give us in finding a plan to resolve the problems as we saw them before the consultant appeared on the scene. And, of course, the new look at images, goals and problems also opens up whole new areas in which relevant, feasible alternatives may be found.

Images, Information, and Models

This brings us to the very special kind of consultant we find ourselves calling on today more and more — the economic analyst, the systems analyst, or the operations researcher. In urban planning, in transportation planning, and in outdoor recreation planning, we are finding that much more precise images are needed for some of the more precise parts of the planning process.

First, we are concentrating more attention on better images of existing situations against which to compare goal-criteria in order to identify our problems. Second, we are developing better models for projecting probable future situations which we cannot control, like what kinds and how much demand there will be for outdoor recreation facilities. Third, we want to make better projections of the expected outcome of our various plan alternatives as a firmer base from which to choose preferred plans.

In my planning model I have placed the image step first to suggest that each of us starts out with some prior image, some storehouse of organized information about ourselves and our environments. It means that our current efforts to improve our images, by building sophisticated models and collecting and processing huge amounts of information, involve us in a cycling back to reconsider our current images, to search for and generate new or modified alternative images, to evaluate the expected outcomes of such alternatives, and to select some preferred image or set of images.

Though the stress is now on mathematical models, the need is for getting and organizing better information of all kinds, shapes, and forms. We need better information about the outcome of our own organizational efforts. We seek better information about the people we are serving and the groups that support our agencies and their programs. We want better information about the goals and problems, the satisfactions and dissatisfactions of our own personnel and those we serve. We search for better strategies for building support, and for bargaining to resolve goal conflicts. Most of all we are looking for better ways to reduce our uncertainties about the things we cannot control (though we sometimes do just the opposite — we avoid or ignore them where we find we cannot do much about them).

I will now make one last addition to my planning model, which is becoming not-so-simplified. I feel it is vital that we pay more attention to the postvaluation of outcomes when we carry out preferred plans. And I include here some keeping track of results on a continuing basis. Which suggests the need to develop and carry out monitoring plans. As shown in Figure 7, the primary step of developing such a plan will come after the action plan is chosen and before the operations and outcome occur. This monitoring plan must include measures of performance, and these will be reflected in many of the subtests embedded within the actual operations, but also in the outcome plan. For a structural outcome like a capital facility, some plan for testing progress in achieving the outcome must be spelled out in the blueprints and working drawings. For the action involved in construction we will also need a series of subtests to keep track of scheduling and programming operations. And for the many kinds of action programs to achieve behavioral outcomes — such as supervised recreation activities and other direct service to people — some subtests will be needed for the continuous monitoring of service performance and consumer satisfaction. In each case, the purpose of the monitoring plan is to provide feedback which will suggest adjustment and alteration of plans and programs before unwanted characteristics get built into the outcomes.

As members of organizations our images include the full store of accumulated information found in files, records, and data tapes, as well as those stored in our personal memories and those of our peers. One current concern of planning agencies is how to make that information more widely available since it tends to get locked off into inaccessible corners.

Planning agencies are asked to look at problems that were not previously the responsibility of any subgroup in an organization or even of an organization in the community. In this sense the planning agency becomes a deliberate adaptive mechanism for the organization or the community at large.

We are beginning to expect each organization in the community to recognize its interdependencies with many other organizations and to ask how its operations affect others around it. We can no longer plan for and operate our schools, parks, homes, or industries on the assumption that nature will take care of most major consequences and people will just have to learn to live with all the rest. Unavoidably, each organization must understand, plan for, and operate within something less than the total environment. Still the boundaries of what we are holding them responsible for are fast expanding. The environment in which our images, information, and models must enable us to reduce uncertainties grows steadily larger and more complex.

There are many kinds of models, and some are more useful in the planning process than others. As we search for or generate models, we must keep in mind that they are to be used for both describing present situations and generating information about probable future situations, as well as for the very special case of projecting the expected outcomes of alternative plans. Not all model forms are directly concerned with the goals, problems, plans and outcomes which will concern us in the planning process. And not all model forms will explicitly include the factors which we know we must manipulate as we develop outcome and action plans. Thus, there will be a set of tests derived from the need for models in other parts of the planning process, and these tests must be used in searching for and generating alternative models, evaluating them, and selecting the preferred models which will be used.

Conclusion

I have tried to suggest here some ways to look at the steps in a rational planning process. I have described planning as a complex network of feedback loops with carefully stated tests for determining which loops to use and which paths to follow in any given instance. It is a general model, intended to apply to any kind of planning process or any given planning operation. But a specific planning operation will not follow all the loops and all the alternative pathways. A given operation will follow one specific path through my model, skipping some loops and repeating others. We should be able to describe any actual planning operation, or the plan for it, using network planning techniques, such as "critical path" or PERT. And, of course, there are real advantages to using those techniques to deal with complex planning behavior in a group of people.

My planning model emphasizes the general at the expense of the specific. In order to allow for all major possibilities the model has had to ignore many minor realities of any real planning situation. But this general approach makes it possible to emphasize the significant interrelations within the planning process. It goes beyond the normal linear sequence of steps describing the planning process to suggest how those significant interrelations are involved no matter where we are or where we start in the planning process.

In closing, I would like to stress some key considerations about organization and support for planning. Organization implies some division of labor, in this case dividing the planning tasks into fairly independent subsets that can go on simultaneously. This is both a strength and a weakness for planning in an organization within a complex society. I have spoken before of the prevalence of both logical sequences and interdependency feedbacks in the rational planning process. Both make it hard to divide the planning job into mutually-exclusive sets of simultaneous activities. Yet it is so obvious that much more can be accomplished if many people work on parts of planning. The critical problem is seeing that the separate efforts get coordinated and built back together, guided by something like the general approach suggested here. Perhaps an organizational planning step might be added in which these coordinating and synthesizing problems get tackled in a systematic manner. In any case, coordination of planning activities in an organization cannot be expected to meet the same tests that would be expected to make sense for an individual. Adding the complexities of planning to all the uncertainties of human behavior suggest that we should expect to find considerable duplications and overlap.

The problem of building support for programs, even programs for better planning, relates largely to the problems of shared or conflicting goals I have already discussed. But here as elsewhere it also stresses the need on our part

256

to develop better images of the goals of present and potential supporters and support groups. This can come partly from better ways to monitor and analyze actual goal satisfactions. But the major part must probably continue to come from keeping the whole planning process open to review by interested parties. Only in this way can people register their approval or disapproval of how correctly we are viewing their goals and problems, along with their reactions to what we do or propose. Exposing our planning to review, at all steps from images to outcomes, may also be necessary if we are to discover and encourage the new support groups which may be forming around new goals, images and plans.

I hope that I have gotten across my image of the planning process as one that is embedded in the larger and much more complex maze of conflicting goals and shifting coalitions. I will leave with you the challenge of finding new ways to make rational analysis effective amid the human conditions of conflict.

Footnotes

1. This whole section draws heavily on Miller, G. A., E. Galanter and K. Pribram, *Plans and the Structure of Behavior,* Holt, 1960.

2. Here I am using the term "goal" to refer to all kinds of desired outcomes, with primary emphasis on outcomes required or desired by individual human beings. I prefer to reserve "goal" for individuals and use "objective" for groups of individuals, to make it clear that groups do not have goals in the same sense that individuals do — that group objectives are nothing more than some combination of goals of individuals in that group. Some people use "goal" to refer to more specific operational statements, which I will refer to as "goal-based-criteria." Other people use the term "goal" much more broadly and vaguely. I will not try to resolve all the confusions here. My main point is that some kind of highly-specific statement describing a desired outcome is needed to serve as the test to determine whether or not that outcome has been accomplished in any given instance.

References

1. Miller, G.A.; E. Galanter; and K. Pribram: *Plans and the Structure of Behavior.* Holt, 1960.

2. Boulding, Kenneth E.: *The Image.* University of Michigan Press, 1956.

3. March, J.G. and H.A. Simon: *Organizations.* Wiley, 1958.

4. Simon, Herbert A.: "On the Concept of Organizational Goal," *Administrative Science Quarterly.* 9-1, June 1964; 1-22.

5. Cyert, R.M. and J.G. March: *A Behavioral Theory of the Firm.* Prentice-Hall, 1963.

ESTABLISHMENT OF GOALS AND DEFINITION OF OBJECTIVES

by

Robert C. Young

Planning Director

Windham Regional Planning Agency

Willimantic, Connecticut

When I first read the initial draft of this paper I was appalled to realize that I could reduce what to me is an interesting subject to such tedium. But on further consideration I realized that this can happen to any subject, no matter how inherently fascinating, which is broken down into constituent parts and over-analyzed. The subject of goals lends itself to a dramatic treatment that can fire the hearts and minds of the audience but my purpose is otherwise. What I hope to do is to establish a conceptual framework and discuss workable procedures which will help outdoor recreation planners choose meaningful goals and then convert them to real hardware and programs.

The heart of this subject is really policy planning and the procedures involved in converting broad policy into definitive and unquestionable guidelines. It involves the determination of what we want to do before we decide how to do it. If this seems like the usual way of doing things, a few moments of reflection will certainly bring to mind a number of recent and dramatic examples of rather expensive things we are doing as a nation simply because we *can* do them. But whether we are flying to the moon or designing a park, this is an increasingly dangerous practice. Precisely because our technology and wealth have made so many more things technically and economically possible, it becomes more important to decide *why* we want to do them or if, indeed, we want to do them at all. Nowadays, we can get what we *do not* want with great ease and efficiency. This is a somewhat new condition in civilization — previously, a great deal of struggle was involved in making any kind of change.

As a society we have not yet developed the social or governmental mechanisms for making basic decisions. When the automobile was invented, for instance, there could not have been a conscious choice between this mode of transportation and another. Something was needed to replace the horse, and the automobile was the only thing that would work. Today, however, there are probably dozens of suggested new modes of transport. These may very well affect our cities and our society — even outdoor recreation — in ways as profound as the automobile, but while we are presented with a choice, the mechanisms of formulating transportation policy with full attention to its social, economic and political ramifications are weak indeed.

The choices in outdoor recreation are likewise broadening. In the thirties, to my family on Long Island, a visit to a beach forty miles away was a major expedition that involved all kinds of advance planning. More recently I took an evening flight from New York to Hartford with a bathing suit in my bag, that was still wet from an afternoon dip at Montego Bay, Jamaica, and I talked to a stewardess who said she had been playing golf in Los Angeles that morning. In point of time Montego Bay is almost where Jones' Beach was thirty years ago — not quite, perhaps, but it is getting close. The implication is that we will soon have to decide what once remote recreational resources we are going to allocate for what purposes and for whom. Who knows at what not-too-distant date it might be possible to put a bunch of kids on a skybus and transport them, say from Watts to Padre Island or from Detroit to Cape Hatteras for a day's swim?

This widening choice inevitably involves multiple values, and it is the conscious and agonizing choice between these values that makes policy planning so difficult. We must often now choose between mass enjoyment and maintenance of natural environment or between active use and unviolated scenery. In the last thirty years or so, a number of factors such as heated cars, snow tires and ski lifts have made skiing almost a national sport to the delight of some and the chagrin of others who hate to see their favorite mountains bear the scars of ski trails. Here again is a choice that did not have to be made until affluence and technology made more things possible.

In the field of recreation planning very little thought appears to have been given to the problem of setting goals; those that were more or less pursued by various programs had not only been around for a long time but were poorly defined. Let me hasten to add that I am not singling out recreation planners. Urban planners have historically paid more attention to the "hows" rather than the "whys" and have only recently become concerned with the purposes that should underlie reasoned programming. But the day is over when one can plan for a traditional market. New concepts of social and economic equity, new realizations of the importance of social dynamics and, of course, the much vaunted increase in leisure and wealth mean that a whole new set of factors have to be cranked into planning considerations.

The Planning Process

The idea that a plan is a reasoned strategy to pursue goals is not a new one, although it would appear a new concept that there is a definite methodology and prodecure involved in setting the goals themselves. Although the planning process is competently discussed by Mr. Marquis in the preceeding paper, I would like to review briefly my own particular interpretation.

The planning process follows a universal pattern, whether a revolution, a neighborhood park or a family cook-out is being planned. Differences exist according to the nature of the subject matter and the administrative structure of the organization doing the planning, but the process remains the same in spite of how the work-flow might be designed. Also, some steps may be covered without a great amount of conscious thought so that the process may appear different.

As I have previously indicated, a plan is a reasoned strategy to pursue reasoned goals. Consequently, the planning process is simply the process of determining these goals and working out means to achieve them. (A man, through particular thought processes, determines to go fishing; this is his goal.

He then figures out how to get past his wife, what route to take to beat the traffic and what equipment to bring with him; these are the means to realize his goal. Together these decisions constitute a plan.)

In this particular cosmology, the following are the universal steps in planning:

1. Establishment of a goal which states the purpose of the plan.

2. Establishment, by the application of standards, of objectives which state the target for the plan.

3. Investigation into the dynamics of the subject matter and study of available or potential controls.

4. Formulation of strategies designed to reach the objectives in a manner consistent with the goals.

With this kind of structure it can be appreciated that the nature of the goals should determine the nature of the studies and processes that follow. In engineering objectives usually exist as givens, and studies are aimed at acquiring very specific knowledge which is necessary to carry out the requirements of the objectives. Planners are not as fortunate as engineers; they often make extensive studies to gain all information readily available without a clear idea of why they need it. This often leads to a situation where the relative availability of information dictates the goals policy.

Establishment of Goals

Having briefly discussed the framework of planning we can get back to a more detailed discussion of goals and objectives. What I hope to do here is to establish an orderly procedure for the formulation and adoption of fundamental plan policies. A plan, of course, should be sufficiently definitive to lead to very specific action. As such it must eventually deal with real things and real processes. If a plan is a strategy to make things happen — and to happen in a specific way — then the policy that guides the plan must provide a suitably clear guide for the formulation of the strategies. In order to do this the guiding policy must:

1. State an overall purpose.

2. Indicate an awareness of the implications of that purpose or other purposes.

3. Provide a definite target that reflects the overall purpose and whose attainment appears feasible.

4. Infer a course of action.

In the nomenclature that appears to have current general acceptance, these requirements are met by policies that involve goals, standards and objectives. A goal, by stating a value to be pursued, gives the purpose of the action; a standard is a quantitative unit measurement related to the goal, and; an objective is a specific target to be reached. The process of establishing planning policy involves moving from goals to objectives through the employment of standards.

Webster's Collegiate Dictionary defines "goal" as "the end to which a design trends," and gives aim and purpose as synonyms. Note that it says "trends" and not "reaches." A goal provides a traveler with a reason for traveling rather than a destination. Such a goal is often an ideal that is expressed in the abstract terms of values.

An *objective* on the other hand, is capable of both measurement and attainment, but its inherent purpose is implicit rather than explicit. Let me give you an example: a planning agency in a municipality might establish as a simple *goal* the provision of adequate outdoor recreation areas. At this point it can only be guessed as to what is meant by "adequate" or even, for that matter, "outdoor recreation." However, it does state the purpose behind the planning activity. Another community might establish as an *objective* the acquisition of, say, two hundred acres of park land. In this case we know just exactly what the community is after but we do not know why. We can only assume that it is for the purpose of providing adequate (?) outdoor recreation, but the objective might also be for the purpose of preventing low income housing, inflating land values, stalling development, preserving the natural environment, defining the bounds of the city or any number of good or bad motives.

A *standard* as employed here is a unit measurement which "objectifies" a value, insofar as a value can be "objectified." A goal is to be wealthy. The standard of wealth is to have an income of a million dollars a year. The objective is to obtain this income.

As often is the case in the course of defining the terms, the process becomes self-evident. First, a goal is chosen. Then standards are devised to provide measures for the goal. With their use the goal is converted into an objective, which will provide a suitable target for the strategies yet to be devised by the rest of the planning process. In so doing, however, at least one more element must be introduced. That is the element of dimensions. If a standard is usually a unit measurement, it is necessary to determine the number of units involved. This is one of the important and traditional activities of planners.

If, to take a simple case, a particular community takes as its goal the provision of adequate swimming facilities, it must first determine by what standard "adequate" will be measured and then determine the dimensions of the population. Let us say that one of the standards used is that there should be enough water, beach, or such for the simultaneous use of five percent of the population. The dimension in this case is the actual size of the population, and it is up to the planners to determine what this population will be in the design year. If this population turns out to be 10,000 for example, then it is easy to see that it will be necessary to have as an objective provision for 500 persons.

Having shown how goals are made useful for the planning process, we can now dwell at some length on some of the important characteristics of goals themselves. To begin with, this side short of theology, there are no goals that are final ends in themselves. That is, for every goal one can state, the question "why" can be asked. The answer inevitably involves a higher goal which puts the lesser goal in the position of a means to an end. Thus, goals exist in a means-end chain. Moreover, each goal has a number of means-goals serving it so that the final construction is a pyramidal matrix of goals in a means-end hierarchy. The matrix exists by virtue of the fact that most means can be shown to serve a number of goals.

While sorting out the threads of the matrix may be an academic exercise if carried out to any degree, an understanding of the relationship not only helps in the evaluation of goals but helps to indicate possibilities for trade-offs where conflicts may arise. Where such conflicts do arise or where goals appear to be difficult of attainment, it is often useful to take a look at the goal on the next hierarchal level. For instance, it is an often-stated goal to have parks within close proximity of the users. In many cases this may conflict with other goals involving the use of land. In such a situation one should consider that "close proximity" is a means that serves the goal of having the parks used by a particular clientele. This goal might be reached by other means such as those that provide services for longer stays and accomodation for public transportation.

In addition to a hierarchal relationship, goals are often imbued with apparent intrinsic value. While this may be caused by the application of ideology or tradition — and thus more apparent than real — it is an important characteristic. Low taxes, private ownership and free enterprise may indeed be means to an end, but the planner ignores these values at his peril.

Goals are also often competing in that they are mutually exclusive or that they make demands on the same limited resources. One cannot ordinarily aspire to become the greatest football lineman and the greatest high jumper at the same time because they require opposing conditions. For the same reason a tract of land cannot be held in wilderness trust and at the same time be made available for masses of people. On the other hand, a goal to acquire as much recreation land as possible is not logically at odds with the goal to develop presently-held land as much as possible. But they are competitive in that they make demands on the same limited resources — namely public money.

The actual establishment of goals can follow an orderly process in the same manner as planning. Perhaps one of the most widely used methods to establish policy has been the cost-benefit study. While this may be a useful technique if properly and selectively used, it in no way substitutes for an expanded approach to the goal problem. The weak point in a cost-benefit study is the determination of what is a cost and what is a benefit. Clearly, a benefit is something that enhances a goal and a cost is something that negates it. Consequently, a cost-benefit analysis without a prior establishment of goals is pretty useless unless there are only monetary considerations — and it's about time we got away from that particular hang-up.

A second technique often used in recreation planning is a demand study which frequently involves opinion or attitude surveys. These, in my view, are extremely tricky affairs if for no other reason than that they involve human prejudices and motivations which, in their confusion and complexity, warp the results of questionnaires that must remain simple to facilitate mass handling.

In some of the larger cities and metropolitan areas, goals have been propounded by way of committees and conferences. In the New York City metropolitan area, the Regional Plan Association conducted an extensive project involving study groups that responded to "issue" papers and television presentations. Each of these techniques has its drawbacks and limitations, yet each can make a contribution. I would like to suggest, however, that cost-benefit and demand studies and committees and conferences be used within the rational structure required for the establishment of goals.

There are four distinct steps that can be identified in the goal-setting process. These are:

1. Establishment of the perimeter of concern.

2. Establishment of the range of choice.

3. Technical examination of potential goals.

4. Establishment of goals as policy.

In simple terms, before a goal is chosen there must be a will to choose a goal in a particular area of activities. Secondly, if the job is to be done intelligently, one must be aware of the range of possibilities. Further, one must have knowledge of the ramifications and implications of the possible goals and as a last step must come to a firm decision.

Establishment of the Perimeter of Concern

As noted, this is the step in which it is decided for what area goals will be chosen. Outdoor recreation planners are not setting out to establish goals for the totality of society. But, while they have specific responsibilities within the functional area of their purview, they must also be concerned with the relationship of these responsibilities with other aspects of society. The task is to define these responsibilities and relationships.

"Perimeter of concern" may be defined as the bounds of the area covered by the agent's initial responsibility plus the area directly or indirectly affected by the carrying out of that responsibility. At the outset it must be recognized that, thus defined, the area of concern will have to be shared with others. A highway department has the chief responsibility for achieving an efficient highway system, but in so doing, the economic and social fabric of the society is affected. For a highway engineer to say that he has no concern for the social effects of his plans is criminal; for him to say that *he* will establish social goals is insane.

To begin then, the outdoor recreation planner must clearly understand his own responsibilities. I expect that this is not easy as it sounds. Legislation and traditional practices are poor guides in this day. Legislation establishing an agency for outdoor recreation is most likely to simply say, "There shall be in the Department of Parks and Forests a Division of Outdoor Recreation which shall be headed by a division chief," and then concern itself with administrative matters. Traditional practices are not much better, as they have been shaped over the years chiefly by those who have been fortunate enough to be able to articulate their demands and influence the policy makers.

No doubt outdoor recreation planners, like others concerned with the public interest, are going through a period of soul-searching in an endeavor to clarify their social responsibilities and define their core responsibilities. In so doing, it would be helpful for them to consider the problem under the general areas of geographical area, scale, functional sector and clientele.

Geographical area may pertain to both facilities and clientele. A YMCA, for instance, is people-oriented and has a clientele from a specific geographic area, but it may operate facilities and programs in a far-flung — even international — geographic distribution. A state park commission, on the other hand, tends to be facilities-oriented and is responsible for facilities within a given geographic area although the users may come from far distant places.

Scale sets the upper and lower limits of responsibility and is more concerned with the significance of a facility or operation than it is with its size. A state park commission is not ordinarily involved with a concern for neighborhood recreation but it may operate certain facilities that are no larger than a neighborhood park. In Connecticut, for instance, a new state park has been established on a very few acres, but these acres contain perhaps one of the two best occurrences of dinosaur tracks in the world — which gives this park significance on an international scale.

If state outdoor recreation planners are to establish goals, they must first decide whether they are interested in activities of a statewide significance, of sub-state significance, or in all non-urban activities. It is even conceivable that state outdoor recreation planners would feel a certain responsibility for urban recreation.

Function is the best word I could think of to describe the purpose for which an outdoor recreation activity is carried out. A by-no-means inclusive list might include play and relaxation, health, education, social rehabilitation and even group therapy. Baseball, for instance, could be said to perform the function of teaching youngsters to cooperate in a social situation. Obviously, in recreation planning, play and relaxation have received the lion's share of attention and this is, without a doubt, an important function, but others should not be ignored. There are many unarticulated needs, and an outdoor recreation program that is designed with some of the aforementioned functions in mind is going to be different from one that has an emphasis on play and relaxation only.

The question of *clientele* has both sectoral and geographical considerations. The determination of clientele on an area basis involves a decision of not just who the customers are but who is being served. There *is* a difference.

In New Hampshire, where I worked as a junior planner, I came to the conclusion that facilities for out-of-state users should not be provided unless an economic gain could be demonstrated. Residents were the clientele; other people were customers. For this reason I argued the state should not provide camping areas that merely amounted to cheap subsidized lodging. (In fairness to New Hampshire it should be noted that it cannot be said that these ideas prevailed.)

By clientele sector I mean the particular group of people that require special attention, who can be categorized by whatever means seems appropriate — age, income, family status, cultural background, etc. In state and national parks everything seems to be geared for the middle-class family unit, but how about: The broken family with no transportation and little organizational experience? The unmarried adult that might like a better place than a cocktail lounge to meet other unmarried adults? The small group of single boys and girls and the hordes of college kids, who before they discovered peace and social justice, used to invade Fort Lauderdale every spring to blow off steam? And the under-privileged family that has no non-urban experience and is fearful of leaving the familiarity of the city slum? These people too are clients.

Once the initial core of the concern has been established, the next step is to determine what other areas of public concern the core impinges on. Some of these obviously are:

1. The effect of recreation as an economic generator through the attraction of tourists.

2. The role of outdoor recreation in education.

3. The relationship between outdoor recreation and conservation.

4. The effect of outdoor recreation on social patterns and structures.

It would be presumptuous to suggest that recreation planners should establish economic, education, conservation and social goals. But on the other hand, the recreation planner cannot do a complete job unless there is policy in these areas, and he can do a genuine service by making these issues known to those in positions of specific or comprehensive responsibility. There is nothing more dangerous to our planned future than the pursuit of single-purpose goals. The original statement of the core responsibility for goal-setting will be greatly enlarged, then, but hopefully it will lead to a meaningful examination of the purposes and missions of outdoor recreation.

Once the perimeter of concern is established, it is possible to give consideration to the *range of choice* which is possible within the encompassed area. This should be in the nature of an exploration trip, and might initially begin with a simple listing of possible goals without, at this time, modifying constraints. While this list should be as inclusive as possible, it should, of course, stop on this side of absurdity. Some examples might be: to provide outdoor recreation for the greatest number of persons possible; to provide high-quality outdoor recreational opportunities; to provide outdoor recreation opportunities that will acquaint participants with conservation principles; to provide outdoor recreation opportunities for the specialized needs of cultural sub-groups; to provide outdoor recreation opportunities that will facilitate the acculturation of minority groups; to maximize outdoor recreation resources as an economic generator; to provide adequate opportunities for those without sufficient resources to provide for themselves.

This should be more than a mechanical exercise for it will be used to indicate the full range of possibilities on one hand and to indicate and clarify points of issue on the other.

Technical Examination of Potential Goals

At this stage the planner has outlined his area or responsibility and is aware of the possibilities within that area. He must now determine which goals are "best" in terms of desirability and feasibility and how the goals interact with each other. The fact that goals have a hierarchal relationship, value, and point of conflict has been previously pointed out. These characteristics must now be determined. In doing so, it is best to treat the goals as real, rather than symbolic, situations; otherwise, the project might end up simply as an exercise in symbol manipulation — a great temptation to those who want to see everything on a computer tape.

In assigning values to goals in terms of desirability, planners should keep in mind: the ultimate personal or societal goal that the outdoor recreation goals will facilitate; the present social and economic conditions of the constituency; the relationship with established goals of a higher jurisdiction; and the relative abundance of related resources. In terms of feasibility, it is worth considering costs in terms of other goals and in terms of new attitudes, institutions or technologies that might be necessary to implement the goal.

With these factors as measures and with a knowledge of the complex inter-relationships of the potential goals, a goals statement can now be drawn up. This cannot be done in terms of absolutes. Neither can it be done by treating goals one at a time. Fanatics are persons who narrowly pursue simple goals; the rest of us realize that, while we have major goals, there are many minor goals that act as constraints that we cannot ignore. We all want to be healthy, but we do not all remove ourselves to Southern California to spend our days eating wheat germ and yogurt in the sea air. Thus, it is not enough to adopt a goal that simply calls for the provision for the greatest number of people; if quality is ignored the goal may be self-defeating. And, too, perhaps the best way to provide for the *maximum* number of people is to provide for the most able and affluent. Goals at this stage must be well thought out and should be fairly lengthy and well qualified statements rather than simple slogans. The issues, costs and consequences should be faced boldly.

Establishment of Goals as Policy

Goals should be established on as formal a basis as possible to become the policy Bible of the agency. In a unified jurisdiction such as a state, it should not be too difficult to find the proper policy body, but if the project is more comprehensive and is taking place in a metropolitan or regional area, the problem of locating the seat of authority becomes more difficult. If there is a mechanism for the adoption of a specialized or comprehensive plan, then the goals should be considered as an official part of the plan and preferably adopted prior to the planning proposals and in the same manner as the plan is adopted.

At this point there is danger that the top administrators, while willing to adopt fine-sounding manifestoes, may pay little attention to the goals once adopted. Such danger is minimized if it is made clear that the goals are built into the planning process and other consequences will follow their adoption. In order to make the issues crystal clear and to provide a firm guide for the continuing technical work, the planner should now have on hand an unequivocal document outlining the purpose, responsibilities and thrust of the mission.

Converting Goals to Objectives

The planner must now find ways to convert the abstract goals to objectives and must later propose very specific measures which will be taken to reach the objectives. In order to be useful the objectives must:

1. Fulfill the spirit and purpose of its correlative goal.

2. Be specific enough so there is no question about when it has been reached.

3. Suggest means of attainment.

4. Be reasonable and feasible in terms of economic and other costs.

It will be recalled that an illustration was given above showing how goals were converted to objectives with the application of standards and dimensions. That is, a goal is expressed in terms of values, and standards are used to quantify the value so that specific objectives can be established. A standard as used here is any measurable criterion that can be used to gauge the relative worth of something that is expressed in value terms. "Pure" water, for instance, is unobtainable outside of the laboratory so that standards must be given in terms of acceptable amounts of various constituents consistent with the particular concept of purity.

If commonly adopted standards are to be used for park planning, there will be a minimum of difficulty because there are a number of sources that state how much acreage of various kinds of parks are needed for population units. These sources do not, however, give standards related to the kinds of goals under discussion. The recent BOR publication, *Outdoor Recreation Standards* (April, 1967) is a case in point. This publication lists adopted and suggested standards for park and play areas and ten separate activities, and cites 135 sources. This is a useful compendium, but it is only a bare beginning. A look at the first item is illustrative. It reads:

1 acre of neighborhood park for each 1,000 persons and 1 acre of neighborhood playground for each 800 persons; or 1 acre of combined park and playground for each 500 persons in a neighborhood. Minimum size is 3 to 5 acres. Park and playground should be within walking distance of every home. Actual service radius in each neighborhood is determined by population density, residential lot sizes and safety access.

Without being critical of the thought that went into the establishment of this standard, it is nevertheless evident that face-value acceptance will be based on a number of uncritiqued assumptions and will leave a number of questions unanswered. It will be assumed that a neighborhood park is a standard facility and that a neighborhood is a standard urban complex housing standard urban people. But a "neighborhood park" in Albuquerque, New Mexico, is going to be different in terms of activities and function from a neighborhood park in Bangor, Maine, or Biloxi, Mississippi, because of climatic conditions if nothing else. And a neighborhood in Watts, California, is different from a neighborhood in Darien, Connecticut, by reason of social, economic and physical differences.

Also, there is no particular reason that I know of which says that all of the activities which are traditionally associated with neighborhood parks need to be all contained within a single space. Nor am I convinced that all of the outdoor recreation activities which we ought to be concerned with *can* be handled in a park, neighborhood, or otherwise. Pedestrian ways, promenades, sidewalk cafes, sidewalk resting places and landscaped private plazas could do many of the things that a park can do in the way of recreation.

Rather than utilize accepted standards for traditional facilities, it would be far better to begin again by examining the goals that have been established and determining the factors that contribute to the desired value. This requires that prime attention be given to the activity rather than the facility. Using the goal "to provide adequate bathing opportunities," as an example, it is not difficult to show how these factors can be identified and appropriate standards arrived at as the principal and associated activities of bathing are well known, as are the requirements for these activities. The chief activities are wading and swimming and the associated activities are sunbathing, picnicking, changing clothes, eating, performing necessary biological functions, responding to the aesthetic environment and traveling to and from the facility. Some of the factors that determine the adequacy of the facility in reference to these activities would be water and beach area per person, water quality and volume, underwater slope and bottom, dressing room space per person, restaurant facilities per person, and distance to the beach, for the population to be served.

Once the factors are identified, the planner is in a position to begin assigning measurable values which become standards. In doing so, he will be concerned with performance characteristics, user characteristics, and environmental characteristics. In reference to bathing, some of these are:

271

Performance Characteristics:

1. Physicial actions of bather in swimming, wading and diving in relation to the need for space and water of specific depth.

2. Actions of bathers on the beach in relation to space and the nature of the beach.

3. Actions in preparation for bathing or trip home.

4. Length of stay at the beach.

User Characteristics:

1. Individual preferences.

2. Individual skills and ability.

3. Economic ability of users.

4. Profile of users (age, family groupings, etc.).

Environmental Characteristics:

1. Climate as it affects length of season and ability to enjoy various activities.

2. Character of the recreational resources and their relative abundance.

3. Character of the urban structure.

With these characteristics in hand — and some may demand a major commitment to research — it should be possible to come up with standards expressing what is meant by "adequate swimming opportunities" and then, by applying the appropriate dimensions, to establish definite objectives.

The provision of adequate bathing was chosen as an illustration because it is relatively simple but no pretense is made that other cases can be so easily handled by the recreation planner. If it is a goal policy that recreation facilities should contribute to the acculturation of minority groups, the planner must seek the help of those who are more familiar with this particular process and can help him find relationships between the process of acculturation, physical facilities and recreation programs.

In the years ahead, much work is going to have to be done on standards simply because planning is becoming more pervasive, comprehensive and formal. This will require more justifiable standards all along the line. If the knowledge does not exist that will help the planner devise standards in all the fields he would like to, it is no cause for dispair. The state of the art is primitive, but it is beginning to contain a healthy mix of idealism, insight and practicality. If the recreation planner does not have all of the answers, he can nevertheless make a tremendous contribution by asking the right questions and demanding that the answers be ultimately useful to the men who cut the trails or pour the concrete.

DECISION-MAKING AND PUBLIC POLICY:
THE PERILS AND POSSIBILITIES OF FRAGMENTATION

by
Jeffrey L. Pressman
Department of Political Science
The University of California, Berkeley

When he participates in the formulation of public policy, a man is called upon to make decisions – conscious choices among alternative courses of action. Not surprisingly, students of public administration have sought to describe the ways in which individuals make decisions and the ways in which they *ought* to make decisions. For the process of choice has important implications for both the structure of governmental machinery and the content of public policy.

The Rational Model

Writing about problem-solving in public administration, Marshall Dimock has endorsed the following method:

> First, there are always the problem and the issues. Second, there are the facts and analyses that need to be applied to the issues. Third, there is the setting forth of alternatives and the pros and cons applicable to each possible solution – all this in the light of larger institutional goals and objectives. Fourth, there is the decision proper, which depends upon choosing among alternatives. . . .[1]

According to this model of rational decision-making, the ideal way to make policy is to choose among alternatives after comprehensive study of all possible courses of action and all possible consequences of those courses – together with an evaluation of the consequences in the light of one's values. Then the alternative which will lead to the most highly-valued consequences is selected.

Now a problem arises: Where may a public administrator or politician obtain a priority list of values against which he can judge consequences of policies? For some,[2] the clear norms of public policy are to be found in "the will of the people." It is the duty of politicians to discover the people's preferences and the duty of public administrators to translate these preferences into policies.

Other writers, while continuing to subscribe to the existence of an identifiable "public interest," are doubtful about finding that interest in the expressed will of the people:

> Living adults share, we must believe, the same public interest. For them, however, the public interest is mixed with, and is often at odds with, their private and special interests. Put this way, we can say, I suggest, that the public interest may be presumed to be

what men would choose if they saw clearly, thought rationally, acted disinterestedly and benevolently.[3]

Statesmen, following natural law and their own higher insights, must lead the people.

Thus, there exists – in the opinion of the above-mentioned observers – a clear "public interest" which can provide guidance to policy-makers in their process of choice. Such a coherent statement of preferences is crucial to the rational decision-maker. Without it he may know each alternative and be able to predict each consequence – but he will have no reason for preferring one consequence to another.

If the best decisions are arrived at through a comprehensive comparison of alternatives "in the light of larger institutional goals and objectives," then a strong case can be made for centralization of policy-making. Only a central decision-maker can receive sufficient information about a wide range of alternatives to be able to make a rational choice. Furthermore, only a decision-maker responsible to a large constituency can choose in the light of broad goals and objectives. Not surprisingly, Dimock himself has proposed that policy-making in the executive branch of American government be centrally co-ordinated in the Cabinet.[4] Others have suggested that centralized political parties are necessary to co-ordinate lower-level interests and make binding decisions in light of the public interest.[5] Finally, it has often been proposed that the Presidency might be strengthened as a central policy-making center.[6] As a national figure from a national constituency, it is argued a President is best able to make policy decisions which concern everybody.

In the area of budgeting, "rationalizing" proposals have often entailed a greater degree of centralization. Arthur Smithies, for example, feels that no claim on the budget should be acted upon until all competing claims can be considered. Of course, this kind of overview must be carried out by a central body – in this case, the Joint (Congressional) Budget Policy Committee. The Committee would be empowered to consider all proposals for revenue and expenditure in a single package, and their recommendations would be made binding by a concurrent resolution.[7] Budgetary decisions would be made *after* every request was weighed against national needs.

For the rationalists, fragmentation of decision-making – whether it occurs in decentralized parties, undisciplined legislatures, or widely-dispersed centers of budgetary power – is evil. To be rational, a decision-making system must be sufficiently centralized to allow one decision-maker (or unit) to evaluate each alternative against an ordering of widely-endorsed priorities. Problems may be factored out to subordinate units, but they must be centrally co-ordinated in the end.

Chinks in the Rationalists' Armor

During the past two decades, social scientists have exposed some embarrassingly large chinks in the armor of the rational decision-making model.[8] To be sure, many proposals for governmental reform continue to be tailored to the rational design. But it is clear that this model contains serious difficulties.

For example, there is the problem of discovering alternatives. According to the rationalists, a decision-maker is called upon to study every alternative choice of action. But from where are those alternatives to come? The rational model simply takes them as given. In fact, it is difficult to imagine how an individual could possibly think of − let alone evaluate − every alternative move on a problem of public policy. The problem is compounded when we consider the plight of a central decision-maker at the top of a hierarchical pyramid, far removed from the grass roots and dependent upon long lines of communication for the gathering of his information.

A second problem is presented by the rationalists' requirement that a decision-maker examine each *consequence* of each alternative. Needless to say, an attempt to take this injunction seriously would be frustrating:

> There is a story to the effect that a statistician once found a very high correlation between the number of old maids and the size of the clover crop in different English counties. After puzzling over this relation for some time, he was able to trace what appeared to him to be the causal chain. Old maids, it appeared, kept cats; and cats ate mice. Field mice, however, were natural enemies of bumblebees, and these latter were, in turn, the chief agents in fertilizing the flowers of the clover plants. The implication, of course, is that the British Parliament should never legislate on the subject of marriage bonuses without first evaluating the effect upon the clover crop of reducing the spinster population.[9]

The chains of consequences are too long and unpredictable to be studied in a comprehensive way.

Furthermore, the problem is deepened by the fact that the consequences for the future of a given policy choice may be very different from the consequences for the present. A country's choice of a missile system this year may result in deterring an enemy attack. However, during the following year advancing technology and military expenditures may give the enemy a sufficiently capable anti-missile defense to make the missile threat less frightening and deterrence less probable. Thus, the estimation of *future* as well as *present* consequences of choices imposes upon the policy-maker a bewilderingly difficult task.

Even if a politician or administrator were able to carry out an all-inclusive overview of alternatives and consequences of policy, the problem of evaluation would still loom large. For it is extremely difficult to conceive of a readily-available and stable listing of values against which a policy-maker could rank the relative desirability of various consequences. It is easy to say that policy decision-makers should be guided by the popular will, but it is much harder to explain how one would determine what the popular will *is* at any given time. Majority votes in campaigns usually provide little guidance on voters' preferences regarding specific policies.[10]

Public policy choices usually involve a multiplicity of values. Consider the following example:

In a recent case in Connecticut, the appropriate choice of location for a new highway between Hartford and New Haven clearly depended on the type of traffic for which the new facility was to be built; hence deciding upon the type of traffic became an inescapable value problem. Should the highway be built primarily for trucks, for inter-city passenger automobiles, or for commuters? Defend any one class of traffic or combination, and one is driven back onto a bewildering variety of relevant rules. Should the highway be for commuters? Is it good for New Haven and Hartford to encourage commutation? What about urban congestion, tax inequalities between central and subsidiary towns, the number of traffic deaths, the amenities of life at the center or the "periphery"? Why does anyone believe a highway is good in the first place? Because citizens should get what they want? Or because social mobility is a good thing? Or because progress demands it? Or because more transportation is good for business? And so forth.[11]

Instead of dealing with an agreed-upon set of values, policy in the public arena is often faced with a large number of conflicting value preferences. There are interests of cities arrayed against interests of farmers, interests in industrial development against conservation interests, and desires for full employment against desires for price stability. Even if the administrator were able to sense all the values which had a bearing on a particular choice, it is not clear which values he should prefer over others. Furthermore, just as today's choice may lead to a different consequence tomorrow, so today's consequence may not be valued so highly tomorrow as it is today. A policy of increased government expenditure, with a subsequent rise in the level of total demand, will be highly valued in a slack economy but not valued in an inflated economy.

It is clear that the requirements of rational decision-making cannot be fulfilled by mortal policy-makers. For man is unable to imagine every alternative, predict every consequence, and judge each consequence against a stable and clear-cut ordering of values. Rational decision-making is not accurate as a description of how man decides, and it is not an entirely worthy statement of how man *should* decide. For political decisions are not technical decisions, merely concerned with finding the "most efficient" solutions in terms of resources expended to accomplish external goals. Political decisions must forge social agreement, accomodate interests, and preserve the structure of the political decision-making process itself. "Political rationality,"[12] the preservation of decision structures, must underlie economic or legal or technical rationality (the efficient expenditures of resources to attain a given goal).

If we find faults with the rational model as both description and ideal, what can we put in its place? Let us turn now to a consideration of some suggested substitutions.

In 1963, David Braybrooke and Charles E. Lindblom[13] collaborated in a devastating attack on the rationalist model and the proposal of an alternative description of decision-making: "disjointed incrementalism." According to the authors, disjointed incrementalism is a set of relatively simple, crude adjustments and adaptations which are made by policy analysts as they make choices in the public realm. Taken together, as a mutually reinforcing set of actions, they constitute a systematic strategy.

Rather than considering the universe as a blank sheet and attempting to imagine a comprehensive range of alternative policies, a decision-maker starts with a knowledge of present and past circumstances and policies. Typically, the only alternatives considered are those which are similar to the status quo.

Not only are the alternatives similar to the status quo; they are also extremely similar to each other. In reaching a decision, a policy-maker in this model carries out a comparative analysis of the marginal or incremental differences between alternative policies. The choice is finally made by evaluating the relative desirability of various increments. A policy-maker "need not ask himself if liberty is precious and, if so, whether it is more precious than security; he need only consider whether an increment of the one value is desirable and whether, when he must choose between the two, an increment of one is worth an increment of the other."[14] In short, the policy analyst acts very much like the consumer in economic theory who chooses among alternative increments of value for which he spends increments of his income. There is no need to produce a comprehensive priorities list of values. Instead, conflicts are expressed in terms of the trading ratios at the margin: how much of one value is worth sacrificing, at the margin in a given situation, to achieve an increment of another?

"Disjointed incrementalism" thus immediately confronts one major difficulty of the rational model — the impossibility of considering (or even discovering) every policy alternative in a given situation. For the only alternatives that will be considered are those which differ incrementally from each other and from the status quo. Besides restricting the number of alternatives considered, disjointed incrementalism also entails a sharp reduction in the number of consequences studied — the second difficulty of the rationalist model. In incrementalism the policy analyst deliberately restricts his examination to certain consequences of his action. An economist may declare that certain aspects of his problem can best be solved by politicians, political scientists, or sociologists. The planner of a federal poverty program may simply not consider the consequences of federal direction of the program for the self-esteem of local elites.

There is no guarantee, of course, that those consequences not considered are unimportant:

> To be sure, incremental analysts do neglect the unimportant consequences of policies, but among those they concede to be important, they often rule out of bounds the uninteresting, (to them), the remote, the imponderable, the intangible, and the

poorly understood, no matter how important. Of course, they also sometimes omit inadvertently some important consequences[15]

Instead of constantly adjusting policy means to ends, say the authors, policy-makers often do the opposite. Objectives shift as policy instruments change. What is *possible* conditions what is aimed for. Policies are continually amended by serial analysis and evaluation, as experience brings new light to bear on the subject under consideration. The social security program, foreign aid, and highway construction programs are amended and revised every few years to take account of changing circumstances and human reactions.

Incremental decision-making is particularly suited to the politics of stable democracies. The authors take almost all their examples from the United States, where social agreement has meant that: "Nonincremental alternatives usually do not lie within the range of choice possible in the society or body politic."[16] Our society, say Braybrooke and Lindblom, could be endangered by change that was too sweeping.

If the slow rate of change in the United States is compatible with incremental decision-making, the dispersion of power in this country is a positive aid to this kind of problem-solving. For, if one man or one group of men is incapable of considering a comprehensive range of policy alternatives and consequences, then a broad consideration of policies requires that decision-making be carried out in a number of centers in society. Besides being incremental, decision-making is disjointed — "in the sense that various aspects of public policy and even various aspects of any one problem or problem area are analyzed at various points, with no apparent co-ordination. . . . "[17] Only through fragmentation can a wide variety of viewpoints be brought to bear on a policy problem and sufficient information be gathered to shape policies in politically realistic ways.

Braybrooke and Lindblom see decision-making in the public arena *not as an intellectual exercise but as a social process.* No central individual or unit must consider each alternative and consequence and then attempt to impose his preferences upon his subordinates. Instead, a large number of dispersed decisions-makers react to specific problems and attempt to influence each other's choices by persuasion, bargaining, negotiation, and the building of alliances. Social agreement is thus forged in the very process of making policy choices.

Disjointed incrementalism represents a radically different alternative to the rational decision-making model. Nonincremental alternatives are neglected, seemingly irrelevant consequences are ignored, and co-ordination is achieved by a social process of negotiation and bargaining. To those who desire order and comprehensiveness, such a model of decision-making may seem frightening. But it appears that this process of "muddling through" characterizes a great deal of choice-making in stable democracies.

Consider the surprise of the House of Commons' Select Committee of Estimates when it found that the supposedly-rational system of Treasury Control of Public Expenditure was in fact characterized by a number of incrementalist habits – the consideration of slightly-differing alternatives, the use of the status quo as a base, the arbitrary exclusion of large areas of budgetary concern. The Committee, not amused, declared:

> It became clear early in the course of the enquiry that it is really an abuse of language to speak of a "system" of Treasury control, if by the word "system" is meant methods and practices that have at one time or another been deliberately planned and instituted. What is called "Treasury control" is better described as a complex of administrative practice that has grown up like a tree over the centuries, natural rather than planned, empiric rather than theoretical.[18]

However, even if much policy-making tends to be characterized by the extremely non-rational style of disjointed incrementalism, it does not follow that all policy decisions *are* or *ought to be* made in this way. It is possible to introduce an element of rationality into less-than-rational decision-making, and the next model attempts to perform this task.

Satisficing and Organizational Decision-Making

For Herbert A. Simon, the model of rational decision-making is clearly out of the question: Man has neither the time, the capacity, nor the information to consider every possible aspect of choice. However, this does not mean that man cannot *intend* to be rational and try to bring some order into his choice-making. We may agree with Simon that "rationality is concerned with the selection of preferred behavior alternatives in terms of some system of values whereby the consequences of behavior can be evaluated."[19] But if it is impossible for each individual to develop a clear priority listing of values to be maximized, then rationality is difficult. A way must be found to make the evaluation of consequences less demanding.

Simon's answer is to replace the rationalists' goal of maximizing – finding the best course of action – with the relatively modest goal of "satisficing" – finding a course of action which is "good enough."[20] In the purely rational model, there exists a set of criteria that permits all alternatives to be ranked: the alternative selected is preferred, by use of these criteria, to all other alternatives. In Simon's model, on the other hand, there exists a set of criteria which describes minimally satisfactory alternatives; the alternative selected is the first one which meets or exceeds all the criteria.

Like Braybrooke and Lindblom, Simon views decision-making as a social process. But unlike the authors of *A Strategy of Decision*, Simon goes on to state that a useful set of "satisfactory" criteria can be constructed for man by his social environment. The creator of this set of criteria is the organization:

> The rational individual is, and must be, an organized and institutionalized individual. If the severe limits imposed by human psychology upon deliberation are to be relaxed, the individual must in his decisions be subject to the influence of the organized group in which he participates.[21]

By specializing administrative functions and goals, the organization sharply reduces the number of values that each portion of the organization (and each man) need consider. Thus, certain consequences are deliberately ignored – not because they are sensed to be "uninteresting" or "remote" or "poorly understood" (Braybrooke and Lindblom) – but because they are outside the jurisdiction of that particular organizational segment. The complexity of the world is reduced to manageable proportions by the declaration and assignment of organizational objectives.

Organizations simplify choice in other ways. By establishing standard practices for accomplishing tasks, the individual is saved from having to discover problem-solving methods *ab nihilo*. Systems of authority prescribe duties and behavioral expectations for the individual, and systems of communication enable him to discover what others have decided and are deciding. Finally, the organization indoctrinates the individual, causing him to view the world in a certain way and greatly reduces the number of environmental stimuli which he will find relevant.[22]

If Lindblom's model seemed to produce a chaos of *laissez-faire* Simon's appears chillingly single-minded and efficient:

> The resources, the input, at the disposal of the administrator are strictly limited. It is not his function to establish a utopia. It is his function to maximize the attainment of the governmental objectives (assuming they have been agreed upon), by the efficient employment of the limited resources that are available to him.[23]

> Once the system of values which is to govern an administrative choice has been specified, there is one and only one "best" decision, and this decision is determined by the organizational values and situation, and not by the personal motives of the member of the organization who makes the decision.[24]

> The task of administration is so to design this environment that the individual will approach as close as practicable to rationality (judged in terms of the organization's goals) in his decisions.[25]

Rationality emerges, not from the omniscient mind of one man, but from the organizational manipulation of a large number of men.

Simon makes a contribution in showing how – even if each individual cannot evaluate a comprehensive range of alternatives and consequences – decision-making can be given some structure in terms of an evaluative framework. Individuals are not entirely rational (as in Dimock), nor do they give up the attempt to be rational (as in Lindblom). Rather, for Simon, individuals in organizations are intendedly rational. That is, they deliberately attempt to select alternatives which are "good enough" in terms of a specific checklist of values. The organization can provide such a checklist and turn the individual's attention toward it.

But there are problems in Simon's "efficiency-oriented" approach. "Efficiency" is a laudable objective; however, an efficient public policy decision involves more than the economic expenditures of resources in order to reach an agreed-upon external purpose. For as we have seen, economic or social rationality in the expenditure of resources is dependent upon *political* rationality — the preservation of the decision-making structures themselves. In making decisions, public organizations must secure agreement with and consent for their choices from groups both inside and outside the organization. They must evolve procedures for benefiting from past mistakes and recovering from present ones. And they must keep the organization itself in good working condition. In a democratic society, decisions must elicit the consent of people they touch; in a pluralistic polity, decisions must forge a certain measure of agreement among diverse power centers.

The goal of technical rationality, without a corresponding political rationality, has been widely criticized during the past few years. Some observers see the deification of technical efficiency as leading to an abdication of major political decision-making to a narrow group of technocrats.[26] The argument of these writers is largely a moral one — concern over the decline of democracy and popular discussion. Others have pointed out the political irrationality of technically "rational" decisions. During the 1950's, for example, the National Security Council produced a number of defense policies which were logically unassailable on paper — but which were not likely to gain political support at home or achieve their desired objectives in the international arena.[27]

It is important, therefore, to consider a third model of less-than-rational decision-making: one that concerns itself with the problem of political rationality and the preservation of decision-making structures themselves.

Heuristic Processes and the Maintenance of the Organization

Like Lindblom and Simon, William J. Gore sees decision-making as the result of a social process.[28] And like Simon, Gore views the organization as the shaper of choice. However, Gore's model of the choice process is much more complex than Simon's. In the Simon model, the organization helped the individual choose more rationally by supplying him with goals, ideologies, and information. Efficiency was seen as the economic use of resources to accomplish given organizational tasks. The organization proposed; the individual disposed.

For Gore, the accomplishment of stated organizational objectives is only one of the tasks of decision-making. Decision-making must attain political as well as economic rationality; that is, it must maintain the organization's existence as well as perform its tasks. According to the author, decision-making is "a pattern of interaction between individuals through which the social mechanisms that sustain effective collective activity are developed and maintained."[29]

This study is no esoteric philosophical exercise; it is based on a close examination of the Lawrence, Kansas Fire Department. Gore notes that rational processes — the setting of goals and the evolution of means to accomplish those goals — are an important part of organizational life.

However, to be successful such processes must be built on heuristic processes (non-logical processes which may aid in the solution of a problem but give no guarantee of doing so). These heuristic processes forge social agreement on policies, and the building of agreement is a hazy and illogical process.

How then does the decision-making process both achieve external tasks and facilitate, at the same time, the necessary agreement to keep the organization functioning? According to Gore, the process of decision-making begins when a tension is produced in an organization's environment (a tension arises when the organization is subjected to a claim which cannot be satisfied). To engage the organization's attention, the tension must satisfactorily pass a number of thresholds (much like the thresholds of "satisficing"). The tension must be articulated and must also be sufficiently relevant to the organization's values. As in Lindblom's model, a decision is typically stimulated by a specific problem — rather than by a long-range plan.

If the stimulus is recognized as relevant the organization must decide how to react. First a few people — usually those most directly involved — try to form the disparate tension stimuli into a coherent and tractable problem. Then, the problem may be evaluated in the light of organizational goals. If the goals offer no guidance in dealing with the problem, the goals themselves may be questioned. A discussion then takes place within the organization, concerning the implications of the problem for organizational structure and purpose.

At this point various power centers within the organization will attempt to influence the nature of the response to the problem by persuasion, negotiation, threats, promises, and appeals to common interest in organizational values. From time to time, "trial balloon" policies will be floated outside the organization in order to obtain a prediction of the extent to which outside elements are favorably inclined toward the move. Thus, "an organization muddles its way into agreement on how it feels about responding to the more or less imminent response-demanding situations."[30]

With internal agreement accomplished, the organization turns to the external environment for active support (or at least, non-hostility). There are a "series of independent discussions going on many places inside and outside the organization at once. Sanction for the response is never a single commitment of support. Rather, it is the sum of dozens, often hundreds, of specific understandings between *people.* "[31]

Gore's model, with its pluralistic fragmentation and disjointedness, appears at first glance to be much like that described by Lindblom. But there are important differences. For Lindblom, decisions to include or exclude certain alternatives or consequences were often arbitrary. In Gore's description, organizational values and processes suggest — but do not dictate in a Simonian manner — the relevant values to be considered. Secondly, Gore relies heavily on the evolution of a goal consensus between individuals and organizations as an aid to producing agreement; Lindblom, considering value consensus an extremely difficult ambition, places more faith in agreement on specific policies.

Thus, Gore's model appears more fluid than the economically "efficient" organization of Herbert Simon, but more ordered (because it includes a fairly regularized organizational process of relating decisions to organizational goals) than Lindblom's "disjointed incrementalism." The agreement forged in the process of decision-making helps to preserve the organization and to achieve "political rationality."

We can see that in the absence of pure rationality, there are a number of ways in which public policy decisions might be made. In Lindblom's model of disjointed incrementalism, each policy-maker focuses on certain policy alternatives and consequences. Values overlooked by one decision-maker will be picked up by another, until all relevant values in our pluralist political system are brought to bear on the policy problem. In Herbert Simon's "intended rationality" model, organizations help individuals to make choices by setting goals, providing information, and supplying needed stimuli. When he bends his action toward organizational goals, the individual decides "rationally," in that he can judge alternatives by examining likely consequences against a "satisfactory" value listing. But "rationality" is not merely an efficient expenditure of resources to achieve defined organizational goals. And in William Gore's heuristic model, we can see how decision-making can help to forge the social agreement which preserves the decision-making structure itself. In the larger society, co-operative discussions *between* decision-making units help to preserve the fabric of the body politic.

All three models represent accurate descriptions of the ways in which *some* decisions – or some parts of decisions – are made in the public arena. Examples are readily available for each model. Disjointed incrementalism is practiced rather heavily in the setting of public expenditure figures in both the United States and Great Britain.[32] Simon's model, in which agreed-upon policies are carried out in standardized "efficient" procedures, seems applicable to lower-level technical decisions in which there is no real clashing of interests. Gore's model, on the other hand, centers around conflicting organizational interests and involves the changing of organizational goals themselves; such a model is an accurate description of major decisions which involve a change of policy direction. An example of such a decision is the recent British Government move to apply for Common Market membership. The Prime Minister announced the Cabinet's decision only after allowing the various interests within and outside the government to pull and tug against each other.

If decision-making cannot be entirely rational, if one man or group of men cannot make a comprehensive evaluation of every alternative and consequence of policy, then what are the implications for the way in which public policy is made and the quality of policies produced? For those who hold a rational model of decision-making, the prescription for good public policy is easy: centralize decision-making machinery; increase the information flow; consider every alternative before taking a step. Dispersion of power is to be shunned, for a broad overview is needed to make a rational choice.

For those who subscribe to a non-rational model of decision-making however, the prescription for effective public policy-making is very different. Now, dispersion of power – as in the fragmented American budgetary process – is seen as a positive aid to calculation. For dispersion of decision-making power means that each choice-maker will have a manageable slice of policy to consider. For Simon, fragmentation is a precondition of intelligent evaluation. For Gore and Lindblom, fragmentation is a prerequisite of the building of agreement and the gathering of information. There is no room, in disjointed decision-making, for an isolated and lofty central co-ordinator. Furthermore, fragmentation often facilitates the faster movement of policies; it is much easier to agree on specific policies or parts of policies than it is to agree on root values.

Thus, civil rights leaders and businessmen have come to various agreements concerning desegregation in Atlanta, Georgia. It is not necessary for these men to agree on an ordering of values or on a national racial policy; it is merely necessary for merchants to recognize that desegregation is "good business." With fragmentation, decisions are not imposed from without; they grow from the interactions among various smaller units. Decision-making, as in the Gore and Lindblom models, involves a simultaneous building of agreement on policies.

Although fragmentation of policy decision-making has its benefits, problems remain. If no man or unit has the ability to make rational central decisions, how can political leadership ever be exercised? Secondly, if decision-making is dispersed over a wide range of power centers, how are the various decisions co-ordinated with one another? Furthermore, how does policy change and improvement take place in non-centralized organizations and political bodies? Do such institutions merely react to emergencies? Finally, what is the quality of public policy which is not subjected to central overview? Are certain interests left unrepresented? Which groups prevail in a fragmented decision-making system? If we endorse a fragmentation of decision-making, these questions demand to be answered.

The Limits and Opportunities of Leadership

If a leader exercising comprehensive overview and direction over the formulation of policy is ruled out, we must search for alternative definitions of leadership in a situation in which decision-making is dispersed. For Herbert Simon, leadership could consist of the erection of an organization's communications network and a division of responsibilities among units. In Gore's model, the "leaders" may be seen as those who thrash out a problem and make sense of it in terms of an organization's goals. (This conception of leadership is non-hierarchical: the leading group – those most affected by a particular tension – could change drastically from one issue to the next.)

However, there is a great deal more we can say about the possibilities of leadership in an organization or political system in which decision-making is fragmented. A distinction between leaders and non-leaders stems from the fact that decisions differ widely in their magnitude; social scientists have often drawn an analytical line between general or crucial decisons (which set the tone and direction) and the specific or routine decisions which carry out the purposes of general decisions.[33] Lindblom distinguishes between large and small change in terms of social opinion: "In any society there develops a strong tendency toward convergence in estimates of what changes are important and unimportant."[34] (Incremental decision-making is suited to small change.) Simon contrasts "broad" decisions regarding values with "day-to-day" decisions concerned with implementation of the value choices.[35] Gore draws a line between ideological decisions and technical decisions.[36]

Leadership can then be defined in terms of making the basic, structural decisions which set the stage for lesser, incremental decisions. Of course, it is very difficult to specify which decisions are basic and which are secondary: the ranking would depend largely on the observer's own value system. But there are certain kinds of decisions which are generally conceded to be basic. One class is made up of decisions which construct and preserve the "rules of the game" in the organizational or political arena. Thus, promulgation of the Constitution and subsequent Supreme Court interpretations of it may be seen as "basic" decisions in that they are concerned with the maintenance of the very constitutional structure of our political system.

Another type of "crucial" decision-making associated with leadership is that which gives purpose and a sense of mission to an organization or political system. It is not required that a leader make centrally-binding substantive decisions after considering the entire terrain of possible actions. Rather he must give to his social organization a sense of what it is and where it is moving (as Stokely Carmichael did in his reorientation of the SNCC to Black Power goals and methods). As Philip Selznick has written:

> The executive becomes a statesman as he makes the transition from administrative management to institutional leadership.
>
> To "institutionalize" is to *infuse with value beyond the technical requirements of the task at hand.*[37]

In a democratic system, the political leader is rarely in a position to make control decisions on substantive issues after a comprehensive inventory of alternatives. However, he *can* impart a sense of purpose to his country. Observing the difficulties of some contemporary democratic leaders, Walter Lippmann has written recently that:

> Under all the obvious differences between Britain, Germany and the United States there is one thing they have in common in their separate experiences. Granted that Erhard, Johnson and Wilson chose to do unpopular things. What did all three fail to do? They failed, I venture to think, to realize the great human truth that a people will endure if they have become convinced that they are suffering in a great cause. None of the three leaders has been able

to instill in his people a sense that they should rise above their formal conveniences and desires to the great plane of historical necessity and destiny.[38]

Although Franklin Roosevelt was not nearly so observant of civil service niceties as was Dwight Eisenhower, Roosevelt in his speeches and actions gave the federal civil service a sense of its own importance and mission in the formulation of social policy. Eisenhower, although scrupulous about following civil service regulations, was never able to do the same.

Not only does a leader set the goals and purpose of his organization in a system of fragmented decision-making power, he must also adapt these goals to elicit support from outside groups upon whose support his own unit is dependent. For example, Harold Wilson was surely influenced in his decision to commit the Labour Government to an unwavering defense of the pound by the fact that important foreign bankers wished him to do so. A further role of the leader is the settlement of disputes among conflicting organizational units. It is not necessary to survey every policy alternative; the area of dispute provides a leader with a restricted range of policies in which he can work.

An organizational or political leader can do more, however, than simply fashion compromises in which everyone gives up something to get something else. For he can create new situations in which a number of desires can be accomodated without a concomitent surrendering of valued objectives. As Mary Parker Follett has written: "when two desires are *integrated,* that means that a solution has been found in which both desires have found a place, that neither side has had to sacrifice anything."[39]

In a fragmented political system, a leader cannot often simply direct others to follow his instructions and preferences. But he can create situations which will *enable* other decision-makers to support his policies without sacrificing their own objectives. When he was attempting to develop support for the European Recovery Program (Marshall Plan) in 1948, President Truman contributed his administration's prestige and information to Secretary of State George Marshall — thus giving Marshall the resources and support necessary to pursue his objective of designing an effective recovery program. Furthermore, Truman made the issue a strictly non-partisan one, enabling Republican Senator Arthur Vandenberg to support the program and thus take his desired place as a leader of bipartisan foreign policy.[40] Truman's, Marshall's, and Vandenberg's objectives were not compromised — but mutually realized — by the evolution of the policy. The President had not carried out the integrating himself; rather, he had created an integrative situation in which others could act.

At times, instead of seeking to induce agreement, a leader may create situations of "constructive conflict" in order to stimulate new ideas and fresh policy perspectives. President Franklin Roosevelt relied upon fragmented and conflicting information sources, hoping to produce competition. In 1964, to take another example, Prime Minister Harold Wilson created the Department of Economic Affairs to compete with the Treasury in the formulation of

Britain's economic policy. The DEA was supposed to contribute a concern with economic growth; the Treasury would continue to be responsible for price stability and the maintenance of the value of the pound. Out of the resulting conflict, it was assumed that both growth and stability would be considered in planning.

If a recognition of the limits of human capacity leads us to reject a prescription for a central decision-maker in favor of a more fragmented decision-making system, the need for leadership does not disappear. Leaders may not be able to evaluate and control each policy choice, but they are needed to give broad purposes to their social organizations, to adapt goals in order to gain outside support, to settle conflicts, and to create integrative solutions which may satisfy the needs of a number of other decision-makers.

The Problem of Co-ordination: Joining the Fragments Together

Decentralized and fragmented decision-making patterns are appealing to us; the dispersion of power is a fine democratic virtue. But doubts remain: If decision-making is dispersed, how are decisions reached at various places brought together to form broader policies?

In *The Intelligence of Democracy,* Lindblom focuses on the problem of co-ordinating the dispersed incremental decision-makers.[41] For Lindblom, decisions are not first made and then co-ordinated. Rather, the processes of decision-making and co-ordination can occur simultaneously through *partisan mutual adjustment.* An individual decision-maker is seen as a "partisan" who does not assume that there exists a set of knowable criteria for co-ordination which would be acceptable to himself and other decision-makers. Therefore, he does not move toward co-ordination by a co-operative search for common values.[42] (Although Lindblom does not deny that such searches do occur, he concentrates his analysis on the partisan mutual adjustment process.)

Decisions are co-ordinated, without the benefit of a central co-ordinator, by a number of deliberate "adjustments" on the part of the partisans. A decision-maker may make an *adaptive* adjustment, in which he seeks no response from another partisan (he may adjust his decision to past experience or he may defer to the other's expected response). Alternatively, a partisan could make a *manipulated* adjustment, in which he seeks to induce a response from another (he may, in this type of adaptation, engage in bargaining, negotiation, or appeals to a third party).

As partisan decision-makers mutually adjust their decisions to take account of each other, co-ordination takes place and simultaneously facilitates acceptance of the policies produced. In the American political system, there is no highest prescriptive authority who can determine policies for all others. Rather legislators, executives, interest group leaders, and party leaders engage in bilateral and multilateral partisan mutual adjustment with each other.[43] Out of this complex process, co-ordination emerges.

Negotiation, bargaining, threats, promises, and the building of alliances are also used by the decision-makers of Gore's model for influencing and adapting to each other's moves. But decisions in this model are also co-ordinated by co-operative, as well as partisan, discussion. That is, decision-makers seek policies which are compatible with the overriding organizational goals in which all have a stake. Strategic bargaining gives way to co-operative search, a process not emphasized by Lindblom. The direction of the co-operative search is heavily influenced by organizational ideology.

In a system of decentralized decision-making, a pervasive organizational ideology can serve as a strong co-ordinating force by supplying similar decisional premises to the various dispersed units. The result may be the evolution of a system of "illusory decentralization."[44] In the United States Forest Service, for example, nominally decentralized decision-makers are in fact co-ordinated by a pervasive socialization process and common ideology. Organizational belief systems are prime co-ordinating devices in Simon's model; such ideologies are brought to bear on individuals through care-fully-constructed lines of authority and communication.

However, as we have seen, organizational goals do not need to be considered as "givens" which are transmitted downward to the individual. In Gore's view, for example, goals can be modified by the co-operative discussions of individual members. The emphasis on collaboration, co-oper-ation, and mutability of organizational goals is a central thrust of contempor-ary organizational theory.[45] Decisions are not centrally co-ordinated from above, but neither are they co-ordinated by the "partisan" adjustments of bargaining, negotiation, and compromise. Rather, decisions are co-ordinated through the co-operative formulation of superordinate goals to which individuals may bend their efforts. For Gore, such collaborative discussions were often informal and unplanned. Going one step further, a number of modern social scientists have devised systems of *planned* collaboration.

Because they believe that human beings are more creative and more productive in an atmosphere of mutual trust, these social scientists have designed processes to facilitate the emergence of attitudes of co-operation and collaboration in organizational decision-making. "The commitment of members of collaboration-consensus systems is to one another's growth and to superordinate goals on which their growth in part depends."[46]

In such systems, co-ordination is achieved through agreement on goals, through mutual participation in the setting of those goals, and through the development of a communications system to provide continuous feedback and allow for continuous alteration.

A potentially powerful instrument for the transformation of deci-sion-making attitudes from competivite to collaborative has been the laboratory training method, featuring the use of "T-groups." The training process involves the formation of groups of organizational members who are led by an experienced trainer to "unfreeze" competitive attitudes, to analyze interpersonal relations in a free and open manner, and to use the understandings gained to build more collaborative relationships with each other. This method has been found useful in developing attitudes of intergroup as well as interpersonal trust; as individuals apply co-operative attitudes to "outside" groups, there is a common search among formerly competing units for superordinate goals which can facilitate co-operation.[47]

Admittedly, all this has a visionary and unrealistic ring to the uninitiated. And there are difficulties: collaboration between superiors and subordinates appears to presuppose a mass conversion to altruism and the evolution of a reward system for collaboration instead of individual achievement would be no easy task. Nevertheless, the fact that this method has had success in private organizations and is now being used in a public organization like the Peace Corps indicates that some planners of public policy are taking the collaboration-consensus model seriously.

Fragmented decision-making poses problems for overall co-ordination, but there are a number of ways in which co-ordination can be achieved. Decision-makers can adapt to each other by a process of bargaining and negotiation. Alternatively, the common value system of an organization or political system can provide common decisional premises and thus co-ordinate dispersed decision-making units. Co-operative discussion provides a final method of co-ordination; such discussion may be unplanned, as in Gore, or deliberately planned, as in Shepard, Bennis *et al.* Most organizations (and the American political system) are characterized by all three modes of co-ordination. Agencies bargain with each other (for example, there are bitter inter-agency bargaining sessions in the division of an agreed-upon department budgetary total), engage in co-operative discussions with each other (as when the Treasury and Department of Economic Affairs decided to shelve their differences in 1966 and try to salvage the National Plan), and find themselves all drawn together by organizational "rules of the game" (much co-ordination of behavior derives from custom, tradition, and agreed-upon rules which simply eliminate certain types of behavior from consideration).

After decisions are co-ordinated, a smooth-running decision-making system may be achieved. But is this system a stagnant one, or is there possibility of change to new directions? The problem of innovation without an omniscient central innovator must now be faced.

The Temptations of Inertia and the Planning of Change

In the model of disjointed incrementalism, the process of decision-making forges social agreement as fragmented decision-makers are forced to ally with or negotiate with each other. In Simon's model, fragmented decision-making helps individuals make choices and work toward the accomplishment of organizational goals. And in the Gore model, the heuristic processes of problem-solving help to keep the organization together. Not only do these models show how a system is maintained it might also be shown that a system of fragmented decision-making makes it *easier* to produce policy change. After all, it is much easier to agree on small policy shifts than on basic alterations in values or entire programs.

289

Still, fragmented decision-making is open to the charge that it has a built-in bias toward conservatism. If incremental change is the order of the day, how do *large* nonincremental shifts of policy take place? Furthermore, if decisions are so greatly influenced by dominant organizational groups (as in Gore), how can we ever expect divergence from the status quo?

It is true that, in the Lindblom model, special emergencies can call forth policy change. And in Gore's construct, sufficiently important "tensions" can result in both policy alterations and changes in basic goals.[48] But these changes seem merely reactive, and we may ask whether *planned* change might not also be possible.

To these challenges an incrementalist might respond that large policy changes are the results of numerous small ones. In the case of Vietnam, for example, Senator McGovern has pointed out that United States policy has consisted of "a series of steps, each one seemingly prudent and restrained, yet each one unexorably setting in motion the next step to a larger role."[49] A series of unplanned, incremental decisions can move along, unconsciously building momentum, and provide no opportunities for decision-makers to shift gears. It is therefore worthwhile to study ways to bring direction and control to change in a fragmented system.

In 1964, an Israeli Professor of Public Administration, Yehezkel Dror, delivered a stinging attack on Lindblom's theory:

> Although Lindblom's thesis includes a number of reservations, these are insufficient to alter its main impact as an ideological reinforcement of the pro-inertia and anti-innovation forces prevalent in all human organizations, administration and policy making.[50]

To counteract this tendency, Dror proposes a model which includes the preliminary estimation of expected pay-offs of various alternatives. This is followed by a decision on whether a strategy of minimal risk or a strategy of innovation is preferred. If the first, then incrementalism is in order. If the latter, a wide investigation of various alternatives and consequences is carried out.

This model presupposes that it is possible to estimate consequences and risks of alternatives to a greater extent than has been shown to be possible for non-rational man. (We have seen that information about the riskiness and wisdom of an alternative can often be estimated only after trying that choice out in practice.) However, Dror's article is useful in leading to a consideration of possible ways to produce change and improvement in policy.

First, there may be an institutionalization of the consideration of change – of alternatives *more* than incrementally different from present policies. Recent White House Conferences on Education and Civil Rights, for example, were attempts to scan the political landscape for various approaches to policy problems in these areas. An inquiry independent of the usual governmental units would, it was hoped, produce policy ideas which were truly innovative. Independent "think" and "research" units in organizations are also charged

290

with the exploration of new alternatives. There is no attempt to consider *every* alternative, but the field is scanned by a fresh and innovative eye.[51]

A second method of introducing change into a fragmented decision system is provided by "organizational learning." Lindblom shows how experience can lead to change in the substance of policies; we can see that the fruits of experience can also lead to the alteration of decision-making processes themselves. For example, the formulation of plans for public expenditure in Great Britain has been – as we have seen – traditionally a piece-meal, incremental affair. Civil servants proposed expenditure schedules to the Treasury, bargaining ensued, and outstanding issues were settled at the Cabinet level by negotiations between the Chancellor of the Exchequer and the Minister concerned. The years's expenditure total was the result of these assorted partisan mutual adjustments. However, because of a desire to exercise greater control over both the total level and the allocation of expenditure, the decision-making process was fundamentally changed in the period 1961-66.[52] Total annual limits and allocations of expenditure were promulgated in 1965 and were enforced by a committee of non-spending ministers. This was a case of organizational learning; a problem (lack of expenditure control) was identified, and the decision-making process – identified as the source of the problem – was radically altered to produce a different result.

Still, organizational learning may be seen as another "reactive" process. For a method of *institutionalizing* and *planning* for change in the decision-making process, we may turn again to the "planned collaboration" of T-groups:

> . . .a major goal of the change agent is to help participants gain perspective on and insight into themselves and the organization, so that they are free to determine their own behavior, rather than having it determined by their embeddedness in the organization's present structure and culture.[53]

With organizational trappings and status systems temporarily set aside, participants are free to be open and to "think the unthinkable."In this way, change may be institutionalized; the organization's hold over individuals' decision-premises is relaxed.

A final method of inducing change in a system of fragmented decision-making is the creation of a new governmental unit with authority to protect a certain value. (This method of change is allowed for in Lindblom's model.) Thus, the Department of Economic Affairs was created by Harold Wilson to advance the cause of economic growth. (A warning should be noted, however. The mere *creation* of a governmental unit is not sufficient to strengthen a valued objective. For one thing, the unit must be properly staffed. The small size of the DEA staff has hampered this unit's ability to compete with the Treasury. Also, the proposed creation of a new unit must take into account the probability of outside support. President Johnson's plan to bring the business and labor communities together by merging the

Department of Commerce with the Department of Labor ran into harsh opposition from union leaders.)

The building of agreement (Lindblom), the accomplishment of organizational objectives (Simon), and the maintenance of the organization (Gore) are all laudable aims, but they do not insure that decision-making will ever produce policy changes. The possibility of inertia is a great one. However, all hope is not lost: An organization or political system *can* introduce change into its decision-making pattern by the creation of "scanning" units, by organizational learning, by laboratory training, and by the creation of new units charged with the advancement of a certain value. As in the areas of leadership and co-ordination, problems are posed by fragmented decision-making – but a wide range of remedies is at hand.

The Quality and Equality of Public Policy

As we have seen, a system of fragmented decision-making provides aids in calculation to less-than-omniscient human beings. Furthermore, policy evolved in such a system is likely to be more adaptable, more facilitative of agreement, and more "intelligent" (information is gained from experiences at the grass roots and used to improve and reformulate policies) than policy which is centrally initiated and co-ordinated.

But who benefits from public policy formulated in dispersed decisional units? Of the authors we have considered, it is Lindblom who seeks to answer this nagging and important question. In the system of partisan mutual adjustment, the heaviest weight is given to the values, interests and perferences which are (a) most widely shared and (b) most intensely held. But the victory does not simply go the way of the strongest party, for: "In some large part the weight given to a value depends on the authority held by the participants in partisan mutual adjustment who pursue or protect it and by their adversaries."[54] Thus, governmental units have a power in legitimate authority which interest groups do not have. (However, it is important to note that private interest groups have taken over governmental authority in fields like licensing and the regulation of public grazing lands.[55])

To calm any anxieties about weaker groups losing out in the struggle of partisan adjustment, Lindblom declares:

> In partisan mutual adjustment in the United States and in the Western Democracies almost any value that any even relatively small number of citizens moderately or strongly wishes to see weighted into the policy-making process will be weighted in at some value significantly above zero.[56]

However, in order to be "weighed into the policy-making process," it is not enough that a value be supported by a group of citizens who "wish to see" it weighted. (This is a problem which Lindblom does not fully recognize or meet.) Those citizens must also have access to the policy arena. Apparently,

Lindblom assumes free access to the political market place as readily as earlier economists assumed free access to the market.

This is the point at which partisan mutual adjustment among incremental decision-makers begins to show its costs as a method of forming policy. For if we as a nation are committed to equal political rights and the opportunity of all significant groups to be heard (as well as the right of dissenters to speak without harrassment) then we cannot rely on partisan mutual adjustment to produce equitable public policy. Negroes are still denied the vote in parts of the South, and they are excluded from employment, quality education, and self-expression in areas throughout the country. Migrant farm workers have been denied admission to both unions and farm groups. The poor have found it difficult to air their views on the War on Poverty. Welfare recipients have discovered that the scales of justice in welfare boards' quasi-judicial proceedings are firmly tipped against them. Access to the political market place is not free.

It has been shown that the smaller a constituency is, the more dominant are the stronger groups in that constituency.[57] Therefore, decentralization may only exacerbate inequalities. Furthermore, there is no guarantee that the group leaders accurately reflect the views of their followers. Policy in the mutual adjustment process results from the interactions among "party leaders", "interest-group leaders" and so on. Lindblom derides the idea of a "public interest," but he believes in "group interest." The question remains: Are group leaders truly responsive to followers' preferences?

Speaking of access in the context of the civil rights struggle, Lindblom states:

> There is, of course, a limit to the degree to which the remedial and serial character of partisan mutual adjustment makes value aggregation acceptable where they would otherwise be rejected. For millions of American Negroes, for example, no conceivable remedial sequence of decisions and reweighings will, in their lifetimes, raise the value of racial equality to an acceptable level. Even in this case, however, the most active of the discontented are to a degree mollified by their ability to keep a process of reform moving. Their own participation, and that of others, in partisan mutual adjustment gives them some confidence that the weight given the value of racial equality can be, even in their lifetimes, strictly altered.[58]

Since Lindblom wrote those words, the "progress of reform" has largely ground to a halt. In 1967, after the defeat of national fair housing legislation, the heavy liberal losses in the 1966 Congressional elections, and the slowing of the civil rights movement in general, it is doubtful if most Negroes are optimistic about the promise of reform. If Stokely Carmichael is "to a degree mollified," he has been admirably restrained about showing it.

If the United States is committed to freedom of access to the political arena and equality of political rights, and if unregulated decentralization is found to stifle those freedoms, then we may desire the central formulation of national guidelines to protect rights of speech and access. The Supreme Court, in evolving national guidelines for the legal representation of criminals and the educational and political rights of Negroes, has opened routes of access for weaker groups and made democracy more participatory. If the cost of fragmented decision-making is too high, there are times when centralization is in order.

Toward Possibility

If one believes in a rationalist model of decision-making, in which man must evaluate every possible alternative and consequence in the light of a coherent ordering of values, then the prescription for good public policy is easy: centralize decision-making and provide the central decision-maker with enough information to make a fully-informed choice in the light of broad objectives.

However, if one considers that the limits of human capacity make purely rational decision-making impossible, then it seems reasonable to fragment decision-making in order to provide for each choice-maker a manageable section of the world with which to work.

There are perils in piecemeal, fragmented decision-making. Decisions made in dispersed centers may be poorly co-ordinated with each other. Dealing with small segments of small decisions, decentralized choice-makers may succumb to inertia and immobility. Finally, decentralization of decision-making in the political arena can lead to the subjugation of weak minority groups.

However, there are also strengths to be found in fragmentation: decentralized decision-making is likely to be more flexible, more adaptive, more conducive to social agreement, and more "intelligent" in making use of first-hand information and experience. Furthermore, opportunities do exist: opportunities for leadership in terms of goal-setting, definition of purpose, and creation of integrative situations; opportunities for co-ordination in negotiation, bargaining, and the collaborative formulation of superordinate goals; opportunities for change through organizational learning and the formation of new organizational units.

In the world of public policy, the choice is not simply one between rationality and non-rationality. Given human limitations, men and organizations can introduce more rationality into their deliberations by constructing "satisfactory" evaluative frameworks by which to judge policy alternatives. They can explore a wider range of alternatives by creating independent "scanning" units to examine non-incremental policies. Finally, they can use knowledge about the results of decisions to alter the decision-making process itself.

Neither must policy-makers commit themselves to an either-or choice between centralized and decentralized decision-making. Public policy can utilize both methods fruitfully; the choice depends upon the existential situation and the purpose desired. When local information is sought in the evolution of a national War on Poverty, then decentralized decision-making is called for. But when basic constitutional rights — like the right to vote or the freedom of speech — are endangered for any group of citizens, then a strong central decision is required to affirm those rights. Presidential, Congressional, or Supreme Court intervention may be necessary. (A system of decision-making can be decentralized and centralized in sequence. In Britain, under the present Labour Government, economic policy-making was taken out of the Treasury's centralized grasp and split between the Treasury and the DEA. Then in the formulation of the 1965 National Plan and the program for public expenditures, the Government sought to recentralize decision-making in a joint Treasury-DEA group of senior civil servants.)

The choices for decision-makers are not vast ones between "omniscient rationality" and "muddling through," between complete centralization and complete decentralization. To a great extent, the forms of decision-making depend upon the situation in which the policy-maker finds himself — but there is ample room for change and improvement in the decisional process itself. Man can be master of his own fate. The perils are obvious, but the possibilities are enormous.

Footnotes

1) Marshall Dimock, *A Philosophy of Administration* (New York: Harper and Brothers, 1958) p. 140.

2) See Robert M. MacIver, *The Web of Government* (New York: Macmillan Co., 1947) p. 220. Also E.E. Schattschneider, "Political Parties and the Public Interest" *Annals of the American Academy of Political and Social Science.*CCLXXX (1952) p. 22. Also, discussion of the "Rationalist" position in Glendon Schubert, *The Public Interest.* (Glencoe: The Free Press, 1960) pp. 30-79.

3) Walter, Lippmann, *The Public Philosophy* (Boston: Little, Brown, 1955) p. 42.

4) Dimock, *The Executive in Action* (Quoted in Richard F. Fenno, Jr., *The President's Cabinet* [Vintage Books, 1959] p. 263.)

5) See Schattschneider, *op. cit.*, and American Political Science Association, *Toward a More Responsible Two-Party System* (1950).

6) For example, see Grant McConnell, *Private Power and American Democracy* (New York: Alfred A. Knopf, 1966) p. 366.

7) Arthur Smithies, *The Budgetary Process in the United States* (New York: McGraw-Hill, 1955) pp. 192ff.

8) Especially helpful in the preparation of this section were David Braybrooke and Charles E. Lindblom, *A Strategy of Decision* (New York: The Free Press of Glencoe, 1963) pp. 21-57; Herbert A. Simon, *Administrative Behavior* (New York: The Free Press, 1947 – second ed. 1957) pp. 80-84; James G. March and Herbert A. Simon, *Organizations* (New York: John Wiley & Sons, Inc., 1958) pp. 136-141.

9) Simon, *Administrative Behavior,* p. 82.

10) Robert A. Dahl, *A Preface to Democratic Theory* (Chicago: University of Chicago Press, 1956) pp. 124ff.

11) Braybrooke and Lindblom, p. 24.

12) Paul Diesing, *Reason in Society* (Urbana: University of Illinois Press, 1962) p. 198.

13) *A Strategy of Decision.* The model of decision-making is primarily Lindblom's contribution; Braybrooke relates the model to issues in ethical theory. Therefore, I shall refer to disjointed incrementalism as Lindblom's model.

14) Braybrooke and Lindblom, p. 85.

15) *Ibid.* p. 90.

16) *Ibid.* p. 73.

17) *Ibid.* p. 105.

18) *Sixth Report from the Select Committe on Estimates* (Session 1957-58) "Treasury Control of Expenditures" (London: Her Majesty's Stationery Office, 1958) p. xxxvi.

19) Simon, *Administrative Behavior*, p. 75.

20) Simon, *Models of Man* (New York: John Wiley and Sons, Inc. 1957) pp. 204ff.

21) Simon, *Administrative Behavior*, p. 102.

22) *Ibid.* pp. 102-03.

23) *Ibid.* pp. 186-87.

24) *Ibid.* p. 204.

25) *Ibid.* p. 241.

26) For example, see Hans J. Morganthau, "Decisionmaking in the Nuclear Age," *Bulletin of the Atomic Scientists* (December, 1962) pp. 7-8.

27) See Paul Y. Hammond, "The National Security Council as a Device for Interdepartmental Coordination", *American Political Science Review* Vol. LIV (Dec., 1960).

28) W.J. Gore, *Administrative Decision-Making: A Heuristic Model* (New York: John Wiley & Sons, Inc., 1964).

29) *Ibid.* p. 130.

30) *Ibid.* p. 94.

31) *Ibid.* p. 110.

32) See Aaron Wildavsky, *The Politics of the Budgetary Process* (Boston: Little, Brown, 1964) for an examination of the American case; the equivalent British process is discussed in the House of Commons Select Committee report mentioned above.

33) For an excellent discussion of this distinction in terms of the level of generality of decisions, see Andrew S. McFarland, *Power, Critical Decisions, and Leadership: An Analysis of Empirical Pluralist Theory* (Ph.D. dissertation, University of California, Berkeley, 1966) Esp. chapter 4 – "Administrative Theory: Generality and Decisions."

34) Braybrooke and Lindblom, p. 62.

35) Simon, *Administrative Behavior*, p. 96.

36) Gore, p. 99.

37) Selznick, *Leadership in Administration* (New York: Harper and Row, 1957) pp. 4, 11.

38) "The Three Pragmatists." May 8, 1967, p. 29.

39) Henry C. Metcalf and L. Urwick, eds. *Dynamic Administration:* The Collected Papers of Mary Parker Follett (New York: Harper and Brothers Publishers, 1942) p. 32.

40) Richard E. Neustadt, *Presidential Power* (New York: Science Editions, 1962) pp. 46-57.

41) C.E. Lindblom, *The Intelligence of Democracy* (New York: The Free Press, 1965).

42) *Ibid.* pp. 28-29.

43) *Ibid.* pp. 98-99.

44) McFarland, p. 102.

45) See, for example, Chris Argyris, *Integrating the Individual and the Organization* (New York: John Wiley & Sons, Inc., 1964); and Warren G. Bennis, *Changing Organizations* (New York: McGraw-Hill, 1966).

46) Herbert A. Shepard, "Changing Interpersonal and Intergroup Relationships in Organizations," in James G. March, ed. *Handbook of Organizations* (Chicago: Rand-McNally, 1965) pp. 1128-29.

47) *Ibid.* p. 1140.

48) Also see Richard M. Cyert and James G. March, *A Behavioral Theory of the Firm* (Englewood Cliffs: Prentice-Hall, 1963) p. 121, for a discussion of "fire truck tactics" in which business organizational change is stimulated by specific problems.

49) *The Progressive* May 1967, p. 12.

50) Y. Dror, "Muddling Through – 'Science' or Inertia?", *Public Administration Review* (September, 1964) p. 155.

51) Amitai Etzioni has suggested in a review of *The Intelligence of Democracy* ("On the Process of Making Decisions" in *Science* 6 May, 1966, pp. 746-47) that decision-making is typically begun by a process of scanning alternatives and checking them against a list of "obviously crippling disadvantages." Although there is no possibility of studying every alternative, it is helpful to take a preliminary view of the field, using a "broad-angle lens."

52) *Public Expenditure: Planning and Control* (London: Her Majesty's Stationery Office, 1966), Cmnd. 2915.

53) Shepard, p. 1137.

54) Lindblom, *The Intelligence of Democracy*, p. 235.

55) McConnell, p. 361.

56) Lindblom, *The Intelligence of Democracy*, p. 229.

57) McConnell, pp. 342ff.

58) Lindblom, *The Intelligence of Democracy*, p. 217.

PLANS DON'T WORK; PEOPLE DO
by
Dwight F. Rettie

Director, Division of Land Development
U.S. Department of Housing and Urban Development

There is probably no case of "the gap" — from missiles to generations — that is older or more widespread than the gap between plans and performance. In fact, the whole idea of planning as a prelude to intelligent action and decisions has gone sour in some places because some people see very little else except unexecuted plans, plans that have been unable to weather the storm of political controversy and plans that never got beyond the drawing board or the status of a well-prepared publication. Even planners ask out loud whether its all worth it, when so much of the work that goes into planning — collecting the data, analyzing it, drawing up elaborate solutions to problems — seems destined for a waste basket or, at best, a library.

I think part of this frustration with the planning process is based on a continuing misunderstanding of what the planning process and plans are all about. Plans are not decisions — although some plans make the mistake of flying under false colors on this score. Plans should be guides and decision-making tools to help make decisions among various opportunities and competing alternatives. Plans make it more possible to allocate usually scarce resources among competing uses.

Some plans have been raised to the level of immutable law. They are not and should not be. Plans must not only be capable of being changed — plans must be the primary mechanism for institutionalizing the process of change. If not, they are doomed to failure. No man can see clearly enough into the future to plan in ways that take account of all needs and strivings. Even the process of planning for change induces more change.

The problem of relating plans to decisions was posed in a question to me at a university seminar on PPBS recently. After a presentation on agency planning, one student asked:

> How can you plan, if you haven't made a decision on what you're going to do?

The question captures the problem and the paradox of planning for both the planner and the decision-maker. Who plans, and who decides? And, who carries it out?

Let me try to answer these questions by saying that I have great confidence in the arts and abilities of professional planners. Planners now have available to them a wide variety of tools — from the slide rule to the sophisticated computer, and from public opinion polls to broadly engineered census data that no longer ignore the complex inter-relationships between physical and social facts. The art of planning is capable of great innovation when challenged and under proper leadership can be highly pragmatic.

But planners have some other troubles: too many of them disdain the political decision-making process. Sharing part of the progressive tradition in American politics, some recreation planners opt for "keeping planning out of politics." And, in the process of trying to stay "professional" or non-political, they are almost guaranteeing that their plan will have trouble being translated into decisions, and budgets, and staffs, and products.

The art of planning must contain a large measure of involvement by the planner in the political decision-making process. I am here not using the word "political" in a partisan sense — Democratic or Republican — but only within the broad institutional framework of our system of government.

On many occasions I suspect the interchange between the planner and the politician is the most critical communication problem facing either party. If a plan is ever to be a reality, the ideas and alternatives contained in the plan must get to the decision-maker in a form he understands and can use. It must happen at the right time, and (perhaps toughest of all) the exchange must relate to the *real* issues that are of concern to both.

Planners have been well worked-over for what many people regard as too much pipe-dreaming, too many idealized plans that do not come within reasonably predictable budget constraints or plans that ignore other constraints on the decision-maker — personnel and skills, legal limitations, or time pressures. Planners need mechanisms to assure that their plans are not merely blue-sky meanderings.

One way to institutionalize this exchange is through the organizational relationship of the planner and his staff to the decision-maker. There are several schools of thought about where planning should be located in an organizational structure. For me, the specific location of the box is less important than the degree to which its location meets the following three criteria:

1. Is it in direct linkage with the decision-maker?

2. Is it identified with and related to programs and to the end products of the organization?

3. Is it responsive and responsible to the decision-maker?

The first of these criteria relates specifically to the question of communication. Do the planners have easy and continuous exchange with the boss? It is surprising how many do not. The usual stumbling block is a filtering process which takes place through organizational layering — passing communications through one, or two, or three levels of an organization before it reaches the decision level. Another common result is development of the planner's "ivory tower" set aside from the main stream of the organization, where it turns out all too often its work is out of the main stream too.

The second of these criteria relates to substance and to the identity of the organization and staff for planning. Here again the "ivory tower" is all too common, with planning organizations sometimes associated with the

300

budgeting and financial management function (some very strong arguments can be made for close coordination with that function) and with engineering and design staffs.

Effective planning must be focused on the programs and outputs of the organization.

The third criterion is perhaps more controversial — the degree to which the planning organization, and especially its chief, is responsive to political leadership. Here I think an analogy can be made with the role of the city manager. Most city managers serve at the pleasure of the city council or an elected mayor. He is the mayor's man, or the city council's man. If there is marked change in leadership through the political process, there can be change in city managers. At the same time, however, the city manager is recognized as a skilled professional, who brings administrative and executive skills to his job that are not partisan political.

Looking at the top planning job this way could often help make the planning process more relevant to political decision-makers. It means there would normally be more communication, and more of the work of the planning staff would be done in ways that will be more directly useful to the decision-makers. At the same time, I think wider use of such institutional relationships would have the effect of upgrading and enlarging the role and prestige of the top planner and his staff. He ought to be better paid if he sits somewhere nearer the seat of political power than what could be expected if he is set apart and isolated from the community or organization leadership.

The Department of Housing and Urban Development is acutely sensitive to these realities, and technical guidelines for the organization of urban comprehensive planning staffs — especially those whose staffs and operations are funded through the Urban Planning Assistance Programs — give special attention to the relationship between the planning body and the elected political decision-makers.

There are several other closely related levels of communication needed in this process, some of which are too often too weak. I mentioned a minute ago the linkage between planning and financial management, particularly the budgeting process. This link is a key part of the so-called planning-programming-budgeting system (PPBS) concept.

Some of the critics of PPBS assert that it really is not as new or as magical as some of its loudest supporters claim. But I think it is fair to say that the process is a new way of putting together planning, programming, and budgeting in a manner that (1) identifies alternatives, (2) takes into account the long term costs of present decisions, and (3) relates the costs (and budgets) for actions to measures (or at least descriptions) of anticipated outcomes in relation to stated goals. Progressive administration has worked at pieces of this for a long time, but usually in isolation. Too often planning has not been related to budgeting and to the power of the purse strings. PPBS can help pull these elements together.

The three criteria for planning organizational relationships point out that planners need close communication with program administrators and program staffs. In fact, I have heard many arguments assert that planning should be done by the program staffs themselves and should not be relegated to separate staffs or people with non-program interests because plans made by professional planners are unreal or incapable of execution and performance. Unless there are strong avenues and mechanisms for communication between program administrators and the planning staffs, I think this criticism is justified. And as an administrator, I would prefer plans I was sure were related to program realities over plans that may look beautiful on paper but are operationally impossible.

I suspect there is a natural separation of the planning species from the program species in organizations. Educational backgrounds tend to be different (which in turn magnifies the communication problem).

An effective planning, programming and budgeting system of an organization can go a long way toward bridging this communications gap by making certain that planners are brought into major decisions, both early and late. Too often planners retire to the "ivory tower," design a plan — perhaps even a good one — then turn the plan over to the program staffs and decision-makers and walk away from it. One of the reasons this happens is because the temperature in the decision-making kitchen usually gets rather warm. Again, too many recreation planners have been reluctant to sit in these hot seats and subject the results of their work to the "give-and-take" of political compromise.

This leads me to another observation about plan implementation: planners should take less personal offense at the inevitable changes that are made as plans move from paper to performance. It is no reflection on the quality of a plan or on the professional integrity or competence of a planner that plans change. Plans should change. The best analogy I can draw comes from a field in which virtually everybody who has ever done staff work will recognize — letter writing and speech writing. If you have ever written for the boss, you know that draft letters and draft speeches get changed regularly. The staff man who cannot bear to have the boss change a word of a draft is setting himself up for an early case of ulcers or one of those perpetual sour stomachs that comes from too much commitment. Some people call it pride of authorship.

Another important element of the communication process in planning relates to the plan itself. For years planners struggled with budgets that were too thin to permit the use of modern communications media to get across the ideas and alternatives they conceived. In the last 20 years, we have gone through perhaps half a dozen cycles of austerity and affluence in plan presentation. The days of unattractive and almost illegible draft plans are probably (and hopefully) gone. There is at the same time a strong reaction against over-reliance on flashy presentations that are full of color and fancy art but thin on content. The balance between effective communication and the extremes of too much or too little is harder to find that most people appreciate.

Plan communication is made more difficult because audiences are not generally homogeneous and limited. They are mixed and will range from the interested (or even disinterested) lay citizen to the professional administrator and to the protagonistic politician.

As someone who has been professionally involved in the communications process for more than a decade, I have often felt that too much was being asked of a single publication or a single communications item when it alone was used in an attempt to reach and convince all audiences at the same time.

Another phase of plan communication, no less important than the initial dissemination of a plan or idea, is program reporting and follow-up. Here planners frequently fail since they regard this as somebody else's job. And normally the somebody else looks at the problem of progress and performance reporting in terms that are not easily related to the original plan and its goals and objectives.

A comprehensive plan for meeting a state's outdoor recreation needs is geared to statewide dimensions of leisure time, population, mobility, income levels and other factors. By the time the plan is translated into hardware, the recreation agency may only be reporting the number of new campgrounds open or the problems involved in distributing excess capacities on busy weekends. There are, of course, the workload and managerial problems that the agency administrator deals with from day to day, and they are important to him. The work of the agency, however, needs constant restatement in terms that relate to the goals and objectives being served. In the long run, the effectiveness of any plan can only be measured by the degree to which performance serves the plan's objectives.

Data about accomplishments and performance become the basis for evaluation of a plan and for the development of continuing alternatives to account for inevitable change. Here again planners must recognize — as indeed I think most do — that the life expectancy of any plan is necessarily short. Again, one of the major features of the PPBS concept is a return flow of data for program evaluation and replanning on a regular and constant basis. Through such a performance data recycling process the planners learn also.

Most administrators are periodically dismayed by the degree to which so many of the things they do appear to be set in concrete or represent base line operations relatively immune to short-term manipulation. Effective linkage of program decision-making to a plan can change this by focussing attention far enough into the future that the unmoveable base becomes less and less a percentage of the whole. Effective planning should identify these relationships, and through this built-in flexibility substantially increase the odds that the plan can be carried out in the future.

One of the most difficult and yet unsolved elements of the planning process is wrapped up in the catch-all word, "coordination," which all public officials agree is a good thing but which almost universally escapes both definition and practice. Everybody is for it, but few jobs have been set up for people with specific responsibilities for doing it.

If there has been any lesson learned by public administrators in the last 20 years, it is that there is an ecology of the political economy no less complicated than the one biologists have been seeking to describe. The political economy has its own set of food cycles and predatory chains and its own complicated set of interdependent systems and organizations, where the health and success of one system or one reorganization is bound up in what happens to others.

Political scientists and scholars of administration have sensed this complexity for some time, but we are only really beginning to understand it and devise mechanisms that explicitly treat these complexities and interdependencies. Let me be more specific. The history of urban development in the United States has been a highly compartmentalized administrative and political system of unrelated and uncoordinated activities and organizations. No one appreciated the degree to which decisions relating to mass transportation facilities and services could affect both the physical and social environments of housing. We know it now, and we see an enormous job ahead undoing the errors of the past and providing some assurance that we do not ignore these relationships in the future.

In urban development, we have, as a nation, taken land and water and air as inexhaustible resources available for exploitation and contamination. Urban planners have not explicitly treated the quantity and quality of water as a major component of urban dynamics. Only now are we beginning to articulate and act on these relationships.

Planners working in the resource fields — such as those engaged in water resource projects for flood control, irrigation and farm land management — also have tended not to see the relationship of their planning with urban growth and development. Only now are we beginning to tie these unrelated activities together under area-wide comprehensive planning umbrellas that embrace both the rural and urban environment.

In recreation planning we have demonstrated the same case of non-urban bias. Much recreation planning to date has focused on lands and activities largely oriented to a rural economy and to values that are expressions of our rural and agrarian heritage. Expenditures by governments for outdoor recreation have focused on hunting, fishing, camping, and other outdoor activities that reflect rural systems from our past.

One of the consequences of this focus has been to shortchange the recreation opportunities for the 70 some percent of the American population that lives in our cities and metropolitan areas. We have almost ignored the large number of urban citizens who lack the mobility or the income or the leisure time to make use of the recreational assets set aside in the rural hinterlands.

Recreation planning, even some of the best of it, has failed to be comprehensive because it has failed to come adequately to grips with the urban realities of the United States in the late 1960's and beyond. It is impossible for outdoor recreation planning to succeed in being comprehensive if it ignores its relationship to transportation systems or its relationship to housing, to employment, to wage levels, and to the availability of leisure time.

One of the most important outcomes of the studies made by the Outdoor Recreation Resources Review Commission was the beginning of an awareness of the relationships between outdoor recreation planning and the total ecology of our national development. Studies of leisure time and incomes were important contributions of the Commission but ones which we have only made partial use of so far. I am sure the National Outdoor Recreation Plan, now in preparation by the Bureau of Outdoor Recreation, will take this system another major step down the road.

The coordination of outdoor recreation planning and programming with other activities at all levels of government is a new burden and opportunity for planners and administrators. We see this in planning for model cities right now. As communities are putting together the broadly based programs to attack the physical and social problems of our cities, recreational facilities and programs are being recognized as important ingredients of the planning process. They will be important aspects of the physical developmental processes as well. This awareness was documented in what for many people was a surprising conclusion of the National Advisory Commission on Civil Disorders which concluded that inadequate recreation facilities and services was the fifth most frequently mentioned grievance in a list of possible causative factors leading to last summer's riots and disorders.

Among the 20 cities that accounted for the 24 most serious disorders, grievances relating to recreation were found in 15 cities and were ranked of first importance in three, second in one, and third in four cities.

The Commission examined ghetto grievances and identified those complaints which seemed most causal. Of the 12 most significant kinds of grievances, poor recreation facilities and programs ranked fifth — behind police practices, unemployment, housing, and education. Recreation was regarded as a more significant grievance than the ineffectiveness of the political structure, discriminatory administration of justice, inadequate municipal services, and inadequate welfare programs. In several cases dissatisfactions with recreational facilities were the proximate cause or issue in a violent outbreak.

As model cities planning goes on, and as there are more model cities, new demands are going to be placed on professional outdoor recreation planners to coordinate their interests and activities with the broad spectrum of urban programs focused on model neighborhoods. But, if we are working at model neighborhoods and continuing to strengthen traditional outdoor recreation activities, there is a middle ground that needs more attention also. Here, for example, we might provide opportunities for people who live in major metropolitan areas to use outdoor recreation facilities outside the cities through public transport operations that increase the mobility of city people and open up whole new areas for their activity — through relating outdoor recreation planning to transportation planning.

Other new dimensions of outdoor recreation coordination involve the uses of land and facilities now ignored or underutilized.

Better coordination between outdoor recreation programs and school systems can offer opportunities to open school grounds and play areas during the evenings, weekends, and summers. Such areas may now be locked or unlighted or otherwise unavailable.

There are tens of thousands of acres of municipal watershed lands surrounding many metropolitan areas (some owned by public agencies, the balance by private water companies) that have enormous outdoor recreation potential not now being used and sometimes not even being planned for. On this count many administrators of recreation agencies must get over the traditional notion that they have no interest in the utilization of lands they do not own.

The success of translating recreation plans into useful new opportunities on the American landscape depends, however, far less on the plan itself and more on the people who make it, who will decide whether to carry it out, and who will put it into operation.

Plans don't work; people do!

The needs for new skills and new people doing recreation planning will place severe strains on the existing capacity we now have in the United States. There is too much to do now and too few people to do it.

Outdoor recreation planners will continue to be challenged by problems that seem insurmountable in dimension, particularly when related to the resources available to tackle them. As a nation we have not yet caught up with the outdoor recreation deficit created by the depression of the thirties and by the diversion of funds and resources during World War II. As a consequence much of what we now do in outdoor recreation is geared only to catching up with past needs, and we are making disappointingly little progress in fulfilling the conservation orator's challenge to meet the needs of future generations of Americans for parks, open space, wilderness, wildlife and nature.

Our performance in outdoor recreation closely parallels what we do with highways. We build new ones, and as soon as the opening day ribbon is cut, we are bumper to bumper and worrying about overuse. Parks are no different.

Part of this problem stems from the pressures (some of which are our own creation) to develop new open space areas soon after they are designated and acquired. These pressures are very difficult to meet and often impossible to ignore.

We need to explore whole new sets of outdoor recreation alternatives, particularly those involving land acquisition, if we are effectively to set aside and have available outdoor recreation resources for the 300 million people of our population in the year 2000.

We are in no danger of running out of land. As one of my colleagues pointed out to me a few days ago, if the entire United States population were moved into the state of Texas today, Texas would still be less densely populated than England. Stated another way, the United States can support a population of one billion people and still be less densely populated than Switzerland.

The problem is not with the basic configuration of our planet; the problem is the way we use our land and its resources. The cities on Lake Erie and the effluent which they produce are in the process of making that lake a dead cesspool. The impact of our population, of urbanization and of our technology far exceeds the spread of our cities or the land which we occupy. We are capable of contaminating entire airsheds covering thousands of square miles. We are polluting entire river systems from land uses that occupy almost negligible percentages of the land area.

We can no longer claim ignorance of the problems. In many cases we have rather clear plans by which we can solve them. Now, today, it is for the planners and the decision-makers to put together that effective team which can assure performance for the future.

SOME BROAD IMPLICATIONS
OF OUTDOOR RECREATION PLANNING

by
Roman H. Koenings
Regional Director, Lake Central Region,
Bureau of Outdoor Recreation, U.S. Department of the Interior,
Ann Arbor, Michigan

The purpose of this paper is to discuss briefly a few aspects of outdoor recreation and outdoor recreation planning not covered in the other papers in these proceedings. But first, I would like to emphasize several points that have been made.

I would like to reemphasize that conditions are constantly changing, and, therefore, it is next to impossible to identify a plan per se, for planning is a constant effort which must adjust to changing conditions.

The second point I would like to reemphasize is that the action phase of a plan is as important as any other phase of the plan. Actually, if there is no action program set forth to accomplish the needs identified in the rest of the plan, you really do not have a plan. Too many plans are gathering dust for there is no program for implementation which makes them a collection of information rather than a plan.

The plan must be presented in such a way that it is a usable document to the decision-makers. Too often planners attempt to make the decisions. This is the responsibility of those employed to make the decisions or those who have been elected to do so.

With those few remarks, I would like to move into another area of outdoor recreation. Many people consider outdoor recreation as lying on a river bank in the sun with a fishing pole. The use of leisure time and that part of leisure time utilized in outdoor recreation pursuits may well be a social problem for this nation. All too often people look only at the benefits of leisure time rather than at some of the problems it might create. There are many historians, including Arnold Toynbee, who maintain that if the work week in this nation continues to be reduced in terms of number of hours, the use of leisure time in this country may be one of the greatest problems this nation may have to face in the future. Obviously, this leisure time, associated with increased income, will result in more participation in outdoor activities.

I would also like to point out in this regard, that although the Outdoor Recreation Resource Review Commission identified six classifications of areas, they basically fall into three categories. The first of these categories are those areas we set aside to preserve our *national* heritage. These are the historic and archeological and areas of unique natural splendor. I use the word "unique" as defined in the dictionary, which means "one of a kind" rather than unusual. The second category is those areas we acquire to preserve our *natural* heritage, such as Yosemite, the Grand Tetons, Glacier, and many others. The third category is the activity oriented areas, both passive and active.

The first two categories — those areas we preserve for our national heritage and those areas we preserve for our natural heritage — are really not necessary for what normally is considered outdoor recreational pursuits. They are extremely important in the overall well-being of the people of this nation, for as most of you realize, we are a young nation, and we do not have the pure ethnic background you will find in France, Italy, Germany, and many other nations. It is necessary that we acquire and preserve these areas as part of our heritage so future generations will realize the tremendous effort which was made to make this nation what it is. In your planning efforts you should be well aware of the importance of these areas.

The third point I would like to make in this brief discussion is that the leisure time spent in outdoor activities does have a tremendous economic impact on this nation. The President stated in a recent speech that tourism alone in this nation amounted to $33 billion. It has also been reported by Michigan and Wisconsin that the tourist industry in each of those two states amounts to $1 billion a year. These figures do not include the amount of money spent by the recreationists themselves for various types of equipment, boats, motors, cameras, binoculars, golfing and fishing equipment, and a host of other types of gear necessary or desirable to participate in outdoor recreational pursuits. I would suggest that each of you, when you have time, try to prepare such a list for your edification. I am sure you will be surprised at how long it will become.

As a fourth point, I would strongly urge that during the planning process, you remain constantly aware of the social and economic factors involved and that you bring these to the attention of the decision-makers.

My last comment is that you give due consideration to the quality of the total environment as well as to specific recreational areas. There is a need to provide the people of this nation with a pleasant place to live as well as beautiful areas in which to recreate. I am certain you realize that your tasks as outdoor recreation planners are not small and easy nor your responsibilities insignificant.

CONCLUDING REMARKS
by
Stanley A. Cain
Assistant Secretary for Fish and Wildlife and Parks
U.S. Department of the Interior, Washington, D.C.*

Observers of the contemporary scene warn us of dangers to modern man. These warnings often are based on the rapidity of the technological changes that affect man, his society, and his environment. The engineer is busily applying physics and chemistry, the physician his knowledge of biology, the social scientist his understanding of cause and effect, while the humanist laments a lost Eden or dreams of Utopia.

As President Howard W. Johnson of the Massachusetts Institute of Technology has said recently, "Technology is at once our blessing and our bane, the well-spring of our aspirations, yet the threat to our well-being. Technology is both social benefactor and social calamity."

Yet the danger to modern man does not arise from his growing capacity to *induce* change but, rather, from his poor ability to *control* sensibly his new powers. Whether or not the scientist feels aloof and not responsible for the applications others make of the new knowledge, we are not ready to let him run the country; yet much of present fear for the future is a result of society's lack of control of technical developments. To quote Howard Johnson again, technology "offers us nuclear power and the specter of thermonuclear destruction, personal transportation and urban pollution, computers which multiply our creative power and threaten our privacy, mass communication and mass propaganda...the potential of the good life, but seems unable to lessen the poverty around us."

If we are not willing to let the scientist and engineer run the country, neither are we ready to let the economist or the social psychologist do it. And as for the planner, he is in demand by every municipality and at higher levels of government, too — yet the planner is an adviser without authority.

We have outgrown the tribal council and its ability in simpler times to act sensibly, and the town meeting is not a practical mechanism for a meeting of minds in a modern nation of two hundred million persons. The power of decision has been delegated to the politicians on one side and the administrator in the middle.

It is somewhere in the interface of these three sectors — the political, the administrative, and the technical — that society has lost control of its destiny. We cannot regret the growth of knowledge, for ignorance is no protection, although we have not searched with equal diligence all areas of our need. The human population explosion, for example, is a consequence of application of biological and social knowledge to the causes of death while we have neglected the birth rate. We have advanced our knowledge of nuclear fission and fusion and are applying it to peaceful purposes without having learned how to avoid the catastrophe of ultimate war. We have developed mechanical

*Now with the Department of Resource Planning and Conservation, University of Michigan.

means of changing the face of the earth without being able to control the bulldozer. We have developed tens of thousands of physical machines and gadgets and hundreds of thousands of chemicals without learning how to maintain clean air and water, keep pesticides out of our food, and dangerous drugs off the market. We have built and rebuilt cities without knowing how to maintain a livable environment, and everywhere in the countryside nature is degraded. As Dave Brower has said, "Man cannot make a wilderness but he can make a desert."

I have overstated the case for this moment in history, but I have not overstated the direction of movement. The present question is whether the stirrings can swell to a crescendo that will reverse the trends that have existed since the start of the scientific-technological revolution. Can human population be stabilized at a level commensurate with a limited physical world and man's ability to supply himself with a level of living appropriate to his humanness? Can we have the many advantages of urbanization and cities fit to live in? Can we wrest from the environment the raw materials to supply our needs without its total degradation?

To focus on our present concern, we have never before shown so much concern for urban open space, rural wildlands, and opportunity for outdoor recreation. While this concern has generated some action, the difficulties are tremendous. Why is it, we might ask ourselves, that we so often say of an ungenerous and even despicable behavior, "that is human nature," when at the same time we take fuller pride in expressions of social conscience than ever before in human history?

We can look for light on this paradox in our ancient biological roots. The survival value of the social group has been tested through time. The first point is simple. As a member of a flock or herd the individual has some invisibility that he would not have standing alone. The group multiplies the individual's chances of being overlooked by a predator — wildebeast and lion on the East African plain, duck and hunter in a Louisiana marsh. Among the primates man himself is not without this instinct for the security of the group.

Under simpler conditions, the conservative character of the group provided survival value. Groups were small, problems elementary, and structure simple. Food and water and territoriality in that connection were the necessities. Innovation was absent or change, if it occurred, was on the imperceptible geological time-scale of biological evolution. For early man it was little different. Through most of history social groups have been few, clearly drawn, and subject only to slow change. It is only for modern man that groups are exceedingly numerous, yet each such collective serves the same basic needs that are both material and psychological.

We are born into some groups — family, church, and political units from town to nation. Others we join according to how we make a living, what we believe in, what we enjoy. Whatever their nature, one individual may be a member of dozens of groups. We find advantages in this collectivism — political party, business firm, profession, social group. We unite for common purposes; we comply for mutual benefit.

For early man the kinds of groups were few — the warrior group, the hunter or farmer group, perhaps a few craft groups, the priesthood, and some form of nobility or ruling council. A tribe or a primitive nation with such simple structure made decisions easy, compliance sure, and individual security high, for every man knew both his position and his obligation.

As modern human society has become more complex, it has done so by multiplication of the number and variety of groups as well as by the individual's participation in many different groups for different purposes. While the biologically rooted human need for belonging has not been lost, the complexity of structure makes it difficult to translate the group power into effective social action. There are too many interfaces!

The group is inherently conservative. If not concerned just with maintaining the status quo, it is at least self-centered and usually directed toward a single goal. These groups have been described as "complacent conspiracies of judgment." Because they are numerous and because goals are different, the subgroup structure leads to conflict of purpose. The threats that face us today arise from these conflicts. Whereas we can and have expressed national goals in resounding terms, it has been difficult to harmonize our diverse actions with them. So we stand, a mixture of good and bad, wisdom and foolishness, belief and incredulity, conservative and radical, social and antisocial, progressive and retrogressive.

We need to find the means and the mass courage to define and accept humanistic as well as technological goals. Somehow we must create the mores (perhaps like Leopold's "land ethic") and effective legislation to influence the herd tendency. We cannot dispense with society's group structure except at the cost of chaos and anarchy, yet we cannot stand still as technology changes the real world about us as well as our lives in it. The conservatism of the group must be met by individuals with the faculty of discrimination. Here is the point and counterpoint of conformity and individuality. There can be no real progress toward solution of our present problems without individuals who take the risk of discriminatory judgments. In these times of burgeoning science and technology that have so changed the world, the self-interest of the group is at least partly in opposition to the social interest. Somehow we must translate our knowledge and technology into effective social action.

The orthodoxy of quantitative science and the materialism of technological development are little less limiting to understanding than the orthodoxy based on decree or revelation. In the contrast of the conservative group and the discriminating critic, we are faced with a dilemma and the means of resolving it. In the face of the systems of nature, which have been disrupted by our attack upon them, and the efficient machines of technology, we must devise political-economic-social-legal systems that work smoothly for the general welfare.

Somehow the national power structure must be changed so that the single-mindedness of road and dam builders, thermal-electric power developers, real estate developers, natural resource processers, and all other special-interest groups — private and public — are amenable to the social need. The gap between what we profess and what we do must be narrowed. Only the discriminating critic can bring this about, and he needs to be a generalist if not a universalist.

Long before this you must have wondered what all this has to do with outdoor recreation planning. I hope now to suggest that there is a connection. The spirit of play is a human attribute. The desire, perhaps the need, for recreation is deep-seated in all of us. Yet recreation is not one activity and the multitudinous recreational interests have their own single-mindedness as truly as economic and other human interests.

In a very real sense, the demand for recreational opportunities is expressed by groups, groups that tend to be as conservative as their group interests are narrow. The bird-watcher, whose success one might suppose is diminished directly as his companions are multiplied, knows that if there are to be birds to be watched, he must see to it that bird habitats are preserved. So he unites with fellow enthusiasts in the National Audubon Society. And the hunter who runs the risk of being shot in mistake for a deer, a risk in proportion to the number of hunters in the field at the same time, belongs to sportsmen's organizations in order to promote his interests. And so it is with every kind of outdoor recreational activity — fishermen, swimmers, sailors, motor boaters, waterskiers, hikers, mountain climbers, skiers, horsemen, bicyclists and motorcyclists, tote-goaters, campers, rock-hounds, amateur naturalists, ecologists and other scientists, photographers — all have found it useful to belong to organizations concerned with promotion of their special interests in the outdoors.

This is the way that demand gets verbalized and effectuated. With every passing year the opportunity for individual enjoyment is lessened and the need for group solidarity is increased if opportunity is to be had. Each group is essentially self-centered, but the groups can and do join forces to provide for private or public opportunity to bird watch, or hunt, fish or swim, and several of the national organizations that began with a limited interest in the outdoors have broadened their scope to encompass the entire field of conservation. Representatives of Audubon, Isaac Walton League, the Wilderness Society and Sierra Club, for example, testify before legislatures and Congress on pending bills concerning air or water pollution, the creation of a park, the building of a dam, the dredging and filling of estuaries, the use of pesticides, changes in hunting regulations, and so on.

So it is that the relations between supply and demand for outdoor recreation opportunity get expressed. There are conservative hard-core groups in every instance, and there are the discriminatory thinkers who may over time shift somewhat the center of gravity of a traditional position.

But the phenomenon is not just that of recreational interests, many of which may be in direct conflict under certain circumstances, as between the white-water canoeist who needs a free-flowing river, and the waterskier who needs the slack-water pool behind a dam, or the wilderness lover who wants nature left alone and the camper who wants the conveniences of home. The matter is not that simple because the landscape that the recreationist needs is useful to many others — the miner, the lumberman, the rancher, the farmer, the power developer, the highway builder, the real estate developer, and commercial and industrial interests.

Just as the recreation groups may join temporarily in support of a conservation interest, so the resource exploiters back up one another's interests.

Out of such confrontations interests get defined and clarified and, sometimes, an overriding public interest is made clear. Since the public interest, which is the goal of the nation as a group, is by its nature a compromise, it follows that no special subgroup interest can be fully satisfied. I think it is a measure of our growing maturity that in recent decades we are arriving at compromises that give something for everyone but not everything for anyone.

We are establishing more national parks, national seashores, wildlife refuges, and wilderness areas than ever before, and there will certainly be a national system of scenic and wild rivers and national foot-trails. The last few years have seen many states appropriate funds and float large bond issues for state areas, as have some counties and municipalities. An impetus to this has come from the Land and Water Conservation Fund, shared by these different levels of government. But more important than this fact alone, I believe, is that every gain along these lines has produced a corresponding limitation on consumptive resource exploitation. When a piece of landscape is set aside for a park, the lumberman and the miner have lost some of their former base. When a stretch of seashore becomes a recreation area or refuge, it is no longer available for private homes or commercial development.

Most of our national life has been lived in an economy of private enterprise. Although there has been some regulation of private enterprise and even considerable governmental assistance to it, land and water and the natural resources they contain have mostly been used in a way determined solely by the owner irrespective of what other private or public uses might have been in the public interest. The significant change of recent years, so it seems to me, is that public enterprise, government that is, is accomplishing what individuals couldn't have done for themselves.

Despite the protestations one always hears when any private action is restrained for public purposes, recent history does not spell the doom of lumbering, mining, ranching, irrigation farming, the development of roads, airfields, private homes, or anything else we need as a nation. What is being worked out is a sort of equitable balance among the many personal and public needs. Not all uses of landscape are compatible at a given place. That being the case, incompatible uses must be separated from each other without any one use being denied some opportunity somewhere. Let us notice also that this is not being done by expropriation of private property. Quite the opposite. It is typical that the government has to pay much more to acquire private property for public purposes than such property is worth as measured by appraised sale value in the absence of a governmental interest. Let me put it more clearly; it is typical that private owners of land get an unearned windfall of profit for the simple reason that the market ceases to operate when there is a public declaration of interest to establish a park or recreation area.

In closing I return to the theme I developed at the start. The tendency, in fact the necessity, to form social groups lies deep in human history. This tendency is an indispensible feature of human society, a necessary conservative force, a sort of social balance wheel. But if that characteristic stood alone our species would be unable to meet the challenges of change — natural changes in the environment, but above all, changes that man himself has induced especially by his growing technological competence. If we find ourselves unable to meet the challenges of technological change, it will be because we have failed to generate the discriminating thinkers who challenge the herd psychology and modify it enough to preserve the group structure by shifting, perhaps only slightly, the centers of traditional belief.